fluency *with*

Information Technology

Skills, Concepts, & Capabilities

LAWRENCE SNYDER

University of Washington

Brief Edition

PEARSON

Addison
Wesley

Boston San Francisco New York
London Toronto Sydney Tokyo Singapore Madrid
Mexico City Munich Paris Cape Town Hong Kong Montreal

Executive Editor:	Susan Hartman Sullivan
Development Editor:	Pat Mahtani
Assistant Editor:	Elizabeth Paquin
Marketing Manager:	Nathan Schultz
Production Supervisor:	Marilyn Lloyd
Composition:	Gillian Hall, The Aardvark Group
Text Designer:	Joyce Cosentino Wells
Cover Designer:	Regina Hagen Kolenda
Text and Cover Image:	© 2003 Vince Cavataio/Index Stock Imagery
Prepress and Manufacturing:	Caroline Fell

Access the latest information about Addison-Wesley titles from our World Wide Web site:
http://www.aw-bc.com/computing

Many of the designations used by manufacturers and sellers to distinguish their products are claimed as trademarks. Where those designations appear in this book, and Addison-Wesley was aware of a trademark claim, the designations have been printed in initial caps or all caps.

The programs and applications presented in this book have been included for their instructional value. They have been tested with care, but are not guaranteed for any particular purpose. The publisher does not offer any warranties or representations, nor does it accept any liabilities with respect to the programs or applications.

Library of Congress Cataloging-in-Publication Data

A catalog record for this book is on file at the Library of Congress.

ISBN 0-321-26846-6

1 2 3 4 5 6 7 8 9 10-DOW-07 06 05 04

For Julie Ann, Dan, and Dave

Preface

WELCOME to the brief edition of *Fluency with Information Technology: Skills, Concepts, and Capabilities*. I am delighted to introduce to you a book that moves beyond the click-here-click-there form of technology instruction to one firmly founded on ideas. The time is right for a new introduction to IT because today the majority of college and post-secondary students are already familiar with computers, the Internet, and the World Wide Web. They do not need rudimentary instruction in double-clicking and resizing windows. Rather, they need to be taught to be confident, in-control users of IT. They need to know how to navigate independently in the ever-changing worlds of information and technology, to solve their problems on their own, and to be capable of fully applying the power of IT tools in the service of their personal and career goals. They must be more than literate; they must be fluent with IT.

What's Fluency with Information Technology?

The inspiration for writing this book comes from a report by the National Research Council (NRC), *Being Fluent with Information Technology*. In that study, commissioned by the National Science Foundation, the committee asserted that traditional computer literacy does not have the "staying power" students need to keep pace with the rapid changes in IT. The study concluded that the educational "bar needs to be raised" if students' knowledge is to evolve and adapt to that change. The recommended alternative, dubbed *fluency with information technology*, or FIT, was a package of skills, concepts, and capabilities wrapped in a project-oriented learning approach that ensures that the content is fully integrated. The goal is to help people become effective users immediately, and to prepare them for lifelong learning.

The Vision

Because fluency with information technology—I usually shorten it to *Fluency*—is a new concept that largely implements the vision of the NRC committee, I'll introduce the main components: the three-part content, the integration mechanism of projects, and the role of programming.

Three-part Content

To make students immediately effective and launch them on the path of lifelong learning, they need to be taught three types of knowledge: Skills, Concepts, and Capabilities.

> *Skills* refers to proficiency with contemporary computer applications such as email, word processing, Web searching, etc. Skills make the technology immediately useful to students and give them practical experience on which to base other learning. The Skills component approximates traditional computer literacy content; that is, Fluency *includes* literacy.

> *Concepts* refers to the fundamental knowledge underpinning IT, such as how a computer works, digital representation of information, assessing information authenticity, etc. Concepts provide the principles on which students will build new understanding as IT evolves.

> *Capabilities* refers to higher-level thinking processes such as problem solving, reasoning, complexity management, troubleshooting, etc. Capabilities embody modes of thinking that are essential to exploiting IT, but they apply broadly. Reasoning, problem solving, etc. are standard components of education; their heavy use in IT makes them topics of emphasis in the Fluency approach.

For each component, the NRC report lists ten recommended items. These are shown in the accompanying table.

Projects

The Skills, Concepts, and Capabilities represent different kinds of knowledge that are co-equal in their contribution to IT fluency. They span separate dimensions of understanding. The overall strategy is to focus on the Skills instruction in the lab, the Concepts instruction in lecture/reading material, and the Capabilities instruction in lecture/lab demonstrations. The projects are the opportunity to use the three kinds of knowledge for a specific purpose. They illustrate IT as it is often applied in practice—to solve information processing tasks of a substantial nature.

A project is a multiweek assignment to achieve a specific IT goal. An example of a project is to create a database to track medical patients in a walk-in clinic, and to give a presentation to convince an audience that patient privacy has been preserved. Students apply a variety of Skills such as using database design software, Web searching, and presentation facilities. They rely on their understanding of Concepts such as database keys, table structure, and the Join query operator. And they use Capabilities such as reasoning, debugging, complexity management, testing, and others. The components are applied together to produce the final result, leading students to an integrated understanding of IT and preparing them for significant "real life" applications of IT.

The NRC's List of Top Ten Skills, Concepts, and Capabilities

Fluency with Information Technology

Skills

1. Set-up a personal computer
2. Use basic operating system facilities
3. Use a word processor to create a document
4. Use a graphics or artwork package to manipulate an image
5. Connect a computer to the Internet
6. Use the Internet to locate information
7. Use a computer to communicate with others
8. Use a spreadsheet to model a simple process
9. Use a database to access information
10. Use on-line help and instructional materials

Concepts

1. Fundamentals of computers
2. Organization of information systems
3. Fundamentals of networks
4. Digital representation of information
5. Structuring information
6. Modeling and abstraction
7. Algorithmic thinking and programming
8. Universality
9. Limitations of Information Technology
10. Social impact of computers and technology

Capabilities

1. Engage in sustained reasoning
2. Manage complexity
3. Test a solution
4. Find problems in a faulty use of IT
5. Navigate a collection and assess quality of the information
6. Collaborate using IT
7. Communicate using IT about IT
8. Expect the unexpected
9. Anticipate technological change
10. Think abstractly about Information Technology

Relationship to Full Fluency

The present volume is the first half of *Fluency with Information Technology*, and as such includes a mix of about half of the recommended Skills, Concepts and Capabilities: Chapter 2, "What the Digerati Know," covers such Skills topics as consistent interface and menus; Chapter 3, "Making the Connection," covers Concepts related to networking such as Internet routing and the http protocol; Chapter 7, "To Err Is Human ...," covers Capabilities related to debugging and troubleshooting. This volume also includes a case study, Chapter 6, illustrating the use of the World Wide Web for research. This book launches students on the Fluency path by presenting an essential foundation for using computers today, and is the ideal preparation for learning the remainder of the Fluency curriculum, which is dedicated to lifelong learning.

Audience

This book is designed for freshmen "non-techies," students who will not be majoring in science, engineering, or math. Except for one short paragraph about encryption, which can be skipped, no mathematical skills are required beyond arithmetic.

There are no prerequisites. Most students who take Fluency will have used email, surfed the Web, and perhaps word processed, which is more than enough preparation to be successful. Students with no experience are advised to spend a few hours acquiring some exposure to IT prior to starting Fluency.

Chapter Dependencies

I have written *Fluency with Information Technology* so it can be taught in a variety of ways. After the introductory Chapters 1 and 2, the overall structure is a series of standalone chapters with few dependencies arranged in small chapter sequences devoted to a sustained topic. The sequences are:

> 3, 4, 5 networking, HTML, and information

> 8, 9, 10, 11 data representations, computers, and algorithms

One effective way to use this design is to present one of the chapter sequences as the basis for a project assignment. Then, while the students are working on the project—projects may span two or more weeks—material from standalone chapters is covered.

Though there are various arrangements, two sequences stand out to me as especially good ways to present the material:

> *Internet forward.* This is the given chapter sequence. The approach begins with networking and HTML, and progresses through to algorithms and multimedia. The strategy is compatible with the logistics of teaching the class in a short amount of time. For example, a build-a-Web-page project can be assigned after Chapter 5 or 6.

> *Traditional.* In this approach, the material unfolds in the time sequence of its creation. So, information representation and computers come before networking. In this case, the order is 1–2, 8–10, 3–7, 11.

Both of these strategies have a compelling pedagogical justification. Which is chosen depends more on instructor taste and class logistics than on any need to present material in a specific order.

Pedagogical Features

Learning Objectives: Each chapter opens with a list of the key concepts that readers should master after reading the chapter.

There are several boxed features that appear throughout the text to aid in understanding of the material. These are:

FITtip: Practical hints and suggestions for every day computer use.
FITbyte: Interesting facts and statistics.
FITcaution: Warnings and explanations of common mistakes.
Try It: Short, in-chapter exercises with solutions provided.
Checklists: A useful list of steps for completing a specific task.

Throughout the text, I also distinguish notable material by the following features:

FITlink: Shows students a practical application of some of the abstract concepts presented in the text.
Great Moments: A historical look at some of the major milestones in computing.
Great Minds: This feature takes a closer look at some of the influential pioneers in technology.

Reference material includes the following:

Glossary: Important words and phrases appear in boldface type throughout the text. A glossary of these terms is included at the end of the book.
Answers: Solutions are provided to the odd numbered exercises for the multiple choice and short answer questions.
Appendix A: HTML reference including a chart of web safe colors.

Supplements

The companion Web site for *Fluency with Information Technology* is at www.aw.com/snyder/, where you can find all the supplements available for this book, as well as the various HTML sources, database designs, programs used in the textbook examples, and an extended glossary. Students are encouraged to retrieve these files to explore along with the text.

The following instructor supplements are available to qualified instructors at the texts website. Please contact your local Addison-Wesley Sales Representative, or send email to aw.cse@aw.com for information about how to access them. You can also request an Instructor's Resource CD-Rom with these materials from your sales representative.

> *Laboratory Materials with solutions.* Learning Fluency is a hands-on activity, so a complete set of laboratory exercises are available.

> *PowerPoint slides.* A convenient resource for teaching Fluency is the collection of PowerPoint slides available at the site.

> *Instructor's manual with solutions.*

> *Test bank.*

> *Test generator.*

Note to Students

Fluency is a somewhat unusual topic, making this a somewhat unusual book. There are two things that I think you should know about using this book.

> *Learn Skills in the lab.* Of the three kinds of knowledge that define Fluency—Skills, Concepts, and Capabilities—very little of the Skills material is included in this book. The Skills content, which is mostly about how to use contemporary computer applications, changes very rapidly, making it difficult to keep up to date. But the main reason few skills are included is that they are best learned in the lab, seated in front of a computer. The lab exercises, which are online and are up to date, provide an excellent introduction to contemporary applications. They provide great coverage of the Skills.

> *Study Fluency steadily.* If this book is successful, it will change the way you think, making you a better problem solver, better at reasoning, better at debugging, etc. These Capabilities are useful in IT and elsewhere in life, so they make learning Fluency really worthwhile. But changing how you think won't happen by just putting the book under your pillow. It'll take some studying. To learn Fluency you must apply good study habits: read the book, do the end of chapter exercises (answers to odd-number exercises are printed at the back of the book), start on your assignments early, ask questions, etc. I think it's best if you spend some time in the lab studying Fluency (not reading email) *every day*, because it takes some time for the ideas to sink in. Students with good study habits tend to do well in Fluency class, and because it improves their problem-solving abilities, etc., they become even better students! It takes some discipline but it pays.

Finally, some sections of the book are best read with a computer handy so that you can try things out. I have marked those chapters in the Table of Contents with a small wave. Good luck! Writing this book has truly been a pleasure. I hope reading it is equally enjoyable.

Acknowledgments

Many people have contributed to this work. First to be thanked are my collaborators in the creation of the Fluency concept, the NRC Committee on Computer Literacy: Al Aho, Marcia Linn, Arnie Packer, Allen Tucker, Jeff Ullman, and Andy van Dam. Special thanks go to Herb Lin of the NRC staff who assisted throughout the Fluency effort, tirelessly and in his usual great good humor. Two enthusiastic supporters of Fluency: Bill Wulf of the National Academy of Engineering and John Cherniavski of the National Science Foundation have continually supported this effort in more ways than I am aware. It has been a pleasure to know and work with this team.

As the material was developed for this book, many have contributed: Ken Yasuhara and Brian Bannon, teaching assistants on the first offering of CSE100, contributed in innumerable ways and injected a needed dose of practicality into my ideas. Grace Whiteaker, Alan Borning, and Batya Friedman have been generous with their ideas regarding Fluency. Martin Dickey of CSE and Mark Donovan of UWired have been constant sources of support. The original offerings of CSE100 benefited greatly from contributions by Nana Lowell, Anne Zald, Mike Eisenberg, and Fred Videon. Colleagues who have contributed include Frank Tompa, Martin Tompa, Carl Ebeling, Brian Kerninghan, Dotty Smith, Calvin Lin and David Mizell.

I am particularly grateful for the keen insights and valuable feedback from the reviewers of this project: Nazih Abdallah, University of Central Florida; Robert M. Aiken, Temple University; Diane M. Cassidy, University of North Carolina at Charlotte; Anne Condon, University of British Columbia; Lee D. Cornell, Minnesota State University, Mankato; Nicholas Cravotta, University of California, Berkeley; Gordon Davies, Open University; Peter J. Denning, George Mason University; Rory J. DeSimone, University of Florida; Richard C. Detmer, Middle Tennessee State University; David L. Doss, Illinois State University; John P. Dougherty, Haverford College; Philip East, University of Northern Iowa; Michael B. Eisenberg, University of Washington; Robert S. Fenchel, University of Wisconsin, Madison; Michael Gildersleeve, University of New Hampshire; Jennifer Golbeck; Michael H. Goldner; Esther Grassian, UCLA College Library; Raymond Greenlaw, Armstrong Atlantic State University; A. J. Hurst, Monash University, Australia; Malcolm G. Lane, James Madison University; Doris K. Lidtke, Towson University; Wen Liu, ITT Technical Institute; Daniela Marghitu, Auburn University; C. Dianne Martin, George Washington University; Peter B. Miller, University of Virginia; Namdar Mogharreban, Southern Illinois University, Carbondale; Paul M. Mullins, Slippery Rock University; David R. Musicant, Carleton College; Alexander Nakhimovsky, Colgate University; Brenda C. Parker, Middle Tennessee State University; Dee Parks, Appalachian State University; Laurie J. Patterson, University of North Carolina, Wilmington; Roger Priebe, University of Texas, Austin; Paul Quan, Albuquerque Technical Vocational Institute; John Rosenberg, Monash University, Australia; Robert T. Ross, California Polytechnic State University; Zhizhang Shen, Plymouth State College; Robert J. Shive, Jr.,

Millsaps College; Patrick Tantalo, University of California, Santa Cruz; and Mark Urban-Lurain, Michigan State University.

Thank you to Jim McKeown and Sandra Macke for contributing to the end of chapter exercises.

The Fluency material has been a topic of discussion with many international colleagues. Discussions with Hans Hinterberger, John Rosenberg, and John Hirsch have been especially valuable in critiquing the material from an overseas perspective. Other helpful international commentary came from Anne Condon, Hannes Jonsson, Jerg Nievergelt, Clark Thomberson, Barbara Thomberson, Ewan Tempero, and Kazuo Iwama.

Among the many thoughtful computer users who have either generously described their misunderstandings about IT or patiently listened to my explanations about IT, I wish to thank Esther Snyder, Helene Fowler, Judy Watson, Brendan Healey, Victory Grund, Shelley Burr, Ken Burr, and Noelle Lamb.

It is my great pleasure to thank my editors, Susan Hartman Sulllivan, Pat Mahtani, and Mary Clare McEwing. Their enthusiasm for the project and their devotion to perfection have been inspirational. And working with them is fun. Joyce Wells has done a fantastic job with the design. Others of the Addison-Wesley team to whom I owe thanks are Michael Hirsch, Regina Kolenda, Marilyn Lloyd, Elizabeth Paquin, and Lesly Hershman. Thanks especially to Bobbie Lewis and Daniel Rausch.

Finally, my wife Julie, and sons, Dan and Dave, have been patient, encouraging, and, most important, a continual source of good humor throughout this effort. It is with my deepest appreciation that I thank them for everything.

Contents

The Master said: "To learn something and then put it into practice at the right time. Is this not a joy?

—THE ANALECTS OF CONFUCIUS

fluency
Information Technology
Skills, Concepts, & Capabilities

Brief Edition

part 1

BECOMING SKILLED
AT INFORMATION TECHNOLOGY

Our study of information technology begins with an introduction to both information and technology. If your contact with computers has been limited, an introduction is essential. If you are like most readers, you've used computers enough to be familiar with email, Web surfing, and perhaps word processing; but, you think, there must be many other cool and interesting ways to use information technology. You're right! And getting a firm foundation is the fastest way forward.

In this first part of our study we focus on becoming skilled at using an Internet-connected personal computer. You will learn new applications—in fact, you will learn how to learn new applications—and you will find out about the Internet and World Wide Web. By the end of this part you will be able to apply information technology to your studies, work, and recreation.

The goal is for you to become a confident, skilled user. You can achieve this goal by combining the information in Part I with daily use of computers and the Internet. We present practical, useful information that requires practice and use, making Fluency a subject in which you can immediately apply what you learn.

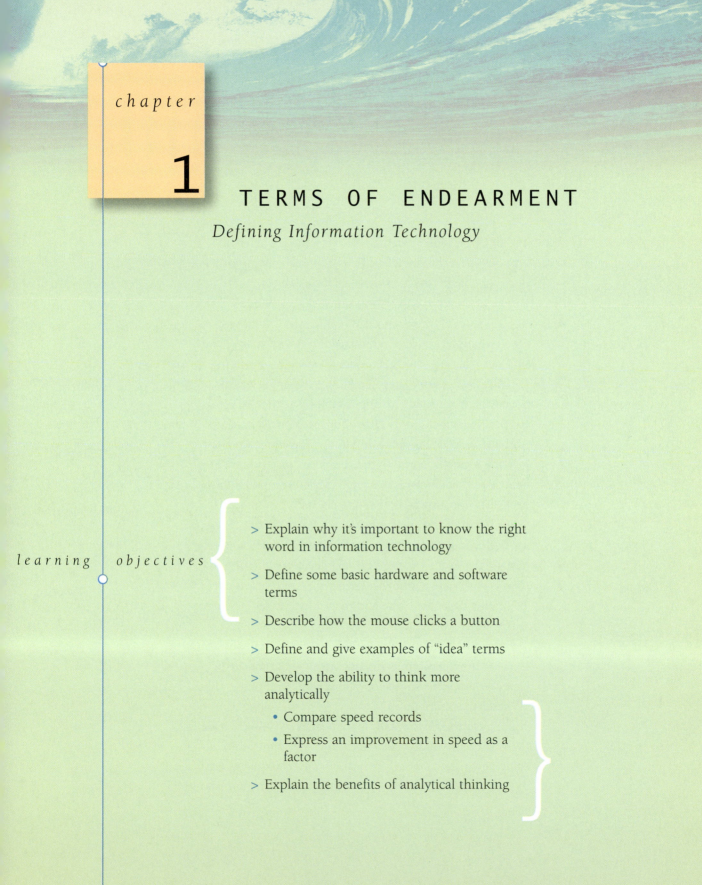

chapter

1

TERMS OF ENDEARMENT

Defining Information Technology

learning | *objectives*

> Explain why it's important to know the right word in information technology

> Define some basic hardware and software terms

> Describe how the mouse clicks a button

> Define and give examples of "idea" terms

> Develop the ability to think more analytically
  • Compare speed records
  • Express an improvement in speed as a factor

> Explain the benefits of analytical thinking

It would appear that we have [as a society] reached the limits of what it is possible to achieve with computer technology, although one should be careful with such statements as they tend to sound pretty silly in 5 years.

—JOHN VON NEUMANN,
COMPUTER PIONEER 1947

TO BECOME Fluent, we need to learn the language of information technology. The people who created information technology (IT) are notorious for using acronyms, jargon, and everyday words in unusual ways. Acronyms like WYSIWYG (pronounced *WHIZ·zee·wig*), "what you see is what you get," are often meaningless even after you find out what the letters stand for. (We'll come back to the WYSIWYG story later.) Jargon like "clicking around" for navigating through an application or a series of Web pages is meaningful only after you have actually done it. And an everyday term like **window**, originally chosen to give the idea of a portal to the computer, may no longer be a good metaphor for the sophisticated computer concept. It is not surprising that people coming across these terms for the first time are confused. But is such technospeak any more weird than, say, medical or musical terms? (For example, the terms *bilirubin* in medicine and *hemidemisemiquaver* in music seem very odd to us, too.) Technology, like medicine and music, makes better sense with a little explanation.

Our first goal in this chapter is to understand why learning the right term is essential to any new endeavor. Next, we ask some simple questions about computers (like "Where's the Start button?") as a way of reviewing terms you may already know. But, for almost every familiar term, there is a new word or idea to learn. We also introduce some new words for the physical or computational aspects of the computer. These are mostly terms you have probably already heard, so finding out exactly what they mean will help you make them part of your everyday vocabulary. Along the way, we explain basic ideas like how buttons are created and how they are clicked. This starts to demystify how the computer's virtual world works and it introduces the ideas of process and algorithm. Then we introduce the "idea" terms of IT, words like *abstraction* and *generalization*. These terms refer to deep concepts, and devoting a few minutes to understanding them will pay off throughout the rest of our Fluency study. Finally, we close with interesting stories about how people and computers have advanced, as we become more analytical thinkers.

WHY KNOW JUST THE RIGHT WORD IN IT

Why has information technology adopted so many strange terms? Because an enormous number of new ideas, concepts, and devices have been invented for IT. These phenomena had to be named so that their creators could describe them and explain them to others. Acronyms are common, because as engineers and scientists develop ideas, they often abbreviate them with the letters of the concept's description. The abbreviation sticks, and if the concept is important, its use extends beyond the laboratory. For example, when engineers invented the "small computer system interface," they abbreviated it SCSI. People began to pronounce it "skuzzy" rather than saying S-C-S-I. Naming-by-abbreviation makes a terminology full of acronyms. Critics call it "alphabet soup." But we can understand it once we understand what all those letters stand for. For example, ROM is short for "read-only memory." Even without knowing much about computers, you can guess that it is a special type of memory that cannot be written to.

Using exactly the right word at the right time is one characteristic of an educated person. Perhaps the best term to learn to use well is the French (now also English) term *le mot juste* (luh mo·joost), which means the right word or exact phrasing.

There are two important reasons for knowing and using le mot juste. First, understanding the terminology is basic to learning any new subject. In learning what these new words mean, we learn the ideas and concepts that they stand for. Our brains seem to be organized so that when we give a thing or idea a name, we remember it more easily. For example, in ice hockey, *icing* is the term for hitting the puck across the blue lines and across the opponent's goal line. We might not even notice this amid all the passing and slap shots. By knowing this new definition for the familiar word *icing*, we start watching for it, increasing our understanding and enjoyment of the game. Precision in using the term means precision in understanding the idea. Eventually the word stops sounding weird and becomes a part of our normal vocabulary. At that point, we use the right word without even thinking about it.

The second reason for knowing and using the right word is to communicate with others. If we use the terms properly, they'll understand us. We'll be able to ask questions and get help—something everyone starting out in a field needs to do. In information technology, using the right word to get help is especially important, because we must often get help by email, on the telephone, or through an online help facility. We have to be precise and articulate because no one will be by our side to help us describe it. If we cannot say what's wrong, we won't get the help we need. Indeed, a goal of Fluency is to be able to get help from such resources. The ability to use *le mot juste* allows us to communicate, get help, and ultimately to be self-reliant.

You could learn vocabulary by reading a computer dictionary, of course, but that's *waaay* too boring. Rather, we introduce the basic terminology by answering some of the nagging questions about IT that have unexpected answers.

WHERE'S THE START BUTTON?

Most computers are on all the time, which is why screen savers were invented. Screen savers—animations such as a kitten prancing around the screen or a changing geometric design—are programs that sleep when the computer is in use but wake up when the computer is idle for a while. They "save the screen" because a single, unchanging image could be "burned into the screen"; that is, it could permanently change the phosphorous surface of the screen, creating a "ghost" of the image that interferes with viewing. The ever-changing image keeps this from happening. (Recent technological advances have made burn-in less of a problem, but screen savers remain; also, many computers simply turn off the screen.) You can reactivate a computer by moving or clicking the mouse, or by pressing any key.

If computers are usually on, why bother to learn where the Start button is? Because sometimes they are off, and as we will see later, we might need to **cycle power**—turn the computer off and then back on. To know where to look for the power button, we need to know the different organizations of a computer.

Two Basic Organizations: Monolithic or Component

Some computers are sold as **components** with a separate monitor, computer and hard drive, speakers, and other devices. (We'll discuss the individual devices later.) Many desktop PCs are organized this way. The **monolithic** package, like an iMac or a laptop, has all the devices bundled together, as shown in Figure 1.1(a). The component approach lets you mix and match parts to fit your needs, as shown in Figure 1.1b. The all-in-one monolithic design is simpler because manufacturers decide for you which components will form a balanced, effective system. Laptops are monolithic, of course, because it is inconvenient to carry around multiple parts. Expect to use both.

(a)   **(b)**

Figure 1.1. Examples of the monolithic (a) and component (b) systems.

In the monolithic design, the **power switch** (⏻) is on the chassis or, often for Macs, on the keyboard. For component systems, the power switch is usually on a separate box near the display containing the CD and/or floppy disk drives. Most component monitors also have their own power switch, but it turns off only the monitor, not the whole computer.

The Monitor

The **monitor** is a video screen like a TV, of course. But there are many differences. Unlike passive TVs, computers are interactive, so the monitor becomes more like a blackboard showing the information created by both the computer and the user as they communicate. Modern monitors are **bit-mapped**, meaning that they display information stored in (the bits of) the computer's memory, as illustrated in Figure 1.2. TVs generally display images live or from recorded tape, captured with a camera. The big, bulky monitors are **cathode ray tubes**, abbreviated CRTs, whereas the slim, flat displays are **liquid crystal displays** (LCDs).

To emphasize the contrast between TVs and computers, notice that television can only show "reality," the images *recorded* through the camera's lens. But a computer creates the images it displays in its memory; they don't have to exist in physical reality. When a computer creates its own world, it's called **virtual reality**.

Figure 1.2. An enlargement of a monitor's display of the word bitmap and the corresponding bits for each pixel.

Cables

The components and the computer must be connected to each other, of course, and they must be connected to an electrical power source. For power-hungry devices like monitors, separate **power cables** are usually used, which is why there is a separate power switch. For simple devices like the keyboard or mouse, the **signal** and power wires are combined into a single cable. To help us plug in the cables correctly, the computer's sockets and the cable's plugs are often labeled with icons, as shown in Figure 1.3. So, we simply match icons.

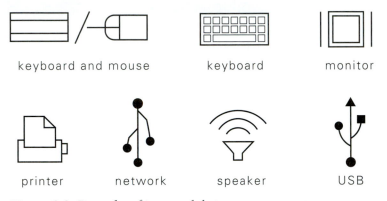

| keyboard and mouse | keyboard | monitor |

| printer | network | speaker | USB |

Figure 1.3. *Examples of icons and their component parts.*

<table>
<tr><td>FITCAUTION</td><td>**Damage Control.** When connecting computer components (or other electronic devices), plug in the power connection last. When disconnecting, remove the power connection first. Briefly, PILPOF—plug in last, pull out first.</td></tr>
</table>

Computer component plugs fit into their sockets in only one way. After you figure out which way around the plug goes in, insert it into the socket gently at first to make sure that the pins—the stiff wires making the connections—align and do not become bent. Once the plug is inserted, **seat** it by pushing it in firmly.

Notice that connectors like the red, green, blue (RGB) cable on a monitor are usually held in place by screws or a clasp, which you should tighten after seating the cable.

Colors: RGB

Combining different amounts of the primary colors of light—red, green, and blue (RGB)—produces the colors you see on your computer monitor, as shown in Figure 1.4. The computer tells the monitor the right proportions of light to display with signals sent through the RGB cable. Any color can be created with some combination of intensities of these three colors. In computer applications, when we select a color from a "palette"—to change the color of text, for example—we are really telling the computer how much of these three colors of light to use.

Figure 1.4. The RGB color scheme.

Pixels

The monitor's screen is divided into a grid of small units called **picture elements**, or **pixels**. A pixel is about the size of the dot on an *i* in 10-point type. (Check this out on your monitor.) The computer displays information on the screen by drawing each pixel the color needed for the intended figure or image. For example, the pixels forming an *i* are colored black and the surrounding pixels are colored white when showing text. The size of the grid in pixels—1024 × 768 is typical for a laptop—is important when choosing a monitor because the more pixels in each row and column, the higher the resolution of the image on the screen; that is, the smoother and crisper it can be.

The computer must first create in its memory everything displayed on the screen, pixel by pixel. For computer-animated movies like *Toy Story*, creating images of dancing toys is extremely difficult. But the appearance of reality that we see on the screen when we use a computer is much easier to generate, as we demonstrate in the FITLINK beginning on page 9.

FITTIP | **Image Change.** The size of the pixel grid displayed on the screen can be increased or decreased using the Control Panel for the Display (Windows) or Monitor (Mac).

WHERE IS THE COMPUTER?

This may seem like an odd question to ask, but it's not. In casual conversation, most of us call the monitor sitting on a desk "the computer." Technically speaking, we're usually wrong. For the monolithic organization such as a laptop or iMac, the part that actually does the computing *is* inside the same unit as the monitor, of course. So for those cases we're right. But for component systems, the computer is

{ FITLINK }

A Virtual Button > >

It is simple to color the screen's pixels to make a figure that looks like a believable button. On a medium-gray background, the designer colors the top and left sides of a rectangle white and the bottom and right sides black. This makes the interior of the rectangle appear to project out from the surface, because the white seems to be highlights and the dark seems to be shadows from a light source at the upper left. (If the figure doesn't look much like a button, look at it from a distance.) There is nothing special about the medium-gray/white/black combination except that it gives the lighted/shadowed effect. Other colors work, too. And, by using colors with less contrast, it is possible to give the button a different "feel"; for example, less metallic, as shown in Figure 1.5.

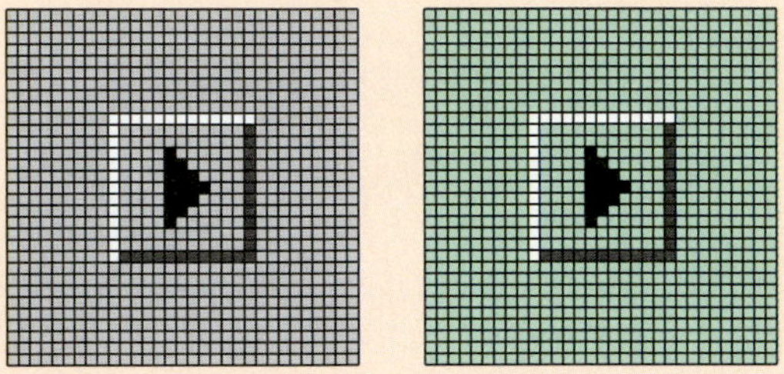

Figure 1.5. *Two virtual buttons with different "feels."*

THE ILLUSION OF BUTTON MOTION

To show that the button has been pressed reverse the black and white colors and translate the icon one position down and to the right. To **translate** a figure means to move it, unchanged, to a new position. Because our brains assume that the light source's position stays the same, the reversal of the colors changes the highlights and shadows to make the inside of the rectangle appear to be pushed in. The translation of the icon creates motion that our eyes notice, completing the illusion that the button is depressed, as shown in Figure 1.6. Notice, however, that the translation of the icon down and to the right is not really a correct motion for a button "pushed into the screen." But accuracy is less important than is the cue to our brains that there is motion.

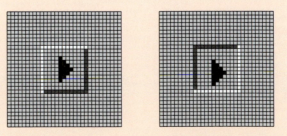

Figure 1.6. *The translation of a button icon.*

We must emphasize that there is no button anywhere inside the computer. The bits of the computer's memory have been set so that when they are displayed on the screen, the pixels appear to be a picture of a button. The computer can change the bits when necessary so that the next time they are displayed, the button looks as if it has been pushed in. Adding a "click" sound makes the illusion even more real. But there is still no button.

PRESSING A VIRTUAL BUTTON

If there is only a picture of a button, how can we "click" it with the mouse? That's a good question, which we can answer without becoming too technical.

Of course, the place to begin is with the mouse pointer. The mouse pointer is a white arrow point with a black border and, like the button, must be created by the computer. When the mouse is moved, the computer finds out in which direction it is moving and redraws the pointer translated a short distance in that direction. By repeatedly redrawing the pointer in new positions that are redisplayed rapidly, the computer produces the illusion that the pointer moves smoothly across the screen. It's the same idea as cartoon flipbooks or motion pictures: A series of still pictures, progressively different and rapidly displayed, creates motion. The frequency of display changes is called the **refresh rate** and, like motion-picture frames, is typically 30 times per second. At that rate, the human eye sees the sequence of still frames as smooth motion.

As the mouse pointer moves across the screen, the computer keeps track of which pixel is at the point of the arrow. In Figure 1.7, the computer records the position by the row and column coordinates, because the pixel grid is like graph paper. So (141, 1003) in Figure 1.7(a) means that the point pixel is in the 141st pixel row from the top of the screen and at the 1003rd pixel column from the left side of the screen. With each new position, the coordinates are updated. When the mouse is clicked, as shown in Figure 1.7(d), the computer determines which button the mouse pointer is over, and then redraws the button to look pushed in.

COORDINATING THE BUTTON AND THE MOUSE

How does the computer know which button the mouse pointer is over? It keeps a list of every button drawn on the screen, recording the coordinates of the button's upper-left and lower-right corners. So, in Figure 1.7, the button would have its upper-left corner at pixel (132, 1010) and its lower-right corner at pixel (145, 1022) (see Figure 1.8). The two corners, call them (x_1, y_1) and (x_2, y_2), determine the position of the rectangle that defines the button: the top row of white pixels is in row x_1, the left-side column of white pixels is in column y_1, the bottom row of black pixels is in row x_2, and the right-side column of black pixels is in column y_2.

Now, if the mouse pointer's point has a row coordinate between x_1 and x_2, the pointer is somewhere between the top and bottom of the button, though it may be to the left or right of the button rather than on it. But if the pointer's point also has a column coordinate between y_1 and y_2, the pointer is between the left and right sides of the button; that is, it is somewhere on the button. So, for each button with coordinates (x_1, y_1) and (x_2, y_2), the computer tests whether

$$x_1 < \text{row coordinate of mouse pointer point} < x_2$$

and

$$y_1 < \text{column coordinate of mouse pointer point} < y_2$$

are *both* true. If so, the mouse pointer's point is over that button, and the button is redrawn in the "clicked configuration." Also, other software is told that the user just clicked on the button, so it can do whatever action the button commands.

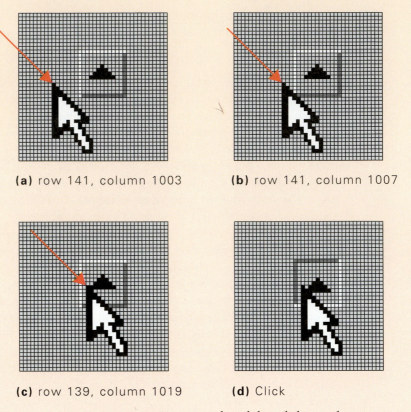

(a) row 141, column 1003   **(b)** row 141, column 1007

(c) row 139, column 1019   **(d)** Click

Figure 1.7. *Mouse pointer moving toward, and then clicking, a button;*
the coordinates of the point of the pointer are given by their row, column positions.

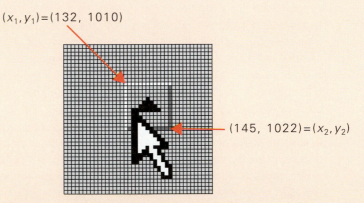

Figure 1.8. *A button's location is completely determined*
by the positions of its upper-left and lower-right corners.

Creating a button and keeping track of the positions of the button and the mouse pointer may seem like a lot of work, but it makes using a computer easier (and more fun) for us. The metaphor of pressing a button to cause an action is so natural that going to the trouble of making buttons greatly simplifies our work.

not in the monitor unit, but rather in a separate box that is often on the floor below the desk or somewhere else nearby. Calling the monitor the computer is not so much a mistake as an acknowledgment that the monitor is our interface to the computer, wherever it may be physically.

In the component approach, the computer and many of its components (for example, hard disk, floppy disk drive, and CD drive) are packaged together in a box that is called the **processor box**, though it often has a fancy marketing name (for example, minitower) that has no technical meaning; see Figure 1.9. For the monolithic approach, of course, the associated disks and drives are in the same package as the monitor. It's as if the monitor were attached to the processor box, so everything in this section applies.

Motherboard

Inside the processor box is the **motherboard**, a printed circuit board containing most of the circuitry of a personal computer system, as shown in Figure 1.10. The name comes from the fact that smaller printed circuit boards, sometimes called **daughter boards**, but more often called **cards**, are plugged into the motherboard for added functionality. A motherboard is impressive to look at with all of its fine wire patterns, colorful resistors, economy of space, and so forth. (Ask your computer dealer to show you one—it's safer than looking at the one in your computer and risking harm to it.) The motherboard is a **printed circuit** or PC board. (This use of "PC" predates "PC" used for "personal computer" by decades.) Of the many parts on this PC board, only the microprocessor chip and the memory are of interest to us at the moment.

Microprocessor

The **microprocessor**, found on the motherboard, is the part of a personal computer system that computes. The microprocessor is involved in every activity of the system, everything from making the mouse pointer appear to move around the screen to locating information stored on the hard disk. The microprocessor is the "smart" part of the system, so engineers often describe the other parts of a computer as "dumb." It is surprisingly easy for a computer to be "smart," as we will see. Eventually, we will even ask, "Can a computer think?"

The "micro" part of microprocessor is archaic and no longer accurate. The term "microprocessor" was adopted around 1980 when all of the circuitry for a computer first fit onto a single silicon chip. These were technically computer processors, but they were small and primitive compared to the mainframes and the "minicomputers" of the day, so they were called *micro*processors. But improvements came so quickly that in a few years microprocessors were more powerful than the largest computers of 1980. Today's microprocessors are fast, highly optimized, loaded with features, and very sophisticated. In fact, microprocessors spend most of their time doing nothing, just waiting for us. Because there is nothing "micro" about today's microprocessors, we will simply use the proper term **processor** for the rest of this book.

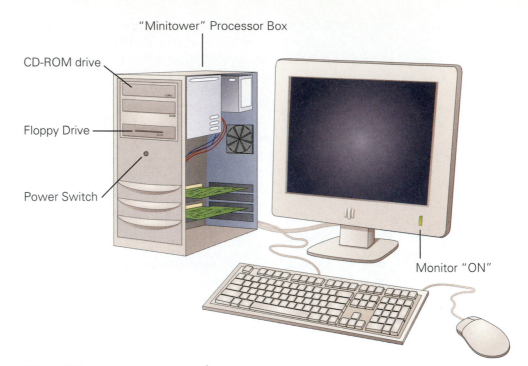

Figure 1.9. *A component-approach computer.*

Figure 1.10. *A motherboard.*

Memory

The **memory** of a computer is where a program and its data are located while the program is running. For example, when you are using a word processor, the word processing program and the document being edited are stored in the memory. (When they're not in memory, programs and data are stored on the hard disk; see the next section.) Computer memory is also called **RAM**, short for **random access memory**. The basic unit of memory is a **byte**, which will be described in Chapter 8. Today's personal computers have millions of bytes of RAM memory, or **megabytes**, from the Greek prefix **mega-** for million. (See Figure 9.9 in Chapter 9 for a list of prefixes.)

There are two basic ways to locate and retrieve, or *access*, information: sequential and random. Information stored sequentially is arranged in a line, so that when you want to get a specific item, you have to skip everything else stored before it, as shown in Figure 1.11. Cassette tapes, VCR tapes, and so on are examples of **sequential access**. **Random access** means that any item can be retrieved directly. Finding dictionary entries, library books, and numbers in a phonebook are examples of random access. Random access is faster than sequential access, as anyone wanting to watch the last scene on a VCR tape well knows.

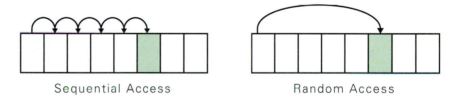

Sequential Access   Random Access

Figure 1.11. Sequential versus random access.

Hard Disk

The **hard disk** is not really part of a computer—it is technically a high-capacity, persistent peripheral storage device. But it is so fundamental to personal computer systems that it's helpful to think of it as a basic part. The hard disk is also referred to as the **hard drive**, and was once simply known as a **disk** before floppy disks were invented. The hard disk stores programs and data when they are not in immediate use by a computer. Disks are made from an iron compound that can be magnetized. Because the magnetism remains even when the power is off, the encoded information is still there when the power comes back on. So a disk is said to be *permanent* or *persistent* storage. A hard disk is usually located in the same box as the processor, because without access to permanent storage, the processor is crippled.

The hard disk looks like a small stack of bright metal washers with an arm that can sweep across them, as shown in Figure 1.12. The "popping" or "clicking" sound we sometimes hear is the arm moving back and forth as it accesses information on various tracks of the disk.

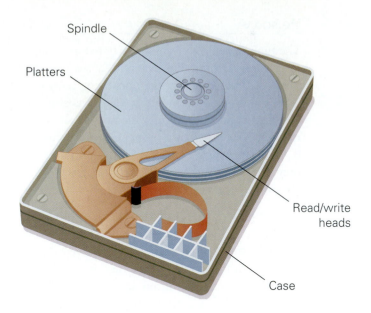

Spindle

Platters

Read/write
heads

Case

Figure 1.12. A hard disk.

Hard-disk Memory vs. RAM. A successful computer user must understand an important difference between the RAM memory and the hard disk memory. Today's RAM is made from integrated circuit (IC) technology, informally called **microchips**. One property of IC memory is that it is **volatile**, meaning that the information is lost when the power is turned off. So all of the information that must be permanently saved must be on the hard disk. *The point is to save your work often, which copies it from the RAM to the disk.* This limits the amount of work that will be lost if the computer crashes for some reason. If your computer crashes, you have to restart it, which may mean cycling power (turning the power off and on). When the power goes off, the information in the volatile RAM is lost, but the information saved on the nonvolatile disk will be reloaded when the computer restarts.

HOW SOFT IS SOFTWARE?

The term hardware predates computers by centuries. Originally it meant metal items like hinges and nails, used in construction. There was no need for the word software until computers were invented.

Software

Software is a collective term for programs. The name contrasts with hardware, of course, but what does it mean for software to be "soft"? When a computer function is implemented in software, the computer does the operation by following instructions. A program that figures out income taxes is an example. If the function is implemented in **hardware**, the computer does the operations directly with wires and transistors. (We say it is **hard-wired**.) The multiplication operation is an example.

The difference between "hard" and "soft" is like the difference between an innate ability, such as coughing, and a learned ability, such as reading. Innate abilities are "built in" biologically, and they're impossible to change, like hardware. Learned abilities can be easily changed and expanded. We can change from reading English to reading French, *n'est-ce pas*? A computer cannot change how it multiplies, but one minute a computer can be following the instructions to figure U.S. income tax, and the next moment it can be following instructions to compute Canadian income tax. (Computers don't *learn* to perform soft operations, of course, the way we learn to read. Rather, they are simply given the instructions and told to follow them.)

FITBYTE

The Hard Reality. The difference between hardware and software was dramatically illustrated in 1994 when a bug was discovered in the hard-wired divide operation of Intel's Pentium processor, an approximately $200 chip. Though the wrong answers were rare and tiny, the error had to be fixed. If divide had been implemented in software, as had been the usual approach in computing's early years, Intel could have sent everyone a simple patch for $1 or $2. But hardware cannot be changed, so the Pentium chips had to be recalled at a total cost of about $500 million.

Algorithms and Programs

An **algorithm** is a precise and systematic method for solving a problem. Another term for a systematic method is a **process**. Some familiar algorithms are the arithmetic operations like addition, subtraction, multiplication, and division; the process for sending a greeting card to a parent; and the method for finding a number in the telephone book. The method for determining when a mouse pointer is over a button is an algorithm. Because an algorithm's instructions are written down for some other agent (a person or a computer) to follow, precision is important.

Though we are sometimes taught algorithms, like the arithmetic algorithms, we figure out many algorithms on our own, like finding phone numbers. In Chapter 10, we introduce **algorithmic thinking**, the act of thinking up algorithms. Writing out the steps of an algorithm is **programming**, and **programs** are simply algorithms written in a specific programming language for a specific set of conditions.

When we ask a computer to do something for us, we ask it to **run** a program. This is literally what we are asking when we click on the icon for an application like Netscape. We are saying, "Run the program from the Netscape company to browse the Internet." *Run* is a correct term that has been used since the invention of computers. But a slightly better term is *execute*, because it emphasizes an important property of computing.

Execute

A computer **executes** a program when it performs instructions. The word **execute** means following a set of orders exactly as they are written. Indeed, computer pioneers used the word *orders* for what we now call instructions. The orders tell the computer to act in a specific way and in no other. When orders are given, the faithful agent is *not* supposed to think. There is no possibility for optional or independent behavior. "Following instructions literally" is what computers do when they run programs, and it is that aspect that makes "execute" a slightly better term than "run."

In addition to run and execute, **interpret** is also a correct term for following a program's instructions, as explained in Chapter 9.

Boot

Finally, the term **booting** means to start a computer and **rebooting** means to restart it. Because booting most often happens after a catastrophic error or a crash, you might guess that the term is motivated by frustration—we want to kick the computer like a football. But *booting* comes from *bootstrap*. Computers were originally started by an operator who entered a few instructions into the computer's empty memory using console push buttons. Those instructions told the computer to read in a few more instructions—a very simple operating system—from punch cards. This operating system could then read in the instructions of the real operating system from magnetic tape, similar to a VCR tape. Finally, the computer was able to start doing useful work. This incremental process was called **bootstrapping**, from the phrase "pulling yourself up by your bootstraps," because the computer basically started itself. Today this process is in the boot ROM.

THE WORDS FOR IDEAS

Though understanding the physical parts of IT—monitors, motherboards, and memory—seems very important to our success with IT, we will not be so concerned with them. Rather, we will mostly use **concept** words such as those in this section.

"Abstract"

One of the most important "idea" words used in this book is the verb *to abstract*. It has several meanings. In British mysteries, *to abstract* means *to remove*, as in *to steal*: "The thief abstracted the pearl necklace while the jeweler looked at the diamond ring." The meanings of *to abstract* in information technology share the idea of removal, but the thing being removed is not physical. The thing being removed is an idea or a process, and it is extracted from some form of information.

To **abstract** is to remove the basic concept, idea, or process from a situation. The removed concept is usually expressed in another, more succinct and usually more general form, called an **abstraction**.

We are familiar with abstraction in this sense. For example, parables and fables, which teach lessons in the form of stories, require us to abstract the essential point of the story. When we are told about a fox who can't reach a bunch of grapes and so calls them sour, we abstract an idea from the story: When people try but fail to reach a goal, they often change their view of the desirability of the goal.

Notice two key points here. First, many but not all of the details of the story are irrelevant to the concept. In the process of abstracting, we must decide which details of the story are relevant and which are irrelevant. The "grapes" and the "fox" are unimportant, but "failure" is important to the point. Being able to tell the difference between important and unimportant details is essential to understanding the point of a story, and to abstraction generally. Second, the idea—the abstraction—has meaning beyond the story. The point of repeating the parable, of course, is to convey an idea that applies to many situations.

"Generalize"

A process similar to abstraction is to recognize the common idea in two or more situations. Recognizing how different situations have something basic in common is why we create parables, rules, and so on.

To **generalize** is to express an idea, concept, or process that applies in many situations. The statement summing up that idea is called a **generalization**.

For example, most of us notice that twisting a faucet handle left turns water on and twisting it right turns it off. Not always—some water taps have only a single "joy stick" handle, and others have horizontal bars that pull forward—but it is true most of the time. We generalize that "on" is to the left; "off" is to the right. Perhaps we also notice that twisting lids, caps, screws, and nuts to the left usually loosens them, and right usually tightens them. Again, we generalize that left means loosen, right means tighten. We probably also generalize that both situations are really examples the same thing! A generalization of generalizations.

Noticing patterns and generalizing about them is a very valuable habit. Though generalizations do not always apply, recognizing them gives us a way to begin in a new but similar situation.

"Operationally Attuned"

Another term related to extracting concepts and processes refers to being aware of how a gadget works. To be **operationally attuned** is to apply what we know about how a device or system works as an aid to simplifying its use.

For example, we previously generalized that with few exceptions all caps, lids, screws, and nuts tighten by turning right, and loosen by turning left. We might know this intuitively, but knowing it *explicitly* makes us operationally attuned. That is, knowing this fact as a rule—some kids learn "righty-tighty, lefty loosey"—means that when a lid or nut is stuck, we can twist it very hard in the correct direction, making sure we are loosening rather than tightening it.

The term operationally attuned has been introduced here to emphasize that thinking about how information technology works makes it simpler to use. We don't expect to be experts on all of IT—no one can be. But by asking ourselves, "How does this work?" and using what we learn by thinking about the answer, we are likely to be more successful at applying IT. Our Fluency study will focus on learning enough to answer many of the "How does this work?" questions.

{ F I T LINK }

Tuning In > >

In our daily lives, we use hundreds of devices, systems, and processes. For some, like the ignition on the car, we quickly learn which way to turn the key because it only turns in one direction. We don't think about how it works. Using it becomes a habit. Other gadgets, however, have more leeway, and for them it helps to be attuned to their operation. One example is a deadbolt lock, which moves a metal bar from the door to the doorframe to lock the door. Thinking about how the lock works can tell us whether the door is locked or not. Referring to Figure 1.13(a), notice which way the knob is turned. By visualizing the internal works of the lock, we can imagine that the top of the knob is attached to the bar. When the knob is pointing left, the bar must be pulled back—that is, unlocked. When the knob is positioned to the right, the bar is extended, so the door is locked. (Not all deadbolt locks are this simple, nor are they all installed right side up.) We may not know how the lock really works, but explaining its operation in our own terms means that we can see at a distance whether the door is locked or unlocked. It's not a big deal, but it might save us from getting up off the sofa and trying the door to see if it's locked.

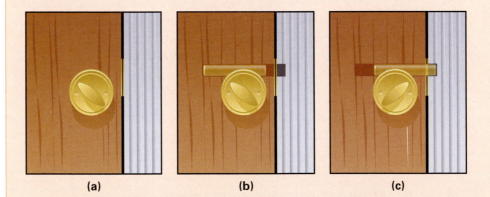

(a)   **(b)**   **(c)**

Figure 1.13. Deadbolt lock. (a) The external view. (b) Internal components, unlocked. (c) Internal components, locked. Thinking about how the deadbolt works allows us to see at a glance whether the door is locked or not.

"Mnemonic"

Finally, **mnemonic** is a rather unusual term that we use in IT, and in other fields as well. The silent *m* implies it's a word with an unusual past.

A mnemonic (*ni-´mă-nik*) is an aid to remembering something. The reminder can take many forms, such as pronounceable words or phrases. North Americans remember the five Great Lakes with HOMES—Huron, Ontario, Michigan, Erie, and Superior. Earlier in this chapter, we mentioned PILPOF—plug in last, pull out first—for remembering when to connect and disconnect the power cable.

There are many details about IT that we need to know only occasionally, like when to connect power. They're not worth memorizing, but they're inconvenient to look up. So, if we can think of a mnemonic that helps us remember the details when we need them, we make using technology simpler.

ANALYTICAL THINKING

Using the right terms makes learning IT simpler, but an equally valuable habit to acquire is becoming more analytical. When we say that the world record in the mile run has been improving or computer performance has been improving, we are making only very weak statements. They simply assert that things have changed over time for the better. But has the change been infinitesimally small, or has it been gigantic? How does the change compare to other changes? Since we can easily find information—that's one of the benefits, for example, of the World Wide Web—we can know an earlier measure of performance and a recent measure. Then we can compare them. Thinking analytically is essential to becoming Fluent in IT, but it is also useful in our other studies, our careers, and throughout life.

Consider the mile run as an illustration.

Mile Runs

When Moroccan miler Hicham El Guerrouj broke the world record on July 7, 1999, the news reports trumpeted that he "smashed," "eclipsed," and "shattered" the world's record set six years earlier by Noureddine Moreceli of Algeria (see Figure 1.14). El Guerrouj had run a mile in an astonishing 3 minutes, 43.13 seconds, an impressive 1.26 seconds faster than Moreceli. The descriptions were not hyperbole. People around the world truly marveled at El Guerrouj's accomplishment, even though 1.26 seconds seems like a small amount of time.

To put El Guerrouj's run into perspective, notice that 45 years had passed since Englishman Roger Bannister attracted world attention as the first man in recorded history to run a mile in less than 4 minutes (see Figure 1.14). His time was 3:59.4. In 45 years, the world's best runners improved the time for the mile by an astonishing 16.27 seconds. (Notice that El Guerrouj's 1.26 seconds was a large part of that.) As a rate, 16.27 seconds represents an improvement from 15.038 miles per hour to 16.134 miles per hour, or just over 7 percent. Given that Bannister's world-class time was the starting point, an improvement in human performance of that size is truly something to be admired.

Comparing to 20-year-olds

How do these world champions compare to average people? Most healthy people in their early 20s—the age group of the world record setters—can run a mile in 7.5 minutes. This number was chosen because it covers the ability of a majority of the people in the age range, and is approximately twice the time El Guerrouj needed. To say El Guerrouj is twice as fast as an average person is to say he is faster by a factor of 2. (The factor is found by dividing the new rate by the old.)

This factor-of-2 difference is a rough rule for the performance gap between an average person and a world champion for most physical strength activities such as running, swimming, jumping, and pole vaulting. The factor-of-2 rule tells us that no matter how hard most people try at physical activities, their performance can improve by at most twice. Of course, most of us can only dream of achieving even part of that factor-of-2 potential. Nevertheless, the factor-of-2 rule is an important benchmark.

Figure 1.14. *The runners Hicham El Guerrouj (left) and Roger Bannister (right).*

Factor of Improvememt

When we compared world champions, we said there was a 7 percent improvement and that El Guerrouj's speed was about a factor-of-2 times faster than the speed of an average person. There is a difference between expressing improvement as a **percentage** and expressing improvement as a factor. We find a **factor of improvement** by dividing the new rate by the old rate. So, to find El Guerrouj's improvement over Bannister's, we divide their rates (16.134/15.038) to get 1.07. Percentages are a closely related computation found by dividing the *amount of change* by the old rate (16.134 – 15.038) / 15.038 = 0.07 and multiplying the result by 100. The added complexity of percentage is potentially confusing, so we use the simpler factor-of-improvement method. El Guerrouj was a factor-of-1.07 times faster than Bannister and about a factor-of-2 times faster than an average person.

TRY IT

Computing the Factor of Improvement. Flyer 1, the aircraft Orville and Wilbur Wright flew at Kitty Hawk, North Carolina, went so slowly (10 mph) that the brother who wasn't piloting could run alongside as it flew just off the ground. The SR-71 Blackbird, probably the world's fastest plane, flies at 2200 mph, three times the speed of sound.

What is the factor of improvement between Blackbird and Flyer 1?

Speed of Blackbird = 2200 mph

Speed of Flyer 1 = 10 mph

Factor of improvement = 2200/10 = 220

The Blackbird is a factor-of-220 faster than Flyer 1.

Super Computers

As another example of analytical thinking, let's compare computer speeds. The UNIVAC I, the first commercial computer, unveiled in 1951 (and current when Bannister set his record), operated at a rate of nearly 100,000 addition operations (adds) per second. By comparison, a typical PC today—say, the portable IBM ThinkPad—can perform a billion additions per second or so. This factor-of-10,000 improvement over UNIVAC I (1,000,000,000/100,000) is truly remarkable. But, consider this—the ThinkPad is no record setter. It's the sort of computer a college student can afford to buy. Engineering workstations can easily do several billion adds per second, boosting the factor even higher. And an Intel computer called ASCI Red, built for Sandia National Laboratory, held the world record for computer speed in 1999, when El Guerrouj set his record. ASCI Red ran at an astonishing 2.1 trillion floating-point adds per second. (Floating-point adds are decimal arithmetic operations that are more complex than the additions used to measure the speed of the UNIVAC I.) Compared to the UNIVAC I, ASCI Red is a factor of 21 million times faster!

Perhaps nothing else in human experience has improved so dramatically. In roughly the same time period that human performance improved by a factor of 1.07 as measured by the mile run, computer performance improved by a factor of 21,000,000. Can we comprehend such a huge factor of improvement, or even the raw speed of ASCI Red?

FITTIP

Faster Still. ASCI Red was the fastest of its day, but its day has passed. Several computers have eclipsed its performance, and better designs continue to emerge. For the latest speed tests, see `www.netlib.org/benchmark/top500.html`.

FITBYTE

Think About It. Most of us can appreciate the 7 percent improvement of El Guerrouj's run over Bannister's, and probably the factor-of-2 improvement in average versus world champion performance. Those we can imagine. But factors of improvement in the thousands or millions are beyond comprehension. Notice that if El Guerrouj had improved on Bannister by a factor of 21,000,000, he'd have run the mile in 11.4 microseconds. That's 11.4 millionths of a second. What does that mean?

> Human visual perception is so slow that El Guerrouj could run 3000 miles at that rate before anyone could even notice he had moved.

> The sound would still be "inside" the starting gun 11.4 microseconds after the trigger was pulled.

> Light travels only twice as fast.

Both the raw power of today's computers and their improvement over the last half-century are almost beyond comprehension.

Benefits of Analytical Thinking

To summarize, we have made our understanding of recent speed improvements crisper by applying simple analysis. Rather than accepting the statement that the mile run and computers have improved, we found out the facts given as two measurements of performance. But once we had the data, we did not leave it as two separate observations: 100,000 additions in 1951 versus 2.1 trillion additions in 1999. Instead, we analyzed their relationship by figuring the factor of improvement: 2,100,000,000,000/100,000. ASCI Red is faster by a factor of 21 million.

This analysis let us compare the improvement to other advancements, and to put them all into perspective. The mile run, though improving by an apparently small factor of 1.07 times in 45 years, is still very impressive when we recall that champions are only about a factor-of-2 better than average people. Computer performance has improved by unimaginable amounts. Though our original statement, "the mile run and computers have improved," is correct, our analysis helps us to be much more expressive and precise. Analytical thinking helps us understand more deeply the world of information technology and the physical world in which we live.

The Story Behind WYSIWYG

The only remaining task is to define the first acronym mentioned in the chapter, **WYSIWYG**. Remember that it stands for "what you see is what you get." To understand the term, recall that the computer creates the virtual world we see on our screens. The representation the computer uses to keep track of the things on the screen is very different from the picture it shows us. For example, the text you are reading was stored in the computer as one very long line of letters, numbers, punctuation, and other characters, but it is displayed to me as a nicely formatted page like the one you are reading. The computer processes its representation—the long sequence of characters—to create the nicely formatted page. The original text editors couldn't do that, so users had to work with the long string. If you wanted to change anything, you had to imagine what it would look like printed out.

Eventually text editing systems were programmed to show the user the page as it would appear when printed. Changing the text became much easier. This property was described as "what you see [when editing] is what you get [when its printed]" or WYSIWYG. Text editors with the WYSIWYG property became known as **word processors**.

SUMMARY

In this chapter we have focused on learning IT terms in context. We started by recognizing that knowing and using *le mot juste* is important in IT for two reasons. Our brains seem to organize knowledge around words, so as we learn the words, we learn the ideas. Also, knowing the right terms helps us communicate with others in the field. Then we learned some basic terminology using questions like "Where is the Start button?" and "How soft is software?" These questions helped us review basic terms that were probably already familiar—monitor, screen saver, RAM, software, and so on. Mixed in with these discussions were new words that perhaps you didn't know—sequential access, volatile, motherboard, and so on. You will use some of these terms, like *software*, daily. Others, like *volatile*, you may never use. But the idea that it names—information is lost when the power is switched off—is very important to your everyday use of IT, making the term a secure site to anchor practical advice, "Save your work regularly." We also considered a brief list of "idea" words, such as *abstract*. These words and ideas will be used throughout our study of IT. Finally, we illustrated analytical thinking by looking at improvements in the mile run and computer speed.

We're not done, however. All of the chapters of this book introduce new terms when new ideas are introduced. Learning and remembering the terms can help you learn and remember the ideas. All of the new terms have been collected in the glossary at the end of the book. Check the glossary when a term slips your mind. In addition to the glossary in this book, there are several good online glossaries, and it's probably a good idea to find one with your Web browser and bookmark it—that is, save its URL. (Whoops, have we defined **URL** yet? No, but we will in Chapter 3. Meanwhile, check the glossary to find out what it stands for.)

EXERCISES

Multiple Choice

1. Computer monitors are different from TVs because:
   A. monitors are bit-mapped whereas TVs are not
   B. TVs are interactive whereas monitors are not
   C. monitors are CRTs whereas TVs are not
   D. more than one of the above

2. Screen savers:
   A. are useful because they prevent burn-in
   B. save energy
   C. can be turned off with a key press or a mouse click
   D. all of the above

3. The display for a laptop is most likely a:
   A. TV
   B. RGB display
   C. LCD
   D. CRT display

4. Mice and keyboards do not have power cords because:
   A. they are not electrical
   B. the power and the signal wires are in one cable
   C. they run on batteries
   D. none of the above

5. The last cable you plug in should be the:
   A. monitor cable
   B. keyboard cable
   C. printer cable
   D. power cable

6. RGB stands for:
   A. red, green, black
   B. red, gray, blue
   C. rust, black, brown
   D. red, green, blue

7. A typical monitor:
   A. has over a million pixels
   B. has a 1024×768 pixel grid
   C. displays pixels that are generated on the hard drive
   D. all of the above

8. How many pixels make up the button in Figure 1.8 (page 12)?
   A. 19×19
   B. 304
   C. 1024×768
   D. none of the above

9. If the computer redraws every pixel on the screen of a laptop 30 times a second, how many pixels get redrawn in a minute?
   A. 23,592,960
   B. $1024 \times 768 \times 30$
   C. $1024 \times 768 \times 60$
   D. more than one of the above

10. How is the process for clicking a check box similar to clicking a button?
   A. The tip of the arrow must be inside the x, y coordinates that make up the check box.
   B. The user must click the mouse button.
   C. The configuration of the check box must change from unchecked to checked or vice versa.
   D. all of the above

Short Answer

1. The _____ is involved in every activity of the computer system.

2. Knowing _____ is important to understanding technology and being understood when talking about it.

3. A _____ saves energy by shutting off the monitor when it is not in use.

4. The last cable you should plug in should be the _____.

5. How many pixels are on a typical laptop?

6. The number of times a second that images on the screen are redrawn is called the _____.

7. The _____ is the active point of the mouse pointer.

8. A specified result sought through the use of a precise and systematic method is a(n) _____.

9. _____ is the proper term used when a computer performs the instructions in a program.

10. The process of starting a computer is called _____.

11. Gleaning the central idea or concept from a situation is called _____.

12. A device that helps you remember a fact or concept is a _____.

13. A WYSIWYG text editor is called a _____.

14. On the computer, programs and information are stored on the _____.

15. The formulation of an idea, concept, or process that can be applied in many situations is called a _____.

Exercises

1. Here are some of the acronyms found in this chapter. Next to each, write its name and its meaning.

   SCSI
   IT
   CRT
   LCD
   RGB
   CD
   RAM
   ROM
   PC
   IC

2. Create a list of mnemonics that you know and their meanings.

3. Find the details of the computer system you are using. If you do not have the manual, use an ad from a newspaper, flyer, or a Web site. Write down the specifications for your system, paying close attention to the terms and specs that are unfamiliar. Make a note to learn more about these in further chapters.

4. It took Magellan's expedition three years to circumnavigate the globe. The space shuttle makes an orbit in about 90 minutes. Calculate the factor of improvement.

5. Ellery Clark of the United States won the long jump in the 1896 Olympiad in Athens, Greece with a jump of 20 feet 9 3/4 inches. The current world record is held by Mike Powell of the United States, who jumped a distance of 8.95 meters. What is the factor of improvement? Be sure to convert between feet and meters.

6. Ray Harroun won the first Indianapolis 500 in 1911 with a speed of 74.59 miles per hour. The 2002 race was won by Helio Castroneves with a speed of 166.499 mph. What is the factor of improvement?

7. In 2003, Svetlana Feofanova set the world pole vault record at 4.76 meters. William Hoyt set the record in 1896 with a vault of 3.30 meters. What is the factor of improvement that she made over the men's record of 1896? What is the percentage increase?

WHAT THE DIGERATI KNOW

Exploring the Human-Computer Interface

> Explain key ideas familiar to experienced users (the digerati):

- The advantages of having common features in information technology
- The benefits of using feedback of "clicking around" and "blazing away" in exploring new applications
- The basic principle of IT: Form follows function

> Explain how a basic search is done

> Use common methods to search and edit text:

- Find (words, characters, spaces)
- Shift-select
- The placeholder technique
- Search-and-replace (substitution)

> Demonstrate an ability to think abstactly about techology by using the basic rules of IT to learn about information technology new to you

PERHAPS the most uncomfortable part of being an inexperienced computer user is the suspicion that everyone but you is born knowing how to use technology. They seem to know automatically what to do in any situation. Maybe, you think, they have all come from the same alien planet that computers have come from.

Of course, experienced users don't really have a technology gene. Through experience, however, they have learned a certain kind of knowledge that lets them figure out what to do in most situations. Most people do not "know" this information explicitly—it is not usually taught in class. They just learn it through experience. But, you can avoid long hours of stumbling around gaining experience. In this chapter, we reveal some secrets of the digerati so that you, too, can "join the club." (Digerati is a new word for people who understand digital technology, from the word *literati*.)

The major goal for this chapter is to show you how to think about technology abstractly. We do this by asking how people learn technical skills and by considering what the creators of technology expect from us as users. This chapter will also help you understand that:

> Computer systems use consistent interfaces, standard metaphors, and common operations.
> Computer systems always give feedback while they are working.
> Making mistakes will not break the computer.
> The best way to learn to use new computer software is to try it out, expecting to make mistakes.
> Asking questions of other computer users is not evidence of being a dummy, but proof of an inquiring mind.

These ideas can help you learn new software quickly. A key abstract idea about software is that it obeys fundamental laws. This deep idea can help you in your everyday software usage, as we illustrate when we explain the principle "form follows function." We show how this principle applies to basic text searching, which helps you learn the subject without using any specific vendor's software. Such knowledge applies to every system and makes us versatile users. You, too, can become one of the digerati.

LEARNING ABOUT TECHNOLOGY

Human beings are born knowing how to chew, cough, stand, blink, smile, and so forth. They are not born knowing how to ride a bicycle, drive a car, use a food processor, or start a lawnmower. For any tool more complicated than a stick, we need some explanation about how it works and possibly some training in its use. Parents teach their children how to ride bicycles, driver's training classes explain to teenagers how to drive safely, and most products come with an owner's manual.

Some tools such as portable CD players are so intuitive that most people living in our technological society find their use "obvious." We don't need to look at the owner's manual. We can guess what the controls do because we know what operations are needed to play recordings. (Without this knowledge, the icons on the buttons would probably be meaningless.) And we can usually recover from mistakes. For example, if you were to insert a CD upside-down, it wouldn't work, so you'd turn it over and try again.

But the fact that we live in a technological society and can figure out how a CD works doesn't mean that we have any innate technological abilities. Instead, it emphasizes two facts about technology:

> Our experience using (related) devices guides us in what to expect.

> The designers who create these devices know we have that experience and design their products to match what we already know.

These two facts are key to success with information technology.

A Perfect Interface

On certain Apple Macintosh computers, when a user loads an audio CD into the computer's CD drive, the **graphical user interface** (**GUI**) shown in Figure 2.1 appears on the screen. A GUI, pronounced "*GOO-ey*," is the medium by which users interact with programs running on a personal computer. This GUI appears on the screen because the Macintosh's operating system, noting that a CD has just been inserted into the drive and recognizing that it is an audio CD, assumes the user wants to listen to it. So, it starts the software that plays audio CDs, shows the user the GUI to find out what he or she wants to play, and waits for a response.

Figure 2.1. Graphical user interface for one version of an Apple Macintosh audio CD player.

Using Analogy

As first-time users of this software, we look at the GUI wondering what the software does and how to use it. There is an online user's manual, but we will not need it. The GUI tells the whole story. This GUI shows us a familiar picture of a CD player, complete with digital readout in green LCD numerals, "metallic" buttons with the standard icons, and so on. No physical CD player looks exactly like this one—for example, the CD slot is the wrong size—but it is so much like a real CD player that anyone who has seen one recognizes this image immediately. So we guess that pressing the button with the Play icon (▶) will cause the computer to play the CD. But, because this is a GUI, we can't really press a button. The action analogous to "pressing" for a computer is "clicking" with the mouse. We know this from experience. Clicking on the button with the icon for Play starts the CD playing. Because it worked, we know that the analogy of the GUI to a physical CD player is correct, and from then on we have a basic idea of how to operate the software. We didn't need lessons; no one had to help us.

Understanding the Designer's Intent

The use of the physical analogy to guide the user in learning to operate the CD player software may seem obvious, but it demonstrates a basic idea of consumer software. Like anyone who invents a new tool, software designers have to teach users how to operate their inventions. They can and do write manuals explaining all of the software's slick features, but it's much better if users can figure out the software without studying the manual. So, software designers, like physical CD player designers, try to pick easy-to-understand user interfaces. Instead of creating a GUI that requires explanation, the designers guessed that an analogy with the familiar physical CD player would be intuitive. They put a lot of time and effort into making their GUI look real by using LCD numerals, "metallic" buttons, the standard button icons, a "slot" for the CD (which plays no role but to make the metaphor more believable), a slider volume control, and so forth. And they guessed right. Anyone who has used a CD player will know how this software works, at least its basics. (The Microsoft Windows operating system audio CD player for the same software generation also uses some of these features of the physical analogy, as shown in Figure 2.2.)

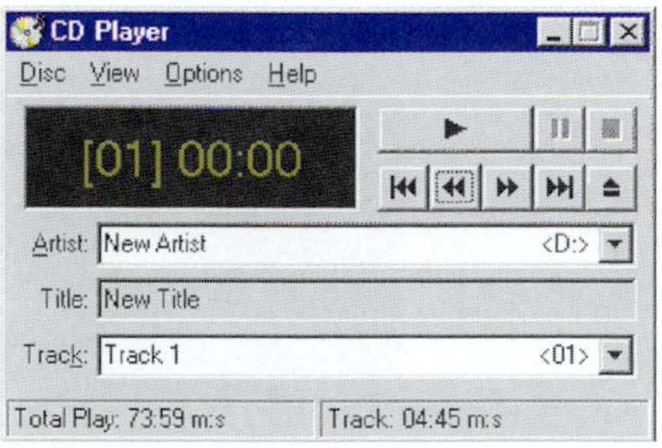

Figure 2.2. *Audio CD player GUI for the Windows operating system.*

To summarize, it is in a software designer's interest to make the GUI intuitive enough for us to figure out on our own. Though they do not always succeed as brilliantly as the designer(s) of the Macintosh audio CD GUI, we should expect as users that the software has been well crafted and that we can "brain out" how it works. We use this idea every time we need to use new software.

BASIC METAPHORS OF SOFTWARE

In software, a metaphor is an object or idea used as an analogy for a computation.

It is clear from a physical analogy how to play a CD with the audio CD player GUIs, but there is more to this software than just the seven standard buttons: Play, Stop, Eject, Last Track, Next Track, Forward, and Backward. How are we supposed to know about those other features? We can guess what some of them do, like Shuffle, because physical CD players have this feature. But we can figure out other parts of this software based on standard metaphors used in almost all consumer software GUIs. Most have suggestive graphic forms, and we see them in the audio CD player. Once we become familiar with these metaphors, we can easily guess how to interact with the software.

The following basic metaphors are used by almost all computer systems. They generally have a consistent meaning, though sometimes slightly different graphic forms.

Command Buttons

As shown in Figures 2.1 and 2.2, a command button usually looks like a 3D rectangle, highlighted and with an icon or text centered on the button, as explained in Chapter 1. This text label says what the command does. To invoke the command—that is, to tell the software to perform the operation shown on the label—we are expected to "press" the button by clicking on it with the mouse. We then get feedback telling us that the button has clicked, usually a change of color, shadow, or highlight; a text/icon change; or other indicator, such as an audible "click." (Some people think such indicators are obsessive attempts at realism, but some form of feedback is essential to effective computer use, as explained below.)

A Click Is Enough. When clicking on a button, it is not a good idea to press down on the mouse button for a long time, because the computer may interpret a too-long click as another action.

Slider Control

The volume control, in Figure 2.3(a), is a slider control. A **slider control** sets a value from a "continuous" range, such as volume. To move the slider, place the mouse pointer on the slider, hold down the (left) mouse button, and move in the direction of change. The most common examples of sliders are the scroll bars in a window display, usually shown at the right and bottom of the window, as shown in Figure 2.3(b). When the window is not large enough to display all of the information in the horizontal or vertical direction, a scroll bar is shown for each direction in which information has been clipped. For example, for a word processor document that doesn't all fit in a window, a scroll bar lets you move up and down or side to side to read all the text. The range is the length—the number of lines in the document—and the width—the length of the (maximum) line. Often the size of the slider of the scroll bar is scaled to show what proportion of information is displayed. Thus, if the slider takes up half of the length of the "slot," about half of the information is displayed. There are usually directional triangles (▾ ▴) at one or both ends of the scroll bar; clicking on them moves the slider one "unit" in the chosen direction.

(a)   **(b)**

Figure 2.3. Slider controls. (a) A volume control. (b) A scroll bar.

Triangle Pointers

To reduce clutter, GUIs hide information until the user needs or wants to see it. A triangle pointer indicates the presence of hidden information. Clicking on the triangle reveals the information. You can see triangles in Figure 2.1 (below the Normal button ▾) and in Figure 2.2 (at the ends of the Artist and Track text boxes ▾). Clicking on the triangle pointer in Figure 2.1, for example, would result in Figure 2.4. Notice that now the direction of the pointer is reversed. Clicking on that triangle again hides the information.

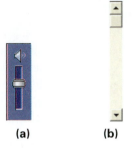

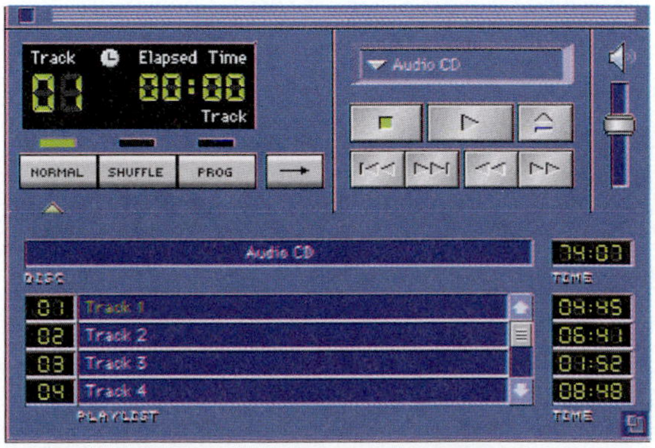

Figure 2.4. Audio CD GUI displaying the hidden titles and track information.

Close

Any open window can be closed, and most GUIs give the user a way to do it with a click. On the Macintosh (see Figure 2.1), clicking on the empty box (▣) in the upper-left corner closes the window. On Windows systems (see Figure 2.2), clicking on the X button ☒ in the upper-right corner closes the window. A Windows application ends when its main (or only) window is closed, but if just subwindows are closed, the application generally keeps running.

These are just a few of the metaphors to illustrate the concept. There are many others, and beginning users should get to know them quickly. The point here is to emphasize that computer applications have many operations in common, and software designers purposely use these **consistent interfaces** so that they can take advantage of the user's knowledge and experience. Experienced users look for familiar metaphors, and when they recognize a new metaphor, they add it to their repertoire.

FITBYTE

Mac or PC? Is the Macintosh better than the PC, or vice versa? The question usually sets off a pointless argument. Listening to the battle, many wrongly decide that the other system must be very different and hard to use. In fact, the two systems are much more alike than they are different, sharing the concepts of this chapter and much, much more. Any competent user of one can quickly and easily learn to use the other. And *every* Fluent user should.

Menus

The primary way users interface with software is through menu choices. A **menu** lists the operations that the software can perform. A menu groups operations that are similar. A menu is either listed across the top of a window, in which case it is called a **pull-down** or **drop-down** menu, or it appears wherever the mouse is pointing when a mouse button is clicked, in which case it is called a **pop-up** menu. Both menu types work the same way.

Pulling down or popping up a menu reveals a list of operations. Sliding the mouse down the list causes the items to be highlighted as it passes over them, and clicking or releasing the mouse button selects a menu item. If the software has enough information, it does the operation immediately and the window closes. If not, it asks for more information by opening a new window. Answering these questions may mean more information is needed. Eventually the command will be fully specified and can be performed. You can stop the dialog at any time by simply moving your mouse pointer away from the menu or clicking on **Cancel**. That is, clicking on **Cancel** is the same as never having looked at the menu in the first place, no matter how much information has been entered.

Menus in most consumer software give more information that just the item list. They tell you which operations are available, say when more input is needed, and sometimes give you shortcuts. Refer to Figure 2.5 as you read these descriptions.

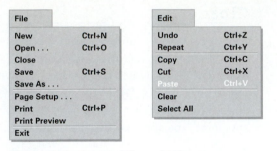

Figure 2.5. *Generic File and Edit menus.*

Which Operations Are Available? Unlike restaurant menus that are printed once and reused, occasionally requiring the server to explain that certain items are not available, GUI menus are created each time they are opened. So they specify exactly which operations are available. An operation may not apply in every context. For example, **Paste** is not available if nothing has been cut or copied using the **Cut** or **Copy** commands. Operations that are available are usually shown in solid color, and operations that are not available are shown in a lighter color or "gray," as shown for the **Paste** operation in Figure 2.5. Unavailable items are not highlighted as the cursor passes over them, and, of course, they cannot be selected.

Is More Input Needed? Some operations need further specification or more input from the user. Menu items that need further specification have a triangle pointer (▶) at the right end of the entry (see Figure 2.6). Selecting such an item pops up a menu with the additional choices. Making the selection causes the operation to be performed unless it needs still more specification. Menu items show that they need more input with an ellipsis (⋯) after their name. Selecting the item opens a dialog box for specifying the input. For example, in Figure 2.6, the operation **Symbol** has an ellipsis because it needs the user to specify which symbol should be inserted.

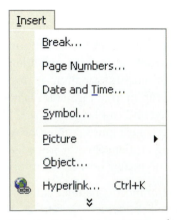

Figure 2.6. *An insert menu showing ellipses and triangle pointer.*

Is There a Shortcut? Sometimes it is more convenient to type a keyboard character than to pull down a window with the mouse. So some menu items have shortcuts. A **shortcut** is a combination of keyboard characters, shown next to the menu item, which has the same effect. For example, in Microsoft Windows, the menu choice **Copy** has the shortcut **Ctrl-C**, and **Paste** has the shortcut **Ctrl-V**. (Like the Shift key, the Control key Ctrl is held down while typing the associated character. Though the character is shown as a capital, you should not press the Shift key.) A **Ctrl**-plus-character combination is required so that the operating system can distinguish between the menu choice and a plain character. The Macintosh uses **Command-C** and **Command-V** for these operations—that is, the same letters. (The Command key is labeled with the "clover" symbol, ⌘.) Notice the consistency between different operating systems.

Shortcuts are not very important for a casual user, but they are extremely handy for people who use a single application intensively. The shortcut key combination can be set or changed in some systems.

Menu entries can give even more information about shortcuts. For example, Windows includes an icon as a visual cue for some operations (such as a floppy disk for **Save** and a printer for **Print**). See the Hyperlink icon in Figure 2.6.

FITBYTE

> **A Win for Users.** The Microsoft Windows operating system includes most of the GUI metaphors developed for the Apple Macintosh, so in 1988 Apple sued Microsoft for patent infringement. Apple claimed Microsoft illegally used the "look and feel" of its Mac. The legal issues were complex, but the judge ruled that Microsoft could freely use the metaphors Apple had developed. This might not seem fair to Apple, but it was a great win for users, because it meant that GUIs could work pretty much the same on the Mac and the PC.

STANDARD GUI FUNCTIONALITY

There are some operations that almost all personal computer applications should be expected to do simply because they process information. That is, whether the information is text or spreadsheets or circuit diagrams or digitized photographs, the fact that it is information stored in a computer means that certain operations will be available in the software. We call these operations the **standard functionality**. For example, it should be possible to save the information to a file, open a file containing the saved information, create a new instance, print the file, and so on. You should expect to find these functions in almost every software application.

File Operations

To help users, the standard operations are grouped—usually with other operations specific to the application—into two menus labeled **File** and **Edit**. Generally, the operations under the **File** menu apply to whole instances of the information being processed by an application. An **instance** is one of whatever kind of information the application processes. For example, for word processors, an instance is a document; for MP3 players, an instance is a song; for photo editors, an instance is an image. So, the **File** menu items treat a whole document. The operations you can expect to see under the **File** menu and their meanings are as follows:

> > **New** Create a "blank" instance of the information.

> > **Open** Locate a file on the disk containing an instance of the information and read it in.

> > **Close** Stop processing the current instance of the information, but keep the program available to process other instances.

> > **Save** Write the current instance to the hard disk or a floppy disk, using the previous name and location.

> > **Save As** Write the current instance to the hard disk or a floppy disk with a new name or location.

> > **Page Setup** Specify how the printing should appear on paper; changes to the setup are rare.

> > **Print** Print a copy of the current instance of the information.

> > **Print Preview** Show the information as it will appear on the printout.

> > **Exit** or **Quit** End the entire application.

Notice in Figure 2.5 that lines group the operations.

Edit Operations

The **Edit** operations let you make changes within an instance. They often involve selection and cursor placement. The operations are performed in a standard sequence: Select-Cut/Copy-Indicate-Paste-Revise. Selection identifies the information to be moved or copied. Selection is usually done by moving the cursor to a particular position in the instance and, while holding down either the mouse button or keyboard keys, moving the cursor to a new position. All information between the two positions is selected. Highlighting, usually color reversal, identifies the selection. If the information is to be recorded and deleted from its current position, the **Cut** command is used. The **Copy** command records but does not delete the information. Next, the new location for the information is indicated in preparation for pasting it into position, although in many applications the Indicate step is skipped and the selected information is placed in a standard position. The **Paste** command copies the information recorded in memory into the indicated position. Because a copy is made in memory, the information can be pasted again and again. Often, revisions or repositioning are required to complete the editing operation.

The operations under the **Edit** menu and their meanings are as follows:

> **Undo** Cancel the most recent editing change, returning the instance to its previous form.

> **Repeat** Apply the most recent editing change again.

> **Copy** Store a copy of the selected information in temporary storage, ready for pasting.

> **Cut** Remove the selected information and save it in temporary storage, ready for pasting.

> **Paste** Insert into the instance the information saved in the temporary storage by **Cut** or **Copy**; the information is placed either at the cursor position or at a standard position, depending on the application.

> **Clear** Delete the selected information.

> **Select All** Make the selection be the entire instance.

Notice that **Undo** is not always available because not all operations are reversible.

Because these operations are standard—available for most applications and consistent across operating systems—it is a good idea to learn their shortcuts, given in Table 2.1. (**Clear** often does not have a shortcut, to prevent accidents.) In addition, "double-click"—two (rapid) clicks with the (left) mouse button—often means **Open**.

Table 2.1 *Standard Shortcuts. These common shortcut letters for standard software operations combine with "Command"* (⌘) *for Mac OS or "Control"* (Ctrl) *for Windows.*

File Functions		Edit Functions	
New	N	Cut	X
Open	O	Copy	C
Save	S	Paste	V
Print	P	Select All	A
Quit	Q	Undo	Z
Redo	Y	Find	F

FITTIP

Be Selective. New users can get confused when an operation they want to use is not available (that is, it is shown in gray). Often this is because the operation needs the user to select something and nothing is selected. For example, the computer cannot perform **Copy** until you have selected what you want copied.

New Instance. Finally, notice that **New** under the **File** menu creates a "blank" **instance**. What is "blank information"? To understand this fundamental idea, notice that all information is grouped into **types**, based on its properties. So, photographs—digital images—are a type of information, and among the properties of every image is its length and width in pixels. Monthly calendars are a type of information with properties such as the number of days, year, and day of the week on which the first day falls. Text documents are another type, and the length of a document in characters is one property. Any specific piece of information—an image, month, or document—is an instance of its type. Your term paper is an instance of the document type of information; June 2003 is an instance of calendar type information. To store or process information of a given type, the computer sets up a structure to record all of the properties and store its content. A "new" or "blank" instance is simply the structure without any properties or content filled in. As an example, imagine a blank monthly calendar—seven columns of squares headed with the days of the week, a place to enter the month name, and so on. That's a **New** month, ready to receive its content. See Figure 2.7.

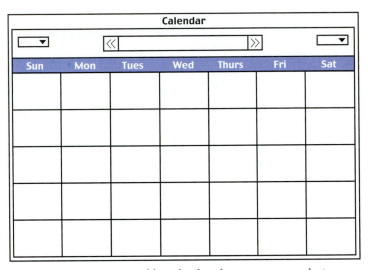

Figure 2.7. A **New** *monthly calendar showing one month, i.e., a "blank instance."*

Expecting Feedback

A computer is the user's assistant, ready to do whatever it is told to do. It is natural that when any assistant performs an operation, he, she, or it should report back to the person who made the request, describing the progress. This is especially true when the assistant is a computer (and therefore not very clever), because the person needs to know that the task was done and when to give the next command. So a user interface will always give the user feedback about "what's happenin'."

Feedback takes many forms, depending on what operation a user has commanded. If the operation can be performed instantaneously—that is, so fast that a person would not have to wait for it to complete—the user interface will simply indicate that the operation is complete. When the operation is an editing change, the proof that it is done is that the user can see the revision. When the effect of the command is not obvious—say, when one clicks on a button—then there is some other indication provided; for example, highlighting, shading, graying, or some other color change, or underlining.

The most common form of feedback is the indication that the computer is continuing to perform a time-consuming operation. As the operation is being carried out, the cursor is replaced with an icon such as an hourglass on Windows systems ⌛, or a wristwatch 🕐 or rainbow spinner 🌈 on Macintosh systems. Applications can also give the user custom feedback. A common indicator is the busy spinner ◔, a circle divided into quarters, two white and two black, that "revolves." The file transfer application Fetch turns the cursor into a running dog 🐕. When the completion time can be predicted, applications show a meter that is "filled" as the operation progresses. Often these displays give a time estimate for when 100 percent will be reached. Finally, when an operation is processing a series of inputs, the "completion count" gives the tally of the completed instances.

FITTIP

Following Protocol. Our normal interactive use of computers alternates between our commanding the computer to do something and the computer doing it. If the computer can't finish immediately, it gives feedback showing the operation is in progress. If the computer is finished, we can see the effects of the command. Be attuned to this protocol. If nothing seems to be happening, the computer is waiting for you to give a command.

"CLICKING AROUND"

When the digerati encounter new software, they expect a consistent interface. They expect to see the basic metaphors, find standard operations, and get feedback while the application is working. Digerati automatically look for these features of the interface and begin exploring. The purpose of the exploration is to learn what the software can do.

We call the act of exploring a user interface **clicking around**. It involves noting the basic features presented by the GUI and checking each menu to see what operations are available. So, for example, on seeing a slider bar, the experienced user's response is to slide it to see what happens. On the Mac audio CD GUI shown in Figure 2.1, when we slide the bar up and down, the speaker icon above it shows—following the feedback principle—more-and-larger or fewer-and-smaller white arcs to its right. We might guess these arcs indicate more or less sound coming from the speaker. If the CD is playing, we'll also notice that the volume increases or decreases. Either way, we know that this is the volume control.

FITTIP

A Fast Start. When you're using software for the first time, practice "clicking around":

> Take a minute to study the graphics of the GUI.

> Open each window to see what operations are available.

> Determine the purpose of icons and controls.

> Have "balloon help" or "what's this?" turned on for a short explanation of icons and controls when the cursor hovers over them.

"Clicking around" can help you figure out what operations are available with the software without having to be taught or read the manual. Software manuals are notoriously dull reading and hard to use. But "clicking around" does not make them obsolete. Manuals—they're mostly online and called **Help**—are still necessary and useful. "Clicking around" works because (a) we come to the new software with technological experience, and (b) software designers try to build on what we know by using metaphors, consistent interfaces, and so forth. When the new software works like the last software did, we already "know" how to use it. The manual is usually needed only to understand advanced features or subtleties of operation. Ironically, then, the manual is most useful for experienced users, not beginners.

Returning to the audio CD GUI of Figure 2.1, when we click on the down triangle, we reveal the track list shown in Figure 2.4. As new users of this software, we may not immediately understand what the list is for, especially if the physical CD players we are familiar with do not have a play list. But, by "clicking around," we notice either that "Track 1" can be selected like text or that the cursor when moved across the text changes into the "I-beam" text editing cursor. Both indicate that we can add text. Or, perhaps, we just guess that listing off the tracks wouldn't require a large text box reading "Track 1," etc., so there must be some other purpose for it. No matter how "clicking around" cues us, we discover that we can edit the entries. We can customize the title and songs on each track to get the results shown in Figure 2.8.

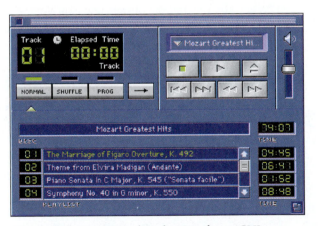

Figure 2.8. *Customized Audio CD player GUI.*

"Clicking around" is exploration and as such it may not tell us all the features of the software. We may need to experiment and test repeatedly, or give up and try again later. But the technique will usually give results. And if it doesn't, the software product designer has undoubtedly failed to some extent.

"BLAZING AWAY"

After getting to know a software application by "clicking around," the next step is to try it out. We will call this **blazing away**. The term suggests a user trying out an application assertively—exploring features even without a clear idea of what they will do. "Blazing away" can be difficult for beginning users, because they're afraid something will break if they make a mistake. A basic rule of information processing is: *Nothing will break!* If you make a mistake, the software is not going to screech and grind to a halt and then plop onto the floor with a clunk. When you make a mistake, the software may "crash" or "hang," but nothing will actually break. Most of the time, nothing happens. The software catches the mistake before doing something wrong and displays an error message. By paying attention to these messages, you can quickly learn what's legal and what isn't. Therefore, "blazing away" can be an effective way to learn about the application even if you make mistakes.

Of course, saying that nothing will break is not the same as saying that it's impossible to get into a terrible mess by "blazing away." Creating a mess is often very easy. Beginners and experts do it all the time. The difference between the two is that the experts know another basic rule of information technology: *When stuck, start over.* That may mean exiting the software. It may mean rebooting the computer. It may simply mean "undoing" a series of edits and repeating them. The simple point is that the mess has no value. It does not have to be straightened out, because it didn't cost anything to create in the first place, except for your time. Because that time will be chalked up to "experience" or "user training," there is no harm in throwing the mess out. Thus, an experienced user who is "blazing away" on a new software system will probably exit the software and restart the application over and over, without saving anything.

FITBYTE

Getting Out and Getting Back In. Starting over is so common for computer users—it's called, *getting out and getting back in*—that it's become the subject of some geek humor. A mechanical engineer, an electrical engineer, and a computer engineer are camped at Mt. Rainier. In the morning, they pack up to leave and get into their car, but it doesn't start. The ME says, "The starter motor is broken, but I can fix it," and he gets out of the car. The EE says, "No way. It's the battery, but I know what to do," and she gets out of the car. The CE says while getting out of the car, "Now, let's get back in."

Usually, we are working with new software because we have something specific we want to do, so it pays to focus on getting that task done. This means that we should "blaze away" on those operations that will contribute to completing the task. We don't have to become experts, only complete the task. Indeed, it is common for Fluent users to know only the most basic functions of the software systems they use infrequently. And, because they are not regular users, they usually forget how the applications work and have to "click around" and "blaze away" all over again.

Obviously, when you are "blazing away" and throwing away your efforts when you get into trouble, you shouldn't spend too much time creating complicated inputs. For example, if the software asks for text input and gives you space for several paragraphs, just enter `Test text` and go on exploring. Once you understand the system, you can focus on using the software productively.

"WATCHING OTHERS"

"Clicking around" and "blazing away" are the first steps when learning new software because we are likely to be successful using only our own observation and reasoning skills. And, if we need to know something very specific about the software, we can always read the manual or online help. However, these two extremes may not cover all of the possibilities. Complicated software systems usually have some features that are not obvious, too advanced or too specialized to the particular application to learn on our own. They are GUI features that most of us would not think to look for, and they provide capabilities that we may not even know we need.

The Shift-Select Operation

An example of such a not-so-obvious feature is the use of the Shift key in selection operations. Suppose we want to select the red and green circles of the stoplight in Figure 2.9(a) so that we can change their color, but not the yellow circle. Clicking on the red circle selects it (Figure 2.9(b)), as shown by the small boxes around the circle. Clicking on the green circle selects it and deselects the red circle (Figure 2.9(c)). Dragging the cursor across the red to the green selects all the circles (Figure 2.9(d)). So how do we select just red and green without the yellow? The problem is that when we select something (e.g., the green circle), anything that is already selected (e.g., the red circle) becomes deselected automatically. We need some way to bypass that automatic protocol.

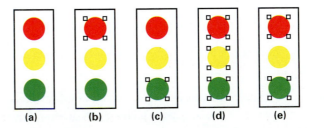

(a)   (b)   (c)   (d)   (e)

Figure 2.9. Examples of selection.

The solution is to select the first item (e.g., the red circle) and then hold down the Shift key while selecting the second item (e.g., the green circle). Using the Shift key during a selection has come to mean "continue selecting everything that is already selected." Because the red circle is already selected when the green circle is Shift-clicked, both become selected, completing the task.

Learning from Others

The **Shift-select** operation, meaning "continue to select the item(s) already selected," is a common feature in commercial software. Without knowing about Shift-select, however, we probably wouldn't discover it by "clicking around" or "blazing away." We would not think to try it. We might not even know that we need the feature in the first place. So how do we learn about this kind of feature?

FITTIP

Toggling Shift-select. Generally when you use Shift-select, one or more additional items will be selected, because you usually click on an unselected item. But what happens when you use Shift-select on an item that is already selected? It deselects that item only, leaving all other items selected. This property of changing to the opposite state—selecting if not selected, deselecting if selected—is called **toggling**. It is a handy feature in many situations.

We could take a course on the specific software or read the user's manual. But an alternative is to get in the habit of watching others when they use a system we are familiar with. As we watch, we should be able to follow what they are doing, though it might seem very fast. If we see an operation that we do not understand, we ask what the person did. Instead of thinking we're dummies, most people are eager to show off their know-how. Many an obscure feature, trick, or shortcut is learned while looking over the shoulder of an experienced user, so it pays to pay attention.

FITTIP

One Text Selection. Notice that for text, Shift-select usually results in the selection of all the text between the cursor's previous position and its new position; it is not usually possible to select disconnected sequences of text.

A BASIC PRINCIPLE: FORM FOLLOWS FUNCTION

A theme of this chapter is that computer systems are very much the same because software designers want users to be able to figure out how to use their systems on their own. To help this self-instruction process, designers use consistent interfaces and suggestive metaphors. Designers could be extremely creative, thinking up wild new interfaces and unusual operations. Such GUIs might be quite interesting and very cool, rather like video games with a practical purpose, but it might take years to learn and be effective with such tools. Few of us can take that much time to be productive. So instead, designers make use of the fact that consistency and familiarity help users learn quickly.

But a much deeper principle is also at work here. Designers are not just using good sense. There are limits on what information can be recorded or what operations can be computed. Many of the principles governing information and computation are too complicated for us to cover in this textbook, but these principles tell us an important fact about information technology: The task—*not* the specific software implementation—dictates the behavior of a solution. We should expect different software implementations for a task to be similar, not only because designers want them to be easy to learn, but also because they perform the same basic functions. We describe this property by the rule **form follows function**.

When we say "form follows function" in software, we do not mean that the systems look alike. Applications software from different vendors can look and feel very different even though it is for the same task. The form we are talking about is the way the basic operations of the software work.

Similar Applications Have Similar Features

So, for example, word processors all do the same sorts of things in similar ways, no matter which software company created them. The differences (and there are always differences, often big differences) are limited to the look, feel, and convenience of the software; the core functions are still the same. Word Perfect, Word, NotePad, Apple Works, Simple Text, BBText, and a dozen other systems give you a basic set of operations on text characters. They let you move a cursor around the text, select text characters, and create, copy, insert, and delete characters. They let you create an "empty" file of text—systems use the term *new*—as well as save it, name it, display it, and print it. All of those features are fundamental to text processing—they were not invented by the software companies. These features share a common functionality that determines the way all word processors work.

The same thing applies to browser programs, spreadsheet programs, drawing programs, and so on. When we learn to use an application from one software maker, we learn the core operations for that task and the features and quirks of that vendor's product. When we use software from a different vendor, we should look for and expect to recognize immediately the same basic operations. They may have a different look and feel in the second vendor's software, but they will still be there.

Take Advantage of Similarities

What's the advantage of having similarities in features and applications? Knowing that common, basic operations in programs do the same task frees us in at least three ways:

> When a new version of software is released, we should expect to learn it very quickly because it will share the core functions and many of the quirks of the earlier version.

> When we get another vendor's software for an application we know well, we should expect to use its basic features immediately.

> When we are frustrated by one vendor's software, we should try another vendor's software. Using our experience with the first system, we will learn the new system quickly. (And "voting" by buying better software should help improve overall software quality.)

In summary, because the function controls how a system works, different software implementations must share basic characteristics. You don't need to feel tied to a particular software system that you learned years ago. You should experiment with new systems; you already know the basic functional behavior.

SEARCHING TEXT USING FIND

The concept that form follows function has another advantage: It lets us learn how certain computations work without referring to any specific software system. Of course, we must focus only on the basic processing behavior rather than on the "bells and whistles" of the GUI, but learning in this way lets us apply our knowledge to any implementation. We illustrate this idea with text searching.

Many applications let us search text. Text searching, often called **Find**, is used by word processors, browsers (to look through the text of the current page), email readers, operating systems, and so on. **Find** is typically available under the **Edit** menu, because locating text is often the first step in editing it. In cases where editing doesn't make sense—say, when looking through a file structure in an operating system—**Find** may be listed under the File menu or as a "top level" application. The shortcut for Find—Command-F for Mac OS and Ctrl-F for Windows—is standard with most applications.

The things to be searched are called **tokens**. Most often, the tokens are simply the letters, numbers, and special symbols like @ and & from the keyboard, which are called **characters**. However, sometimes we search for composite items, such as dates, that we want to treat as a whole. In such cases, the date would be the token, not its letters and digits. For the purposes of searching, tokens form a sequence, called the **search text**, and the tokens to be found are called the **search string**. One property of the search string is that it can be made of any tokens that could be in the text. That is, if the text can contain unprintable characters like tabs, the search string is allowed to have those characters.

How to Search

To illustrate searching, suppose the search string is `content` and the text is a sentence from Martin Luther King's "I Have a Dream" speech:

```
I have a dream that my four little children will one day
live in a nation where they will not be judged by the color
of their skin, but by the content of their character.
```

Searching begins at the beginning, or at the current cursor position if there is a cursor. Though computers use many clever ways to search text, the easiest one to understand is to think of "sliding" the search string along the text. At each position, compare to see if there is a token match. This simply means looking at corresponding token pairs to see if they are the same:

```
I have a dream ...
▲▲▲▲▲▲▲
│││││││
▼▼▼▼▼▼▼
content
```

(Notice that spaces are characters, too.) If there is a match, then the process stops and you are shown the found instance. But if there is no match, slide the search string one position along and repeat:

```
... by the content of ...
     ▲▲▲▲▲▲▲▲▲▲▲▲▲▲
     ││││││││││││││
     ▼▼▼▼▼▼▼▼▼▼▼▼▼▼
... ccccccccontent
```

If the search string is not found when the end of the text is reached, the search stops and is unsuccessful. (Search facilities typically give you the option to continue searching from the beginning of the text if the search did not start there.) The search ends where it began when the search string is not found.

Search Complications

Character searching is easy, but to be completely successful, you should be operationally attuned. There are four things to keep in mind when you are searching: case sensitivity, hidden text, substrings, and multiword strings.

Case Sensitivity.

One complication is that the characters stored in a computer are case sensitive, meaning that the uppercase letters, such as `R`, and lowercase letters, such as `r`, are different. So a match occurs only when the letters *and* the case are identical. A case-sensitive search for `unalienable rights` fails on Jefferson's most famous sentence from the *Declaration of Independence*:

```
We hold these truths to be self-evident, that all men are cre-
ated equal, that they are endowed by their Creator with certain
unalienable Rights, that among these are Life, Liberty and the
pursuit of Happiness.
```

To find `unalienable rights` in a text that uses the original capitalization, we would have to ignore the case. Search tools will be case sensitive if case is important to the application. For example, word processors are usually case sensitive, but operating systems may not be. If the search can be case sensitive, the user will have the option to ignore case.

Hidden Text.

Characters are stored in the computer as one continuous sequence. The characters are of two types: the keyboard characters that we type, and formatting information added by the software application. Because every system uses a different method for the formatting information and because it is usually not important to the search anyhow, we will show the formatting information here using our own invented tags.

Tags are abbreviations in paired angle brackets, such as `<Ital>`, that describe additional information about the characters (in this case, that they should be printed in italics). Tags generally come in pairs so that they can enclose text like parentheses. The second of the pair is like the first, except with a slash(/) or back-slash(\) in it. (Tags will be needed often in our study, so backslash (\) will be used here for the tags of our generic application to distinguish them from later uses of slash in HTML, the OED digitization, and XML.) For example, to show that the word "Enter" should be printed in italics, a software application might represent it as `<Ital>Enter<\Ital>`. The application won't show these formatting tags to the user, but they are there.

For example, the balcony scene from *Romeo and Juliet* appears in a book of Shakespeare's plays as

> SCENE II.   *Capulet's orchard.*
>
>   *Enter* Romeo.
>
> *Romeo.*   He jests at scars that never felt a wound.
>   [*Juliet appears above at a window.*
> But, soft ! what light through yonder window breaks?
> It is the east, and Juliet is the sun.

But, this scene might be stored in the computer as follows:

```
SCENE·II.·▶<Ital>Capulet's·orchard.<\Ital>↵↵<Center><Ital>
Enter<\Ital>Romeo.<\Center>↵↵<Ital>Romeo.<\Ital>▶He·jests·
at·scars·that·never·felt·a·wound.↵<Right>[<Ital>Juliet·app
ears·above·at·a·window.<\Ital><\Right>↵But,··soft·!·what·l
ight·through·yonder·window·breaks?·↵It·is·the·east,·and·Ju
liet·is·the·sun.↵
```

The word processor's tags surround the italic text (`<Ital>`, `<\Ital>`), and the text to be centered (`<Center>`, `<\Center>`) or right-justified (`<Right>`, `<\Right>`). The user typed the other characters, and they are the ones we are interested in now. These characters include the text we see as well as formatting characters we can't see: **spaces** (·), **tabs** (▶), and **new-lines** (↵). Because these characters control formatting and have no printable form, there is no standard for how they are displayed; for example, the new-line character is the **paragraph symbol** (¶) in some systems. Users can ask that all the characters they type be displayed:

```
SCENE·II.·▶  Capulet's·orchard.↵
↵
                           Enter·Romeo.↵
↵
Romeo.▶        He·jests·at·scars·that·never·felt·a·wound.↵
                      [Juliet·appears·above·at·a·window.
↵
But,··soft·!·what·light·through·yonder·window·breaks?↵
It·is·the·east,·and·Juliet·is·the·sun.↵
```

Because the effects of the formatting are shown, it is easy to see where the non-printed formatting characters are. During a search, the software's formatting tags are generally ignored, but all of the characters typed by the user are considered. Some systems do allow tags to be searched by giving you a way to search for formatted text such as, for example, italic.

Substrings.   It gets more complicated when we think of search strings as having a meaning more complex than tokens. For example, we often look for words, though the tokens are characters. The problem is that the software searches for token sequences, not the more complicated objects that we may have in mind. So searches for the search string **you** in President John Kennedy's inaugural address turn up five hits:

```
And so, my fellow Americans: ask not what
your country can do for you-ask what you
can do for your country.
My fellow citizens of the world: ask not
what America will do for you, but what
together we can do for the freedom of man.
```

Of the five hits, only three are the actual word we're looking for; the other two hits *contain* the search string. To avoid finding **your**, we could search for ·**you**· because words in text are usually surrounded by spaces. However, that search discovers *no* hits in this quote because **you** doesn't appear with spaces on both sides. The five hits for **you** are followed by **r**, a dash, a new-line, an **r**, and a comma, respectively. The **you** at the end of the second line probably should have had a space between it and the new-line, but the typist left it out. Because looking only for the word **you** and avoiding **your** would mean checking for all of the possible starting and ending punctuation characters as well as blank, it is probably better to give up on finding the exact word matches and simply ignore the cases where the search string is part of another word. If the search is part of the system, such as a word processor, where words are a basic element, the ability to search for words will be available. Such cases are the same as changing the tokens from characters to words.

Multiword Strings. A similar problem happens with multiword search strings. The words of a multiword string are separated by spaces, but if the number of spaces in the search string is different from the number in the text being searched, no match will be found. For example, the search string

```
That's·one·small·step·for·man
```

Neil Armstrong's words on first stepping on the moon, will not be found in the quote

```
That's·one·small·step·for··man,·one·giant·leap·for·mankind.
```

because there are two spaces between `for` and `man` in the text. We could be careful about separating words by only one space when we type, but everyone makes mistakes. And more to the point, we may not have typed the text we're searching.

> **FITTIP**
>
> **One Small Step.** It is a good idea to look for single words in your search instead of longer phrases. For example, looking for `leap` or `mankind` might work because they were probably not used again in the transcript from the moon walk.

In summary, searching is the process of locating a sequence of tokens, the search string, in a longer sequence of tokens, the text. Character searches are usually limited to the characters the user has typed, though other characters may be present. User-typed characters can include nonprintable formatting characters like new-line characters. Searches look for token sequences, and the tokens (for example, characters) are often more basic than what we can build from them (for example, words). To be successful, we must think up search strings so that we find all the matches we're interested in.

EDITING TEXT USING SUBSTITUTION

Search-and-replace, also known as **substitution**, is a combination of searching and editing to make corrections in documents. The string replacing the search string is called the **replacement string**. Though substitution can apply to only one occurrence of the search string in the text, there is little advantage to using search-and-replace facility over simply searching and editing the occurrence directly. The real power of substitution comes from applying it to all occurrences of the search string. For example, if you typed "west coast" in your term paper but forgot that regions are usually capitalized, it is a simple matter to search for all occurrences of `west coast` and replace them with `West Coast`.

Because substitution can be a powerful tool that we want to study closely, we will express it in this book using a left-pointing arrow (←) between the search string and the replacement string. The capitalization example is shown as

```
west coast ← West Coast
```

Such an expression can be read, "`west coast` *is replaced by* `West Coast`" or "`West Coast` *substitutes for* `west coast`." Another example is

```
Norma Jeane Mortensen ← Marilyn Monroe
```

describing her 1946 name change when she signed her first movie contract.

We emphasize that the arrow is only a **notation** that helps us discuss substitutions in this book; it doesn't appear within the application. When using an application, a GUI is used to specify the replacement. For example the two text windows of the GUI correspond to the information on each side of the arrow. **Find** is the left side of the arrow, and **Replace** is the right side. We don't type the arrow in applications. It is only for our use here.

Unwanted Spaces

In the last section, we noted that multiple spaces separating words in a text complicates searching for multiword strings. Substitution can fix the "multiple spaces in a document" problem: Simply collapse double spaces to single spaces. That is, if the search string is ·· and the replacement string is ·, a search-and-replace over the whole document results in all pairs of spaces becoming single spaces. Expressed using the arrow notation, the "two spaces are replaced by one" substitution is

```
·· ← ·
```

Of course, in some places, such as at the end of sentences, we might want double spaces. Such cases can be fixed with substitutions of the form

```
·· ← ···
```

```
?· ← ?··
```

```
!· ← !··
```

which will restore the sentence-ending double blanks after the three punctuation characters. Performing multiple changes on text is a valuable technique.

Formatting Text

One situation where substitution is particularly handy is when text is imported into a document from another source and the formatting becomes messed up. For example, suppose you find the Articles from the UN's Universal Declaration of Human Rights on the Web:

Article 1 All human beings are born free and equal in dignity and rights. They are endowed with reason and conscience and should act towards one another in a spirit of brotherhood.

Article 2 Everyone is entitled to all the rights and freedoms set forth in this Declaration, without distinction of any kind, such as race, color, sex, language, religion, political, or other opinion, national or social origin, property, birth or other status.

Furthermore, no distinction shall be made on the basis of political, jurisdictional or international status of the country or territory to which a person belongs, whether it be independent, trust, non-self-governing, or under any other limitation of sovereignty.

Article 3 Everyone has the right to life, liberty and security of person.

But when you copy the first three articles and paste them into your document, they come out looking this way:

> Article 1 All human beings are born free and equal in dignity and
> rights. They are endowed with reason and
> conscience and should act towards one another in a spirit
> of brotherhood.
>
> Article 2 Everyone is entitled to all the rights and freedoms set forth
> in this Declaration, without distinction of any
> kind, such as race, color, sex, language, religion, political
> or other opinion, national or social origin,
> property, birth or other status.
>
> Furthermore, no distinction shall be made on the basis of
> political, jurisdictional or international status of
> the country or territory to which a person belongs, whether
> it be independent, trust, non-self-governing,
> or under any other limitation of sovereignty.
>
> Article 3 Everyone has the right to life, liberty and security of person.

The formatting is a mess. Displaying the text with the formatting characters reveals:

> ········Article·1··All·human·beings·are·born·free·and·equal·in·dignity·and·↵
> rights.··They·are·endowed·with·reason·and·↵
> ········conscience·and·should·act·towards·one·another·in·a·spirit·↵
> of·brotherhood.··↵
> ↵
> ········Article·2··Everyone·is·entitled·to·all·the·rights·and·freedoms·set·forth↵
> ·in·this·Declaration,·without·distinction·of·any↵
> ········kind,·such·as·race,·color,·sex,·language,·religion,·political·↵
> or·other·opinion,·national·or·social·origin,·↵
> ········property,·birth·or·other·status.··↵
> ↵
> ········Furthermore,·no·distinction·shall·be·made·on·the·basis·of·↵
> political,·jurisdictional·or·international·status·of·↵
> ········the·country·or·territory·to·which·a·person·belongs,·whether·↵
> it·be·independent,·trust,·non-self-governing,·↵
> ········or·under·any·other·limitation·of·sovereignty.··↵
> ↵
> ········Article·3··Everyone·has·the·right·to·life,·liberty·and·security·of·person.··↵

We see that extra spaces and new-line characters have been inserted when we imported the text into the document.

Clearly, removing the groups of eight leading blanks is simple: replace them with nothing. When writing the substitution expression, we express "nothing" with the Greek letter epsilon, which is called the empty string; that is, the string with no letters. (Notice that epsilon is used only for writing out substitution expressions for ourselves. In the Find-and-Replace facility of an application, simply leave the replacement string empty.)

········ ← ε

Removing the leading blanks was easy because they are only at the beginning of the lines and nowhere else. Correcting the new-line characters is more of a problem.

We want to get rid of the new-lines that have been inserted within a paragraph and keep the paired new-lines that separate the paragraphs. But getting rid of single new-lines

↵ ← ε

will also get rid of *all* the new-lines! How can we keep the paired new-lines but remove the singles?

The Placeholder Technique

An easy strategy, called the **placeholder technique**, solves such problems. It begins by substituting a placeholder character for the strings we want to keep; that is, the new-line pairs. We pick # as the placeholder because it doesn't appear anywhere else in the document, but any unused character or character string will work. The substitution expression is

↵↵ ← #

Our text without the leading blanks and double new-lines now looks like this:

Article·1··All·human·beings·are·born·free·and·equal·in·dignity·and·↵
rights.·They·are·endowed·with·reason·and·↵
conscience·and·should·act·towards·one·another·in·a·spirit·↵
of·brotherhood.#Article·2··Everyone·is·entitled·to·all·the·rights·and·freedoms·set·forth·↵
in·this·Declaration,·without·distinction·of·any↵
kind,·such·as·race,·color,·sex,·language,·religion,·political·↵
or·other·opinion,·national·or·social·origin,·↵
property,·birth·or·other·status.#Furthermore,·no·distinction·shall·be·made·on·the·basis·of·↵
political,·jurisdictional·or·international·status·of·↵
the·country·or·territory·to·which·a·person·belongs,·whether·↵
it·be·independent,·trust,·non-self-governing,·↵
or·under·any·other·limitation·of·sovereignty.#Article·3··Everyone·has·the·right·to·life,·liberty·and·security·of·person.

The new-lines that remain are the ones to be removed, so we need to replace them by nothing

↵ ← ε

The resulting text has no new-line characters left:

> Article·1··All·human·beings·are·born·free·and·equal·in·dignity·and·rights.··They·are·endowed·
> with·reason·and·conscience·and·should·act·towards·one·another·in·a·spirit·of·brotherhood.#
> Article·2··Everyone·is·entitled·to·all·the·rights·and·freedoms·set·forth·in·this·Declaration,·
> without·distinction·of·any·kind,·such·as·race,·color,·sex,·language,·religion,·political·or·
> other·opinion,·national·or·social·origin,·property,·birth·or·other·status.#Furthermore,·no·
> distinction·shall·be·made·on·the·basis·of·political,·jurisdictional·or·international·status·of·the·
> country·or·territory·to·which·a·person·belongs,·whether·it·be·independent,·trust,·non-self-
> governing,·or·under·any·other·limitation·of·sovereignty.#Article·3··Everyone·has·the·right·to·
> life,·liberty·and·security·of·person.

Finally, replace the placeholder with the desired character string

\# ← ↵↵

which gives us

> Article·1··All·human·beings·are·born·free·and·equal·in·dignity·and·rights.··They·are·endowed·
> with·reason·and·conscience·and·should·act·towards·one·another·in·a·spirit·of·brotherhood.·
>
> Article·2··Everyone·is·entitled·to·all·the·rights·and·freedoms·set·forth·in·this·Declaration,·
> without·distinction·of·any·kind,·such·as·race,·color,·sex,·language,·religion,·political·or·
> other·opinion,·national·or·social·origin,·property,·birth·or·other·status.··
>
> Furthermore,·no·distinction·shall·be·made·on·the·basis·of·political,·jurisdictional·or·
> international·status·of·the·country·or·territory·to·which·a·person·belongs,·whether·it·be·
> independent,·trust,·non-self-governing,·or·under·any·other·limitation·of·sovereignty.
>
> Article·3··Everyone·has·the·right·to·life,·liberty·and·security·of·person.

Except for the bold form of **Article** and its accompanying number, the result looks like the original document with only new-line pairs and no new-line singletons. The final replacements

Article 1 ← **Article 1**

Article 2 ← **Article 2**

Article 3 ← **Article 3**

completes the task.

To summarize, the placeholder technique is used to remove short search strings that are part of longer strings that we want to keep. If we were to remove the short strings directly, we'd trash the longer strings. The idea is to convert the longer strings into the placeholder temporarily. Of course, a single placeholder character can replace the long strings because all we're keeping track of is the position of the longer string. With the longer strings replaced by the placeholder, it is safe to remove the short strings. Once they are gone, the longer string can replace the placeholder. The substitution expressions

LongStringsContainingInstance(s)OfAShortString ← *Placeholder*

ShortString ← **ε**

Placeholder ← *LongStringsContainingInstance(s)OfAShortString*

summarize the idea.

THINKING ABOUT INFORMATION TECHNOLOGY ABSTRACTLY

We began this chapter promising to reveal some secrets known to expert computer users. And we have. Now, it is not so miraculous that the digerati appear to know how to use software they have never seen before.

We observed that application software systems must behave in ways governed by the functions they provide. Form follows function was our description of it. So, creating and editing keyboard input requires a small set of basic operations that all editing and word processing systems must have. The same applies to browsers, to spreadsheets, and so forth. This means that when we learn specific software for a specific task, we are learning both its core operations, common to all software for that task, as well as the "bells and whistles" of its GUI. So, once we've learned one vendor's software for an application, we should expect to be able to use another company's application without much difficulty. Our introduction to the core ideas of searching and substitution illustrated the point: We learned the basics without needing to look at any specific software. In addition, we learned some useful skills, such as the placeholder technique.

But the chapter's topic really concerns information technology more abstractly. We considered how people learn technology generally, and information technology in particular. Because no one is born knowing how to use technology, users must learn each new tool. The best case is when the training is simply a user's previous experience with technology. In such cases, the technology operates exactly the way users expect. Software designers try for this by using familiar features when they design computer–human interfaces and applications. They use consistent interfaces, recognizable metaphors, standard operations, and so on. So one way to explore new software is to "click around," learning it by applying what we already know, and by not being afraid to make mistakes. Thinking from the abstract to the specific guided us to using technology well. The larger lesson of this chapter, then, is to think about information technology abstractly, which is key to becoming a member of the digerati.

As you become a member of the digerati, you can think about technology abstractly, and be more likely to ask questions such as

☑ *"What do I have to learn about this software to do my task?"*

☑ *"What does the designer of this software expect me to know?"*

☑ *"What does the designer expect me to do?"*

☑ *"What metaphor is the software showing me?"*

☑ *"What additional information does this software need to do its task?"*

☑ *"Have I seen these operations in other software?"*

When you think about information technology in terms of your personal or workplace needs, you may ask questions such as

☑ *"Is there information technology that I am not now using that could help me with my task?"*

☑ *"Am I more or less productive using this technological solution for my task?"*

☑ *"Can I customize the technology I'm using to make myself more productive?"*

☑ *"Have I assessed my uses of information technology recently?"*

These and similar questions can help you use technology more effectively. Information technology, being a means rather than an end, should be continually assessed to ensure that it is fulfilling your needs as the technology changes and evolves.

SUMMARY

This chapter began by exploring how people learn to use technology. The conclusion was that people must either be taught technology or figure it out on their own. We can figure out software because designers use consistent interfaces, suggestive metaphors, standard functionality, and so on. We applied our previous experience to learn new applications, just like the digerati. We admired how the "perfect GUI" was perfectly intuitive. We learned that in computer software, nothing will break when we make mistakes, so we should explore a new application by "clicking around." We should also try it out by "blazing away," knowing that we will mess up; when we do we will throw away our work by exiting and starting over—getting out and getting back in.

Exploration is not the only way to learn, however. Some functions of a new application, like Shift-select, are not obvious, so we should watch other users and ask questions. You're not a dummy if you ask, only if you don't. We also learned that *form follows function*, so although software systems for a given task might have different icons and colors, there are basic operations that they must have in common. Thus, if we look past the "flash" of the GUI to these core operations, we can easily learn to use another manufacturer's software for the task. To demonstrate this commonality, we studied searching and substitution, which are available with many applications. As part of our discussion on editing text, we used the placeholder technique. Finally, we discussed thinking abstractly about technology. We applied general principles and ideas so that we would come to know what the digerati know and become more expert users.

EXERCISES

Multiple Choice

1. Experienced computer users are known as:
   A. digerati
   B. literati
   C. mazzerati
   D. culturati

2. What is a GUI?
   A. graphical update identification
   B. general user identification
   C. graphical user interface
   D. general update interface

3. Software designers use analogies to help a user understand software because doing so:
   A. makes it easier for the user to learn and use the software
   B. makes the software more popular
   C. is required by law
   D. more than one of the above

4. An example of a metaphor is:
   A. The player played with the heart of a lion.
   B. The silence was deafening.
   C. The computer played chess as well as the best humans.
   D. all of the above

5. Which of the following is not a common computer metaphor?
   A. buttons
   B. door handles
   C. menus
   D. sliders

6. A slider control is used for selecting:
   A. one of several options
   B. one or more of several options
   C. within a continuous range of options
   D. one or more items from a list

7. In Windows, closing a subwindow:
   A. is not allowed
   B. leaves the application running
   C. quits the application
   D. automatically saves your file

8. A dialog will open when a menu has a(n) _____ in it.
   A. shortcut
   B. ellipsis
   C. check mark
   D. separator

9. Which of the menu options in Figure 2.5 will always open a dialog?
   A. Open and Print
   B. File and Edit
   C. Clear and Exit
   D. Paste

10. Menu options that are unavailable:
    A. have a check mark by them
    B. are gray
    C. have a line through them
    D. are hidden

Short Answer

1. _____ is the word used to describe people who understand digital technology.

2. GUI stands for _____.

3. Software designers help users understand their software through the use of _____.

4. A _____ is a figure of speech where one object is likened to another.

5. _____ are used to indicate there is information available that is usually hidden.

6. Open, New, Close, and Save can usually be found in the _____ menu.

7. To avoid cluttering the screen with commands, software designers put most of their commands in _____.

8. Undo, Cut, Copy, and Paste can usually be found in the _____ menu.

9. The online manual can usually be found in the _____ menu.

10. Menus that can show up anywhere on the screen are called _____.

11. Another name for a pull-down menu is a _____.

12. When the computer needs more information from the user before it completes an action, it gets the information via a _____.

13. Menus that are unavailable are generally colored _____.

14. Menu options that will open a dialog display can be identified because they contain a(n) _____.

15. The clover-shaped shortcut key on a Macintosh is called the _____ key.

Exercises

1. Discuss the advantages of a consistent interface. Look at it from the consumer's view and from the developer's view.

2. List the technology tools you can typically use without reading the owner's manual.

3. What are the two keys to success with information technology?

4. Match the buttons on the two CD interfaces in Figures 2.1 and 2.2. Label the commands. Speculate on how the features found on only one are implemented on the other.

5. What happens when we apply the ** ← * replacement to *****? Try this out with your text editor. How many times did it find and replace? How many were left? Explain how this process worked.

6. Describe the similarities and differences between the Windows CD Player and the Windows Media Player. If you have a Mac, use the CD Player and the QuickTime Player.

7. Using Lincoln's Gettysburg Address, what appears more often, "that" or "here"?

8. How many times does the word "the" appear in Lincoln's Gettysburg Address? How many times do the letters "the" appear together in it?

MAKING THE CONNECTION

The Basics of Networking

learning | *objectives*

{

> Describe changes that networked computers have brought to society

> Tell whether a communication technology (Internet, radio, LAN, etc.) is synchronous or asynchronous, broadcast or point-to-point

> Explain the roles of Internet addresses, domain names, and DNS servers in networking

> Distinguish between types of protocols (TCP/IP and Ethernet)

> Describe how computers are interconnected by an ISP; by a LAN

> Distinguish between the Internet and the World Wide Web

}

*The presence of humans in a system containing high-speed
electronic computers and high-speed accurate communications
is quite inhibiting.*

—STUART LUMAN SEATON, 1958

COMPUTERS alone are useful. Computers connected
together are even more useful. Proof of this came dramatically in the mid-1990s when the Internet, long available to
researchers, became generally available to the public. The
Internet is the totality of all the wires, fibers, switches,
routers, satellite links, and other hardware for transporting
information between addressed computers, as shown in
Figure 3.1. For the first time, people could conveniently
and inexpensively connect their computers to the Internet
and thereby connect to all other computers attached to the
Internet. They could send email and surf the Web from
home. This convenient access to volumes of information,
eCommerce, chatrooms, and other capabilities greatly
expanded the benefits people derived from computers.

This chapter begins by considering how connecting
computers together with the Internet has changed the
world. We identify five of the most significant effects of
the Internet—not all of them clearly good. After we've
looked at the impact of the Internet, we define some communication terms. These will help you compare the
Internet with other forms of communication. Some topics
are designed to give you a sense of how the Internet works
without the technical details: naming computers, packets,
the TCP/IP and Ethernet protocols, and connecting your
computer to the Internet. Next, the World Wide Web and
file structures are explained in preparation for Chapter 4
on HTML.

NETWORKED COMPUTERS CHANGE OUR LIVES

A skeptic might wonder whether all of the excitement and frenzy surrounding the Internet is anything more than hype. After all, for a hundred years, average citizens in developed countries have had access to great repositories of information in libraries, have been able to communicate with each other via telephones or the post, and have enjoyed the benefits of retail commerce. Wire services brought the news from distant locales, and broadcast media such as newspapers, radio, and television conveyed that news widely. Has anything actually changed? Very definitely.

The interconnection of computers—networking—has brought us the Information Age and with it profound changes. Now:

> Nowhere is remote.

> People are more interconnected.

> Social relationships are changing.

> English is becoming a universal language.

> Freedom of speech and of assembly have expanded.

Consider each change in detail.

Nowhere Is Remote

In the past, centers of commerce, learning, and government justly claimed a difference from more remote places in the world based on the ready access to information. But today, because of information technology, nowhere is remote any longer. For instance, comparing a person's access to information in New York, New York to Unalakleet, Alaska, we see few differences. In the past, to find a Prague subway map for vacation planning, a New Yorker might have gone to the New York City Public Library, whereas someone from Unalakleet may have been out of luck. But now, both places have the same access to information, because the best, up-to-date map is available online from the Prague subway system. Similarly, to get a share price from the NASDAQ stock exchange, both places are equal. And to find out what people think "about them Mets," it's possible either to listen to NYC radio online or join a sports chatroom of other fans.

Differences remain, of course. For example, the entire holdings of the New York City Public Library will not soon be online, so scholars and others will continue to visit the library in person. But the vast amount of new information people want or need is available electronically from the nearest Internet connection. It's as easy to read the *Sydney Morning Herald* in Sydney, Nova Scotia, as it is in Sydney, New South Wales, and unlike distributing a physical copy of the paper, readers can peruse it electronically at the same time on both sides of the world.

It may be that the claim "nowhere is remote" looks at the question backwards. Perhaps everywhere is remote in the sense of being the same distance from most information sources. For example, in many companies, information workers can choose to telecommute. Though they may be at home, physically remote from their employer, they are electronically at the same distance as if sitting in the office. Telecommuting is obviously attractive to the employee, but the employer may see advantages, too. A worker may be more productive at home in a bathrobe and fuzzy slippers than at the office choked by a power tie and fuming from a terrible commute. One result of telecommuting may be that people will choose to live in remote, picturesque places. That might ease the population burden on already congested cities, but raise the burden in places like Port Douglas, Australia; Banff, Canada; or Hania, Greece.

People Are More Interconnected

Though there may be no studies to prove it, the anecdotal evidence is that people keep in closer, more frequent contact with friends and family across the country or in foreign lands via the Internet than by telephone or mail. The advantages are that email generally costs less than the telephone and is faster than the postal mail. You can email friends or family to find out what they are having for dinner, if you're interested. Such a simple question might not be worth a phone call, especially because time differences complicate long-distance telephone communication—both parties must be connected simultaneously. The Internet gives everyone the choice of treating email as a message by reading it later or as a conversation by being online and answering it immediately.

The Web also provides the opportunity for people to meet passively. By creating a Web page describing our interests, hobbies, free-time activities, and other descriptive information, we are publishing an "advertisement" for ourselves that can be read from anywhere in the world. Most important, the Web page can be seen by "Web search engines"—programs that cruise the Internet, locating the pages on which various descriptive terms appear. Suppose you create a Web page about growing bonsai trees from *Sequoia sempervirens*. If someone else also interested in Sequoia bonsai asks a Web search engine to look for pages containing information about that topic, your page may be found. The searcher can contact you, and a friendship or collaboration based on this shared interest may blossom. In this way, people can become acquainted with others sharing similar interests without ever meeting face-to-face. The benefit of passive meeting is that it can be based on extremely narrow interests or specialties that would not support an organization or society. And associations of this form can form rapidly—a whole interest group could form around an event that is unfolding, such as a typhoon or election.

Social Interactions Are Changing

Not all aspects of information technology can be considered good. A possible dark side is that time spent in using a computer displaces other activities—the displacement effect. If people spend time with a computer surfing the Web, playing games, or engaging in other activities that displace in-person social interaction, the outcome may be less desirable. Recent studies from Carnegie-Mellon and Stanford Universities seem to show a decline in social interactions after people become intensive computer users. Claims were even made for an "increase in depression." The topic is complicated and further study is needed, but the displacement effect of using computers is certainly a potential risk.

As an example of how the problem can quickly become complicated, consider that a person's time online might be spent participating in chatrooms or sending email to friends and family. Isn't this simply a modern form of in-person social interaction? Possibly, but possibly not. Maybe we know our electronic acquaintances only superficially compared to our in-the-flesh friends. On the other hand, maybe we "open up" and speak more candidly to someone we only know anonymously. Also, the possibility of keeping in close electronic contact with family or meeting others passively who have similar interests may be more rewarding than meeting with our face-to-face acquaintances, which are limited to people who are physically nearby. The Internet is changing people's social interactions, but the long-term effects are still to be seen.

English Is Becoming a Universal Language

Since the end of World War II, there have been growing indications that English may become the universal language. Many reasons exist for this shift, including the huge influence of U.S. movies and pop culture, and the dominance of science and technology in English-speaking countries since that war. English is not yet the universal language, of course, but it is the leading candidate. IT is giving it a huge push.

Though Microsoft Windows is available in German and Japanese editions, much software is available only in English; and the non-English options are limited to only a few major languages. Still, the driving force behind people's desire to read and understand English is not software, but the World Wide Web. Most Web pages are in English, and when they are multilingual, English is usually among the choices. English is also widely used for eCommerce. The bias toward English encourages Web pages in English, reinforcing English's status as a universal language. People fluent in English have greater access to IT's benefits. Of course, computer translation can convert from English to another language, but so far these translations have not been very faithful, and they are available for only a few widely spoken languages. There will likely be no computer translators for most of the world's languages.

Interestingly, it seems that adopting English as a universal language for IT could have little effect on other languages. In non-English-speaking countries, English would be taught as a second language and the population would be bilingual. This is already the case in many countries. There is no real threat to the native language because it is used in most other aspects of daily life.

Freedom of Speech and of Assembly Have Expanded

Creating a Web page is a means of identifying ourselves. We can state who we are (or think we are) and what we believe in. The Web page can be viewed from anywhere and located by a Web search engine. Most important, it is not subject to any editorial oversight or significant restrictions. Such an unfettered, worldwide communication medium presents an unprecedented degree of freedom of speech, previously available only to those who owned broadcast channels or printing presses. It allows political and artistic expression (within the limits of the medium), and any form of self-promotion (including shameless). As with freedoms generally, free speech on the World Wide Web can be abused, leading to hate propaganda or instructions on building bombs. The opportunity for *unmediated* expression to such a large audience, however, would seem to be a new benefit of information technology and the Internet.

Along with free speech, the Internet also promotes freer association. Like-minded people can find each other by searching the Web. Once connected, they can communicate by email or form chatrooms and newsgroups. They are electronically close regardless of how far apart they are in physical space. Unlike ham radio, which relies on broadcast to connect a group, email can be private. Electronic assembly is unique in overcoming the problems of place and time for bringing people together.

There are other benefits—sensitive information on topics like contraception or religion can be accessed privately—but the five changes just described surely establish that the wonders of the Internet are not simply hype.

Internet. The present-day Internet is the commercial descendant of the ARPANET, developed for the U.S. Department of Defense Advanced Research Projects Agency (DARPA). The ARPANET sent its first messages in 1969.

COMMUNICATION TYPES: SOME COMPARISONS

To understand the Internet, it is necessary to explain some basic vocabulary of communication.

Communication between two entities, be they people or computers, can be separated into two broad classes: synchronous and asynchronous. **Synchronous communication** requires that both the sender and the receiver are active at the same time. A telephone conversation is an example of synchronous communication. Both people in the conversation must perform one of the two parts of the communication—sending (talking) or receiving (listening)—at the same time. In **asynchronous communication**, the sending and the receiving occur at different times. A postcard is an example of asynchronous communication because it is written at one time and read sometime later. An answering machine or voice mail make telephones asynchronous in the sense that the caller leaves a message that the receiver listens to later. Email is also asynchronous.

> **Spamming.** Spam is unsolicited email. Spam is often sent by people promoting get-rich-quick schemes. Spam email once had subject lines like "Earn Big $$$," but spammers have become more subtle, choosing innocent subject lines to snare readers. The term is widely believed to derive from a *Monty Python* skit in which the word "spam" was chanted by Vikings to drown out restaurant conversation; that is, unwanted input harms legitimate communication. State legislatures have attempted to outlaw spam.

Another property of communication concerns the number of receivers. A single sender and many receivers is **broadcast communication**. Radio and television are examples of broadcast communication, of course. The term **multicast** is also used when there are many receivers, but the intended recipients are not the whole population. Magazines, often specialized to a topic, are an example of multicast communication. The opposite of broadcasting and multicasting is **point-to-point communication**. Telephone communication is point-to-point. The property of broadcast *versus* point-to-point communication is separate from the property of synchronous *versus* asynchronous communication.

A fundamental feature of the Internet is that it provides a general communication "fabric" linking all computers connected to it. (See Figure 3.1.) That is, the computers and the network become a single medium that can be applied in many ways to produce alternatives to established forms of communication The Internet's point-to-point asynchronous communication is like the postal system, for example, but at electronic speeds. In fact, the Internet is fast enough to mimic synchronous communication. Two or more people can have a conversation by the rapid exchange of asynchronous messages. Instant messaging is an example. So the Internet can be used like a phone. (With special software, an Internet-connected computer can *be* a phone, too.) Also, multicasting is possible, enabling small to modest-size groups to communicate via chatrooms. Finally, because it is possible to post a Web page that can be accessed by anyone, the Internet offers a form of broadcasting that compares with radio or television. The Internet is truly a universal communications medium.

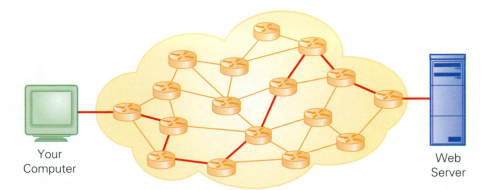

Your Computer

Web Server

Figure 3.1. *A diagram of the Internet.*

The Internet also becomes more effective with each additional computer added to it. That is, if *x* computers are already attached to the Internet, adding one more computer results in *x* potential new connections—that computer with each of the original machines.

THE MEDIUM OF THE MESSAGE

How does the Internet transmit information such as email messages and Web pages? Complex and sophisticated technologies are used to make today's Internet work, but the basic idea is extremely simple.

The Name Game of Computer Addresses

To begin, remember that the Internet uses point-to-point communication. When anything is sent point-to-point—a phone conversation, a letter, or furniture—the destination address is required.

IP Addresses. Each computer connected to the Internet is given a unique address called its **IP address**, short for **Internet Protocol Address**. An IP address is a series of four numbers separated by dots, as shown in Figure 3.2. For example, the IP address of the computer on which I am typing this sentence is `128.95.1.207`, and the machine to which my email is usually sent is `128.95.1.4`. Although the range of each of these numbers (0–255) allows for billions of Internet addresses, IP addresses are actually in short supply.

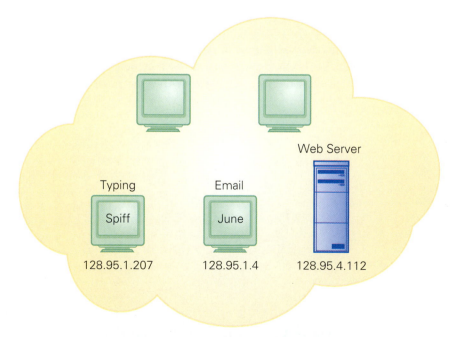

Figure 3.2. *Computers connected to the Internet are given IP addresses.*

Change of Address. Since the 1970s we've used Internet Protocol Version 4 (IPv4). IPv4 specifies 4-byte IP-addresses, plenty for the days when only about 200 computers were networked. Now about 200 million computers are networked, motivating development of Internet Protocol Version 6 (IPv6). IPv6 specifies 16 byte IP-addresses, solving the IP-address problem for good.

Domain Names.

Suppose we needed to know the four-number IP addresses of our friends' computers in order to send them email; the process would be very annoying and uncivilized. Instead, the Internet uses human-readable symbolic names for computers that are based on a hierarchy of *domains*. A **domain** is a related group of networked computers. For example, the name of my computer is `spiff.cs.washington.edu`, which reveals its domain membership by its structure. Pulling apart the name, my computer (`spiff`) is a member of the Computer Science and Engineering Department domain (`cs`), which is part of the University of Washington domain (`washington`), which is part of the educational domain (`edu`), as shown in Figure 3.3(a) and (b). This is a hierarchy of domains because each is a member of the next larger domain. Another of my computers, `tracer.cs.washington.edu`, has a name with a similar structure, so it is apparently a member of the same domain. Other departments at the University of Washington, such as Astronomy (`astro.washington.edu`), have names that are peers of `cs` (on the same level) within the `washington` domain, and other schools (for example, `princeton.edu`) have names that are peers with `washington` within the `edu` domain. These names are symbolic and meaningful, making them easier to read than numbers, and being arranged in a hierarchy makes them easier to remember.

Where It's @. Email addresses, like domain names, have a structure. For example: `president@whitehouse.gov`. The portion to the right of the @ sign is the **destination address**, and it has domain structure. It is processed by the sending computer(s). The information to the left of the @ sign is the **user ID**, and it is processed by the receiving computer.

DNS Servers.

How do the convenient domain names like `spiff.cs.washington.edu` get converted into the IP addresses (for example, `128.95.1.207`) that computers need? The **Domain Name System** (**DNS**) translates the hierarchical, human-readable names into the four-number IP addresses, as shown in Figure 3.4. This allows both people and computers to use their preferred scheme. Every Internet host (a computer connected to the Internet) knows the IP address of its nearest **Domain Name System server**, a computer that keeps a list of the symbolic names and the corresponding IP addresses. Whenever you use the hierarchical symbolic name to send information to some destination, your computer asks the DNS server to look up the corresponding IP address. It then uses that IP address to send the information. The DNS servers keep their information up to date dynamically (that is, on-the-fly), making the existence of IP addresses almost invisible to users.

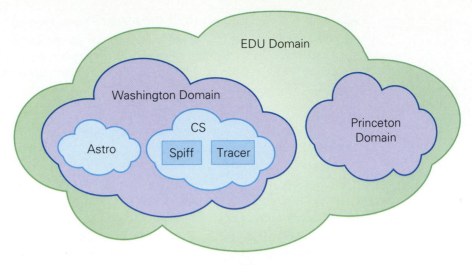

(a)

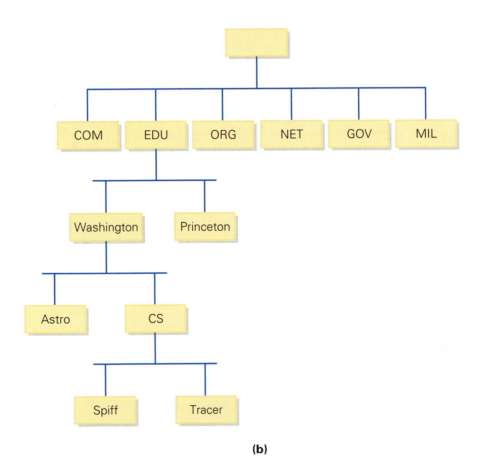

(b)

Figure 3.3. *Two diagrams of domain hierarchy.*

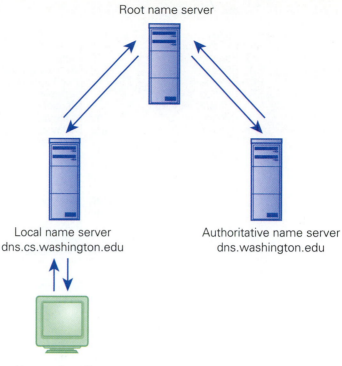

Root name server

Local name server
dns.cs.washington.edu

Authoritative name server
dns.washington.edu

Requesting client
spiff.cs.washington.edu

Figure 3.4. Hosts like Spiff make requests to a local DNS server. If it knows the IP-address it replies, but if not, it asks one of 13 Root name servers. They usually know, but if not they ask the Authoritative name server. When the answer returns, all servers update their records.

Top-level Domains. The `.edu` domain for educational institutions is one of several **top-level domain** names. With `.edu` the following is the original set:

`.com` for commercial enterprises

`.org` for organizations

`.net` for networks

`.mil` for the military

`.gov` for government agencies

This set of top-level domains has recently been expanded. The original domains all apply to organizations in the United States. There is also a set of mnemonic two-letter country designators, such as `.ca` (Canada), `.uk` (United Kingdom), `.fr` (France), `.de` (Germany, as in Deutschland), `.es` (Spain, as in España), `.us` (United States), and so on. (See Table 3.1 for a complete list.) These allow domain names to be grouped by their country of origin. The period, always pronounced *dot*, simply separates the levels of the domains, and was chosen to be easy to type and say.

Table 3.1. *Top-level Country Domain Abbreviations*

AF	Afghanistan	EG	Egypt	LT	Lithuania	SN	Senegal
AL	Albania	SV	El Salvador	LU	Luxembourg	SC	Seychelles
DZ	Algeria	GQ	Equatorial Guinea	MO	Macau	SL	Sierra Leone
AS	American Samoa	ER	Eritrea	MK	Macedonia, the for-	SG	Singapore
AD	Andorra	EE	Estonia		mer Yugoslav	SK	Slovakia (Slovak
AO	Angola	ET	Ethiopia		Republic of		Republic)
AI	Anguilla	FK	Falkland Islands	MG	Madagascar	SI	Slovenia
AQ	Antarctica		(Malvinas)	MW	Malawi	SB	Solomon Islands
AG	Antigua & Barbuda	FO	Faroe Islands	MY	Malaysia	SO	Somalia
AR	Argentina	FJ	Fiji	MV	Maldives	ZA	South Africa
AM	Armenia	FI	Finland	ML	Mali	GS	South Georgia &
AW	Aruba	FR	France	MT	Malta		South Sandwiches
AU	Australia	FX	France, Metropolitan	MH	Marshall Islands	ES	Spain
AT	Austria	GF	French Guiana	MQ	Martinique	LK	Sri Lanka
AZ	Azerbaijan	PF	French Polynesia	MR	Mauritania	SH	St. Helena
BS	Bahamas	TF	French Southern	MU	Mauritius	PM	St. Pierre &
BH	Bahrain		Territories	YT	Mayotte		Miquelon
BD	Bangladesh	GA	Gabon	MX	Mexico	SD	Sudan
BB	Barbados	GM	Gambia	FM	Micronesia	SR	Suriname
BY	Belarus	GE	Georgia	MD	Moldova, Republic	SJ	Svalbard & Jan
BE	Belgium	DE	Germany		of		Mayen Islands
BZ	Belize	GH	Ghana	MC	Monaco	SZ	Swaziland
BJ	Benin	GI	Gibraltar	MN	Mongolia	SE	Sweden
BM	Bermuda	GR	Greece	MS	Montserrat	CH	Switzerland
BT	Bhutan	GL	Greenland	MA	Morocco	SY	Syrian Arab Republic
BO	Bolivia	GD	Grenada	MZ	Mozambique	TW	Taiwan, Province of
BA	Bosnia &	GP	Guadeloupe	MM	Myanmar		China
	Herzegovina	GU	Guam	NA	Namibia	TJ	Tajikistan
BW	Botswana	GT	Guatemala	NR	Nauru	TZ	Tanzania, United
BV	Bouvet Island	GN	Guinea	NP	Nepal		Republic of
BR	Brazil	GW	Guinea-Bissau	NL	Netherlands	TH	Thailand
IO	British Indian Ocean	GY	Guyana	NC	New Caledonia	TG	Togo
	Territory	HT	Haiti	NZ	New Zealand	TK	Tokelau
BN	Brunei Darussalam	HM	Heard & McDonald	NI	Nicaragua	TO	Tonga
BG	Bulgaria		Islands	NE	Niger	TT	Trinidad & Tobago
BF	Burkina Faso	HN	Honduras	NG	Nigeria	TN	Tunisia
BI	Burundi	HK	Hong Kong	NU	Niue	TR	Turkey
KH	Cambodia	HU	Hungary	NF	Norfolk Island	TM	Turkmenistan
CM	Cameroon	IS	Iceland	MP	Northern Mariana	TC	Turks & Caicos
CA	Canada	IN	India		Islands		Islands
CV	Cape Verde	ID	Indonesia	NO	Norway	TV	Tuvalu
KY	Cayman Islands	IR	Iran (Islamic	OM	Oman	UG	Uganda
CF	Central African		Republic of)	PK	Pakistan	UA	Ukraine
	Republic	IQ	Iraq	PW	Palau	AE	United Arab
TD	Chad	IE	Ireland	PA	Panama		Emirates
CL	Chile	IL	Israel	PG	Papua New Guinea	GB	United Kingdom
CN	China	IT	Italy	PY	Paraguay	US	United States
CX	Christmas Island	JM	Jamaica	PE	Peru	UM	United States Minor
CC	Cocos (Keeling)	JP	Japan	PH	Philippines		Outlying Islands
	Islands	JO	Jordan	PN	Pitcairn	UY	Uruguay
CO	Colombia	KZ	Kazakhstan	PL	Poland	UZ	Uzbekistan
KM	Comoros	KE	Kenya	PT	Portugal	VU	Vanuatu
CG	Congo	KI	Kiribati	PR	Puerto Rico	VA	Vatican City State
CK	Cook Islands	KP	Korea, Democratic	QA	Qatar	VE	Venezuela
CR	Costa Rica		People's Republic of	RE	Reunion	VN	Vietnam
CI	Cote d'Ivoire	KR	Korea, Republic of	RO	Romania	VG	Virgin Islands
HR	Croatia (local name:	KW	Kuwait	RU	Russian Federation	VI	Virgin Islands (U.S.)
	Hrvatska)	KG	Kyrgyzstan	RW	Rwanda	WF	Wallis & Futuna
CU	Cuba	LA	Lao People's	KN	Saint Kitts & Nevis		Islands
CY	Cyprus		Democratic Republic	LC	Saint Lucia	EH	Western Sahara
CZ	Czech Republic	LV	Latvia	VC	Saint Vincent & the	YE	Yemen
DK	Denmark	LB	Lebanon		Grenadines	YU	Yugoslavia
DJ	Djibouti	LS	Lesotho	WS	Samoa	ZR	Zaire
DM	Dominica	LR	Liberia	SM	San Marino	ZM	Zambia
DO	Dominican Republic	LY	Libyan Arab	ST	Sao Tome &	ZW	Zimbabwe
TP	East Timor		Jamahiriya		Principe		
EC	Ecuador	LI	Liechtenstein	SA	Saudi Arabia		

Following Protocol

Having figured out how a computer addresses other computers to send them information, we still need to describe how the information is actually sent. The sending process uses **Transmission Control Protocol/Internet Protocol** or **TCP/IP**. It sounds technical, and is. But the concept is easy to understand.

TCP/IP Postcard Analogy. To explain how TCP/IP works, we repeat an analogy used by Vincent Cerf, one of the pioneers of IP: Sending a message, say, an email message, is like sending your novel from Tahiti to your publisher in New York City using only postcards. How could you do that? Begin by breaking up the novel into small units, only a few sentences long, so that each unit fits on a postcard. Number each postcard to indicate where in the sequence of the novel the sentences belong, and write the publisher's address on each. As you complete the postcards, drop them into a mailbox. The postal service in Tahiti will send them to the publisher (eventually), but the cards will not be kept together, nor will they all take the same route to the publisher. Some postcards may go west, via Hong Kong, when an airplane that can carry mail is headed in that direction. Others may go east, via Los Angeles, when there is an aircraft headed in that direction. From Hong Kong and Los Angeles, there are multiple routes to New York City. Eventually the postcards arrive at the publisher, who uses the numbers to put the postcards in order and reconstruct the novel, as shown in Figure 3.5.

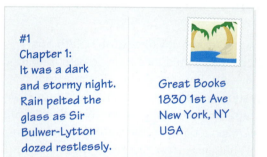

#1
Chapter 1:
It was a dark
and stormy night.
Rain pelted the
glass as Sir
Bulwer-Lytton
dozed restlessly.

Great Books
1830 1st Ave
New York, NY
USA

Figure 3.5. The TCP/IP postcard analogy.

Cerf's postcard analogy makes the concept of TCP/IP clear. Sending any amount of information, including a whole novel, can be done by breaking it into a sequence of small fixed-size units. An **IP packet**, like the postcard, has space for the unit, a destination IP address, and a sequence number. IP packets are filled in order and assigned sequence numbers. The packets are sent over the Internet one at a time using whatever route is available, as shown in Figure 3.6. At the destination, they are reordered by sequence number to assemble the information.

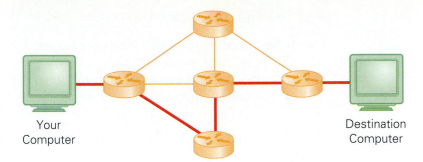

Figure 3.6. *The Internet makes use of whatever routes are available to deliver packets.*

Packets Are Independent.   Consider the advantages of TCP/IP. For example, it is natural to assume that IP packets would take a single path to their destinations, like conventional telephone calls, but they do not. Because each packet can take a different route, congestion and service interruptions do not delay transmissions. If sending the first postcard via Hong Kong meant that all following postcards had to be sent via Hong Kong, then a typhoon preventing aircraft from flying between Tahiti and Hong Kong would delay transmission of the novel. But if the postcards can take any available route, the transmission can continue via Los Angeles. As a result, all of the novel might be delivered via LA before airline service is restored between Tahiti and Hong Kong. This idea motivated engineers to decide to make TCP/IP packets independent.

Moving Packets: Wires and More.   Although Cerf's analogy uses postcards and airplanes, the Internet uses electrical, electronic, and optical means for communication. The original ARPAnet used long-distance telephone lines, and the Internet continues to rely on telephone carriers for long-distance connections. However, as the Internet has grown and as new technologies such as fiber optics have matured, the Internet now uses separate dedicated lines as well. Because the TCP/IP protocol describes exactly how IP packets are structured and how they are to be handled, the technology used to move the packets only concerns the carrier. The computers at each end of the communication do not know or care what medium is used because they simply send and receive IP packets. Indeed, transmissions often rely on multiple technologies as the packets move through the Internet.

Ironically, with the growth of Internet capacity, telephone companies are also sending telephone conversations over the Internet. The speech is digitized, stuffed into IP packets at the speaker's end, sent over the Internet, unpacked at the listener's end, and converted back to the analog form acceptable to a phone set. This suggests that the Internet is fast becoming the universal information carrier.

Far and Near: WAN and LAN

The Internet is a collection of **wide area networks** (**WAN**), meaning networks designed to send information between two locations widely separated and not directly connected. In our postcard analogy, Tahiti and New York City are not directly connected; that is, there is no single airline flight that goes between Tahiti and the Big Apple. So each postcard takes a sequence of airline flights to reach New York City. In the same way, the Internet is a collection of point-to-point channels, and packets must visit a sequence of computers to reach their destination. In networking terms, packets take several **hops** to be delivered. The trace in Figure 3.7 shows that a ping—a "please reply" message—from my machine `spiff` to `eth.ch`, the Swiss Federal Technical University, takes 18 hops on its route from Seattle to Zürich.

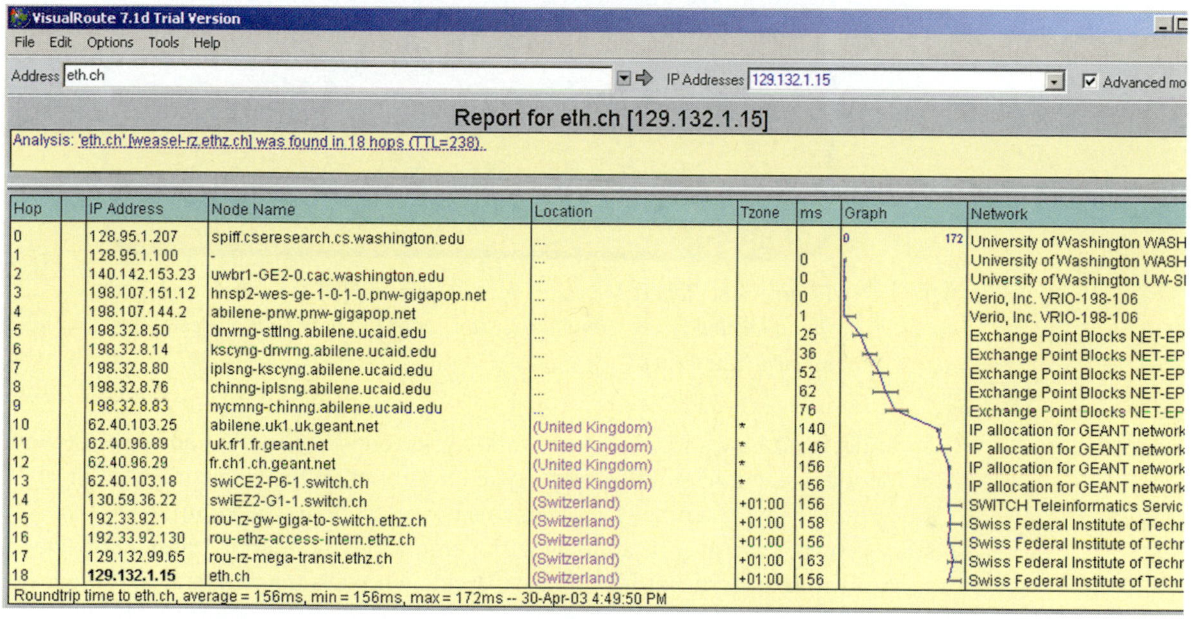

Hop	IP Address	Node Name	Location	Tzone	ms	Graph		Network
0	128.95.1.207	spiff.cseresearch.cs.washington.edu	...			0	172	University of Washington WASH
1	128.95.1.100	-	...		0			University of Washington WASH
2	140.142.153.23	uwbr1-GE2-0.cac.washington.edu	...		0			University of Washington UW-SI
3	198.107.151.12	hnsp2-wes-ge-1-0-1-0.pnw-gigapop.net	...		0			Verio, Inc. VRIO-198-106
4	198.107.144.2	abilene-pnw.pnw-gigapop.net	...		1			Verio, Inc. VRIO-198-106
5	198.32.8.50	dnvrng-sttlng.abilene.ucaid.edu	...		25			Exchange Point Blocks NET-EP
6	198.32.8.14	kscyng-dnvrng.abilene.ucaid.edu	...		36			Exchange Point Blocks NET-EP
7	198.32.8.80	iplsng-kscyng.abilene.ucaid.edu	...		52			Exchange Point Blocks NET-EP
8	198.32.8.76	chinng-iplsng.abilene.ucaid.edu	...		62			Exchange Point Blocks NET-EP
9	198.32.8.83	nycmng-chinng.abilene.ucaid.edu	...		76			Exchange Point Blocks NET-EP
10	62.40.103.25	abilene.uk1.uk.geant.net	(United Kingdom)	*	140			IP allocation for GEANT network
11	62.40.96.89	uk.fr1.fr.geant.net	(United Kingdom)	*	146			IP allocation for GEANT network
12	62.40.96.29	fr.ch1.ch.geant.net	(United Kingdom)	*	156			IP allocation for GEANT network
13	62.40.103.18	swiCE2-P6-1.switch.ch	(United Kingdom)	*	156			IP allocation for GEANT network
14	130.59.36.22	swiEZ2-G1-1.switch.ch	(Switzerland)	+01:00	156			SWITCH Teleinformatics Servic
15	192.33.92.1	rou-rz-gw-giga-to-switch.ethz.ch	(Switzerland)	+01:00	158			Swiss Federal Institute of Techr
16	192.33.92.130	rou-ethz-access-intern.ethz.ch	(Switzerland)	+01:00	156			Swiss Federal Institute of Techr
17	129.132.99.65	rou-rz-mega-transit.ethz.ch	(Switzerland)	+01:00	163			Swiss Federal Institute of Techr
18	129.132.1.15	eth.ch	(Switzerland)	+01:00	156			Swiss Federal Institute of Techr

Roundtrip time to eth.ch, average = 156ms, min = 156ms, max = 172ms -- 30-Apr-03 4:49:50 PM

Figure 3.7. *A ping from the author's machine to eth.ch.*

When computers are close enough to be linked by a single cable or pair of wires, the interconnection is referred to as a **local area network** (**LAN**). Ethernet is the main technology for local area networks, and is appropriate for connecting all the computers in a lab or building. An Ethernet network uses a radically different approach than the Internet, but it is equally easy to understand.

Ethernet Party Analogy. Depending on the technology, the physical setup for an Ethernet network is a wire, wire pair, or optical fiber, called the **channel**, that winds past a set of computers. (Robert Metcalfe, the inventor described the channel as the "The Ether," giving the technology its name; see Figure 3.8) Engineers "tap" the channel to connect a computer, allowing it to send a signal (that is, drive an electronic pulse or light flash onto the channel). All computers connected to the channel can detect the signal, including the sender. Thus the channel supports broadcast communication.

Getting Ether.   Robert Metcalfe described the Ethernet (1973) as a "multipoint data communication channel with collision detection." Though *ether* refers to the medium the ancients believed held the stars and planets, Metcalfe used a co-axial cable in his first implementation, the 100-node *Alto Aloha Network* at Xerox's Palo Alto Research Center.

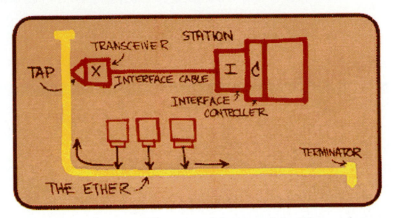

Figure 3.8. Robert Metcalfe's original drawing of the Ethernet design; the unlabeled boxes, computers, "tap" onto the wire that Metcalfe has labeled "The Ether."

To understand how an Ethernet network works, consider another analogy. A group of friends is standing around at a party telling stories. While someone is telling a story, everyone is listening. The speaker is broadcasting to the group. When the story is over, there may be a momentary pause while the friends wait for someone to start the next story. But how do they decide who tells the next story? There is no plan or agreement as to who should speak next. Typically someone just begins talking, "I remember the time. . . ." If no one else begins talking, that speaker continues telling the story to completion. At the end of the story, there may be a pause, and then someone else will start talking. If two or more people begin talking after the pause, they will notice that others are speaking and immediately stop. There is a pause while everyone waits for someone to go ahead. Assuming speakers tend to wait a random length of time, someone will begin talking. It is possible that two or more speakers will again start at the same time, notice the situation, stop, and wait a random length of time. Eventually one person will begin telling another story.

In this analogy we have assumed all the friends are equal; that is, there is no difference in status, nor does anyone have an especially loud or soft voice. Even so, the system isn't fair, because it favors the person who waits the shortest length of time at the end of a story. Of course, we all know such people!

Ethernet communication works like the party protocol. When the channel is in use, as when someone is telling a story, all of the computers listen to it. Unlike storytelling, however, only one computer typically keeps the transmitted information; that is, this broadcast medium is being used for point-to-point communication. A pause indicates the end of the transmission when no computer is sending signals and the channel is quiet. A computer wanting to transmit starts to send signals and, at the same time, starts to listen to the channel to detect what is being transmitted on the channel. If it is exactly the information the computer sent, the computer must be the only one sending, and it completes its transmission. If not, its signals are being mixed in with signals from one or more other computers. It notices that the data is garbled, and so it stops sending immediately. The other computer(s) will stop, too. Each machine pauses for a random length of time. The computer that waits the shortest length of time begins sending, and if there are no conflicting computers, it continues. If not, the colliders repeat the process.

FITBYTE

Many Versus One. There is an important difference between the way the Internet works and the way an Ethernet works. The Internet uses a point-to-point network to implement point-to-point communication. An Ethernet uses a broadcast network for point-to-point communication. The difference is that with the Internet multiple communications can take place at once over different wires, but with the Ethernet only one communication can take place at a time. This limitation is usually not a problem, because Ethernets usually carry much less traffic.

Connecting a Computer to the Internet

How are computers actually connected to the Internet? Today there are two basic methods:

> By an Internet service provider (ISP)

> By a campus or enterprise network

Most of us use both kinds of connections in one day, depending on where we study or work. Let's look at each approach.

Connections by ISP.
As the name implies, Internet service providers sell connections to the Internet. Examples of ISPs are `AOL.com` and `Earthlink.net`, but there are thousands of providers. Most home users connect to the Internet by ISPs. Here's how an ISP connection usually works:

Users plug their computer into the telephone system just as they would connect an extension telephone. (The plug, called an RJ-11, is universal in North America, but an adapter may be needed in some foreign countries.) Then the computer's modem, which is generally built into modern personal computers, can dial up the ISP and establish a connection. This operation is similar to a fax machine dialing another fax machine. (An alternative to a dial-up line is a dedicated connection to the ISP, such as a digital subscriber line or DSL.) The modems—one at each end of the telephone connection— enable the home computer to talk to the ISP's computer so that they can send and receive information. The ISP's computer is connected to the Internet, so it relays information for its customers. For example, when you surf around the Web and click on a remote link (that is, a page stored on a distant computer), the request for the page is sent from your computer to the

ISP's computer, across the Internet to the remote computer, which then sends the Web page back across the Internet to the computer at the ISP. From there, the page is sent over the phone line to your computer and displayed on your screen.

Enterprise Network Connections (LAN). The other way to connect to the Internet is as a user of a larger networked organization such as a school, business, or governmental unit. In this case, the organization's system administrators have connected the computers in a local area network. The Ethernet technology mentioned earlier is an example of a local area network. These local networks, known as **intranets**, support communication within the organization, but they also connect to the Internet by a gateway. Information from a distant Web computer is sent across the Internet, through the gateway to the organization's intranet, and across the LAN to the user's computer.

With either method, ISP or LAN, you usually send and receive information across the Internet transparently—that is, without knowing or caring which method is used.

FITBYTE

> **Should I know my computer's IP address?** No. If you are dialing into the Internet via an ISP, your computer is assigned a temporary IP address for use until you log out. If you access the Internet via an intranet, one of two cases applies. Your network administrator could have assigned your computer an IP address when it was set up. Alternatively, no permanent address was assigned, and your computer gets one each time it is turned on, using the Dynamic Host Computer Protocol (DHCP). In any case, the IP address is nothing you have to worry about.

THE WORLD WIDE WEB

Some of the computers connected to the Internet are **Web servers**. That is, they are computers programmed to send files to browsers running on other computers connected to the Internet. Together these Web servers and their files are the **World Wide Web** (**WWW**). The files are Web pages, but Web servers store and send many other kinds of files, too. These files are often used to create the Web page (for example, images or animations) or to help with other Web services (for example, software to play audio).

When described in these terms, the Web doesn't seem like much. And technically, it's not. What makes the World Wide Web so significant is the information contained in the files and the ability of the client and server computers to process it.

FITBYTE

> **No Confusion.** The World Wide Web and the Internet are different: The Internet is all of the wires and routers connecting named computers. The World Wide Web is a subset of those computers (Web servers) and their files.

Requesting a Web Page

When you request a Web page, such as my university Web page (`http://www.cs.washington.edu/homes/snyder/index.html`), your browser asks for the file from a Web server computer. The Web page address, called a **Universal Resource Locator**, or **URL**, has three main parts:

Protocol. The `http://` part, which stands for Hypertext Transfer Protocol, tells the computers how to handle the file. There are other ways to send files, such as `ftp`, the File Transfer Protocol.

Server computer's name. The name is the server's IP address given by the domain, `www.cs.washington.edu`. Your computer uses the name to send a request to the server computer for the page.

Page's pathname. The pathname is the sequence following the IP address, `/homes/snyder/index.html`. The pathname tells the server which file (page) is requested and where to find it. Its structure is explained below.

All URLs have this structure, although you may not think so, because in some cases you can leave parts out and the software will fill in the missing part. (However, it is never a mistake to use the full form.)

The World Wide Web is built on a client/server relationship between computers. When you request a page, your browser is a client of the Web server. The idea is that the client is asking for some service that the server is handing out. The client/server relationship is a brief relationship that usually involves only two communications. Your computer sends the request for the page, and the server computer sends it back. That's it. In the next moment the server will answer the request of some other client, and your computer may make a request of a different server when you type in a different URL. As we learn in Chapter 16, the client/server structure is very powerful.

FITBYTE

Punctuating the Internet. Notice the structure of email addresses and URLs, and their punctuation:

Email: `receiver@domain.address`

URLs: `http://domain.address/pathname`

The `domain.address` has one or more dots, no `@`, and no slashes. Email has an `@`, but URLs do not. The `receiver` can have dots, dashes (`-`), and underscores (`_`). Spaces are not allowed in either email or URLs.

Describing a Web Page

As you know, servers do not store Web pages in the form seen on our screens. Instead, the pages are stored as a *description* of how they should appear on the screen. When the Web browser receives the description file, known as the **source** file, it creates the Web page image that we see. There are two advantages to storing and sending the source rather than the image itself:

> A description file usually requires less information.

> The browser can adapt the source image to your computer more easily than a literal pixel-by-pixel description.

For example, it is easier to shrink or expand the page from its description than by using the image itself. Though browsers show the image, they always give you the option of seeing the description, too. Next time you are online, look under **View** and find **Source** or **Page Source** in your browser. Figure 3.9 shows a simple Web page and its source.

Hypertext

To describe how a Web page should look, we usually use the **Hypertext Markup Language** (**HTML**). Markup languages, long a staple of publishing and graphic design, describe the layout of a document, such as margin width, font, whether text is left justified or centered, whether text is italic or bold, where images go, and so on. Hypertext began as an experiment to break away from the straight sequence of normal text: first paragraph, second paragraph, etc. With hypertext, it is possible to jump from a point in the text to somewhere else in the text or to some other document, and then return. This feature, which breaks a document's linear sequence, gives it a more complex structure. The (usually blue) highlighted words of Web pages are *hyperlinks*, the points from which we can (optionally) jump and return. Hypertext got its name in the late 1960s from Theodore Nelson, though in his *Literary Machines* Nelson credits the original idea to computer pioneer Vannevar Bush. Combining the two ideas—markup languages and hypertext—lets us build nonlinear documents, ideal for the dynamic and highly interconnected Internet. The World Wide Web was born.

 FITBYTE

Accelerating Ideas. Tim Berners-Lee invented HTML, a markup language that includes hypertext, in 1990 while he was working at CERN, the European Laboratory for Particle Physics.

In Chapter 4 we study HTML to learn how Web pages are created and processed. In Chapters 5 and 6, we explore the content of the WWW, and in Chapter 16 we consider more sophisticated Web applications.

FILE STRUCTURE

To use networks well, we need to understand file structures, though the topic is not technically part of networking. Recall from your experience using a personal computer that a **directory**—also known as a **folder**—is a named collection of files or other directories.

```
<html>
   <head> <title> Alto Computer </title> </head>
   <body bgcolor="white"><font face="Helvetica">
     <img align="right" src="alto.jpg">
     <h1>Alto, A Computer of Note</h1>

     <p>The Alto, built at (and named after) the Xerox Palo
       Alto Research Center (PARC), was the first networked
       personal computer.  Ethernet technology, also invented
       at PARC, was first used to connect Altos. Created by
       the team of Ed McCreight, Chuck Thacker, Butler
       Lampson, Bob Sproull and Dave Boggs to explore office
       automation, the Alto was the first production machine
       to have a bit-mapped display and a mouse.</p>

      <p>Though Xerox was unable to market the Alto
        — they cost $32,000 in 1979 — the computer impressed
        many others who did push the technologies. For
        example, Apple Computer co-founder Steve Jobs was so
        impressed when he saw the Alto, he created the
        revolutionary Apple Macintosh in its image.</p>

   </body>
</html>
```

Figure 3.9. A Web page and the HTML source that produced it. Notice that an additional image file, `alto.jpg`, is also required to display the page.

Directory Hierarchy

Because directories can contain directories, which can contain files and other directories, and on and on, the whole scheme—called the **file structure** of the computer—forms the **directory hierarchy**. Think of any hierarchy as a tree, and in the case of the file structures, directories are the branch points and files are the leaves. Hierarchy trees are often drawn in odd ways, such as sideways or upside down, but in all cases two terms are standard:

> > *Down or deeper* in the hierarchy means into subdirectories; that is, toward the leaves.

> > *Up or higher* in the hierarchy means into enclosing directories; that is, toward the root.

Figure 3.10 shows the path between the a file, `xerox-alto.jpg`, a leaf in the directory hierarchy, and the `desktop`, a directory and the root in the directory hierarchy. For example, from `NextLevelDown`, "deeper" is towards `xerox-alto.jpg` and "higher" is towards `Desktop`.

Figure 3.10. *A hierarchy diagram showing the path between* `xerox-alto.jpg` *and the* `desktop`.

Learning the "directionality" of hierarchical references makes navigating the Web simpler.

Part of the directory hierarchy is shown in the pathnames of URLs. For example, the National Air and Space Museum's URL for a brief description of Pioneer 10, the first man-made object to leave the solar system, is `http://www.nasm.si.edu/galleries/gal100/pioneer.html`. The page is given by a pathname, `/galleries/gal100/pioneer.html`, that tells the computer how to navigate through the Air and Space Museum's directory hierarchy to the file, as shown in Figure 3.11. Each time we pass a slash (`/`), reading the pathname from left to right, we move into a subdirectory. That is, we go deeper into the hierarchy. We start at a top-level directory called `galleries`. (The NASM has 23 exhibit rooms called galleries, and we might assume that this directory contains information about each of them.) Within the `galleries` directory, there is a subdirectory called `gal100`, which we might assume refers to Gallery 100, the room containing famous "firsts" in air and space exploration. And in the `gal100` directory, there is a file called `pioneer.html`, the Web page we want.

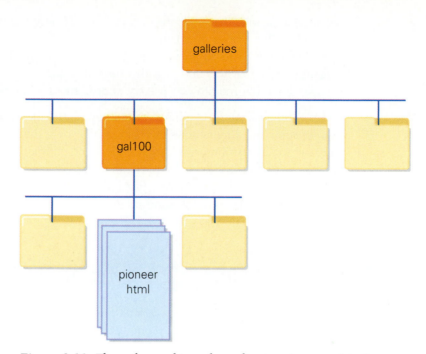

Figure 3.11. The pathname hierarchy ending in `pioneer.html`.

Case In Point. Remember that case sensitivity means computers treat upper- and lowercase letters as different. In URLs domains are not case sensitive, because they are standardized for DNS lookup. Pathnames can be case sensitive, because they tell how to navigate through the Web server's file structure, which may be case sensitive. Be careful when typing pathnames, and when in doubt, try lowercase first.

In general, the path in a URL tells the server computer where to find the requested file in the server's file structure. The server computer follows the hierarchical structure just as we did in the NASM example.

Organizing the Directory

A common way to organize the information in a directory is to list or index the files that are in the directory. The information about NASM's Gallery 100 is organized this way. There is a file in the `gal100` directory, `gal100.html`, that lists the links to Web pages about exhibits in the gallery. Because an index linking to the files in a directory is common, browsers know to look for such a file. When a URL ends in a slash (which means the last item on the path is a directory rather than a filename), the browser automatically looks for a file called `index.html` in that directory. So, a request for the URL

`http://www.cs.washington.edu/homes/snyder/index.html`

to my university Web page is the same as

`http://www.cs.washington.edu/homes/snyder/`

because a browser that finds the directory named `snyder` will automatically look for a file called `index.html` in it. Of course, the `index.html` file will exist only if the person who set up the Web pages and built the file hierarchy decided to organize them that way and provided the index pages. Some people do and some people don't, but the browser will try `index.html` when necessary.

Why build a hierarchy at all? Why not lump all the files into one huge directory? Most people build hierarchies to organize their own thinking and work. For example, the gallery-exhibit organization is clear and simple. Because directories cost nothing, there is no reason not to use them, and it is highly recommended. (In this book, when we create a Web page, for example, we will always use a subdirectory for organizing the pictures on the page.)

THE INTERNET AND THE WEB

Some Web servers have `www` as part of their domain name, some don't. Some Web servers, like `www.cs.washington.edu`, seem to add on the `www` if you leave it out, and some, like New York City's Museum of Modern Art (MoMA), work either way; both `www.moma.org` and `moma.org` give the same Web page. When is the `www` required and when is it optional?

First remember that names like `www.cs.washington.edu` are simply names. That is, like `spiff`, `www` is the name of a computer, the Web server, in the `cs.washington.edu` domain. And, like all computers connected to the Internet, Web servers have IP addresses. To refer to a Web server, you *must* give its name exactly, because your computer will ask the DNS server for the Web server's IP address using that name. If the name is wrong, either you get back the IP address for the wrong computer or, more typically, the DNS lookup will fail. Your browser will give you an error message saying it could not locate the server and directing you to check the address. So, there is no option: You must give the name exactly.

But no organization taking the trouble to put a Web server on the Internet wants visitors to fail, so their Web administrators try to save users from mistakes. For example, if you try to access my Web page but forget the `www`, your request to `cs.washington.edu` will reach the wrong computer. However, that computer has been programmed to notice `http://` requests and to return to your browser a reply, "You probably meant `www.cs.washington.edu`." This is called a **redirection**.

Browsers are designed to try again with the recommended address. So, if when you type `http://cs.washington.edu/homes/snyder`, your location window quickly changes to `http://www.cs.washington.edu/homes/snyder`, making it seem that the www has been added. But all you are seeing is your browser try-ing the redirection address. The redirection could have been `http://www.aw.com/snyder/`, the URL for this book. In that case, the redirec-tion looks like a replacement, which is what it really is. Redirection is used exten-sively at Web sites to avoid telling users that they made a mistake and to get them to where they want to be.

Rather than using redirection, some organizations, like the Museum of Modern Art simply make several names work. That is, MoMA has registered both `moma.org` and `www.moma.org` to the IP address `4.43.114.168`, saving us from making a mistake no matter which choice we make and avoiding redirection. Both names produce the same result because they connect to the same computer.

Web servers don't have to be named www. It's just what people usually name their Web servers. The reason that so many Web servers are named www is because as the Web got started, many domains added another computer to be their Web server. The server needed a name that people could remember, because redirection was not yet in wide use. Because the first groups named their servers www, it helped everyone's memory if later groups did, too. Now it seems like a requirement, but it is only tradition.

SUMMARY

The chapter opened with a discussion of five fundamental ways networked comput-ers have changed the world and our lives. Next, basic types of communication were presented: point-to-point, multicast, broadcast, synchronous, and asynchronous. Most forms of communication apply a combination of these types. For example, tele-phones are synchronous and point-to-point. An overview of networking included IP addresses, domains, IP packets, the IP-protocol, wide area versus local area networks, Ethernet protocol, ISPs, and enterprise networks. From there we explained the differ-ence between the Internet and the World Wide Web, terms that are commonly con-fused. Finally, we explained where HTML came from and reviewed file hierarchies in preparation for our study of HTML in Chapter 4.

EXERCISES

Multiple Choice

1. Passive interaction via the Internet allows interaction of individuals:
   A. separated by distance
   B. separated by time
   C. with a shared interest
   D. all of the above

2. English is becoming the universal language as a result of all of the following except:
   A. American pop culture
   B. the dominance of science and technology in English-speaking countries
   C. information technology's predominant use of English
   D. the Alto Project

3. Overall, the ability of individuals to create and publish Web pages:
   A. presents an enormous security risk
   B. extends human expression
   C. has led to a proliferation of hate pages and pornographic sites
   D. has unduly diverted huge sums from other IT projects

4. Spamming is like:
   A. telemarketing
   B. junk mail
   C. advertising inserts
   D. all of the above

5. If the Internet consisted of four computers, there would be six possible connections. If it consisted of five computers, there would be ten possible connections. How many connections are possible with ten computers?
   A. 10
   B. 30
   C. 45
   D. infinite

6. What is the potential number of IP address available?
   A. 65,536
   B. 16,777,216
   C. 4,294,967,296
   D. limitless

7. The part of an email address to the right of the @ is most like a:
   A. mailbox
   B. post office
   C. letter
   D. return address

8. DNS stands for:
   A. Determined Name of Sender
   B. Determined Not Spam
   C. Domain Name System
   D. Domain Number Sequence

9. The origins of the Internet can be traced to:
   A. news services sending wire stories to local newspapers
   B. phone companies creating the long distance system
   C. government, big business, and educational institutions conducting Cold War research
   D. the United States and USSR creating a hotline

10. As an aspiring TV exec, the ideal country to locate the top-level domain for your new quiz show "What's My IP?" would be:
    A. Papua New Guinea
    B. Cocos Islands
    C. Tuvalu
    D. Nauru

Short Answer

1. eCommerce is the shortened term for _____.

2. The interconnection of computers has led to an era called the _____.

3. A communication that goes out to many people within a specific target audience is called a _____.

4. A hierarchy of related computers on a network is called a _____.

5. Computers on the same level of a domain are known as _____.

6. A "please reply" message sent over the Internet is called a _____.

7. Computers on an Ethernet network "tap" into a cable called a _____.

8. A company that supplies connections to the Internet is called a(n) _____.

9. Intranets connect to the Internet via _____.

10. Local networks that support communications wholly within an organization are called _____.

11. Special computers that send files to Web browsers elsewhere on the Internet are known as _____.

12. The http:// in a Web address is the _____.

13. Files are often sent over the Internet via a process known by the acronym _____.

14. The source file for a Web page contains the _____ of the page, not the actual image of the page.

15. HTML stands for _____.

Exercises

1. How have networked computers made your life different from the life of your parents?

2. Discuss five changes the Information Age has brought.

3. There's an adage, "Guns don't kill people. People kill people." How does this relate to human nature and the Internet?

4. Label the following with either an S to indicate synchronous communication or an A to indicate asynchronous communication.

   _____ movie   _____ book
   _____ chat session   _____ concert
   _____ email   _____ text messaging
   _____ video conference   _____ Web board
   _____ Web page

5. Go to `www.mids.org/mapsale/world/index.html` and check out the Internet maps of the world. Where is most of the traffic? Plot the course of a packet from Tahiti to New York. What routes are available and where are the bottlenecks?

6. Try the Web address above without the file name. What do you get?

7. Describe how the Internet is like a bus route, a subway route, UPS or Federal Express. How is it different from these? Go to `www.mta.nyc.ny.us/nyct/maps/submap.htm` to see a map of the NYC subway system. How does it compare? Compare the Internet to the Prague subway map by going to `www.odyssey.on.ca/~europrail/prague.htm`.

8. What industries have prospered and which ones might have suffered because of the growth of the Internet? Why?

chapter

4

MARKING UP WITH HTML

A Hypertext Markup Language Primer

learning objectives {

> Know the meaning of and use hypertext terms

> Use HTML tags to structure a document

> Use the basics of HTML tag attributes

> Use HTML tags to link to other files

> Explain the differences between absolute and relative path names

> Use HTML to encode lists and tables

Most of the fundamental ideas of science are essentially simple and may as a rule be expressed in a language comprehensible to everyone.

—ALBERT EINSTEIN

WEB PAGES are created, stored, and sent in encoded form; a browser converts them into the image we see on the screen. The Hypertext Markup Language (HTML) is the main language for defining how a Web page should look. Features like background color, font, and layout are all specified in HTML. Learning to "speak" HTML is easy. So easy, in fact, that most Web pages are not created by writing HTML directly, but by using Web authoring software; that is, programs that write the HTML automatically. We will still learn HTML because it helps us understand the World Wide Web, gives us experience directing a computer to do tasks for us, and prepares us for other topics in our Fluency study. When we are finished, we will speak a new "foreign" language!

This chapter begins by reviewing the concept of tags, which we learned about in Chapter 2, and we introduce the dozen most basic HTML tags. Next comes document structuring, including details such as headings and alignment. After discussing special characters, we create an example of a text-only Web page. We decide that the page should have an image and hyperlinks, so we learn about placing images and links and how to connect them. With this knowledge we improve our example page. Finally, we introduce the basics of lists, tables, and colors, which give us more control over the "look and feel" of our Web pages.

MARKING UP WITH HTML

HTML is straightforward. The words that will appear on the Web page are simply surrounded by formatting tags describing how they should look.

Formatting with Tags

Remember from Chapter 2 that tags are words or abbreviations enclosed in angle brackets, `<` and `>`, like `<title>`, and that tags come in pairs, the second with a slash (`/`), like `</title>`. The tag pair surrounds the text to be formatted like parentheses. So the title, which every HTML Web page has, would be written as

`<title>Tiger Woods, Masters Champion</title>`

These two tags can be read as "beginning of title text" and "end of title text." The title is shown on the title bar of the browser when the page is being displayed (the very top of the window where the close button is). In HTML, the tags are not case sensitive, but the actual text is. So, in this example, we could have used `<TITLE>`, `<Title>`, `<tITle>`, or any other mix of lower- and uppercase letters. We will follow tradition and use only lowercase letters in tags.

Tags for Bold and Italic

HTML has tags for bold text, `<b>` and `</b>`, for italic text, `<i>` and `</i>`, and for paragraphs, `<p>` and `</p>`. You can use more than one kind of formatting at a time, such as italic bold text, by "nesting" the tags, as in

`<p><b><i>Veni, Vidi, Vici!</i></b></p>`

which produces

Veni, Vidi, Vici!

It doesn't matter in which order you put the tags. You get the same result if you put the bold before the italic:

`<p><i><b>Veni, Vidi, Vici!</b></i></p>`

The key is to make sure the tags are nested correctly. All the tags between a starting tag and its ending tag should be matched. So, in the *Veni, Vidi, Vici* example, between the starting `<p>` tag and its ending tag `</p>` all the tags match in both cases.

FITTIP

HTML is relaxed about some of these rules, but when and how is often complicated. So in this book we ignore any relaxed rules to avoid complication, because they don't make a difference in the pages you can create.

A few tags are not paired and so do not have a / ending form. One example is the horizontal rule tag, `<hr>`, which displays a horizontal line. Another example is break, `<br>`, which continues the text on the next line and is useful for ending each line of an address. These tags do not apply to multiple characters, so they don't need to surround anything.

An HTML Web page file begins with the `<html>` tag, ends with the `</html>` tag, and has the following structure:

```
<html>
   <head>
        preliminary material goes here
   </head>
   <body>
        the main content of the page goes here
   </body>
</html>
```

The section surrounded by `<head>` and `</head>` contains the beginning material like the title, and the section surrounded by `<body>` and `</body>` contains the content of the page. *This form must always be followed, and all of these tags are required.*

FITCAUTION

Use Simple Text Editors. While we are giving ignore-at-your-own-peril rules about a Web page's form, we should offer a caution about text editors. HTML must be written using basic ASCII characters. We discuss these in Chapter 8, but for now, think of them as the characters from the keyboard. As we learned in Chapter 2, standard word processors (e.g., WordPerfect, Word, and Claris Works) produce files of such characters, but they also include special formatting information that browsers do not like. For that reason, you *must* write HTML using a basic text editor such as NotePad (Windows), Simple Text (Mac), BBText (UNIX), or the like. And always make sure that you save the file using Text format. This way the HTML file will make sense to Web browsers. Also, always make sure that the file name ends with the `.html` extension, so that the browser knows that it is reading an HTML document.

There's not very much to HTML. By the end of the next section, we will have created a respectable Web page—our first!

STRUCTURING DOCUMENTS

The point of a markup language is to describe how a document's parts fit together. Because those parts are mostly paragraphs, headings, and text styles like italic and bold, the tags of this section are the most common and most useful.

Headings in HTML

Because documents have headings, subheadings, and so on, HTML gives us several levels of heading tags to choose from, from level one (the highest) headings, `<h1>`

and `</h1>`, to level two, `<h2>` and `</h2>`, all the way to level eight, `<h8>` and `</h8>`. The headings display the material in large font on a new line. For example,

```
<h1>Pope</h1> <h2>Cardinal</h2> <h3>Archbishop</h3>
```

would print as

Pope

Cardinal

Archbishop

You should use the heading levels in numerical order without skipping a level, although you don't have to start at 1. Notice that the headings are bold and get less "strong" (smaller and perhaps less bold) as the level number increases.

HTML Format vs. Display Format

Notice as well that although the HTML text was run together on one line, it was displayed formatted on separate lines. This illustrates the important point that the HTML source tells the browser how to produce the formatted image based on the *meanings* of the tags, not on how the source instructions look. Though the source's form is unimportant, we usually write HTML in a structured way to make it easier for people to understand. There is no agreed-upon form, but the example might have been written with indenting to emphasize the levels:

```
<h1>Pope</h1>
   <h2>Cardinal</h2>
       <h3>Archbishop</h3>
```

White Space

The two forms give us the same result. Computer experts call space that has been inserted for readability **white space**. We create white space with spaces, tabs, and new lines. HTML ignores white space. The browser turns any sequence of white space characters into a single space before it begins processing the HTML. The only exception is **preformatted** information contained within `<pre>` and `</pre>` tags, which is displayed as it appears.

The fact that white space is ignored is important when the browser formats paragraphs. All text within paragraph tags, `<p>` and `</p>`, is treated as a paragraph, and any sequence of white space characters turn into a single space. So

```
<p> <b>Xeno's Paradox: </b>
Achilles and a turtle were to run a race. Achilles could
run twice as fast as the turtle. The turtle,
being a slower runner,
```

```
got a 10 meter head start, whereupon
Achilles started and ran the 10 meter distance. At that
moment the turtle was 5 meters farther. When Achilles had run
that distance the turtle had gone another 2.5 meters,
and so forth. Paradoxically, the turtle always remained
ahead. </p>
```

would appear as

Xeno's Paradox: Achilles and a turtle were to run a race. Achilles could run twice as fast as the turtle. The turtle, being a slower runner, got a 10 meter head start, whereupon Achilles started and ran the 10 meter distance. At that moment the turtle was 5 meters farther. When Achilles had run that distance the turtle had gone another 2.5 meters, and so forth. Paradoxically, the turtle always remained ahead.

The width of the line is determined by the width of the browser window. Of course, a narrower or wider browser window makes the lines break in different places, which is why HTML ignores white space and changes the paragraph's formatting to fit the space available. Table 4.1 summarizes the basic HTML tags.

Table 4.1. *Basic HTML Tags*

Start Tag	End Tag	Meaning	Required
`<html>`	`</html>`	HTML document; first and last tags in an HTML file	✔
`<title>`	`</title>`	Title bar text; describes page	✔
`<head>`	`</head>`	Preliminary material; e.g., title, at start of page	✔
`<body>`	`</body>`	The main part of the page	✔
`<p>`	`</p>`	Paragraph, can use `align` attribute	
`<hr>`		Line (horiz. rule), can use `width` and `size` attributes	
`<h1>` . . . `<h8>`	`</h1>` . . . `</h8>`	Headings, eight levels, use in order, can use `align` attribute	
`<b>`	`</b>`	Bold	
`<i>`	`</i>`	Italic	
`<a href="fn">`	`</a>`	Anchor reference, *fn* must be a pathname to an HTML file	
`<img src="fn">`		Image source reference, *fn* must be pathname to `.jpg` or `.gif` file	
` `		Break, continue text on a new line	

Brackets in HTML: The Escape Symbol

Notice that there would be a problem if our Web page had to show a math relationship such as $0 < p > r$, because the browser would misinterpret $< p >$ as a paragraph tag and not display it. To show angle brackets, we use an *escape* symbol—the ampersand (`&`)—followed by an abbreviation, followed by a semicolon. For example:

> `&lt;` displays as <
>
> `&gt;` displays as >
>
> `&amp;` displays as &

Notice that the escape symbol, the ampersand, needs an escape, too! So, our math problem would be solved in HTML by

`<i>0 &lt; p &gt; r</i>`

Accent Marks in HTML

Letters with accent marks also use the escape symbol. The general form is an ampersand followed by the letter—and whether it is upper- or lowercase makes a difference—followed by the name of the accent mark. So, for example, `&eacute` displays as é, `&Egrave` displays as È, `&ntilde` displays as ñ, and `&ouml` displays as ö. Table 4.2 lists a few useful special symbols for some Western European languages. You can find a complete list at

`www.w3.org/MarkUp/html13/latin1.html`

Table 4.2. Special Symbols for Western European Language Accent Marks

à	&agrave;	á	&aacute;	â	&acirc;	ã	&atilde;	ä	&auml;
å	&aring;	ç	&ccedil;	è	&egrave;	é	&eacute;	ê	&ecirc;
ë	&euml;	ì	&igrave;	í	&iacute;	î	&icirc;	ï	&iuml;
ñ	&ntilde;	ò	&ograve;	ó	&oacute;	ô	&ocirc;	õ	&otilde;
ö	&ouml;	ø	&oslash;	ù	&ugrave;	ú	&uacute;	û	&ucirc;
ü	&uuml;								

Note: For an accent mark on a uppercase letter, make the letter following the & uppercase.

Attributes in HTML

Though most text properties are a single key term or abbreviation, some properties, such as how to align text, need more information. For example, we can't just say we want text justified; we have to say that we want it left justified, centered, or right justified. We do this by using the tag's attributes. Attributes, which are generally optional, appear inside the angle brackets.

Align, Justify. For example, paragraphs and headings have an align attribute specifying whether the text should be left justified, centered, or right justified. The attribute follows the tag word, separated by a space, and is separated from its value (in double quotes) by an equal sign. So

```
<p align = "center"> <b>Winston Churchill once observed:</b>
</p>
<p> If at 20 you are not liberal, you have no heart. </p>
<p align = "right"> If at 40 you are not conservative, you
have no mind.</p>
```

would display as

> **Winston Churchill once observed:**
>
> If at 20 you are not liberal, you have no heart.
>
> If at 40 you are not conservative, you have no mind.

Notice that when we don't specify the alignment attribute, as in the second line, the default is left justified.

Horizontal Rule Attribute. The horizontal rule tag, `<hr>`, mentioned earlier, also has attributes. One attribute, width, specifies how wide the line should be as a percentage of the browser window's width; another attribute, `size`, says how thick the line should be. So `<hr width="50%" size=1>` displays a horizontal line that takes up half of the horizontal width and is the minimum thickness, as in

---

The default size is 2. Experiment to find the size that works best for your application. Notice that the width, `50%`, is enclosed in quotation marks, but the size specification, 1, is not. This has been done for illustration purposes. HTML does not need the quotes *if a browser can figure out what is intended.* But don't take chances—put quotes around anything that follows the equal sign.

FITCAUTION

Misquotes. Quotation marks are the cause of many HTML errors. Of course, quotes must match, and it is easy to forget one of the pair. But, there are also different kinds of quotes: The simple quotes (" and ') are the kind HTML likes; the fancy, curving quotes, called "smart quotes," (as shown) are the kind HTML doesn't like. Check *carefully* for messed-up quotes when the HTML produces the wrong Web page.

Though we have introduced only a few HTML tags so far, we can already create Web pages, as shown in Figure 4.1. Study the HTML and notice the following points:

> The title is shown on the title bar of the browser window.

> The alignment attribute has been used in the level 1 heading to center the heading.

> The level 2 headings are left justified because that is the default.

> The statement of Russell's Paradox is in bold.

> The HTML source paragraphs are indented more than the `<h2>` heading lines to make them more readable.

> The line between the two paragraphs is three quarters the width of the browser window.

> Acute accents are used in Magritte's first name.

> The French phrase from the painting is in italics.

> The word *picture* is in italics for emphasis.

It's a simple page, and it was simple to produce.

FITBYTE

Compose and Check. It's a good idea always to write the text first and then format it in HTML. A productive way to work is with two windows open, your editor and your browser. After writing a few HTML formatting tags in the editor, *save* them and then check the result with the browser by *reloading* the source.

MARKING LINKS WITH ANCHOR TAGS

The example shown in Figure 4.1 may be an interesting Web page, but it doesn't use hypertext at all. It would be more informative, perhaps, if it linked to biographies of Russell and Magritte. Also, it would be easier to understand if it showed Magritte's painting or linked to it.

Two Sides of a Link

In this section we learn how to make hyperlinks. When a user clicks on a hyperlink, the browser loads a new Web page. This means there must be two parts to a hyperlink: the text in the current document that is highlighted, called the **anchor text**, and the address of the other Web page, called the **hyperlink reference**.

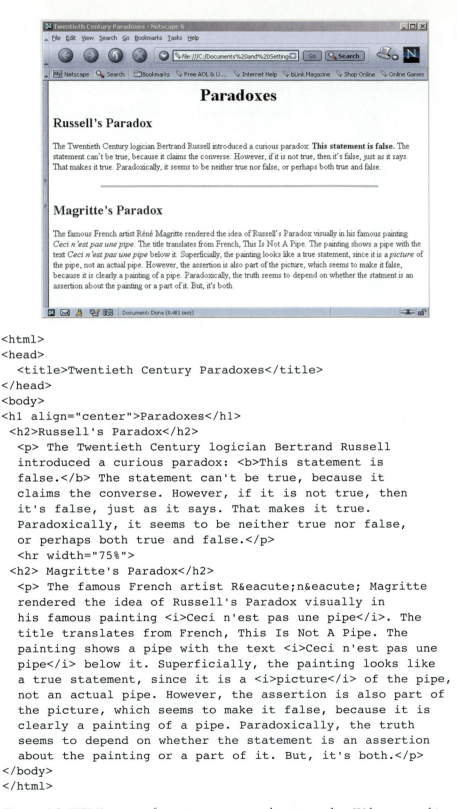

```
<html>
<head>
  <title>Twentieth Century Paradoxes</title>
</head>
<body>
<h1 align="center">Paradoxes</h1>
 <h2>Russell's Paradox</h2>
  <p> The Twentieth Century logician Bertrand Russell
  introduced a curious paradox: <b>This statement is
  false.</b> The statement can't be true, because it
  claims the converse. However, if it is not true, then
  it's false, just as it says. That makes it true.
  Paradoxically, it seems to be neither true nor false,
  or perhaps both true and false.</p>
  <hr width="75%">
 <h2> Magritte's Paradox</h2>
  <p> The famous French artist R&eacute;n&eacute; Magritte
  rendered the idea of Russell's Paradox visually in
  his famous painting <i>Ceci n'est pas une pipe</i>. The
  title translates from French, This Is Not A Pipe. The
  painting shows a pipe with the text <i>Ceci n'est pas une
  pipe</i> below it. Superficially, the painting looks like
  a true statement, since it is a <i>picture</i> of the pipe,
  not an actual pipe. However, the assertion is also part of
  the picture, which seems to make it false, because it is
  clearly a painting of a pipe. Paradoxically, the truth
  seems to depend on whether the statement is an assertion
  about the painting or a part of it. But, it's both.</p>
</body>
</html>
```

Figure 4.1. HTML source of `paradoxes.html` *and corresponding Web page resulting from its interpretation by a browser.*

Both parts of the hyperlink are specified in the **anchor tag**, constructed as follows:

- ☑ *Begin with* <a *making sure there's a space after the* a*. The* a *is for anchor.*
- ☑ *Give the hyperlink reference using* href="*filename*"*, making sure to include the double quotes.*
- ☑ *Close the anchor tag with the* > *symbol.*
- ☑ *Specify the anchor text, which will be highlighted when it is displayed by the browser.*
- ☑ *End the hyperlink with the* </a> *tag.*

For example, suppose `http://www.bios.com/bios/sci/russell.html` were the URL for a Web biography of Bertrand Russell; we would anchor it to his last name on our Web page with the anchor tag

```
Bertrand <a href="http://www.bios.com/bios/sci/russell.html">Russell</a>
```

normal text   hyperlink reference   anchor

This hyperlink would be displayed with Russell's last name highlighted as

Bertrand Russell

When the browser displays the page and the user clicks on Russell, the browser downloads the bio page given in the href. As another example, if Magritte's biography were at the same site, the text

```
<a href="http://www.bios.com/bios/art/magritte.html">Magritte</a>
```

would give the reference and anchor for his hyperlink.

Absolute Pathnames (URLs)

In these anchor tag examples, the hyperlink reference is an entire URL because the Web browser needs to know how to find the page. Remember from Chapter 3 that the URL is made from a protocol specification, `http://`, a domain or IP address, `www.bios.com`, and a path to the file, `/bios/sci/russell.html`. The files are two levels down in the directory (folder) hierarchy of the site.

From the Russell and Magritte examples, we guess that at the Bios Company site, the biographies have been grouped together in a top-level directory (see Chapter 3) called `bios`. Probably the scientists, like Russell, are grouped together in the subdirectory called `sci`, and the artists are grouped together under the subdirectory called `art`. Within these directories are the individual biography files, `russell.html` and `magritte.html`. The slash (/) separates levels in the directory hierarchy, and "crossing a slash" moves us lower in the hierarchy into a subfolder. Such complete URLs are called **absolute pathnames**, and they are the right way to reference pages at other Web sites.

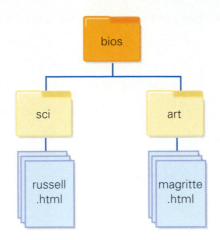

Relative Pathnames

Often a link refers to other Web pages on the same site. Because these pages will all be stored in the same or nearby directories, their anchor tags use **relative pathnames**. A relative pathname describes how to find the referenced file *relative* to the file in which the anchor tag appears. So, for example, if the anchor tag is in an HTML file in directory X, and the anchor references another file also in directory X, only the name of the file is given, not the whole path.

Suppose that we have written our own biographies for Russell and Magritte for our `paradoxes.html` page. If the files are named `russellbio.html` and `magrittebio.html`, and they are in the same directory as the `paradoxes.html`, the anchor tags of the Paradoxes page can use relative references:

```
<a href="russellbio.html">Russell</a>
```

and

```
<a href="magrittebio.html">Magritte</a>
```

This saves us typing the protocol part, the domain part, and the path to the folder part, but that's not why we like relative pathnames. Relative pathnames are more flexible, because they let us move Web files around as a group without having to change the references. This flexibility will become important when you begin managing your own Web page.

Going "Deeper" in a Directory.
Relative pathnames are very simple when the file containing the anchor and the referenced file are in the same directory—we just give the file name. When the referenced file is "deeper" in the directory hierarchy, perhaps in a folder or in a folder in a folder, we simply give the path from the current directory down to the file. For example, in the directory containing `paradoxes.html` we create a subdirectory, `biographies`, which contains the two profiles. Then the anchor for the Russell bio becomes

```
<a href="biographies/russellbio.html">Russell</a>
```

because we must say how to navigate to the file from the Paradoxes page's location. Of course, using relative pathnames means that the files for the pages must be kept together in a fixed structure, but that's the easiest solution anyway.

Going "Higher" in a Hierarchy. The only problem left is how to refer to directories higher up in the hierarchy. The technique for doing this (which comes from the UNIX operating system) is to refer to the next outer level of the hierarchy—that is, the containing directory—as `..` (pronounced "*dot dot*"). So if we imagine that the directory structure has the form

```
mypages
   biographies
      russellbio.html
      magrittebio.html
   coolstuff
      paradoxes.html
```

then, in **paradoxes.html**, the Russell biography anchor would be

```
<a href="../biographies/russellbio.html">Russell</a>
```

because the biography can't be reached by going down from the directory (**coolstuff**) containing **paradoxes.html**. Instead we have to go up to the next higher level to **mypages**. From there, we can navigate down to the bios through the **biographies** directory. We can use a sequence of dots and slashes (`../../`), so that each pair of dots moves the browser up higher in the hierarchy. For example, the reference

```
<a href="../../humorpages/dumbjokes/knockknock4.html">
```

would move up to the directory containing the directory containing the page, then down through the **humorpages** and **dumbjokes** directories to the actual HTML page.

Summarizing, hyperlinks are specified using anchor tags. The path to the file is given as the **href** attribute of the anchor tag, and the text to be highlighted, the anchor, is given between the anchor tag and its closing `</a>`. Paths can be absolute paths—that is, standard URLs—for offsite pages. Relative pathnames should be used for all onsite pages. The relative path can be just a name if the referenced file is in the same directory as the page that links to it, or it can specify a path deeper, through descendant directories, or it can use the `..` notation to move higher in the directory structure. These path rules apply to images as well as hyperlinks.

INCLUDING PICTURES WITH IMAGE TAGS

Pictures are worth a thousand words, as the saying goes, so including them in an HTML document adds to a page's content. To include pictures, we use a tag, but not an anchor tag because we don't want to *refer* to the picture. We want to display it directly on the page. (If you would rather just refer to it, use anchor tags.)

Image Tag Format

An image tag, which is analogous to an anchor tag, specifies a file containing an image. The image tag format is

```
<img src="filename">
```

where **src** stands for "source" and the *filename* uses the same rules for absolute and relative pathnames as anchor tags. So, for example, if the image of Magritte's painting is stored in a file **pipe.jpg**, in the same directory as the Paradoxes page, we can include the image with a relative pathname

```
<img src="pipe.jpg">
```

which finds the image and places it in the document.

GIF and JPEG Images

Images can come in several formats, but two of them are important for Web pages: **GIF** (pronounced either with a hard or soft *g*) and **JPEG** (pronounced *JAY-peg*.) GIF, Graphics Interchange Format, is best for cartoons and simple drawings. JPEG, named for the Joint Photographic Experts Group, is best for high-resolution photographs and complex artwork. To tell the browser which format the image is in, the file name should have the extension **.gif**, **.jpg**, or **.jpeg**.

Positioning the Image in the Document

The big question is, "Where does the image go on the Web page?" To understand how images are placed, notice that HTML lays out text in the browser window from *left to right*, and from *top to bottom*, the same way English is written. If the image is the same size or smaller than the letters, it is placed in line just like a letter at the point where the image tag occurs in the HTML. For example, when we insert a small image █ in the text, it is simply drawn in place. This is convenient

for icons or smiley faces in the text. If the image is larger than the letters █ it is dropped in the text in the same way, but the line spacing is increased to separate it from the neighboring lines. The HTML default rule is: *Images are inserted in the page at the point where the tag is specified in the HTML, and the text lines up with the bottom of the image.*

We can use the **align** attribute in the image tag to line up the top of the image with the top of the text (**align="top"**) or to center the text on the image (**align="middle"**) in the image. In all cases, the **bottom** (default), **middle**, and **top** alignments apply only to the line of text in which the image has been inserted.

 Another common and visually pleasing way to place images in text is to flow the text around them, either by having the image right justified with the text along the left, or vice versa. To make the text flow around the image, use the align attribute in the image tag with the value **"right"** or **"left"**. This forces the image to the right or left of the browser window. The text will continue from left to right, and from top to bottom, in the remaining space, flowing around the image.

Finally, to display an image by itself without any text around it, simply enclose the image tag within paragraph tags. That will separate it from the paragraphs above and below it. You can even center the paragraph to center the image:

FITTIP

Clearer Directions. Notice that there are two sets of tags for alignment attributes. For horizontal alignment, such as paragraph justification, use `left`, `center`, `right`. For vertical alignment, such as for placing images relative to a line of text, use `top`, `middle`, `bottom`.

So how do we put the image of Magritte's painting in the Paradoxes page? Perhaps the most pleasing solution is to right-justify it and let the paragraph flow around it. We can do this by writing

`<img src="pipe.jpg" align="right">`

as long as the picture doesn't take up all or most of the window, which would prevent the text from flowing naturally. To specify how large the picture should be, use the `height` and `width` attributes in the image tag. Give the size in pixels. Thus,

`<img src="pipe.jpg" align="right" height="130" width="192">`

specifies an image that will be about one eighth of the width of a thousand-pixel screen. If the natural size of the image is different from the `height`/`width` specifications, the browser shrinks or stretches it to fit in the allotted space. (The natural size of an image is the best size to use, if possible. However, in our example the natural size is too large, so we divide the dimensions by 3 and round to the nearest whole number.)

FITTIP

Image Size. You can find out the size of an image by checking **File > Properties** (Windows) or **File > Get Info** (Mac) of the image file.

We can also use images to fill in a background by **tiling**, copying a small image over and over to make a background pattern. Use bland, low-contrast, evenly colored images for tiling, so they are not distracting as background. Collections of pictures and graphics just for backgrounds are widely available, such as one that makes the page look like linen paper. The image is specified as the background attribute of the body tag, as in

`<body background="`*filename*`">`

where the *filename* has the same path properties as hyperlink references for anchor tags.

HANDLING COLOR

Color can improve a Web page dramatically, and can be used for both the background and text. The `bgcolor` attribute of the body tag will give you a solid color for the background. You can specify the color either by number, as explained later, or by using a small set of predefined color terms, as in

```
<body bgcolor="silver">
```

The color choices are shown in Table 4.3. The body tag attribute `text` can be used to give the entire document's text a specific color. The example

```
<body text="aqua" link="fuchsia">
```

illustrates controlling the link colors, too. You can change the text in specific places by using the font tag with the color attribute. So, to make Russell's Paradox red, write

```
<b><font color="red">This statement is false.</font></b>
```

Though the predefined colors are handy, you may want more than just 16 colors, and that's where the numeric colors come in.

Table 4.3. *Predefined HTML Colors*

black	silver	white	gray
red	fuchsia	maroon	purple
blue	navy	aqua	teal
lime	green	yellow	olive

Color by Number

As we mentioned briefly in Chapter 1, computer colors are often described by their amounts of red, green, and blue light. The intensity of each color is specified by a number from 0 through 255. So, for example, a zero amount of all three colors (0,0,0) produces the color black. Though it makes no difference for black, the order is always red, green, blue—so we call it **RGB color specification**. If all three colors are at full intensity (255, 255, 255), the color is white because white is a mix of the three colors of light. And, if there is full intensity of one color and none of the other two, as in

(255, 0, 0) Intense Red

(0, 255, 0) Intense Green

(0, 0, 255) Intense Blue

we get the three pure colors.

FITBYTE | **Eye Color.** The original choice of red, green, and blue comes from the color receptors in the human eye.

You can select custom colors for backgrounds and fonts in HTML by giving the three RGB intensity values. The only catch is that you do not specify them as whole numbers between 0 and 255, but as pairs of hex digits between 00 and FF. A **hexadeximal (hex) digit** is one of the symbols {0, 1, 2, 3, 4, 5, 6, 7, 8, 9, A, B, C, D, E, F} from the base-16 or hexadecimal numbering system, which we will discuss in Chapter 11. But we can use them right now without understanding hex. Because the smallest value is 00, which is the same as a normal 0, and the largest value is FF, which is the same to a normal 255, the three pure colors are expressed in HTML as

`#FF0000` Intense Red

`#00FF00` Intense Green

`#0000FF` Intense Blue

The number sign (#) means that what follows is a hexadecimal number. The easiest way to find the values for a custom color, say (255, 142, 42), which is the color of a carrot, is to look up the numbers in Table 4.4 to find their two hex digits. First find the intensity for each color in the table, and then read off the first hex digit from the left end of the row and the second hex digit from the top of the column. Thus the carrot color is

`#FF8E2A` Carrot Orange

because `FF` is 255, `8E` is 142, and `2A` is 42.

Though numeric colors need two levels of translation—first the translation of the color into the three RGB intensities, and then the translation of those values into hex digit pairs—they give us much more flexibility in Web page design. And they work with all browsers. For these reasons, HTML programmers tend to prefer them.

There is one other way to find the numeric specification for a color, and it is the easiest. In Appendix A, Table A.1 shows a standard set of HTML colors and their hex specification. (These colors give best results on most monitors.) Find the color in the table, and read off the hex digits.

With the information learned in the last three sections, it is possible to enhance the Web page of Figure 4.1. The result is shown in Figure 4.2. Notice the local pathnames to our own biographical profiles of Russell and Magritte, the background and text colors, the change of color for the font and for the headings, and, of course, the added image.

Table 4.4. *Hexadecimal Digit Equivalents*

Hex	0	1	2	3	4	5	6	7	8	9	A	B	C	D	E	F
0	0	1	2	3	4	5	6	7	8	9	10	11	12	13	14	15
1	16	17	18	19	20	21	22	23	24	25	26	27	28	29	30	31
2	32	33	34	35	36	37	38	39	40	41	42	43	44	45	46	47
3	48	49	50	51	52	53	54	55	56	57	58	59	60	61	62	63
4	64	65	66	67	68	69	70	71	72	73	74	75	76	77	78	79
5	80	81	82	83	84	85	86	87	88	89	90	91	92	93	94	95
6	96	97	98	99	100	101	102	103	104	105	106	107	108	109	110	111
7	112	113	114	115	116	117	118	119	120	121	122	123	124	125	126	127
8	128	129	130	131	132	133	134	135	136	137	138	139	140	141	142	143
9	144	145	146	147	148	149	150	151	152	153	154	155	156	157	158	159
A	160	161	162	163	164	165	166	167	168	169	170	171	172	173	174	175
B	176	177	178	179	180	181	182	183	184	185	186	187	188	189	190	191
C	192	193	194	195	196	197	198	199	200	201	202	203	204	205	206	207
D	208	209	210	211	212	213	214	215	216	217	218	219	220	221	222	223
E	224	225	226	227	228	229	230	231	232	233	234	235	236	237	238	239
F	240	241	242	243	244	245	246	247	248	249	250	251	252	253	254	255

Note: Find the decimal number in the table, and then combine the entries in the left column and the top row symbols to form the hexadecimal equivalent. Thus decimal 180 is hexadecimal B4.

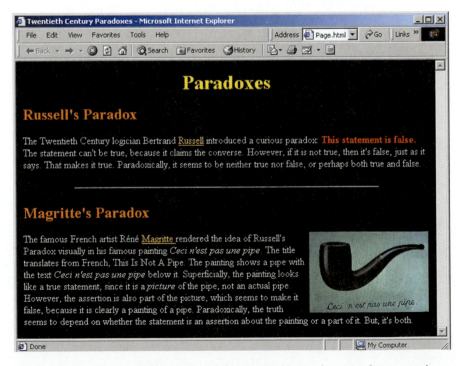

Figure 4.2. *Completed Web page and the HTML source (continued next page).*

```
<html>
  <head>
    <title>Twentieth Century Paradoxes</title>
  </head>
  <body bgcolor="#000000" text="#DDDDDD" link="#FFCC66">
    <h1 align="center"><font COLOR="yellow">Paradoxes</FONT></h1>
      <h2><font color="#FF8E2A">Russell's Paradox</font></h2>
        <p>The Twentieth Century logician Bertrand
        <a href="Russellbio.html">Russell</a> introduced a
        curious paradox: <b><font color="red">This statement
        is false.</font></b> The statement
        can't be true, because it claims the converse.
        However, if it is not true, then it's false, just as
        it says. That makes it true. Paradoxically, it seems
        to be neither true nor false, or perhaps both
        true and false.</p>

<hr width="75%">

    <h2><font color="#FF8E2A">Magritte's Paradox</font></h2>
      <p> <img src="pipe.jpg" height="130" width="192"
      align="right"> The famous French artist
      R&eacute;n&eacute;
      <a href="Magrittebio.html">Magritte</a>
      rendered the idea of Russell's Paradox visually
      in his famous painting <i>Ceci n'est pas une pipe</i>.
      The title translates from French, This Is Not A Pipe.
      The painting shows a pipe with the text <i>Ceci n'est
      pas une pipe</i> below it. Superficially, the painting
      looks like a true statement, since it is a <i>picture</i>
      of the pipe, not an actual pipe. However, the assertion
      is also part of the picture, which seems to make it
      false, because it is clearly a painting of a pipe.
      Paradoxically, the truth seems to depend on whether the
      statement is an assertion about the painting or a part of
      it. But, it's both. </p>
  </body>
</html>
```

Figure 4.2. *Completed Web page and the HTML source (continued).*

HANDLING LISTS

There are many kinds of lists in HTML, the easiest being an unnumbered list. The unnumbered list tags `<ul>` and `</ul>` surround the items of the list, which are themselves enclosed in list item tags, `<li>` and `</li>`. The browser formats the list with each item bulleted, indented, and starting on its own line. As usual, though the form of the HTML doesn't matter to the browser, we write the HTML list instructions in list form. So, for example, the HTML for a movie list would be

```
<ul>
  <li>Luxo Jr.</li>
  <li>Toy Story</li>
  <li>Monsters Inc.</li>
</ul>
```

which would look like

- Luxo Jr.
- Toy Story
- Monsters Inc.

Another kind of list is an ordered list, which uses the tags `<ol>` and `</ol>` and replaces the bullets with numbers. Otherwise, the ordered list behaves just like an unnumbered list. Thus the HTML for the start of the list of chemical elements is

```
<ol>
  <li> Hydrogen, H, 1.008, 1 </li>
  <li> Helium, He, 4.003, 2</li>
  <li> Lithium, Li, 6.941, 2 1 </li>
  <li> Beryllium, Be, 9.012, 2 2 </li>
</ol>
```

which would look like

1. Hydrogen, H, 1.008, 1
2. Helium, He, 4.003, 2
3. Lithium, Li, 6.941, 2 1
4. Beryllium, Be, 9.012, 2 2

We can also have a list within a list, simply by making the sublists items of the main list. Applying this idea in HTML

```
<ul>
  <li>Pear</li>
  <li>Apple</li>
    <ul>
    <li>Granny Smith</li>
    <li>Fuji </li>
    </ul>
  <li>Cherry</li>
</ul>
```

would look like

- Pear
- Apple
  - Granny Smith
  - Fuji
- Cherry

Finally, there is a handy list form called the **definitional list**, indicated by the tags `<dl>` and `</dl>`. A definitional list is usually made up of a sequence of definitional terms, surrounded by the tags `<dt>` and `</dt>`, and definitional data, surrounded by the tags `<dd>` and `</dd>`. So, for example, a definitional list would be expressed in HTML as

```
<dl>
   <dt> Man </dt>
   <dd> <i>Homo sapiens</i>, the greatest achievement
    of evolution. </dd>
   <dt> Woman </dt>
   <dd> <i>Homo sapiens</i>, a greater achievement of
    evolution, and clever enough not to mention it to man.
</dd>
</dl>
```

and would be formatted by browsers as

Man
     Homo sapiens, the greatest achievement of evolution.
Woman
     Homo sapiens, a greater achievement of evolution, and clever enough not to mention it to man.

For especially short terms, a more compact form of the definitional list gives the definition on the same line as the term. Include the **compact** attribute in the `<dl>` tag for this type of list. For example, a definitional list of molecular biology abbreviations would be

```
<dl compact>
   <dt>A</dt>
   <dd>Adenine </dd>
   <dt>C</dt>
   <dd>Cytosine </dd>
   <dt>G</dt>
   <dd>Guanine </dd>
   <dt>T</dt>
   <dd>Thymine </dd>
</dl>
```

which is displayed by browsers as

> A Adenine
>
> C Cytosine
>
> G Guanine
>
> T Thymine

Of course, other formatting commands such as italics and bold can be used within any line items.

HANDLING TABLES

A table is a good way to present certain types of information. Creating a table in HTML is straightforward. It is like defining a list of lists, where each of the main list items, called *rows*, has one or more items, called *cells*. The browser aligns cells to form columns.

The table is enclosed in table tags, `<table>` and `</table>`. If you want the table to have a border around it, use the attribute `border` inside the table tag. Each row is enclosed in table row tags, `<tr>` and `</tr>`. The cells of each row are surrounded by table data tags, `<td>` and `</td>`. So a table with two rows, each with three cells of the form

Canada	Ottawa	English/French
Iceland	Reykjavik	Icelandic

would be defined by

```
<table border>
  <tr>
    <td>Canada</td>
    <td>Ottawa</td>
    <td>English/French</td>
  </tr>
  <tr>
    <td>Iceland</td>
    <td>Reykjavik</td>
    <td>Icelandic</td>
  </tr>
</table>
```

You can give tables captions and column headings. The caption tags are `<caption>` and `</caption>`. You place them within the table tags around the table's caption. The caption is shown centered at the top of the table in bold. You place the column headings as the first row of the table. In the heading row, you replace the table data tags with table heading tags, `<th>` and `</th>`, which also display in bold. The table row tags are `<tr>` and `</tr>` as usual. Thus we can change our example table to give it a caption and column headings:

```
<table border>
   <caption>Country Data</caption>
   <tr>
      <th>Country</th>
      <th>Capital</th>
      <th>Language(s)</th>
   </tr>
   <tr>
      <td>Canada</td>
      <td>Ottawa</td>
      <td>English/French</td>
   </tr>
   <tr>
      <td>Iceland</td>
      <td>Reykjavik</td>
      <td>Icelandic</td>
   </tr>
   <tr>
      <td>Norway</td>
      <td>Oslo</td>
      <td>Norwegian</td>
   </tr>
</table>
```

which will look like this

Country Data

Country	Capital	Language(s)
Canada	Ottawa	English/French
Iceland	Reykjavik	Icelandic
Norway	Oslo	Norwegian

Notice that the first row uses the `<th>` tag rather than the `<td>` tag to specify the headings.

Tables are a handy way to control the arrangement of information on the page. An example where this control might be desirable is when we have a series of links listed across the top of a page. The links only form a one-row table, but the table helps keep the links together. Figures 4.3 and 4.4 show two different HTML sources, one simply listing the links in sequence and the other placing the links into a table. When there is enough window space, the two solutions look the same.

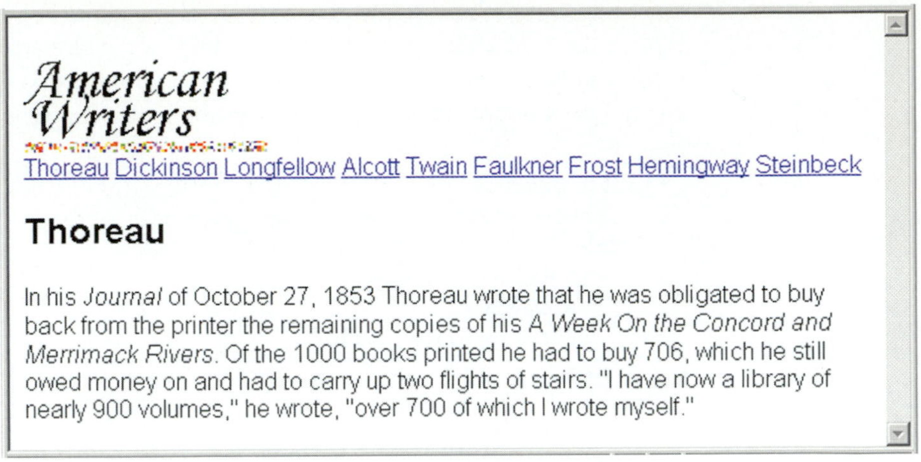

```
<html>
  <head><title>Writer's Anecdotes</title></head>
    <body bgcolor="white" text="black"><font
      face="Helvetica">
        <img src="AWA.gif"v><br>
          <a href="hdt.html">Thoreau</a>
          <a href="ed.html">Dickinson</a>
          <a href="hwl.html">Longfellow</a>
          <a href="lma.html">Alcott</a>
          <a href="sc.html">Twain</a>
          <a href="wf.html">Faulkner</a>
          <a href="rf.html">Frost</a>
          <a href="eh.html">Hemingway</a>
          <a href="js.html">Steinbeck</a>
      <h2>Thoreau</h2>
          <p>In his <i>Journal</i> of October 27, 1853 Thoreau
          wrote that he was obligated to buy back from the
          printer the remaining copies of his <i>A Week On
          the Concord and Merrimack Rivers</i>. Of the 1000
          books printed he had to buy 706, which he still
          owed money on and had to carry up two flights of
          stairs. "I have now a library of nearly 900
          volumes," he wrote, "over 700 of which I wrote
          myself."</p>
  </body>
</html>
```

Figure 4.3. *A page and its HTML for a simple listing of links.*

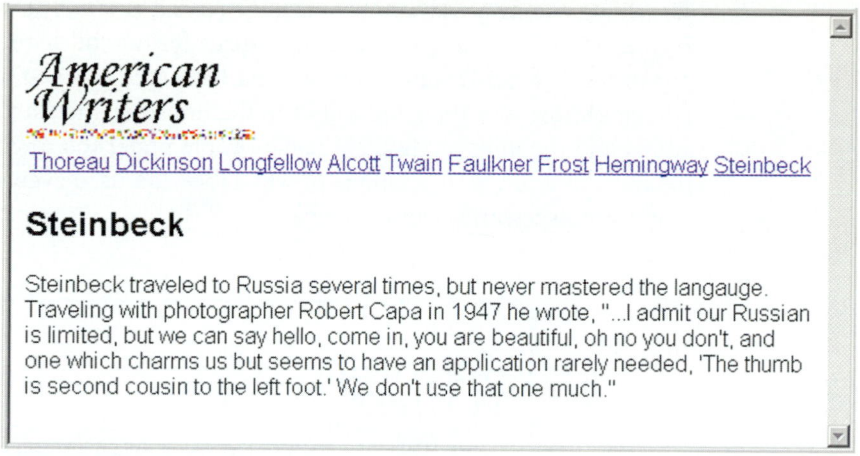

```
<html>
 <head><title>Writer's Anecdotes</title></head>
  <body bgcolor="white" text="black"><fontface="Helvetica">
   <img src="AWA.gif"v>
     <table>
      <tr>
        <td><a href="hdt.html">Thoreau</a></td>
        <td><a href="ed.html">Dickinson</a></td>
        <td><a href="hwl.html">Longfellow</a></td>
        <td><a href="lma.html">Alcott</a></td>
        <td><a href="sc.html">Twain</a></td>
        <td><a href="wf.html">Faulkner</a></td>
        <td><a href="rf.html">Frost</a></td>
        <td><a href="eh.html">Hemingway</a></td>
        <td><a href="js.html">Steinbeck</a></td>
      </tr>
     </table>
 <h2>Steinbeck</h2>
   <p>Steinbeck traveled to Russia several times, but
   never mastered the language. Traveling with
   photographer Robert Capa in 1947 he wrote, "...I
   admit our Russian is limited, but we can say hello,
   come in, you are beautiful, oh no you don't, and one
   which charms us but seems to have an application
   rarely needed, 'The thumb is second cousin to the
   left foot.' We don't use that one much."</p>
 </body>
</html>
```

Figure 4.4. A page and its HTML for listing links in a table.

The difference comes when there is only a small amount of window space. See Figure 4.5. When there is not enough space for the full sequence of links, the browser will **wrap** (continue on the next line) the links just as it wraps normal paragraph text. But the table will keep the links together in a row; scroll bars are added and the links are hidden. Some people prefer the row to the wrap. Keeping the links in a row is an example of why tables are used even when the situation might not necessarily require a table.

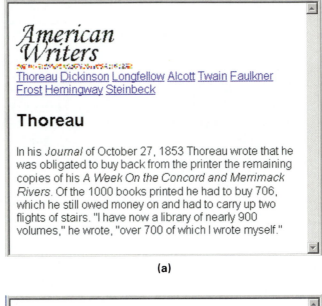

(a)

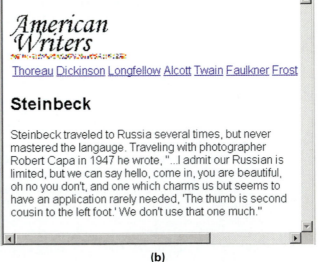

(b)

Figure 4.5. *The display of the two pages from Figures 4.3 and 4.4 in a small window showing that the table (Steinbeck page) keeps the links in a single row rather than wrapping them.*

FITBYTE   **Being Perfectly Correct.** Because computers do only what they are told, the browser follows the HTML commands exactly. So, the page will not look right until every HTML tag is perfectly correct. Perhaps the best advice is to be as careful and accurate as you can be when writing HTML. You have to be exact, and you will make mistakes, but it is also fun!

HTML WRAP-UP

In learning HTML, we have seen how a Web page is encoded. Though HTML has a few more exotic features than those presented here, and the other Web languages have even more powerful features, they are all variations on the same theme: Tags surround all objects that appear on the page, the context is set by specifying global properties of the page (e.g., `<body bgcolor="white">`), and each feature of the format is specified in detail, `<i>isn't it?!</i>`. It's so easy, even a computer could do it!

Indeed, that's what happens most of the time. Web authors usually don't write HTML directly; they use Web authoring tools, such as Macromedia Dreamweaver, or standard text editors like Microsoft Word, or the Composer feature of Netscape. They build the page as it should look on the screen using a WYSIWYG Web authoring program, and then the computer generates the HTML to implement it.

FITBYTE   **Uploading.** Pages are created and tested on a personal computer. To be accessed from other computers on the Internet, the HTML files, the image files, and the directory structure created for them must be uploaded (transmitted) to a Web server, a process often called **publishing**.

SUMMARY

Web pages are stored and transmitted in an encoded form before a browser turns them into the image we see on the screen. HTML is the most widely used form of encoding. The chapter opened by recalling the idea of using tags for formatting. A working set of about a dozen HTML tags was introduced, followed by an explanation of how links are marked with anchor tags. A key point was the use of absolute and relative pathnames. Relative pathnames refer to files deeper and higher in the directory hierarchy. Then we discussed images and their two most popular formatting schemes—JPG and GIF—and how images are placed in a page. The topics of numeric colors, lists, and tables added power to our basic understanding. A full example illustrated the ideas of the chapter. Finally, we noted that although HTML is straightforward, Web pages are usually built with WYSIWYG Web authoring tools, programs that then automatically create the HTML when the page design is complete. You can expect to use both approaches.

EXERCISES

Multiple Choice

1. HTML commands are called:
   A. hops
   B. brackets
   C. tags
   D. tokens

2. HTML tags are words enclosed in:
   A. ( )
   B. // \\
   C. { }
   D. < >

3. Which of the following would put "Sheryl Crow — In Concert" in the title bar of a Web page?
   A. `<title>Sheryl Crow — In Concert</title>`
   B. `</title> Sheryl Crow — In Concert<title>`
   C. `<title> Sheryl Crow — In Concert<title/>`
   D. `<TITLE/> Sheryl Crow — In Concert</TITLE>`

4. Which of the following tags is not paired?
   A. `<hr>`
   B. `<i>`
   C. `<p>`
   D. `<html>`

5. The `<p> </p>` tags indicate the beginning and end of a:
   A. table
   B. picture
   C. paragraph
   D. preformatted text section

6. The `<a. . .>` tag is called an:
   A. anchor
   B. address
   C. add
   D. append

7. Moving lower in a directory hierarchy is called:
   A. dropping a level
   B. crossing a slash
   C. burrowing
   D. drilling through

8. The **..** notation in a relative path of hypertext reference means to:
    A. open a folder and go down a directory
    B. close a folder and open the parent folder
    C. search a folder
    D. create a folder

9. To get an image to sit on the right side of the window with the text filling the area to the left of the image, your tag would need to look like:
    A. `<img src = "mountains.jpg" align = "right">`
    B. `<img src align = "mountains.jpg" "right">`
    C. `<img = "mountains.jpg" src align = "right">`
    D. `<img "mountains.jpg" align src = "right">`

10. The dimensions for an image on a Web page:
    A. are set using the **x** and **y** attributes
    B. are set using the **width** and **height** attributes
    C. must be set to the actual size of the image
    D. are automatically adjusted by the browser to fit in the space allotted

Short Answer

1. Today most Web pages are created using _____.

2. To improve readability of HTML text, the computer experts suggest adding _____ to the source instructions.

3. The _____ tag is a way to get more than one consecutive space in a line of a Web page.

4. _____ tags are tags between other tags.

5. Special commands inside a tag are called _____.

6. _____ are usually used to link to pages on the same site.

7. A **..** in a hypertext reference indicates a _____ path.

8. The **src** in an image tag stands for _____.

9. GIF stands for _____.

10. JPEG stands for _____.

11. To get the RGB color black using hexadecimal numbers, you would write _____.

12. To put the ten greatest inventions of all time, in order, on a Web page, you should use a(n) _____.

Exercises

1. Why learn HTML at all if authoring tools will do the work for you? Give other examples of where you are expected to learn something when there are tools available that will do the work.

2. Use HTML to properly display the following.

General
Colonel
Major
Captain
Lieutenant
Sergeant
Corporal

Private

3. Explain why a page needs to be reloaded in a browser to see the results of editing changes made in the text editor of an HTML document.

4. Indicate the hyperlink reference and the anchor text in this anchor tag. Then break down the hyperlink reference into the protocol, domain, path, and file name.

```
<a href="http://www.nasm.si.edu/nasm/museum/museum.htm">
National Air and Space Museum</a>
```

5. Treat your birthday (mm/dd/yy) as hexadecimal and then determine what color it is.

6. Experiment with hexadecimal colors until you find the seven combinations that will give you the colors of the rainbow.

7. Create a calendar for the current month using a table. Put the month in a caption at the top. Change the color of the text for Sunday and holidays. Make note of any special days during the month. Add an appropriate graphic to one of the blank cells at the end of the calendar.

8. Create a page with your links to your favorite friends on it. Use one column for their names, another for their homepages, and a third column for their email addresses. Link to their homepages. You can link to their email by using a mailto command. It looks like this:

```
<a href="mailto:snyder@cs.washington.edu">Larry
Snyder</a>
```

9. View and then print the source for the author's homepage. It's at **www.cs.washington.edu/homes/snyder/index.html**.

   What is the title of the page? Indicate the heading and the body for the page. Find the table. Find the list. Find the email links. Find the absolute hyperlinks and the relative hyperlinks. How many graphics are on this page?

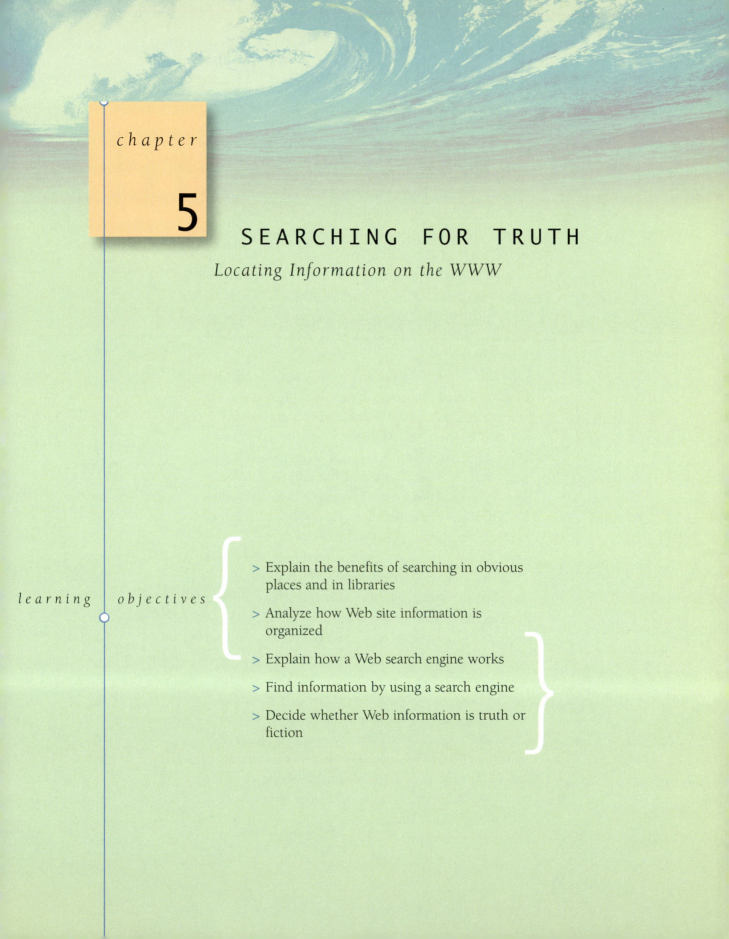

SEARCHING FOR TRUTH

Locating Information on the WWW

learning objectives

> Explain the benefits of searching in obvious places and in libraries

> Analyze how Web site information is organized

> Explain how a Web search engine works

> Find information by using a search engine

> Decide whether Web information is truth or fiction

Know not by hearsay, not tradition, . . ., nor by indulgence in speculation, . . . but know for yourselves.

—BUDDHA

A WELL-KNOWN JOKE tells of a man out for an evening walk. He meets a drunk who is under a streetlight on his hands and knees. "What are you doing?" asks the man. "Looking for my car key," replies the drunk. "You lost it here?" asks the man in conversation as he begins to help look. "No, I dropped it by the tavern." "Then why are you looking over here?" "The light's better," the drunk replies. The joke lampoons a principle—the best place to look for something is where it's likely to be found—that is key to finding information.

In this chapter we discuss searching for information and evaluating its accuracy. To find anything, we have to look where it will be found. Historically, libraries have housed well-organized archives, collections, and other information resources that are good places to look. Now many of those resources are available online, so we can update the "visit the library" advice: Log in to the library. To find what we're looking for we must also understand the hierarchical organization of information. Hierarchy speeds searching, and recognizing hierarchies when we see them helps us find information faster. Of course, using a computer to search greatly extends our reach, so we also need to understand how search engines work, how they organize the information they store, and how to interpret the results of a search. If we are going to use search engines effectively, we need to ask the right questions, which is as important as looking in the right place. But finding information and finding truthful, accurate, insight-ful information are two different things. So we must be aware that deceptive information lurks on the Internet, and learn to recognize accurate sources. Finally, we test our understanding by deciding whether information on a Web page is true or false.

SEARCHING IN ALL THE RIGHT PLACES

Ask a reference librarian where to find a *Scientific American*–type article on black holes and the reply will always be "*Scientific American.*" Yet many of us ask questions like that because we don't think about where to look for the information we want. Reference librarians do think about it, and we can learn from them, becoming better information gatherers. That's important, because on the Web we don't have a librarian's help. The key to finding information is to think logically and creatively.

The Obvious and Familiar

If we're going to "look in the right place," we need to know where the information we want can be found. Like *Scientific American*, many sources are obvious and familiar if we think about it:

> To find tax information, ask the federal (IRS) or state tax office.

> To find the direction to Dover from London, look at a map of the United Kingdom.

> To find out how many shares of stock IBM has outstanding, check the company's annual report.

Many of the answers we want to find have an obvious source, so we can simply guess the online address: `www.irs.gov`, `www.mapquest.com`, and `www.ibm.com`, respectively.

Libraries Online

One advantage that research librarians have over most of us is that they know about many more information sources than we do. Their advantage can be our advantage if we use libraries. Libraries remain substantial information resources despite the growth of the Internet. Most college libraries and many large public libraries let you access not only the online catalog of their own collections, but also many other information resources. These libraries are just a "click away" from us all.

For example, the University of Washington's Libraries, `www.lib.washington.edu`, links to the "Top 20 Databases,"—as well as the catalogs for its and the Library of Congress's collection. See Figures 5.1(a) and (b). Many of these resources are commercial databases that UW subscribes to, so only UW students and faculty can use them. However, your library probably gives you access to similar collections. A quick glance at the resources in that list shows that plenty of specialized information is accessible and searchable online. Checking these sources is a quick and easy way to get information.

UW Libraries Top 20 Databases
ABI/INFORM global: business and management periodicals
Agricola: articles and book chapters from the National Agriculture Library
Aquatic sciences & fisheries abstracts ASFA: marine/brackish/freshwater biology, commerce, engineering, etc., literature
BIOSIS previews: life sciences literature
Books in print: books from North American publishers
Britannica online: searchable encyclopedia
Current Contents: search ® citations and tables of contents from science, social science, arts, and humanities
Electronic Journals list: http://www.lib.washington.edu/types/ejournals/
Engineering village 2: Compendex, CRC Press, Patent Office, Techstreet abstracts
ERIC: education citations covering over 750 professional journals
Expanded academic index: indexing and abstracting of 1500 scholarly journals
GeoRef: geology literature, including North America (back to 1785) and elsewhere (back to 1933)
INSPEC: indexes and abstracts, conference proceedings in physical sciences, EE and CS
LEXIS-NEXIS: full-text newspaper and other popular literature archive
MEDLINE: citations and indexes from 3900 journals in biomedicine
MLA: modern language literature bibliographic information
OCLC WorldCat: world library holdings
PsycINFO: scholarly literature for medicine, psychiatry, nursing, sociology, education, etc.
Research libraries complete: general interest literature from humanities, social science, and science periodicals
Web of science citations database: science citations, and social science citation index, 1980–present

(a)

UW Libraries List of Links	
Biographical Info	Financial Aid & Grants
Bookstores	Geographic Info
Calculators	Libraries
Career Info	News
Consumer Info	Seattle Info
Dictionaries	Statistical Info
Directories	Telephone Directories
Dissertations	Universities Elsewhere
Educational Info	UW Info
Electronic Journals	Web Tools
Encyclopedias	Writing Guides
A-Z List of Reference Tools	

(b)

Figure 5.1. *UW libraries Top 20 Databases (a), and links (b) reference.*

In addition to catalogs and databases, the UW Libraries homepage offers links to reference tools. These links are classified into various groups, shown in Figure 5.1(b).

The last entry, the A-Z List of Reference Tools—the entire list of tools—lists 223 research resources, including a list of Nobel Prize winners. There are links to the *Canadian Yellow Pages*, the *Oxford English Dictionary*, the *Catholic Encyclopedia* (1917 edition), the *Blue Book of Car Prices*, a *Middle English Dictionary*, and the *World Flag Database*. You can find the answers to many questions of burning interest by locating the right link on the list and following it.

The point is not that UW's librarians have done an especially nice job, but that libraries in general provide many online facilities that are well organized and trustworthy. For example, the Chicago Public Library, `www.chipublib.org`, lists similar resources on its Virtual Libraries page, and the Library of Congress, `www.loc.gov/library/`, has huge online collections and services for researchers. These resources are free and open to everyone. So, to find out information, go (electronically) to the library.

Pre-Digital Information

The online digital library is not yet a substitute for going to the physical library and checking out paper books and journals. Despite the billions of Web pages and digital documents, most of the *valuable information typically found in a library is not online*. Most of humankind's pre-1985 knowledge is not yet digitized. And in some cases where paper documents have been digitized, the online version is missing footnotes, references, and appendices, has unreadable equations, or is in other ways incomplete. So, the best place to begin tracking down information is to look at the online library, but don't be surprised if the information you need is not yet digital.

HOW IS INFORMATION ORGANIZED?

To help us find information, librarians, archivists, Web-page designers, and others who organize collections of information give the collections a structure to make them easier to search. The process is simple: All of the information is grouped into a small number of categories, each of which is easily described. This is the top-level *classification*. Then, the information in each category is also divided into a few subcategories, each with a simple description. These are the second-level classifications. See Figure 5.2 Those subcategories are divided, too, into still smaller categories with brief descriptions, the third-level classifications. And on and on. Eventually, the classifications become small enough that it is possible to look through the whole category to find the desired information.

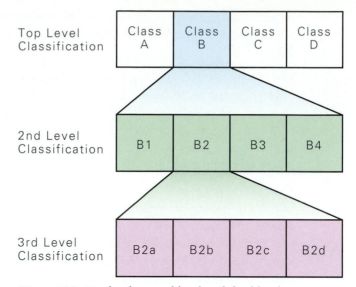

Figure 5.2. *Top level, second level and third level classifications of a collection.*

For example, a source of information about radio stations in the U.S. that carry National Public Radio might use their *geographical region* as its top-level classification, making the top-level categories:

> Northeast, Mid Atlantic, Southeast, North Central, South Central, Mountain, Pacific

Within each region, the second-level classification might use the state, making the Pacific category's subcategories:

> Alaska, California, Hawaii, Oregon, Washington

The third-level categories could be cities for states like California and Texas with several large cities having multiple public radio stations. When the final classification is small enough—Hawaii has only four NPR stations—no finer classification is needed.

There are several important properties to classifications.

> > The descriptive terms must cover all of the information in the category and be easy for a searcher to apply. Region of the country, state, city, etc., have this property.

> > The subcategories do not all have to use the same classification. So, the Pacific category could categorize by states, but the Northeast might categorize by cities.

> > The information in the category defines how best to classify it.

There is no single way to classify information.

This structure is called a *hierarchy*, and as we discussed in Chapter 3 in connection with the directory hierarchy, it is a natural way to organize information. Remember that hierarchies are often drawn as trees. One very famous hierarchy is the "tree of life," the biological taxonomy of organisms. It is too large to display as a tree, but Table 5.1 shows the layers of classification for human beings, from the top level (highest) classification—kingdom—to the last (lowest)—species. Because hierarchies are a logical way to organize information, we find them everywhere. And because they are so intuitive, we don't often consciously notice them. Our goal for the rest of this section is to recognize hierarchies when we see them, because being aware of them speeds up our discovery of information.

FITBYTE

Choose to Exclude. Hierarchies work well not because of what we choose, but what we don't choose. For example, suppose a collection has a million items divided into ten (roughly) equal-size categories. Picking a category eliminates from consideration the 900,000 items in the other categories. If the chosen category is also classified into ten categories, the next choice eliminates another 90,000 items. With two choices we eliminated 990,000 items!

Table 5.1. *The Biological Classification of Human Beings,* Homo sapiens

Taxonomic Level	Name of Classification
Kingdom	Animalia
Phylum	Chordata
Subphylum	Vertebrata
Class	Mammalia
Order	Primates
Family	Hominoidea
Genus	*Homo*
Species	*sapiens*

For example, consider the National Public Radio Web site, `www.npr.org`, shown in Figure 5.3. We might visit this site to find audio information about current news. The site uses hierarchical organization in ways that are sometimes obvious, and sometimes not.

Recognizing a Hierarchy

Looking at the **NPR Programming** pull-down menu (Figure 5.4), we find a list of all of NPR's programs. From the scroll bar on the right, we realize that we are not seeing all of the entries. From the size of the slider, we can guess that we're looking at only about a third of the whole list. The first item (highlighted) is the entire (alphabetized) list of NPR programs, but after that we notice category terms— **Most Requested, NPR News**—separated by lines. Below these are the NPR programs in that category. What we are looking at is a one-level hierarchy of NPR's programming. They have divided all of their programs into five categories:

> Most Requested

> NPR News

> Talk

> Music

> Additional Programming

Figure 5.3. *The National Public Radio (NPR) home page www.npr.org.*

Figure 5.4. *The NPR Programming pull-down menu.*

Figure 5.5 shows the hierarchy drawn as a **tree**. The tree is drawn on its side with the **root** to the left and the **leaves** to the right. Hierarchy trees are often drawn sideways because it's more convenient to write (English) text that way. It is also common to draw them upside down, with the root at the top. Either way, the important part is not the orientation, but the branching metaphor.

Design of Hierarchies

Hierarchies are common and there are general rules for their design and terminology:

> Because hierarchy trees are often drawn with the root at the top, we say "going up in the hierarchy" and "down in the hierarchy." (Similar language—higher and deeper—was used with directory hierarchies in Chapter 3.) The terms are relative to the root being drawn at the top. So "going up" means the classifications become more inclusive. They are moving closer to the root. "Going down" means the classifications become more specific. They are farther from the root.

> The greater-than symbol (>) is a common way to show going down in a hierarchy through levels of classification:

Classification 1 > Classification 2 > . . . > Classification *n*

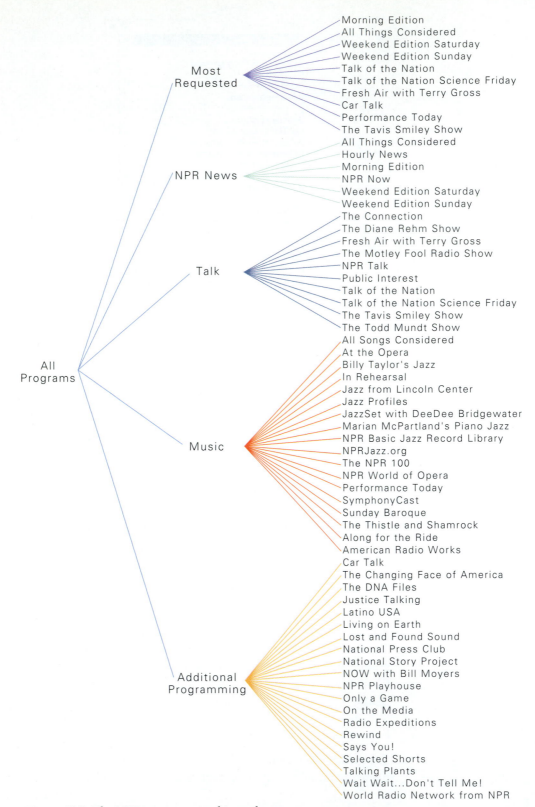

Figure 5.5. *The NPR programming hierarchy tree.*

A One-Level Hierarchy. We call NPR's Programming menu a **one-level hierarchy** because there is only one level of "branching." Counting levels of a hierarchy can be a little confusing sometimes because of all of the connecting lines, but it is easy if we keep two points in mind. First, the tree always has a root—the collection's name. Second, all trees have leaves—the things themselves. Because they exist without any hierarchy, the root and leaves must not count as levels of the hierarchy. When we ignore the root and leaves from Figure 5.5, we see one level of classification.

Partitioning of Levels. Notice that in the NPR menu example, the individual programs can be listed more than once. They can be mentioned both in the **Most Requested** category and in their own category such as **News**. For example, see *All Things Considered*. When every leaf appears once in the hierarchy, the groupings are called **partitionings**. The tree of life is a partitioning because every species is listed once. When the leaves are repeated, groupings "overlap," meaning that an item can be in more than one category. There is no best way to classify information.

Number of Levels May Differ. Finally, the number of classifications of a hierarchy need not be the same for all items. That is, the number of levels of classification between a leaf and root need not be the same for every leaf. Some groupings might require more levels of classification to get the group to a manageable size. For example, if there were many more music programs, we could imagine dividing the **Music** category of Figure 5.5 into three groups: **Jazz**, **Classical**, and **Other**. Then music programs would be reached by two levels of classification, whereas other programs would be reached by only one. A program like Performance Today would be reached by two different paths—a single level through **Most Requested**, or a double level through **Music > Classical**.

HOW IS WEB SITE INFORMATION ORGANIZED?

The NPR Web page designers have used hierarchy to help us find our favorite programs. But they and other Web designers use hierarchy in more basic ways, too.

The NPR homepage itself is the top-level classification for the whole NPR Web site. That is, all of the information on the NPR site must be organized, not just the Web pages for the programs. When we look at the NPR page, we should notice how the information is organized. The page has three basic kinds of information:

> *Classifications* are the roots of hierarchies that organize large volumes of similar types of information. Examples include the row of links listing **news, audio archives, transcripts, discussions, find a station, shop**, and **about NPR**. **contact us** is in this list of classifications, but it is really a single link. Notice that these classifications are also listed at the bottom of the page, and some are available from other places; for example, **more news >** links to **news**.

> *Topic clusters* are sets of related links. Examples include **Editor's Picks**, which shows three of about twenty items listed on another page (**News**), and **Special Features**, which highlights features from other NPR programming. They are not there to help us navigate the site, but to be read immediately. They are available elsewhere at the site, but have been placed on the homepage to make it interesting and immediately useful.

> *Single links* connect to very specialized pages, such as downloads of audio player software, order forms, and the hourly news stream. Single links take us to pages that either are unusual for the site (software downloads) or are popular (the news stream).

This kind of structure is common because many sites offer items of immediate interest as well as access to the rest of the site.

SEARCHING THE WEB FOR INFORMATION

A **search engine** is a collection of computer programs that helps us find information on the World Wide Web. Though programs for text searching existed long before the Web, the explosion of Web-based digital information and its distribution across the planet made the invention of search engines necessary. No one organizes the information posted on the Web, so these programs look around to find out what's out there and organize what they find. It's a big task. How do search engines do it?

How a Search Engine Works

A search engine has two basic parts: a **crawler** and a **query processor**. The crawler visits sites on the Internet, discovering Web pages and building an **index** to the Web's content. The query processor looks up user-submitted keywords in the index and reports back which Web pages the crawler has found containing those words. Popular search engines include Alta Vista, Excite, InfoSeek, Google, and Yahoo!. We will use the Google search engine as our example here (Figure 5.6).

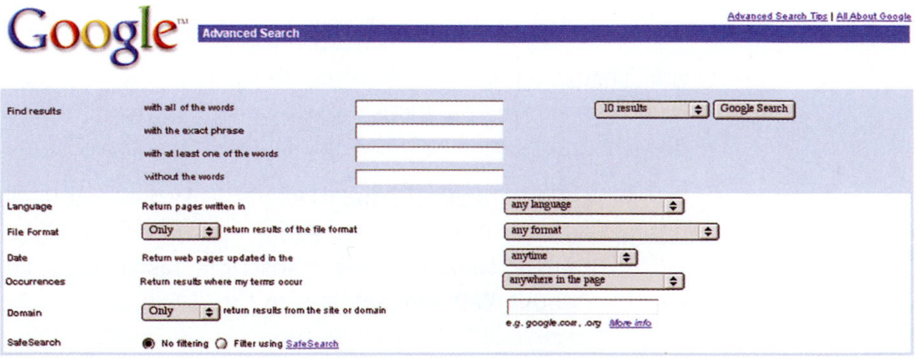

Figure 5.6. The Google search engine's advanced search view.

A Big Name in Searching. "Google" is a variant spelling of googol, a term coined by American mathematician Edward Kasner's nine-year-old nephew Milton Sirotta for the number 10^{100}; that is, 1 followed by one hundred zeros.

Crawlers. When the crawler visits a Web page, it first identifies all the links to other Web pages on that page. It checks in its records to see if it has visited those other pages recently. If not, it adds them to its "To Do" list of pages that must be crawled. Thus crawlers find the pages to look at by saving links to pages not yet visited from pages they've already seen. (Google also lets Web page authors submit their pages to be crawled.)

The crawler also records in an index the keywords used on a page. The words can appear in either the title or the body of the page. For example, the HTML home-page for the Hot Dang! Thai restaurant (`www.hotdang.com`) might have the title block

`<title> Hot Dang! Restaurant, Cuisine of Siam </title>`

so, in the index, the crawler would associate the keywords "hot," "dang," "restaurant," "cuisine," and "siam" with the `www.hotdang.com` URL. Small, unspecific words like "of" are ignored. Crawlers also ignore case.

Shortsightedness. Search engines crawl only a fraction (substantially less than half) of the Web. Because it is growing so fast, there are always new pages not yet visited. Librarians call the pages not crawled, the "Invisible Web." There are other reasons that crawlers miss pages:

> No page points to it, so it never gets on the To Do list

> The page is synthetic—that is, created on-the-fly for each user by software

> The page has no text (images)

> The format is one the crawler does not recognize

Google pioneered the idea of including keywords from the *anchor* (that highlighted text associated with a link) in the index. That is, the words of the highlighted text of a link *to a page* are included among the descriptive terms for that page. For example, if your Web page referenced the Hot Dang! restaurant with the text

`. . . my favorite <a href="http://www.hotdang.com">`
`Thai restaurants </a> . . .`

Thai restaurants would be the highlighted anchor and the terms "Thai" and "restaurants" would be included by Google as keywords associated with `www.hotdang.com`. Anchors help a search engine find relevant pages because the anchors often describe the page better than the page's own content. For example, the Hot Dang! restaurant's motto is "Cuisine of Siam," so the page may not actually say anywhere that it is a Thai restaurant. But your anchor does.

Query Processors. The query processor of a search engine gets keywords from a user and looks them up in the index to find the URLs of pages associated with those keywords. So, for example, when a user asks for "Thai restaurants," all of the URLs associated with those words will be reported back. If Google had crawled your page, the query processor will return `www.hotdang.com` among its responses to the "Thai restaurants" query because your anchor connected "Thai" and "restaurants" with the Hot Dang! site. Notice that in this case the Google crawler might not have crawled the Hot Dang! restaurant's site yet; that site might still be on the To Do list. But it will still know that the site is connected with the terms "Thai" and "restaurants" because of the anchor on your page. If Google had crawled the Hot Dang! site, the query processor would also return `www.hotdang.com` among the responses to the "Thai cuisine" query because "Thai" is in your anchor and "cuisine" is in the restaurant's title.

It is important to give the query processor the right terms to look up. In the next sections, we explain how to create good queries. But even when you choose exactly the right terms, you could get hundreds or thousands of relevant URLs, or **hits**. For example, suppose someone in your hometown of Dallas queries "Thai restaurants in Dallas Texas." There could be a huge list of hits, including (presumably) the homepages for all Thai restaurants, but also your homepage because it uses those words, too. But your page has nothing to do with Thai restaurants, except for your comment about liking Hot Dang!. If the search engine just returns an unordered list of all hits, the user would have to click through the whole list, looking at pages that could be completely irrelevant (see Figure 5.7). We need more help from the search engine!

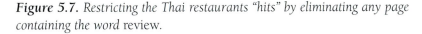

Figure 5.7. *Restricting the Thai restaurants "hits" by eliminating any page containing the word* review.

Page Ranking. Google pioneered another idea called **PageRank** that it uses to order the hits by their importance to the user. (Of course, it cannot have any clue, really, as to what you are looking for.) PageRank is Google's guess about how important a page is. It computes the PageRank by counting how many pages link to a page. The more links there are *to* a page, the more important it must be. As the Google inventors describe it, if page A links to page B, consider the link as a vote by A for B. So, for example, because your page links to `www.hotdang.com`, it "votes" for the restaurant. If many sites vote, it must be of greater interest, so the search engine lists the pages with higher PageRank first. Google also looks at whether the page doing the "voting" is itself highly ranked.

Page Ranking's Limitations. In the previous example, if a restaurant reviewer has a page that many people link to, and the reviewer's page links to Hot Dang!, Google treats that link as a more significant vote than yours, assuming fewer pages link to your homepage. Thus Google would probably list `www.hotdang.com` before your page in the list of hits resulting from the query. Page ranking is highly successful in identifying the pages of greater interest, but, of course, fame isn't everything.

PageRank's idea of one page voting for another exactly captures your purpose of citing Hot Dang! as one of your favorite Thai restaurants. But, if your link had been part of a complaint about food poisoning with the purpose of discouraging others from going to Hot Dang!, Google would still count it as a vote for the restaurant's page. Yea or nay, it's still a vote.

Asking the Right Question

After "Look where the information is to be found," the best advice to someone looking for information is "Ask the right question." The question or **query** we are asking a search engine is, "What pages are associated with the following terms . . . ?" To get the right answer back means not only choosing the right terms but also knowing how the search engine will use them. In this section, we learn how to make effective queries. (All searching facilities have slight syntactic variations.)

> **FITTIP**
>
> **Search Engine Rules.** Most search engines explain their specific rules in a link (located near the search window) called "Advanced" or "Hints" or some similar term. If the query rules you learn in this section don't get you the results you want, check for differences.

Words or Phrases? The first point to understand is that text-searching facilities, including search engines, generally consider each word separately. Though most English speakers think of "Thai restaurants" as a single noun phrase, most search engines treat it as two words. We can ask the search facility to look for the exact phrase by placing quotation marks around it, as in

`"Thai restaurants"`

which has the effect of binding the words together.

But the problem with using the exact-phrase quotes is that the match must be perfect, ignoring spaces and case. Exact matching means information in other forms will be missed. For example, these phrases:

```
Thai restaurant
restaurants featuring Thai cuisine
Thai and Asian restaurants
```

would *not* match the quoted string. For this reason search facilities treat the words as separate and allow them to occur anywhere. It is best to limit the use of exact-match quotes to phrases like titles,

`"Crime and Punishment"`

where the form is always the same. Notice that quoting part of a phrase, say **"Tale of Two Cities"**, is a safe solution when we cannot remember whether it's *The Tale of Two Cities* or *A Tale of Two Cities*.

If the words are treated independently, should the search pick pages with both of the words "Thai" and "restaurants" or pages with just one of them? If it's just one of the words, pages referring to "Thai vacations" and pages referring to "steak restaurants" would also be hits. If we want both, but ask for either, we'll get an enormous number of useless hits.

Logical Operators. So we need to spell out how the words should be processed. We do this by using **logical operators**. The three logical operators are AND, OR, and NOT. They are written using all capital letters to distinguish them from the keywords. Remember that search facilities usually ignore case, so we don't need to capitalize keywords. Capitalizing the logical operators makes them stand out for us. AND and OR are the most commonly used logical operators in queries, and they are **infix operators**, meaning that they are placed between keywords. AND means *both*. OR means *either* or *both*. So, for example, the phrase

Thai AND restaurants

finds pages with both words appearing in any position; that is, they may not be together in the given order. The query

Thai OR Siam

finds pages with either word, including pages where they both appear. Of course, we could write queries that include both operators, but we must be careful. For example, does

Thai OR Siam AND restaurants

mean either a page containing the words *Thai* and *restaurants* or *Siam* and *restaurants* or a page containing either the word *Thai* or the two words *Siam* and *restaurants*? We meant the first. The latter would hit on pages about Thai vacations. Because the query is *ambiguous* (it has more than one interpretation), there is no way of guessing how the search engine will interpret it. So, to be unambiguous, we include parentheses the way we do when we write algebra formulas:

(Thai OR Siam) AND restaurants

Now the search engine will look for pages that have *restaurants* and also either *Thai* or *Siam*.

We can use NOT to exclude pages with the given word. NOT is a prefix operator, meaning that it comes before the word to be excluded. So, to exclude restaurant review pages from the Thai restaurant search, we might write

Thai AND restaurants AND NOT review

Notice that we need the AND to show that three conditions must be met: matching *Thai*, matching *restaurants*, not matching *review*. Most often, NOT is used when we recognize a pattern of unintended interpretations.

So far, we have assumed the simplest case, where the search facility offers only a single window for giving the query. The Google Advanced Search page (recommended) gives us several windows to simplify creating queries with the logical operators. Figure 5.6 shows the GUI of the Advanced Search and each of its windows. There are separate windows for AND words, exact phrases, OR words, and NOT words. In this case, Google saves us from having to type the logical operators. (Though most of the searches illustrated in this book use Google, queries will always be written using the logical operators.) All we need to do is list the search words, separated by blanks, in the correct window. Notice that if more than one window is filled in, the search must fulfill the requirements of all windows together.

FIT CAUTION

> **Misspellings.** Correct spelling is obviously essential to effective searching. Search engines can recognize misspelled words, and ask if you meant to type another word. But it cannot guess that you've made a mistake if you mistype, for example, `trail` for `trial`. It pays to be careful.

Getting Close

We have seen that to be effective at searching, you should pick meaningful and specific keywords. Choosing the right words is sometimes easy, as when you're looking for data on ibuprofen, because the term is unique. At other times, choosing the right words is very difficult, as when you're looking for information on the fuel economy of new cars, because the obvious terms—gas mileage, cars—are extremely common. In any event, thinking for a few moments about a search strategy will really pay off.

Five Tips for an Efficient Search

Here's a recommended process for creating a search:

1. *Be clear about what sort of page you seek.* Ask yourself whether you want a source page from a company or organization (for example, the Hot Dang! restaurant), or a reference page that points to a collection of similar pages (for example, the restaurant reviewer's page), or perhaps a resource page that puts together information on the topic (for example, a guide to Thai cooking). Thinking clearly about the kind of page you want helps to direct the search toward that page.

2. *Think about what type of organization might publish the page you want.* Is the information likely to come from a company, a government agency, a university, some special organization, or another country? You might be able to guess a Web address for the site, and avoid a search altogether. If you can guess a likely URL, for example, `www.hotdang.com`, then try it! Even if you can't guess the URL, you can limit the search by the domain suffix—that is, the "dot com" part of a domain name. (See Figure 5.6.)

3. *List terms that are likely to appear on the pages you are looking for.* You want to find a combination of words that will appear on the the page you want and the fewest number of unwanted pages. You must include words that describe the category (for example, *Thai* and *restaurant)*, and then use AND in limiting words:

> > Location-specific words such as *Dallas* AND *Texas*

> > Time-specific words such as *Monday* because businesses often give the times they're open

> > Activity-specific words such as *entrées*

> > Specialty terms such as *phad* because every Thai restaurant probably serves phad Thai

The pages we seek have many specific properties, each with their characteristic terms. With some thought, we can come up with those terms.

4. *Assess the results.* Before looking at each returned page, check the results to see how effective the search was. Look for the two errors of including too much and not including enough. One way to include too much is to get a type of match you didn't expect. For example, all the pages about vacationing in Thailand probably describe the restaurants where tourists will eat. You can do another search with a NOT keyword (for example, **NOT vacation**) to eliminate these. The other error, not including enough, is possibly harder to recognize. For example, if we include "Monday" in our search, we eliminate all of the restaurants that are open Tuesday to Sunday. So, we must be alert to what we are not finding and consider whether we should drop some of our keywords.

5. *Consider a two-pass strategy.* Because it's hard to get the search terms just right, it is probably a good idea when using the Google search engine to use a "two-pass" strategy. First do a broad topic search, then do one or more searches within your results. Google lets you narrow your search with additional keywords. (See Figure 5.7.) Searching "within results" lets us capture the pages within the category and then try different ways of limiting the search until we find what we are looking for. If we limit the search too much, we can simply back up to the point where the hits are inclusive enough. Notice that the terms in the search-within-results window are more AND terms; that is, they are required on the page. We can force the absence of a term, say, vacation, by writing a minus sign before it like this: **–vacation**.

> **FITTIP**

> **Finding the Needle.** Narrowing the search to the right page is the first task, but finding the information can mean more searching on the page itself. Remember that browsers have a word-search facility, **Find**, under the **Edit** menu. To search on a page, use **Find**.

Using the principles just outlined, imagine that you plan to go windsurfing and need a sailboard. You are thinking of going to Hood River, Oregon, where the

Hood joins the Columbia, a famous windsurfing area. You're flying, so you will need to rent equipment when you arrive. Your queries yield:

sailboards	9180 hits
sailboards AND oregon	342 hits
sailboards AND oregon AND "hood river"	151 hits
sailboards AND oregon AND "hood river" AND rental	23 hits

which includes the shops and tourist facilities pages you want.

In summary, successful searches result from well-thought-out queries based on specific terms. It is wiser to spend time thinking up exact queries, possibly querying several times or searching through results to pinpoint the few pages of interest, than it is to read through many worthless pages from unspecific searches.

WEB INFORMATION: TRUTH OR FICTION?

In Chapter 3 we noted that an increased exercise of freedom of speech is a fundamental change brought about by the World Wide Web. It is possible in many countries of the world to publish anything on the Web, uncensored by companies or governments. This is a benefit, but, like all freedoms, this one carries with it some important responsibilities—not so much for the speaker, but for the reader or listener. Because anyone can publish anything on the World Wide Web, some of what gets published is false, misleading, deceptive, self-serving, slanderous, or simply disgusting. We have to be alert for this and always ask, *"Is this page legitimate, true, and correct?"* In this section we consider whether the pages we've found in our search are giving us reliable information.

Do Not Assume Too Much

The first thing to look for is who or what organization publishes the page. For example, health information from the Centers for Disease Control, the World Health Organization, or the American Medical Association is about the best that can be found. These respected organizations try to publish current and correct information, so we can trust their Web pages. Of course, they publish information based on science, and over time new discoveries might occasionally invalidate something, meaning it wasn't true. But we're not worried about such philosophical aspects of the *nature of truth*. We can assume that respected organizations publish the best information available. We're unlikely to find better.

Checking the organization that publishes the information seems like overkill. After all, if the Web site's domain name is `ama-assn.org`, it claims to be the AMA page, and it's giving out medical information, it must be the American Medical

Association, right? In fact, it is. But, just because a page seems to be from a certain organization and the domain name *seems* plausible, it isn't necessarily true. Domain names are not checked. Anyone could have reserved the domain name `ama-assn.org` and published bogus health information. You must be wary.

To illustrate that sites are not always what they appear to be, consider the hoax perpetrated from the site `www.gatt.org`. The domain name looks like it is related to the General Agreement on Tariffs and Trade, or GATT as it's known, the free-trade agreement of the 1990s. The site looks like the official publication of the World Trade Organization (WTO), the free-trade group that followed on from the GATT treaty. The page shows photographs of Michael Moore, WTO President, quotes him, and posts WTO-related free-trade news. However, the site is actually run by an *anti*-free-trade organization known as the Yes Men.

According to the January 7, 2001, *New York Times*, organizers of a meeting of international trade lawyers in Salzburg, Austria, sent mail to `www.gatt.org` inviting WTO President Moore to speak at their meeting. From `www.gatt.org` came an email reply declining on behalf of Mr. Moore, but offering (a fictitious) speaker, Dr. Andreas Bichlbauer, as a substitute. The meeting organizers accepted Dr. Bichlbauer who came to their October 2000 meeting and gave a very offensive speech critical of Italians and Americans. The perpetrators of the hoax even claimed that a WTO protestor threw a crème pie at Dr. Bichlbauer. They claimed that the pie had contained a *bacillus*, that Bichlbauer had been taken ill and hospitalized, and that he had died. The whole hoax, which caused much embarrassment, began when someone assumed that `www.gatt.org` was a legitimate WTO site.

A Two-Step Check for the Site's Publisher

How can you find out if a site is for real? A two-step process can help:

1. The InterNIC site `www.internic.net/whois.html` lists the company that assigned an IP address (i.e., domain). Type in the domain name, such as `company.com`. Included in the returned InterNIC information about the domain is a site called a `WhoIs Server` maintained by the company that assigned the address. That site will tell you who the domain's owner is.

2. Go to the `WhoIs Server` site and type in the domain name or IP address again. The information returned is the owner's name and physical address.

When checking a Web site, remember to pull out the domain name from the URL.

Elaborate hoaxes like `gatt.org` are rare, though there have been others. A more likely situation is that information is unintentionally wrong or simply fictional. In the first category is information such as "urban legends"—stories like alligators living in the New York City sewer system—that people pass along as true, although they don't have primary evidence or an authoritative basis for believing it. They heard it through a friend of a friend. Urban myths are usually harmless, but not always. In the second category, fiction and humor are meant to entertain us. April Fools' pages, alien spaceships visiting Seattle's Space Needle, and reports of one-ton squirrels fall into this category. They are fun. Every April, National Public Radio, for example, broadcasts a fictitious news story on the program *All Things Considered*. It is best to approach Web pages with some skepticism.

Characteristics of Legitimate Sites

What cues can alert a reader to misinformation? In a recent survey, Internet users thought that a site was more believable if it had these features:

> **Physical existence.** The site provided a street address, telephone number, and legal email address.

> **Expertise.** The site's authors listed references, citations, or credentials, and there were links to related sites.

> **Clarity.** The site was well organized, easy to use, and provided site-searching facilities.

> **Currency.** The site had been recently updated.

> **Professionalism.** The site's grammar, spelling, punctuation, and so forth, were correct; all links worked.

Of course, a site can have these characteristics and still not be legitimate. A site trying to fool people can take care to appear to be legitimate. If you have doubts, check it out. The name and address should be in `www.whitepages.com`. If they are not listed, maybe you should be suspicious. If it's a business, can you find the business in the yellow pages? If the author gives credentials, citations, or other links, check them out, too. By checking, you can feel confident that the information you are getting is reliable.

Check Other Sources

Finally, if the information is important to you, check it on more than one source. After all, it is very easy to use the Internet to find information, so it's equally easy to use it to confirm information. Ask yourself, "If this information were true, what other source could directly or indirectly confirm it?" Of course, we must be equally skeptical about the supporting information. For example, we cannot count the number of sites referencing information as proof that it's true, because by that reasoning the alligators in the sewer urban legend would seem to be supported by the 2050 hits on `alligator AND sewer`. A better approach is to find sites that speak directly to the topic, such as `www.snopes.com`.

THE BURMESE MOUNTAIN DOG PAGE

To test our ability to assess a site, suppose we have found `lme.mnsu.edu/akcj3/bmd.html`, a site describing the Burmese Mountain Dog. (See Figure 5.8.) The page is authoritative looking. It has been posted by someone claiming DVM credentials, probably meaning doctor of veterinary medicine. There are photographs, links to the American Kennel Club, and so on. The page seems completely legitimate and meets most of the criteria the Internet users have listed as indicating authenticity. If we ask Google to find `Burmese AND mountain AND dog`, we get 2350 hits. Many people would probably accept the page as truthful.

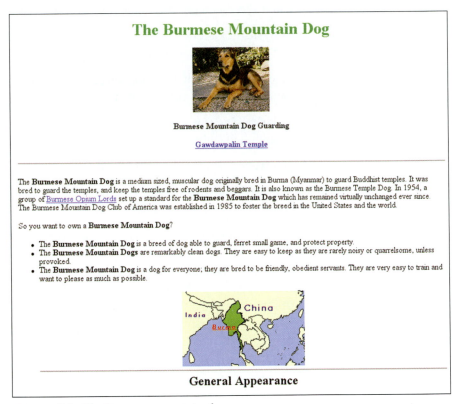

Figure 5.8. *The Burmese mountain dog page.*

Because the page has a link to the American Kennel Club, `akc.org`, which lists all breeds the Club recognizes, it's possible to check out the Burmese Mountain Dog. In the AKC's list of breeds, we find that there is no Burmese Mountain Dog, though there is a Bernese Mountain Dog, named for Berne, Switzerland. What gives? First, we ask if `akc.org` is legitimate by using the `InterNIC WhoIs` service, and find that it is. Next, we check `lme.mnsu.edu` and find it is the Library Media Education department of Mankato State University in Minnesota. This is a surprise. A university is usually a reliable place to get information, but we would expect it to come from the Department of Veterinary Medicine. Accepting that the AKC is giving correct information about the Bernese Mountain Dog, we conclude that either the Burmese page is a fake or the Burmese Mountain Dog is not yet a recognized breed.

It is interesting that there are so many hits on Burmese Mountain Dog, but when we ask Google to look up `bernese AND mountain AND dog` we get 17,800 hits, so the Burmese page gets fewer hits. When we look at photos of the two dogs, we notice that they look very similar. The main difference is that the Bernese has a white chest, while the Burmese has a dark chest with a brown V. Such a striking similarity suggests that someone has made a comparison, so we check for pages citing both. Checking `bernese AND burmese AND mountain AND dog` yields only 175 hits.

A phrase displayed by Google,

It's Bernese, Burmese is a cat

suggests two points: Many of these pages must be listing both cats and dogs, and there is a Burmese cat. (Removing cat (`-cat`) yields only 35 hits.) The other possibility is that people may be mispronouncing or misspelling Bernese as Burmese. A quick look at several of the pages tells us we've guessed right. Some personal pages show a photo of what the AKC calls a Bernese Mountain Dog, but they call it a Burmese Mountain Dog. Another page makes a point of saying it's from Berne rather than Burma. So, we guess that the original page is fiction, and return to it to admire how skillful a hoax it is.

SUMMARY

The secret to finding the information we're looking for is to look in the right place. The first place to look for many types of information is not the Web, but the library. The online resources at large public and university libraries are huge. Libraries not only can give us the needed information in digital form, they can also connect us with the archives of "pre-digital" information—the millions of books, journals, and manuscripts that still exist only in paper form. In many cases the best information only exists in these paper documents. We can expect to use traditional documents for years to come.

Unlike a library, where we can get the help of a reference librarian, we need software and our own intelligence to search the Internet effectively. We create queries using the logical operators of AND, OR, and NOT, and specific terms to pinpoint the information we seek. Once we've found the information, we must judge whether it is correct, to avoid being duped or misled. One way to do this is to check out the organization that publishes the page, including checking the credentials of the people who have written the information. Finally, we need to cross-check the information with other sources, especially when the information is important.

EXERCISES

Multiple Choice

1. One of the downsides of unmediated expression on the Web is:
   A. a need for verification of the accuracy of the content
   B. duplication of information
   C. that very little information is available
   D. all of the above

2. LEXIS-NEXIS would be used to locate:
   A. used-car information
   B. full-text newspapers
   C. personal health information
   D. ancient Egyptian customs

3. Searching through ERIC you would find:
   A. children's names
   B. government Web sites
   C. professional journals
   D. computer information

4. A hierarchy resembles a:
   A. subway map
   B. tree
   C. spoked wheel
   D. list

5. Someone searching with a search engine would use the:
   A. crawler
   B. query processor
   C. index
   D. anchor

6. Most Web pages are not indexed because:
   A. search engines have not crawled them
   B. pages are created on demand and those cannot be indexed
   C. other pages do not point to it
   D. all of the above

7. Google was the first search engine to get its keywords from:
   A. InterNIC
   B. page titles
   C. anchors tags
   D. user submissions

8. The results from a search using AND will be _____ than a search using OR.
   A. larger
   B. the same
   C. smaller
   D. overlapping

9. To omit a word from a search, you would:
   A. put the word MINUS in front of the word
   B. put the word in parentheses
   C. put a minus sign in front of the word
   D. put the word inside quotation marks

10. Which of the following is not a method for testing the believability of a Web site?
   A. professionalism
   B. WWW Consortium approval
   C. expertise
   D. physical existence provided by the site

Short Answer

1. Historically, the _____ has been the repository of information.

2. On the computer, you would look for information using a(n) _____.

3. _____ provide connections to specialized pages.

4. _____ are computer programs that help people find information on the Web.

5. _____ uses the keywords in the anchor link of Web pages to index its pages.

6. Counting the number of pages linked to a page helps to determine that page's _____.

7. AND, OR, and NOT are called _____.

8. Operators placed between words in a query are called _____.

9. A(n) _____ is a method of organizing information by groups.

10. If a word or phrase is enclosed in quotes in a search, the search engine will search for a(n) _____.

11. Web pages found using a search engine are called _____.

12. The _____ operator is used to exclude a word or phrase from a search.

13. In a search, the plus (+) sign is the same as using the word _____.

14. In a search, the minus (−) sign is the same as using the word _____.

15. _____ is a company that tracks information on who owns a Web site.

Exercises

1. Write down the organization chart used by Yahoo! (www.yahoo.com) for its home page. What type of classification is it?

2. Go to InterNIC (`www.internic.net/whois.html`). Type in the name of a Web site and check its information. Do the same for other companies.

3. How would you find a search engine that specializes in European Web sites? Find one and use it. What do you find?

4. Create a classification scheme for clothing items. In your list, what items could be classified in more than one group?

5. Use Switchboard.com (`www.switchboard.com`) to look up your phone number.

6. Use MapQuest (`www.mapquest.com`) to look up your address. Print the map for it.

7. What is the Web address for the New York Public Library?

8. Pick an issue. Find sites on both sides of the issue and analyze their content.

SEARCHING FOR GUINEA PIG B

Case Study in Online Research

learning objectives

> Explain the advantages and disadvantages of online research

> Explain the advantages and disadvantages of primary and secondary sources in research

> Apply the case study example (R. Buckminster Fuller)

- Expand and narrow an online search, as needed

- Use bookmarking

- Locate primary and secondary sources

- Assess the authority of sources

- Use online photos, video clips, and audio clips to enhance the search

- Resolve controversial questions online

- Follow up on interesting side questions

> Use the skills above to be able to do a curiosity-driven online research project

Sometimes I think we are alone [in the universe]. Sometimes I think we are not. In either case, the thought is quite staggering.

—R. BUCKMINSTER FULLER

WE'RE ALL CURIOUS, and the IT knowledge we have developed so far is enough to help us track down the answers to questions we wonder about. Usually these questions are simple: "Is the Colorado ski area Telluride named after the chemical element Tellurium?" With a few clicks we find the answer, perhaps mention it to a friend, and that's that. The World Wide Web has helped us answer the question without visiting the library. Now, with the speed and convenience of the Web, we can easily add to our store of useless facts and amaze our friends.

But information technology offers us more than a simple chance to answer a single question. It lets us find out about substantial topics that interest us and probe deeply wherever our curiosity leads us. This is called **curiosity-driven research**. For centuries now, educated people who were curious about a topic would consult books, but now on-line research expands our opportunities.

Books do have certain advantages: They are generally authoritative, having been carefully researched, usually well written, and permanent. Their disadvantages are that they contain only the information the author selects, so they give us only one point of view; they can take years to produce, so the information they offer may be dated; they are static; and despite so many titles, they cover only a limited number of topics. Books remain excellent sources of information. But the fact is, a book exists because someone else was curious about a topic, researched it, and interpreted the findings. With the World Wide Web, we can pick the topic, we can do our own research, and we can make our own interpretation of what we find. That is, our own curiosity drives the research.

In this chapter we learn to do curiosity-driven research using the WWW. This gives us a chance to use the ideas introduced in earlier chapters. One goal is to explore the limits of the research that can be done on the WWW, because not everything is in digital form yet, and not everything in digital form is worth reading. Another goal is to enjoy a tour through the life and mind of an amazing man, R. Buckminster Fuller, who described himself as both an engineer and a poet. The topic requires using different kinds of information resources. Finally, we learn to fill in the gaps in our knowledge. Though the case study runs to many pages, it represents the search/research activity of a single interesting and enjoyable evening. The conclusion is that curiosity-driven research can be fun, and more interesting and rewarding than watching another rerun of *Friends*.

FITTIP

Student Aid. Curiosity-driven research can be a random process, as different discoveries grab our interest. It appears even more aimless when it's someone else's curiosity doing the driving. Though I explain why we choose the path we take, it is still possible for you to lose track of where we are. If that happens, you may want to check the summary provided at the end of the chapter in Figure 6.19, which gives an overview of the research path followed.

GETTING STARTED WITH ONLINE RESEARCH

Curiosity-driven research usually begins with a name or word we've heard or read. We wonder about it, but often we have too little information at first to begin an informed search with a search engine. In the present case, we wonder about R. Buckminster Fuller, who is a man with a unique name. Even so, performing a Google search on

```
Buckminster AND Fuller
```

produces at least 26,800 hits, way too many to consider. Limiting the search to biographies

```
Buckminster AND Fuller AND biography
```

reduces the hit count to 1600, which is still too many. So, we must gather some identifying information from another source to guide an effective search-engine search. For this case, we make use of the fact that short biographies of famous people are online. Other topics will require different resources.

Narrowing the Search

After going electronically to a convenient library, we find among its research links a list of sources for biographies, including

Biography.com	`www.biography.com/search/`
Biographical Dictionary	`www.s9.com/biography/`
Britannica Lives	`www.eb.com/people/`
Lives, the Biography Resource	`amillionlives.com`

and we try the first one. We have no reason for selecting one resource over another, but if we were to use biographies repeatedly, it would be wise to shop around. The completeness and quality of the entries vary. The response to the `Buckminster Fuller` search request is successful and is shown in Figure 6.1.

Fuller, R(ichard) Buckminster 1895–1983

Inventor, designer, poet, futurist; born in Milton, Massachusetts (great-nephew of Margaret Fuller). Leaving Harvard early, he largely educated himself while working at industrial jobs and serving in the U.S. Navy during World War I. One of the century's most original minds, he free-lanced his talents, solving problems of human shelter, nutrition, transportation, environmental pollution, and decreasing world resources, developing over 2,000 patents in the process. He developed the Dymaxion ("dynamic and maximum efficiency") House in 1927, and the Dymaxion streamlined, omnidirectional car in 1932.

Fuller wrote some 25 books, notably *Nine Chains to the Moon* (1938), *Utopia or Oblivion* (1969), *Operating Manual for Spaceship Earth* (1969), and *Critical Path* (1981). An enthusiastic educationist, he held a chair at Southern Illinois University (1959–75), and in 1962 became professor of poetry at Harvard. In his later decades he was a popular public lecturer, promoting a global strategy of seeking to do more with less through technology. His inventions include the 1927 Dymaxion House, the 1933 Dymaxion Car and, foremost, the 1947 geodesic dome. He has the distinction of having both his names used for a scientific entity, the "fullerene" (also known as a "buckyball"), a form of carbon whose molecule resembles his geodesic dome.

Figure 6.1. Biography.com's biography of Buckminster Fuller.

Expanding the View

Reading Fuller's biography, we learn his name is actually Richard Buckminster Fuller (RFB). The first line mentions that he is the great-nephew of Margaret Fuller. Who's she? Because we are at a biography site, we can look her up. A portion of her Biography.com entry is shown in Figure 6.2. Reading her biography, we note that they both preferred to go by their middle names. More significant parallels in their lives also exist: They were both largely self-taught, they were both intellectually gifted, and they were both concerned about making the world a better place—she through her feminist writings and he through his inventions. Her tragic shipwreck death with her new husband and young child reminds us that Buckminster Fuller's profile doesn't mention if he was married or had children. So, we seek more biographical information. We could check the other three biography sites, but since we've already found the identifying information we need to guide a Google search, we do that.

In the first biography, the term *Dymaxion,* perhaps a term Fuller thought up, is mentioned as a name of both a house and a car that he invented. Surely any biography will mention these inventions, so we search on

`Buckminster AND Fuller AND biography AND Dymaxion`

which reduces the number of hits from more than 1600, when only "biography" is included, to a manageable 149. Interestingly, "Buckminster" and "Dymaxion" are so unusual and so descriptive of this one person that his last name is unnecessary! Searching on `Buckminster AND Dymaxion AND biography` hits 149 times.

Fuller, (Sarah) Margaret 1810–1850

Feminist, literary critic; born in Cambridgeport, Mass. Her father, Timothy Fuller, was a prominent Massachusetts lawyer-politician who, disappointed that his child was not a boy, educated her rigorously in the classical curriculum of the day. Not until age 14 did she get to attend a school for two years (1824–26) and then she returned to Cambridge and her course of reading. Her intellectual precociousness gained her the acquaintance of various Cambridge intellectuals but her assertive and intense manner put many people off. . . . From 1836 to 1837, after visiting Ralph Waldo Emerson in Concord, she taught for Bronson Alcott in Boston, and then at a school in Providence, R.I. All the while she continued to enlarge both her intellectual accomplishments and personal acquaintances. Moving to Jamaica Plain, a suburb of Boston, in 1840, she conducted her famous "Conversations" (1840–44), discussion groups that attracted many prominent people from all around Boston. In 1840, she also joined Emerson and others to found the *Dial*, a journal devoted to the transcendentalist views; she became a contributor from the first issue and its editor (1840–42). . . . She went on to Italy in 1847 where she met Giovanni Angelo, the Marchese d'Ossoli, ten years younger and of liberal principles; they became lovers and married in 1849, but their son was born in 1848. Involved in the Roman revolution of 1848, she and her husband fled to Florence in 1849. They sailed for the U.S.A. in 1850 but the ship ran aground in a storm off Fire Island, N.Y., and Margaret's and her husband's bodies were never found.

Figure 6.2. Exerpt from Biography.com's biography for Margaret Fuller, RBF's great aunt.

Early in the list of hits is another biography from About.com shown in Figure 6.3. Reading this biography reveals something researchers encounter all the time: Different sources differ. Whereas the first biography had described his departure from Harvard as "leaving," this one says he was "expelled." Though we could track down whether he left or was expelled, we will leave it unresolved for now. Despite so many honorary degrees, he obviously didn't take himself too seriously, based on his self-description, *Guinea Pig B*.

The second paragraph emphasizes how he overcame his despair at the death of his daughter, turned his thoughts away from suicide—"his life was not his to throw away"—and went on to see what he could do "on behalf of humanity." He actually worked on the problem of world hunger, a problem most people dismiss as not solvable. His philosophy of treating life as an experiment in "what the little, penniless, unknown individual might be able to do effectively on behalf of all humanity" is inspiring! We need to know more.

Place of Birth: Milton, Massachusetts

Education: Expelled from Harvard University during freshman year

Awards: 44 honorary doctoral degrees, Gold Medal of the American Institute of Architects, Gold Medal of the Royal Institute of British Architects and dozens of other honors. Nominated for Nobel Peace Prize.

Selected Works:

> 1932: The portable Dymaxion house manufactured
> 1934: The Dymaxion car
> 1938: Nine Chains to the Moon
> 1949: Developed the Geodesic Dome
> 1967: US Pavilion at Expo '67, Montreal, Canada
> 1969: Operating Manual for Spaceship Earth
> 1970: Approaching the Benign Environment

Standing only 5′2″ tall, Buckminster Fuller loomed over the twentieth century. Admirers affectionately call him *Bucky*, but the name he gave himself was *Guinea Pig B*. His life, he said, was an experiment.

When he was 32, Buckminster Fuller's life seemed hopeless. He was bankrupt and without a job. He was grief stricken over the death of his first child and he had a wife and a newborn to support. Drinking heavily, he contemplated suicide. Instead, he decided that his life was not his to throw away: It belonged to the universe. He embarked on "an experiment to discover what the little, penniless, unknown individual might be able to do effectively on behalf of all humanity."

To this end, Buckminster Fuller spent the next half-century searching for "ways of doing more with less" so that all people could be fed and sheltered. Although he never obtained a degree in architecture, he was an architect and engineer who designed revolutionary structures. His famous Dymaxion House was a pre-fabricated, pole-supported dwelling. His Dymaxion car was a streamlined, three-wheeled vehicle with the engine in the rear. His Dymaxion Air-Ocean Map projected a spherical world as a flat surface with no visible distortion.

But Fuller is perhaps most famous for his creation of the geodesic dome—a remarkable, sphere-like structure based on theories of "energetic-synergetic geometry," which he developed during WWII. Efficient and economical, the geodesic dome was widely hailed as a possible solution to world housing shortages.

During his lifetime, Buckminster Fuller wrote 28 books and was awarded 25 United States patents. Although his Dymaxion car never caught on and his design for geodesic domes is rarely used for residential dwellings, Fuller made his mark in areas of architecture, mathematics, philosophy, religion, urban development, and design.

Figure 6.3. About.com's biography of Buckminster Fuller.

Searching for Images

Perhaps before going any further we should find out what Fuller looks like. To locate some photographs, we use Google's image search, `www.google.com/ advanced_image_search`. Entering `Buckminster Fuller` yields nearly 500

`.jpg` and `.gif` images. They're not all of RBF—some people have named their cats Buckminster Fuller—but there is a wide range of interesting images of Fuller. Three images from later in life, shown in Figure 6.4, show us an intense man who also seems grandfatherly, the sort of guy who might give you the keys to the Dymaxion car for the weekend.

Figure 6.4. *Three pictures of R. Buckminster Fuller.*

Bookmarking Links

We won't take the time to look through all of these images, nor will we follow all of these links (see Figure 6.5) from the About.com biography site now. But we might want to check these out later. And we have no idea how we will use the information we will discover so we just bookmark the site. (For pictures it's easiest to *save* a copy on our computer rather than book marking the URL.)

Buckminster Fuller: Biography Fast facts about the life and works of Buckminster Fuller, affectionately known as "Bucky."

Buckminster Fuller: Quotes A compendium of quotes and excerpts from Fuller's most famous writings.

What is a Geodesic Dome? From our architecture glossary, illustration and definition of the geodesic dome, conceived by Buckminster Fuller.

Build A Geodesic Dome Model Step-by-step instructions, with diagrams, from Trevor Blake.

Spaceship Earth Facts and photo for the famous dome at Disney Epcot, which is built according to Buckminster Fuller's principles.

Buckminster Fuller: Inventions An extensive collection of resources, illustrations and links, from your Guide to Inventors.

Buckminster Fuller: Net Links Best Buckminster Fuller sites on the Web, selected by your Guide.

Geodesic Domes: Net Links Best Geodesic Dome sites on the Web, selected by your Guide.

Figure 6.5. *Additional links from About.com's biography of R. Buckminster Fuller.*

FITTIP

Online Research Methodology. When using the WWW for research, bookmark every site visited (deleting bookmarks later is trivial) and record the keywords of all searches— both search engine and site searches—in a notebook file. With this information you can revisit the sites and reconstruct the search.

PRIMARY SOURCES

To find out more about Fuller's philosophy and personal life, we decide to do another search on the exact phrase `"Guinea Pig B"`—a name so distinctive there cannot be any others. Recall that Google lets us search for an exact phrase; in this case the search gives 200 hits. When we change the search to `Buckminster AND "Guinea Pig B"` the count drops to 99. This list is a goldmine of specific information about Fuller, and we will return to it.

The first hit for the `Buckminster AND "Guinea Pig B"` search is a page from WNET, New York City's public television station, for a documentary they produced on Fuller's life titled "Buckminster Fuller: Thinking Out Loud." The Guinea Pig B page from this site is shown in Figure 6.6.

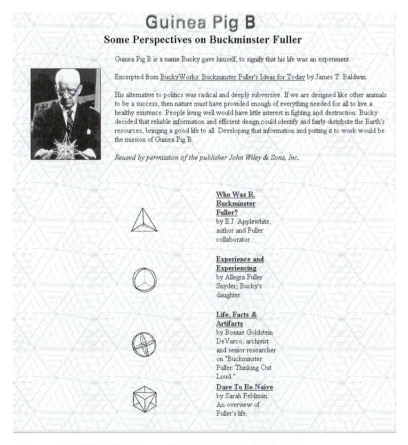

Figure 6.6. WNET's Guinea Pig B page.

The WNET page shows us a new photograph of RBF, cites a recent book about him, and quotes a small excerpt. This is all useful, but the links at the bottom of the page, to four essays, are perhaps more valuable:

Who Was R. Buckminster Fuller? by E. J. Applewhite, author and Fuller collaborator.

Experience and Experiencing by Allegra Fuller Snyder, Bucky's daughter.

Life, Facts and Artifacts by Bonnie Goldstein DeVarco, archivist and senior researcher on "Buckminster Fuller: Thinking Out Loud."

Dare To Be Naïve by Sarah Feldman. An overview of Fuller's life.

From the list we note that Fuller had a daughter, Allegra, who apparently married someone named Snyder. (No relation to the author of this text.)

Assessing the Authenticity of Sources

The importance of these essays is that they are extremely reliable sources of information. Applewhite as a collaborator and Snyder as Fuller's daughter write from direct personal experience. They are known as *primary sources*. Such information is to be preferred for several reasons. First, the information is actual experience and personal impressions. Thus the information is unbiased, except to the degree that anything a person gathers from experience is subject to that person's ability to perceive it, motivation to be objective, and expressiveness. Primary sources are not subject to the distortion or omission that can come when someone else reports information from a primary source. Such a "second-hand" report is considered a **secondary source**. If someone reports from a secondary source, creating a tertiary source, more distortion and omission are possible. Using primary sources helps us get our own impression and point of view on the subject.

Source 1 – An RBF Collaborator.   E. J. Applewhite, a collaborator, is considered a primary source (see Figure 6.7).

Who Was R. Buckminster Fuller?

by E. J. Applewhite

Buckminster Fuller had one of the most fascinating and original minds of his century. Born in 1895 in Milton, Massachusetts, he was the latest—if not the last—of the New England Transcendentalists. Like the transcendentalists, Fuller rejected the established religious and political notions of the past and adhered to an idealistic system of thought based on the essential unity of the natural world and the use of experiment and intuition as a means of understanding it. But, departing from the pattern of his New England predecessors, he proposed that only an understanding of technology in the deepest sense would afford humans a proper guide to individual conduct and the eventual salvation of society. Industrial and scientific technology, despite their disruption of established habits and values, was not a blight on the landscape, but in fact for Fuller they have a redeeming humanitarian role.

Fuller rejected the conventional disciplines of the universities by ignoring them. In their place he imposed his own self-discipline and his own novel way of thinking in a deliberate attempt—as poets and artists do—to change his generation's perception of the world. To this end he created the term Spaceship Earth to convince all his fellow passengers that they would have to work together as the crew of a ship. His was an earnest, even compulsive, program to convince his listeners that humans had a function in universe. Humans have a destiny to serve as "local problem solvers" converting their experience to the highest advantage of others.

. . .

Fuller was an architect, though he never got a degree and in fact didn't even get a license until he was awarded one as an honor when he was in his late 60s. This did not prevent him from designing the geodesic dome: the only kind of building that can be set on the ground as a complete structure—and with no limiting dimension. The strength of the frame actually increases in ratio to its size, enclosing the largest volume of space with the least area of surface. This was his virtuoso invention, and he said it illustrated his strategy of "starting with wholes" rather than parts.

He was also a poet, philosopher, inventor and mathematician, as documented amply in many other web sites on the net.

America has been in the middle of a love-hate affair with technology—and Fuller is right in the middle of it. He introduced not only a unique rationale for technology, but an esthetic of it. Likewise his synergetic geometry bears for Fuller an imperative with an ethical content for humans to reappraise their relationship to the physical universe. Manifest together as design science, they offer the prospect of a kind of secular salvation.

Figure 6.7. Excerpt from the Applewhite essay at the WNET "Guinea Pig B" site.

Source 2 – RFB's Daughter. Buckminster Fuller's daughter Allegra Fuller Snyder is clearly a primary source (see Figure 6.8).

Experience and Experiencing

by Allegra Fuller Snyder

. . .

My father was a warm, concerned and sharing father. As focused as he was on his own work he nevertheless included me in his experiences and experiencing. I remember with great clarity when I was about four years old. I was sick in bed and he was taking care of me. He sat down on the bed beside me, with his pencil in hand, and told me, through wonderful free-hand drawings, a Goldilocks story. I was Goldilocks and with his pencil he transported me, not to the Bear's house, but to universe, to help me understand something of Einstein's Theory of Relativity. What he was telling me was neither remote nor abstract. I was in a newly perceived universe. I was experiencing my father's thoughts and he was experiencing his own thinking as he communicated with me. It was exciting. We were sharing something together and I felt very warm and close to him in that experience. Something of this episode was later remembered in a book called Tetrascroll.

. . .

He loved our island in Maine because it was a physically involving place. We have no fresh water, except cistern-caught rain and well water, which has to be drawn or pumped and then hauled; kerosene and candles for light, a fire in the hearth for heat. Each of these basic requirements involves physical action to produce the needed results. . . . And then, of course, there was sailing, which he loved, where the dialog between nature and human action is so dynamic.

At the heart of each one of these actions, was the sense of the "special case" that would lead to a generalized principle. Any experience would become a "special case," the doorway to larger comprehensivity. When you were around him you were aware how sensitive he was to the smallest experience. His focus could zero in on a pebble on the beach, a twig or flower along a path. Each became the stepping stone to the largest whole.

"The human brain apprehends and stores each sense reported bit of information regarding each special case experience. Only special case experiences are recallable from the memory bank."

. . .

Intuition, imagination, all relate to and are a part of experience. Let me turn for a moment to Bucky's own words on these matters. (What follows are drawn from E.J. Applewhite's wonderful Synergetics Dictionary.)

Intuition is practically physical, the kind of supersensitivity that a child has. Imagination. Image-ination involves rearranging the "furniture" of remembered experience as retrieved from the brain bank.

Speaking with an audience he would say, "All that I can really give you I must always identify by experience." One of his great gifts as a speaker was the fact that he made you experience his ideas and carried you along with the connection between your experience and his experience. "Information is experience. Experience is information."

. . .

Where or how does experience continue to be a part of the picture when, as Bucky pointed out,

"At the dawning of the twentieth century, without warning to humanity, the physical technology of Earthians' affairs was shifted over from a brain-sensed reality into a reality apprehended only by instruments."

His response is that invisibility can be "understood and coped with only by experience-educated mind.

. . .

Figure 6.8. Excerpt from the Allegra Fuller Snyder essay at the WNET "Guinea Pig B" site.

Source 3 – An RFB Archivist. Bonnie Goldstein DeVarco presents a fascinating account of Fuller's archive—he saved everything! Much of the content concerns specifics of the archive that are somewhat tangential to our interest. But two paragraphs stand out in her section on Ephemeralization, quoted here (see Figure 6.9).

> **Life, Facts and Artifacts**
>
> by Bonnie Goldstein DeVarco
>
> **EPHEMERALIZATION**
>
> Although the tactile pleasures of sorting through the physical artifacts of Bucky's life brings a dimension all its own to the discovery of who he was and who he shared his life with, almost the same could be done with the same body of materials available on a computer screen—from drawings, letters and manuscripts to "ephemerabilia," at the touch of a fingertip. In hundreds of letters spanning well over half a century, the love story of Bucky and Anne is told. Anne's letters carry a lilting youthful quality that punctuates even the most fatuous groupings of correspondence to be found in the Chronfile* boxes. Her handwriting is like a beautiful victorian stenciled wallpaper and her ardent and boundless devotion gives life to the saying that behind every great man is a great woman. It is no wonder he personally deemed his most famous geodesic dome, at the 1967 Montreal Exposition, his "Taj Majal to Anne" in honor of their 50th anniversary.
>
> The letters of sculptor Isamu Noguchi, Bucky's lifelong friend, span decades and flavor the correspondence files with Asian subtlety, each page an artwork in and of itself, all on sheer white rice paper written with a brown fountain pen, always poignant, always aesthetically disarming. And how affecting it is to see in a letter to his mother bound into the 1928 Chronfile volume, Fuller's youthful discovery of his Great Aunt Margaret Fuller's thought and its parallels to his own as he writes, "I have been reading much by Margaret Fuller lately. I was astonished to find that some things I have been writing myself are about identical to things I find in her writings. I am terribly interested and am astounded fully that I should have grown to this age and never have read anything of her or grandfather Fuller's."
>
> *RBF kept his correspondence and other documents in a bound file in time order called the Chronfile.

Figure 6.9. *Excerpt from the DeVarco essay at the WNET "Guinea Pig B" site.*

DeVarco's essay is based on information from the archive of Fuller's papers and artifacts, which DeVarco described as "approximately 90,000 pounds of personal history." Fuller produced this information, so it is a primary source. As an archivist and researcher, DeVarco can be presumed to be accurate and reliable. Though her essay is not technically a primary source, we can trust it.

Source 4 – An Institute Developer and Writer. Sara
Feldman's essay has relied on the Fuller archive for its information, so it may be an excellent resource. As researchers, however, we wonder who she is. Her title or relationship to Fuller is not stated with the essay. For example, is she a scholar with academic credentials who we can assume tried to be accurate, or does she write advertising copy for used car companies and perhaps often embellishes the facts? We look her up in Biography.com, but she's not there. We go to the WNET Web site and search their site for her name. We get a link to her bio, which reads

Sarah Feldman

Sarah Feldman is the National Project Director for the National Teacher Training Institute (NTTI) at Thirteen/WNET New York. She is also a content developer and writer for Thirteen's wNetStation and wNetSchool, and other online venues. She taught second grade in the South Bronx and Harlem.

As a director at a national teacher-training institute, content developer, and writer with access to the Fuller archive, Feldman sounds very reliable and so we are confident that her essay is, also. See Figure 6.10 for an excerpt of her essay.

Dare to Be Naïve

by Sarah Feldman

Jobless, without savings or prospects, with a wife and newborn daughter to support, suicidal and drinking heavily, in 1927 Richard Buckminster Fuller had little reason to be optimistic about the future. R. Buckminster Fuller—or "Bucky," as he's affectionately known—transformed that low point in his life into a catalyst for transforming our planet's future as well as his own. A mathematical genius, environmentalist, architect, cartographer, poet, and an engineer of rare foresight and a philosopher of unique insight, Fuller was born in 1895 but can be truly considered a 21st century man.

　Renouncing personal success and financial gain, at age 32 Fuller set out to "search for the principles governing the universe and help advance the evolution of humanity in accordance with them." Central to his mission were the ideas that 1) he had to divest himself of false ideas and "unlearn" everything he could not verify through his own experience, and 2) human nature—and nature itself—could not be reformed and therefore it was the environment—and our response to it—that must be changed. Fuller entered into a two-year period of total seclusion, and began working on design solutions to what he inferred to be mankind's central problems.

　With his goal of "finding ways of doing more with less to the end that all people—everywhere—can have more and more," Fuller began designing a series of revolutionary structures. The most famous of these was the pre-fabricated, pole-suspended single-unit dwelling Dymaxion House. (The term Dymaxion was derived from the words "dynamic," "maximum," and "ion.") . . . Fuller's designs tended to be based [on] a geometry that used triangles, circles and tetrahedrons more than the traditional planes and rectangles. His Dymaxion Air-Ocean Map, which projected a spherical world as a flat surface with no visible distortion, brought him to the attention of the scientific community in 1943, and his map was the first cartographic projection of the world to ever be granted a U.S. patent.

　In 1947 and 1948, Fuller's study of geodesics, "the most economical momentary relationship among a plurality of points and events," led him to his most famous invention, the geodesic dome. A hemispherical structure composed of flat, triangular panels, the domes were inexpensive to produce, lightweight yet strong space-efficient buildings. . . . Today, Fuller's geodesic domes can be found in varying sizes in countries all over the world, from Casablanca to Baton Rouge. Recognized as a landmark achievement in design and architecture, Fuller's dome was described in 1964 by Time magazine as "a kind of benchmark of the universe, what seventeenth century mystic Jakob Boehme might call 'a signature of God.'" In 1959 he joined the faculty of Southern Illinois University in Carbondale and used that as a base of operations for what Fuller called his "toings and froings." For the next two decades, Fuller globe-trotted and lectured and consulted on a variety of projects. During this period of upheaval and great change, Fuller's ideas and work in such areas as ecology, conservation, education and environmental design found an enthusiastic audience among young people all over the world. After a stint at the University Science Center in Philadelphia, in 1972 the non-profit Design Science Institute was formed in Washington, DC to perpetuate Fuller's ideas and designs.

A self-proclaimed "apolitical," Fuller maintained there was "no difference between [the] left and the right." Nevertheless, he admitted he struggled to "dare to be naïve," and retained an optimistic faith that "an omni-integrated, freely intercirculating, omni-literate world society" was within our grasp. A prolific writer, Fuller's magnum opus is undoubtedly "Synergetics: Explorations in the Geometry of Thinking," on which he collaborated with E.J. Applewhite in 1975. The work is considered a major intellectual achievement in its examinations of language, thought and the universe.

Though he only stood 5'2" tall, R. Buckminster Fuller looms large over the 20th century. Though a man of incredible intellect and vision, many of "Bucky's" fans remain most impressed by the man's awe-inspiring humility—and his abiding love for his planet and his fellow human beings. "Above all," said Fuller, "I was motivated in 1927 and ever since by the most mysterious drive we ever experience—that of love. I don't think there's any influence upon my life that compares with . . . love."

R. Buckminster Fuller

July 12, 1895 – July 1, 1983

Figure 6.10.   *Excerpt from the Feldman essay at the WNET "Guinea Pig B" site.*

Assessing Our Progress

So far, we have found four essays (Figures 6.7 through 6.10) about RBF and assessed the quality of their information. We have found them to be either from primary sources or from researchers who used the Fuller archive. This is excellent information, and we will take the time to read it. Notice that we do not mean that secondary or tertiary sources should not be used—we just used two from Biography.com and an About.com profile. They were unsigned biographical sketches that probably relied on generally available information about Fuller. We assumed they are accurate, though we noted a difference—one says Fuller left Harvard and the other says he was expelled. The point is that the two biographies met our need for a quick introduction. Now, because we want to find the most accurate information about Fuller's life and philosophy, we go to the source(s) ourselves.

Reading the essays gives us extraordinary insight into Buckminster Fuller and we can describe him in our own words. He believed, according to Applewhite, that technology is not the "problem" but rather the "solution," and that understanding technology deeply is the key to individual behavior as well as to "saving" society. Snyder's essay emphasized how he only trusted his direct experience as he tried to overcome the bias of conventional wisdom that he believed prevented effective thinking. He tried to do more with less. Feldman quotes Fuller as saying that he turned his life around in 1927, motivated by love, the greatest influence on his life, and DeVarco quotes his description of the Montreal geodesic dome as the "Taj Majal to Anne." It is a personal story of a deep thinker. The geodesic dome was his "virtuoso invention" [Applewhite] and *Synergetics*, a "major intellectual achievement," was his greatest work [Feldman].

And our search also allows us to resolve conflicting information. Snyder describes her father's leaving Harvard as "dismissed," another word for "expelled"—settling that question. Feldman says that Dymaxion stands for "dynamic," "maximum," and "ion," which makes more sense than the "dynamic with maximum efficiency" that we learned in the first biography.

Finding Video Clips

While thinking about this complex man, we cruise the WNET site and discover a page with two short video clips of Fuller. This is also primary information. Though downloading them takes a few moments, they show Fuller describing in his own words some of his most radical ideas. In one he says,

> This is the *real* news of the last century. It is highly feasible to take care of all of humanity at a higher standard of living than anybody has ever experienced or dreamt of, to do so without having anybody profit at the expense of another . . . so that everybody can enjoy the whole earth . . . and it can all be done by 1985.

In the video clip we not only hear what he has to say, but we see the emphasis of his gestures and hear the conviction in his voice. His tone seems to say "not only *can* we raise humanity's standard of living, we *should*." In this way the spoken word is more powerful than the written word. This digitized information has given us valuable insight.

CHRONFILE AND EVERYTHING I KNOW

Recall that the WNET page was the first item in a Google search with the terms `Buckminster AND "Guinea Pig B"`. Having gotten just about everything we could out of that page, we go to the next item, which is a link to the Buckminster Fuller Institute (BFI). See Figure 6.11.

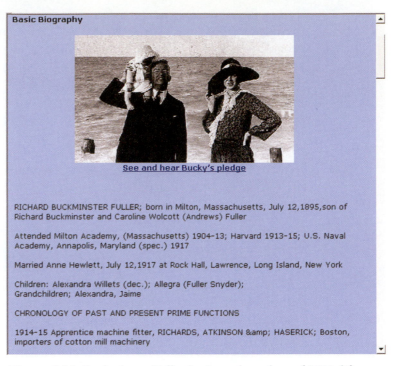

Figure 6.11. Buckminster Fuller Institute chronology of RBF's life.

The BFI timeline of Fuller's life is very interesting, ending with this amazing fact (not shown in the figure): *Anne* [his wife] *and Bucky died within 36 hours of one another one week before their sixty-seventh wedding anniversary!* If this page is what it seems to be—a site associated with the Fuller estate—the information is surely authoritative. Keeping in mind that some sites are hoaxes, we check to see who owns the `bfi.org` domain. Remember that the process of finding out who owns a domain, which takes less than a minute, was explained in Chapter 5. After a few clicks, we learn that the site is owned by the Buckminster Fuller Institute of Santa Barbara, California.

Audio Clips: Everything I Know

Clicking around the site, we find a huge amount of authoritative information, including Chronfile information, copies of whole books by Fuller, and 42 hours' worth of Fuller recordings from 1975 titled *Everything I Know*. This huge archive of online information is divided into 12 parts, each of which is subdivided into paragraph-size units called clips. We listen to a few minutes to get an idea of what *Everything I Know* is like. It's interesting, of course, and we notice from its description that it includes deep, abstract ideas as well as personal stories. Though we're interested in the deep ideas, the personal details are interesting, too. What, we wonder, does he say about Allegra?

If the archive only had the 42 hours of audio clips, we would probably have to listen to most of them to find out. However, JoAnne Ishimine has transcribed them all. This means they can be searched. So we can make a site search for `Allegra`. Among the hits is one where Fuller mentions how Allegra loves to dance and then describes a conversation they had.

> And, when she was twelve, she said "Daddy," we were living in New York at that time, she said "Daddy, you were brought up in Boston with the custom that it is ill mannered for men to make gestures that the man who is properly cultivated is well in possession of his movements, and he just doesn't even move his head, he just talks and sits very motionless, beautifully disciplined to do that." And she said, "I'll tell you, I don't know if I really am a dancer, but whatever I am, my body wants to talk all the time." And she said, "Daddy, I like your ideas very, very much and I want them to prevail, but I think you are frustrating your ideas by your disciplining yourself to sit motionless. I think if you'd just let yourself go things would happen way better for you." She was used to my having a lot of hard luck, nobody was paying any attention to me in those days. And so she seemed so wise that I think I did everything I could to free myself up. . . . But she did make it perfectly clear, a child does move comfortably and uses his body, so I began to let myself do [*sic*] I am utterly unaware of the motions, I assure you, but I have had moving pictures taken of me I've seen myself when I've been giving a lecture and I'm practically going all over the stage like a ballet dancer.

We can see that he *is* an animated speaker in the lectures we watched from the WNET "Buckminster Fuller: Thinking Out Loud" program.

We bookmark the *Everything I Know* archive because it is a rich resource of Fuller information, in his own words. When his ideas pique our interest, we can return to the archives.

Surfing the BFI Site

Looking around the site, we quickly come across Fuller's Dymaxion Map—the surface of the globe projected onto an icosahedron that produces a minimal-distortion flat map. Thinking of an icosahedron inside the earth and imagining the earth's curved surface shrinking down onto the icosahedron's faces gives the idea of the projection. Unfolding the icosahedron, as shown in Figure 6.12, produces the flat map (`www.bfi.org/map_animation.html`). There is an animation by Chris Rywalt (`www.westnet.com/%7Ecrywalt/unfold.html`), and watching the earth unfold a few times gives a good idea of how it works. This minimal-distortion map shows the continents in realistic proportion to one another. The specific unfolding shows the continents as one essentially contiguous island in a single sea. It's Fuller's schematic diagram for Spaceship Earth.

Figure 6.12. *Dymaxion Map—an unfolding of a projection of Earth onto an icosahedron.*

RESOLVING QUESTIONS

There is something confusing here. Fuller invented the geodesic dome (Figure 6.13), as we knew before we started. It's his "virtuoso invention." And he invented the Dymaxion Map (Figure 6.12). The map page tells us that the map projects the globe onto an icosahedron. But we remember the geodesic dome of the Montreal Expo '67 as smoother than an icosahedron. What's the difference? Are they the same idea? If not, how is a geodesic dome related to an icosahedron?

Figure 6.13. *Geodesic Dome—from the U.S. Pavilion at the Montreal Expo '67.*

The local BFI site may be the best place to find information about geodesics and the map's projection. Or maybe we should try a Google search on `difference AND icosahedron AND geodesic`. But, if we think about the question before starting to search, we notice that answering it could be as easy as finding out the two definitions. The best place to find definitions is in a dictionary, so we click up an online dictionary. (Again, if we forget the site name for an online dictionary, we can go to our favorite library's research or reference page to find a link to one.) The two principles at work here are (1) think about what kind of information will answer the question, and (2) look where that type of information may be found. We might be able to answer the question simply by learning the meaning of the two words.

The online dictionaries give the following definitions and drawing (see Figure 6.14):

> **geodesic,** *n*: The shortest line between two points on any mathematically defined surface.
>
> **icosahedron,** *n*: A 20-sided polyhedron.

Figure 6.14. Icosahedron.

Obviously these are not the same. The icosahedron is a solid, and a geodesic is a line. But, this doesn't really explain how a geodesic dome differs from an icosahedron, because the definition we found is for "geodesic," a noun form, and when we refer to the "geodesic dome," we use it as an adjective. Looking further in the dictionary we find

> **geodesic,** *adj:* Made of light straight structural elements mostly in tension <a *geodesic* dome>.
>
> **geodesic dome,** *n:* A domed or vaulted structure of lightweight straight elements that form interlocking polygons.

These definitions help. The icosahedron has just 20 sides, which are triangles, and no matter how large it is—even the size of the earth—it must still have 20 sides or faces. The geodesic dome has any number of faces. From the picture of the Expo dome we can see, first, that the sides are also triangles and, second, that they are interlocking hexagons. That is, the triangles that form one hexagon can be grouped to be parts of other adjacent hexagons. Looking at the icosahedron, we see the triangles forming interlocking pentagons, and because the geodesic definition requires only "straight elements that form interlocking *polygons*," we conclude that an icosahedron is a geodesic solid. It's no surprise that Fuller came up with both the map idea and the dome idea.

We could pursue more detailed questions on structures—it's possible to build a geodesic dome from straws and pipecleaners—but we're more interested in the man than the engineering, so we continue checking the information from the `"Guinea Pig B"` search.

SECONDARY SOURCES

Our search so far has been very successful. It has shown us a complex and productive man, "one of the most original thinkers of the twentieth century." He was rational, sensitive, and used "both sides of his brain." The primary sources have been extensive and rich, including text, photographs, audio clips, video clips, and an animation. Indeed, the information is so extensive it overwhelms us—we've studied only a tiny fraction of it.

Now we have two problems. First, we need to know what is missing in our understanding of Fuller. Second, there seems to be no organization in our thinking. At the moment it is just a collection of facts. One way to solve both problems is to check some secondary sources.

Completing the Picture

Though it's always best to gather information from primary sources, secondary sources are also valuable. Secondary sources can

> Give us a more thorough investigation of the topic—certainly more thorough than ours to this point—and help us fill in gaps.

> Help us organize the information.

> Provide other authors' interpretations, including insights we have not thought of.

As always, we need to check out the sources for authenticity.

From the results of the `Buckminster AND "Guinea Pig B"` search, we find a 3000-word biography by Kirby Urner, who maintains the Synergetics Web page. (From his homepage we find that Urner is a writer and curriculum developer from Portland, Oregon.) The part of the biography shown in Figure 6.15 organizes some of the information that we've found and tells us more about Fuller's navy days. It discusses controversies regarding the independence of Fuller's ideas from those of Ken Snelson, Alexander Graham Bell, and Walter Bauersfield. These controversies are new to us.

A 20th Century Philosopher

by Kirby Urner

Originally posted: May 11, 1998; Last updated: June 19, 2000

. . .

Although the family had a four-generation tradition of sending its sons to Harvard, Fuller was too much the wild romantic to settle in and was expelled for treating an entire New York dance troupe to champagne on his own tab. The family sentenced him to hard labor in a Canadian cotton mill, where he sobered up quite a bit, but he still didn't like Harvard upon giving it a second try and was again expelled. He later returned to Harvard as the Charles Eliot Norton Professor of Poetry (1962).

Given his nautical background as a boy messing about with boats around Bear Island, Fuller was attracted to the navy, and managed to achieve a command with family assistance (1917). His marriage to Anne Hewlett was in grand military style. His native genius as an inventive soul was recognized (he developed a winch for rescuing pilots downed over water) and this led to an appointment at the Annapolis Naval Academy (1918).

At Annapolis, under the tutelage of retired admirals, Fuller felt very much at home, and began to germinate his "Great Pirates" narrative, wherein the big picture thinking then offered to young officers was a culmination of a long tradition of "thinking globally, acting locally" on the part of high seas figures, many of them pirates, and many of them lost to history because operating invisibly, over the horizon from those who kept the historical accounts (mostly landlubbers).

A few years after his honorable discharge, Fuller attempted to make money using his father-in-law's invention, a morterless brick building system, but failed in this enterprise (1926). This failure, which led to joblessness in Chicago, coupled with the trauma of losing his first child Alexandra to prolonged illness in 1922, pushed Fuller to the brink in 1927. He considered suicide but, as he put it, resolved to commit "egocide" instead, and turn the rest of his life into an experiment about what kind of positive difference the "little individual" could make on the world stage. He called himself "Guinea Pig B" (B for Bucky) and resolved to do his own thinking, starting over from scratch. Hugh Kenner likens this to Descartes' resolve to shut himself in a room until he'd discerned God's truth—a kind of archetypal commitment to a solitary journey.

. . .

It was over this concept of "tensegrity" that early divisions over the issue of Fuller's character and integrity came to the foreground. Ken Snelson, a star pupil at Black Mountain College (1948), at first enchanted by Bucky's spell, became highly disillusioned when it appeared that Fuller planned to abscond with the "tensegrity" idea without properly crediting his student.

Fuller's reputation for egomania and improperly seizing upon others' ideas as his own may be traced to this Fuller-Snelson split, and led many to question whether the geodesic dome, widely credited to Fuller (who took out a number of patents around the idea) was another case in point. . . . Alexander Graham Bell had also made extensive use of the octet truss circa 1907, another one of Fuller's key concepts (also patented).

Fuller's own archives, maintained since his death in 1983 by the Buckminster Fuller Institute (BFI) and his estate (EBF), details his side of the story and he seems to have died with a clear conscience regarding these matters—realizing they would remain bones of contention. . . .

Figure 6.15. *Excerpt from Kirby Urner's biography of R. Buckminster Fuller,* `www.grunch.net/synergetics/bio.html`.

Investigating Controversial Questions

The Snelson controversy concerns discoveries that Fuller called tensegrity, for *tension integrity*. Ken Snelson, a sculptor (`www.grunch.net/snelson/`), gives his version of its history in an email to the *International Journal of Space Structures* in answer to their request for information for a planned special publication on tensegrity (`www.grunch.net/snelson/rmoto.html`). The events happened at Black Mountain College in North Carolina in the summer of 1949. Snelson, who had met Fuller at Black Mountain the previous summer, had spent an aimless year building models or artworks (he couldn't decide whether he was an engineer or an artist) that used geometrical ideas he learned from Fuller.

Snelson's email, which we were not permitted to reprint, tells of his first morning at Black Mountain when he showed Fuller his plywood X-Piece (shown in Figure 6.16). Snelson had sent Fuller photos of the sculpture, but based on Fuller's reaction, he concluded that Fuller had not understood the design. Fuller turned it over and over, studying it carefully. Finally, Fuller asked if he could keep it. Relieved that Fuller was not annoyed with him for having used Bucky geometry for an artwork, Snelson agreed, though he hadn't planned to give it away. Later, according to Snelson, Bucky said that the sculpture had "disappeared" from his apartment.

Figure 6.16.
Ken Snelson's structure at the heart of his controversy with RBF.

At the core of Snelson's belief that he contributed to ideas Fuller took credit for is Fuller's apparently slow comprehension of the X-Piece. Snelson offers a second example of Fuller's not fully comprehending the implications of tensegrity. He says that on the next day, Fuller told him that the idea was clever, but that the configuration was wrong. Rather than using compression members in an X structure, they should be arranged in a tetrahedron. Snelson says he'd already used the tetrahedron in a mobile. He'd decided that the X structure was better than the tetrahedron because the X could grow along all three axes rather than the single axis of the tetrahedron. But he was reluctant to challenge Fuller—students just didn't do such things in those days. Again, Snelson believes Bucky didn't fully comprehend the idea, and therefore didn't think of it first.

Snelson says that the next day he built Bucky a model of the tetrahedral structure using adjustable metal curtain rods. He described himself as "wistful" watching Bucky have his picture taken with the model, but he didn't suspect Fuller's motives.

Fuller said in a letter to Snelson that he mentioned Snelson's role in speeches. But, according to Snelson, he never got credit in print. When in 1959 Fuller's tensegrity ideas were displayed at the Museum of Modern Art in New York City, Snelson, knowing the curator, forced Fuller to admit publicly that Snelson had contributed.

Searching at the Buckminster Fuller Institute for **Snelson**, we quickly find Fuller's version of the incident in *Everything I Know*, Vol. 8, though he incorrectly places it in 1958–1959:

> Then in the second summer at Black Mountain, Ken showed me a sculpture that he had made, and, in an abstract world of sculpture, and what he had made was a-a tensegrity structure. And he had a structural member out here two structural members out here, that were not touching the base, and they were being held together held they were in tension. And I explained to Ken that this was a tensegrity. Man, I

had found, had only developed tensegrity structure in wire wheels and in universal joints. . . . When Ken Snelson showed me this little extension thing he did it was really just an arbitrary form, he saw that you could do it [tension integrity], but he was just, as I say, an artistic form or something startling to look at. And I said, "Ken, that really is the tensegrity and it's what I'm looking for because what you've done I can see relates to the octahedron and this gives me a clue of how this goes together in all the energetic geometry.

So Ken opened up my eyes to the way to go into the geometry.

Fuller clearly sees Snelson as having contributed in the form of an artwork one more instance of tensegrity to the two that Fuller already knew. He seems not to be very defensive in his version.

He is also at peace with the fact that Alexander Graham Bell independently invented the octet truss—a key tensegrity structure. Fuller explains as he answers questions in an interview (**www.grunch.net/synergetics/docs/bellnote. html**):

Q. It seems to me that Bell's tetrahedron, which he developed while working on kites, is very like your geodesic structure?

A. Exactly the same.

Q. When you developed your structures, did you know about the work of Alexander Graham Bell?

A. I did not. I was astonished to learn about it later. It is the way nature behaves, so we both discovered nature. It isn't something you invent. You discover.

The Bell case seems to be a case of independent discovery. According to archivist DeVarco, on two different occasions Bell's descendants gave Fuller octet truss models that Bell had made. So, they apparently harbor no disagreement with this view.

Overall, Snelson's criticism of Fuller mutes the rah-rah enthusiasm of the many sites we have found. RBF has a rock-solid reputation still, but even the finest diamonds have tiny imperfections.

EXPLORING SIDE QUESTIONS

Finally, in terms of filling out our profile of Fuller, there is the repeated mention of buckminsterfullerenes. What are they? The first biography (*Biography.com*) we read ends with the statement:

He has the distinction of having both his names used for a scientific entity, the "fullerene" (also known as a "buckyball"), a form of carbon whose molecule resembles his geodesic dome.

It's a carbon molecule. To find more, we ask Google to search on `buckminster-fullerene` and we find many useful links. From a *Scientific American* link we find a page from the State University of New York at Stony Brook, `sbchem.sunysb.edu/msl/fullerene.html`, showing images of the molecule, and we see that the structure fulfills the "interlocking polygons" requirement of the geodesic dome definition (see Figure 6.17). The next link, `www.msu.edu/~hungerf9/bucky1.html`, is to Michigan State University's Nanotechnology Laboratory, which gives us a definition:

> **Buckminsterfullerene**, C_{60}, the third allotrope of Carbon, was discovered in 1985 by Robert Curl, Harold Kroto, and Richard Smalley. Using laser evaporation of graphite they found C_n clusters (where n>20 and even) of which the most common were found to be C_{60} and C_{70}. For this discovery they were awarded the 1996 Nobel Prize in Chemistry.

Checking the online dictionary to find that *allotrope* means "structural form of" (making buckyballs different from graphite and diamond forms of carbon), we've answered the question: A fullerene is a stable molecule of carbon composed of 60 or 70 atoms in the shape of a geodesic sphere (see Figure 6.17). However, the discovery of fullerenes piques our curiosity, and we decide to go to the Nobel Prize site to learn more about the discovery.

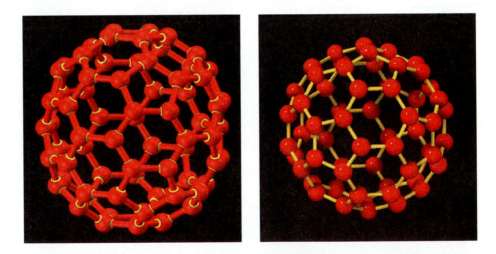

Figure 6.17. *Drawings of buckminster fullerene, C_{60} and C_{70} (also known as fullerenes or buckyballs).*

Recalling that all countries have a country extension, and that Sweden is the home of the Nobel Prize, we correctly guess at the site `www.nobel.se`. There we click `chemistry > laureates >1996` to find the page shown in Figure 6.18. From there we can read the "illustrated presentation" explaining the equipment and experiment that Curl, Kroto, and Smalley used to produce buckyballs and win the Nobel Prize. As it happens, C_{60} has the same structure as a soccer ball: 12 pentagons and 20 hexagons.

Figure 6.18. *The Nobel Prize site for the discovery of the buckminsterfullerene.*

Of course, the mention of soccer gets us to wondering how the A. C. Milan team is doing, so we click up. . . .

CASE STUDY WRAP-UP

We explored Buckminster Fuller's life only because he was an interesting person. We're finished, at least for the moment, so we can put the computer to sleep and get some sleep ourselves. But often the next step is to use the information for some other purpose, say, to write a report. In that case, before turning off the computer we should create a summary file containing:

> Bookmarks from the sites visited—they can be copied from the browser as a group

> Notebook entries of the search terms used with the search engines

> Brief notes on our impressions from the information we found—interesting discoveries, most useful sites, why we followed up on some topics and skipped others, and so forth

This information is our record of the research process, which we can use for writing the report. The reason we should write down our impressions right away is that they won't last. The amazement of new discoveries wears off, we forget things, and time changes our feelings about the content. Though it is important to have time to digest what we've learned and to organize it in our minds, the excitement of learning something new gives a fresh quality that will not be available later.

SUMMARY

The goal of this chapter has been to illustrate curiosity-driven research using the Web, and we have been quite successful (see a summary of our efforts in Figure 6.19). The two main features of this tour through Buckminster Fuller's life were the process of finding the information and the methods of deciding whether the information was authoritative. We tried to use the "right" source for the type of information we wanted.

Searching for Guinea Pig B: The Buckminster Fuller Research Path

The listing below describes the research path followed in this chapter. Most lines represent an access to a WWW document, image, audio or film clip, and so on. Indenting indicates subsidiary actions.

Begin with a Google search because "Buckminster" is a distinctive name; fail—too many hits

Restart by checking online biography sites to find some characterizing term; succeed—find "Dymaxion"

    Learn basic facts about RBF's life, including that he is related to Margaret Fuller

        Check online biography of Margaret Fuller—19th C feminist thinker, died in shipwreck

Check Google for further biographical material using "Dymaxion"; select a highly ranked biography

    Find that he called himself "Guinea Pig B," a characterizing, personal term

    Discover his "little, penniless, and unknown individual" quote and his dream of helping humanity

Check Google for photos to find out what he looks like

Check Google using "Guinea Pig B"

    Find WNET site and four essays: Applewhite, Snyder, DeVarco, Feldman

        Assess sources—Applewhite and Snyder are primary, DeVarco is archivist

        Check on Feldman, first at biography site, then WNET personnel; writer with access to papers

            Read Applewhite's essay for professional assessment—great intellect, creative, influential

            Read Snyder's essay for RBF as father—warm, loving, deeply believed in primary experience

            Read Feldman's essay—threads RFB facts with personal aspects of success, tragedy, family

            Read DeVarco's essay—the "ephemera" of RBF's life; he called Expo dome Taj Majal to Anne

        Summarize our impressions of essays

        View video clip; Fuller passionately argues world hunger/housing woes can be eliminated by 1985

Visit Buckminster Fuller Institute site

    Check BFI's authenticity

Review Basic Chronology—married to Anne; 2 children, one died; many jobs, many awards
Discover *Everything I Know*—42 hours of audio
Listen to Fuller describe Allegra's asking him to become more animated
Discover Dymaxion Map on icosahedron and watch animation
View the Montreal Expo geodesic dome
Wonder how icosahedron and geodesic dome relate
Check dictionaries for definitions—unsatisfactory
Check dictionaries further and interpret definitions relative to map and Expo dome
Assess how complete our knowledge of Fuller is—decide to read another biography
Check the Kirby Urner biography found in the "Guinea Pig B" search
Check out Urner
Discover there is controversy on originality of Fuller's ideas: Snelson, Bell
Check Ken Snelson, the sculptor
Check the *Journal of Space Structures* page giving Snelson's view of discovery
Return to BFI's site and *Everything I Know* for Fuller's view; he acknowledges Snelson
Check an interview with Fuller regarding independent discovery with Bell; he acknowledges it
Conclude our knowledge of Fuller is reasonably complete and balanced
Wonder what a buckminsterfullerene is, and use Google to find citations
Find through *Scientific American* graphic renderings of C_{60} and C_{70}—geodesic spheres, not domes
Find a definition and the discoverers' names from SUNY Stonybrook
Look up *allotrope* in the dictionary and infer the difference from graphite and diamond
Wonder about the discoverers of buckyballs
Navigate Nobel site and find short biographies of the discoverers

Figure 6.19. *Record of the case study search.*

To make the search effective, we wanted to learn enough to ask the right questions. So, we started by checking a brief biography, learned that Fuller had invented something called a Dymaxion house and car, and decided to search for biographical information containing *Dymaxion*. This greatly reduced the hits. In the same way, searching on "Guinea Pig B" led to a rich set of links mostly of primary sources. Later on, "buckminsterfullerene" with its narrow technical meaning led us to that information quickly. We didn't do a Web search each time we wanted information; instead we went directly to a likely source based on the type of information we wanted—dictionary, biography database, WNET personnel, the RFB Institute, the Nobel Prize page. This saved us from "aimless wandering" around the Web.

When we found information, we were always concerned with its authoritativeness. In some cases, it didn't matter much, such as when we checked the short biography to find words like *Dymaxion*. In other cases, we looked for primary sources, knowing that they are the purest forms of information about a topic because they are based on direct experience. For secondary sources, we checked the author's credentials. Secondary sources were valuable because they could both fill in gaps in our knowledge and show us how others interpreted the same information. Our goal was to learn as much as possible from primary sources so that we could interpret the information ourselves, and then to read secondary sources for more viewpoints and information. This strategy helps us to tell other people's opinions from the facts.

Finally, we began the chapter by noting that the Web is better in many ways than reading a book on a particular topic, and it is. In a short time we have found primary data from Fuller, his colleagues, and his family. We have read short biographies, looked at photographs and film clips, heard audio clips, consulted the dictionary, watched animations, and used many other types of reference material. The multimedia resources gave us the chance to form our own opinions based on more than printed words. Computer searches, including global searches with Google, site searches, and page searching, have speeded up our discovery of information. We have read parts of several authors' essays on Fuller. And the links provided by people who found the material before us have connected us to information we might not have known existed. Truly we have discovered Buckminster Fuller based on our own curiosity.

EXERCISES

True/False and Multiple Choice

1. A tertiary source draws directly from personal experience.

2. Each step away from a primary source increases the likelihood of error and omissions.

3. Books have limited research value because they:
   A. take a long time to produce
   B. contain only information the author selects
   C. contain only a single point of view
   D. all of the above

4. Advantages of the Web over a book include:
   A. the Web can be easily updated
   B. easier access
   C. dissemination of information is faster and cheaper
   D. all of the above

5. A primary source is:
   A. the only source on a topic
   B. a source with personal experience
   C. a source that has been verified
   D. all of the above

6. Secondary sources are valuable for all of the following reasons except:
   A. refuting primary sources
   B. organizing information
   C. providing interpretation
   D. filling in gaps

Short Answer

1. _____ is research for the sake of learning.

2. To look for pictures on the Web, you could do a Google search for _____.

3. The _____ folder contains a list of all the Web sites you have visited.

4. _____ are used to save the name and address of a Web site for future reference.

5. Information that comes directly from the source is called a(n) _____.

6. A _____ is someone who reports information from a primary source.

Exercises

1. Find Buckminster Fuller's birthday. Who does he share it with?

2. Do a search for Thomas Jefferson. Find a list of his inventions. Narrow the search to sites on Jefferson and one of those inventions.

3. Play "Six Degrees of Kevin Bacon" and pick two starts to see how many related hits you can find for both of them. Limit the search by ignoring topics such as reviews and books.

4. Perform a search for "Buckminster" and "Dymaxion" to see how many hits there are.

5. Do a search for Ernest Hemmingway. Locate a primary source, a secondary source, and two tertiary sources. Do the sites agree or are there inconsistencies?

6. Do a search for Richard Nixon and his dog, Checkers. Then limit the search until there are less than 100 hits.

7. Do a search for Alaska and coffee plantation. Then limit the search until there are less than 100 hits.

8. Organize the Favorites folder on your computer. Arrange the Favorites into classifications. Create additional folders as needed to organize the files. Copy the Favorites, if needed, so that they can be listed in more than one place.

9. Do a search for Grace Murray Hopper. Find a picture of the first computer bug. Read the stories behind it.

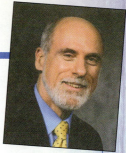

VINTON G. CERF is widely known as the co-designer of the TCP/IP protocols and the architecture of the Internet. As vice president of MCI Digital Information Services from 1982 to 1986, he led the engineering of MCI Mail, the first commercial e-mail service to be connected to the Internet. During his tenure (1976–1982) with the U.S. Department of Defense's Advanced Research Projects Agency (DARPA), he played a key role leading the development of Internet and Internet-related data packet and security technologies. Vinton holds a B.S. in Mathematics from Stanford University and a Ph.D. in Computer Science from UCLA.

How did you get started in all of this?

I was working as a programmer at UCLA in the late 1960s. My job was supported by the U.S. Defense Advanced Research Projects Agency (called ARPA then, called DARPA now). I was working in the laboratory of Prof. Leonard Kleinrock on the Network Measurement Center of the newly-created ARPANET. I was responsible for programming a computer that was used to capture performance information about the ARPANET and to report this information back for comparison with mathematical models and predictions of the performance of the network.

Several of the other graduate students and I were responsible for working on the "host level protocols" of the ARPANET—the procedures that would allow different kinds of computers on the network to interact with each other. It was a fascinating exploration into a new world (for me) of distributed computing and communication.

Did you imagine that the Internet protocol would become as pervasive as it is today when you first designed the protocol?

When Bob Kahn and I first worked on this in 1973, I think we were mostly focused on the central question: how can we make heterogeneous packet networks interoperate with one another, assuming we cannot actually change the networks themselves. We hoped that we could find a way to permit an arbitrary collection of packet-switched networks to be interconnected in a transparent fashion, so that host computers could communicate end-to-end without having to do any translations in between. I think we knew that we were dealing with powerful and expandable technology but I doubt we had a clear image of what the world would be like with 100,000,000's of computers all interlinked on the Internet.

And what do you now envision for the future of the Internet?

I believe the Internet and networks in general will continue to proliferate. There is convincing evidence that there will be billions of Internet-enabled devices on the Internet, including appliances like cell phones, refrigerators, home servers, televisions, as well as the usual array of laptops, servers, and so on.

What are the challenges you are facing?

Big challenges include support for mobility, battery life, capacity of the access links to the network, and ability to scale the optical core of the network in an unlimited fashion. Designing an interplanetary extension of the Internet is a project in which I am deeply engaged at the Jet Propulsion Laboratory. The list is long!

You founded the Internet Society whose motto is "the Internet is for Everyone." What is it doing to achieve that objective?

The Internet Society Task Force was created to analyze and make recommendations on efforts to deal with a range of social issues linked to the Internet's fundamental operation. To be honest, the first attempt to form this group got bogged down in administrivia and arguments over how the task force would operate, be governed and tasks and publications suitably monitored. I believe there are many social issues that can be addressed, in part, through the voluntary cooperation of the ISOC chapters and members. More access to Internet is high on my list of agenda items.

What surprises you most about how the Internet is used today?

The things that surprise me most include:

1. The use of the Internet for proxy voting at annual meetings.
2. Instant messaging and its use during voice conference calls.
3. The amount and variety of information-sharing that goes on, not even counting Napster. For example, the sharing of information via personal web pages.
4. The popularity of online role-playing games (including Sims, Everquest, etc.)
5. The failure to effectually apply the Internet for health care paperwork.
6. The slow process by which Education has made use of the Internet.
7. The increasing popularity of streaming audio (and video where speeds allow).

Do you have any advice for students studying IT?

Think outside the limitations of existing systems—imagine what might be possible; but then do the hard work of figuring out how to get there from the current state of affairs. Dare to dream: a half dozen colleagues and I at the Jet Propulsion Laboratory have been working on the design of an interplanetary extension of the terrestrial Internet. It may take decades to implement this, mission by mission, but to paraphrase:

"A man's reach should exceed his grasp, or what are the heavens for?"

An interplanetary Internet?

It is an effort to standardize communication protocols used in space exploration so that each new mission can make use of earlier mission communication resources. Eventually a kind of interplanetary backbone network would arise from the accumulation of these standardized communication capabilities. This will allow investigators to have direct access to their instruments and robotic vehicles, to control sensor systems, and capture information for further analysis. I am excited by the thought that we might have nearly continuous communication with sensor systems on other planets and their satellites. It will transform space science.

interview
VINTON G. CERF

ALGORITHMS AND DIGITIZING INFORMATION

Having now become more skillful with information technology, it is time to learn a few of the underlying concepts that make IT possible. Like black holes in astronomy or natural selection in ecology, the underlying phenomena of IT are interesting to learn about. The difference is, IT concepts can have direct applicability to your daily use of IT.

In Part II we learn about how information is represented, from basic bits through sound and video to virtual reality. We also explain what a transistor is, and how a few million of them could process information. And we introduce the fundamental idea of an algorithm, though you've already seen several in Part I. At the end you will have a basic idea of what's happening inside a computer and how it stores your information.

In your experience so far, you have known the frustration when some aspect of IT is not working the way you want. So, you know that figuring out what's wrong is one of the most important capabilities a computer user can possess. Though we cannot give you a guaranteed, works-every-time algorithm to debug your problems, we do give useful guidelines that can help you more quickly solve any IT mystery.

TO ERR IS HUMAN

An Introduction to Debugging

> Explain how ordinary precision differs from precision required in IT

> Describe the five-step strategy for debugging
> - Explain the purpose of each step
> - Give an example of each step

> Apply the five-step strategy for debugging the HTML code for a Web page
> - State what changes you made during debugging
> - State what changes were unnecessary

> Learn how to approach debugging when you don't understand the system

One item could not be deleted because it was missing.
                    —MAC OS SYSTEM 7.0 ERROR MESSAGE

You are not thinking. You are merely being logical.
                    — NEILS BOHR TO ALBERT EINSTEIN

A COMMON saying among computer users is "To err is human, but to really foul things up takes a computer." One characteristic that makes a computer so useful—and sometimes so frustrating—is that it does exactly what it is told to do, and nothing more. Because it will follow each instruction "to the letter" and continually check itself, it operates almost perfectly. So, in truth, the computer doesn't foul things up at all. We humans—those of us who write the software and those of us who use it—are not perfect, of course. And that combination *can* really foul things up. So we have to learn how to discover what's wrong and to get ourselves out of our difficulties. Learning debugging techniques—the subject of this chapter—is perhaps the best way to deal successfully with mistakes and errors, and to avoid the foul-ups in the first place.

The first goal of this chapter is to recognize that the greatest, most common source of problems is our lack of precision. Computers never get what we *mean*, only what we *say*. So we must say exactly what we mean. The next objective is to understand what debugging is in modern IT systems. We then introduce the debugging process using a student/parent scenario. This lets us analyze the process during the student/parent interaction. The next goal is to abstract from the story the principles of debugging. The principles do not give a mechanical procedure guarantee-ing success, but rather a reliable set of guidelines. We then apply the principles to debugging a faulty Web page design. This detective work will not reveal *who*dunit because we're the most likely "perps," but rather *what*-dunit, our error. The final objective is to illustrate debug-ging a system when we have no idea how the system works.

PRECISION: THE HIGH STANDARDS OF IT

When using information technology, we must be precise. The standards of accuracy in IT are extremely high, much higher than many people's usual level of precision.

Precision in Everyday Life

In normal conversation, for example, when giving telephone numbers, many North Americans will say "oh" rather than "zero," as in "five-five-five-oh-oh-one-two" for 555-0012. Of course, the listener knows that phone numbers are all numeric, and simply makes the mental conversion. A computer does not know that fact unless it has been specifically programmed to know it and to make the conversion. The "oh" and "zero" are different (bit sequences) to a computer. So, if we type "oh" for "zero," a computer would simply accept the input, try to use it literally, and cause an error.

Merrily Mistaken. Sometimes we use this confusion on purpose, as in Canada's alternating letter-numeral postal code for Santa Claus, H0H 0H0.

The "oh" for "zero" substitution is probably used by North Americans because it is easier to say, having only one syllable. (Other English speakers say "*naught*" for "*zero.*") It is probably not the sort of error we would make if we were asked to type a phone number into a database system or modem software. And, even if it were, the software would catch the error, because some software systems *have* been programmed to know that phone numbers are all numeric. Rather than converting "oh" to "zero," however, they usually just object to being given nonnumeric input. But there are many cases in which the computer cannot help us when we make an error.

EXACTLY HOW ACCURATE IS "PRECISE"?

New email or Web users often type in an incorrect email address or URL. A common error is to confuse "oh" and "zero," or "el" and "one," though there are many other mistakes new users can make. If computers can catch mistakes like "oh" for "zero" in modem software or databases, why can't they catch them in email addresses and URLs? The reason is simple: Although "oh" and "el" are illegal in all phone numbers, they are not illegal in all email addresses or URLs. For example, `flo@exisp.com` and `f10@exisp.com` could both be legitimate email addresses. If the software made "zero" for "oh" and "one" for "el" substitutions, poor Flo would never get any email. So, computers must accept the letters or numbers as typed for email addresses or URLs. Corrections are not possible. Users must be as precise as they can be when entering such information.

FITCAUTION

Be Sensitive. Be alert to case sensitivity—the difference between lower- and upper-case—in email addresses and URLs. To computers, *C* and *c* are different in some cases, and in others they have been programmed to ignore case. For example, case does not matter in Internet domain names—`flo@exisp.com` and `flo@ExISP.COM` are the same—because case is normalized for DNS lookup. But frequently the "local" information in URLs—that is, the text after / symbols—is case sensitive because it is processed by the destination Web server. So, `www.exisp.com/flo/home/` and `www.exisp.com/FLO/HOME/` may be different. When in doubt, assume that case matters.

Lexical Structures

The general principle operating is this: Call the kinds of inputs just discussed **field inputs** because they are the sorts of information that are entered into boxes on forms that are used for names, code numbers, user IDs, files, folder names, and so on. All such field inputs are governed by some **lexical structure**, rules about the legal form for input fields. The lexical structure limits the symbols that can be used in specific positions, possibly how many symbols can be used (i.e., a length limit), and possibly which punctuation symbols can be used. Lexical constraints can be very restrictive. For example, the lexical structure for inputting course grades is limited to at most two symbols: the first symbol must be chosen from {A, B, C, D, F} and the second symbol must be chosen from {+, −, ♭}. (The ♭ denotes *blank*.) So, A+ is OK, but C++ is wrong. Lexical constraints can be loose, too, allowing any sequence of symbols of any length. Computers check to see that the lexical constraints are met, preventing lexical errors. But if the lexical structure permits both alternatives of a commonly confused symbol, no check can be made. Both alternatives are legal, as in UserIDs. Precision is essential.

FITTIP

Spacing Out. The ♭ represents blank or space. This solves the problem that spaces must be visible in some cases so that we know that they're there. "Multiplication dots," •, are used by word processors (Chapter 2), but when they are easily confused with other symbols, we use ♭ to represent blank.

Because we have to be accurate when supplying any input to a computer, we can avoid considerable grief by being as exact as we possibly can be. It is obviously faster and less frustrating to enter information exactly than to be sloppy, to have to find the mistake and enter it correctly.

DEBUGGING: WHAT'S THE PROBLEM?

Debugging is the method of figuring out why a process or system doesn't work properly. Debugging is usually applied to computer or communication systems, especially software, but the techniques are the same whether the systems are mechanical, architectural, business, or others. Though debugging relies on logical reasoning and is usually "learned from experience," there are debugging principles and effective strategies that we can learn. Knowing these techniques is important in information technology because a major part of using IT systems is figuring out why things are not working properly.

Debugging in Everyday Life

People debug or **troubleshoot** all the time. When their cars don't start, they figure out whether the battery is dead or whether there is no fuel in the tank. Faults and failures in everyday life usually involve correct, working systems with a broken or worn-out part. That is, the system is properly designed and constructed, but some part failed. The car's dead battery keeps it from starting, for example. When the part is replaced, the system works.

Debugging in Information Technology

Debugging an information system is slightly different. In information systems, we might have entered wrong data or wrong configuration information in a working system. When it's corrected, the system works. But another possibility with information systems is that they might have a **logical design error.** An analogy in car design would be if the backup lights, which should only work when the car is in reverse, come on when we step on the brakes. This would be a design or construction error. In software, such logical errors are quite possible even in commercial software, and users must be aware that a correct, working system cannot always be relied upon. Despite that fact, we will always first assume we have a "correct, working system."

Wrong Data or Wrong Command?

Remember that when we are debugging an information system, we are generally part of the problem. In an information system, we command the computer to do a task, and give it input. When this input gets the computer into an error state despite our belief that the input should have worked, the two possibilities—wrong data or command—involve us. Our commands or data led to the problem, and so we'll have to fix it. Computers cannot debug themselves, though they do detect and correct low-level errors such as memory errors. The two types of mistakes are treated differently.

Fixing Wrong Data. When our wrong data creates an error, either we *understand* the system and just goofed up, or we *don't understand* the system and goofed up. If we understand the system, we just begin afresh and navigate through the data entry again, being more careful. Typically, in these cases, we have some idea where we might have made the mistake, and fixing it is easy. If we don't understand the system, the problem is almost certainly *our* conceptual error. In such cases, debugging will rely more on the how-to-learn-a-new-system guidelines given in Chapter 2 than on the debugging guidelines here, though we'll probably need the debugging principles, too. Of course, the situation is not always so neatly divided. Often we *think* we understand the system, but don't. Then we still have a conceptual error, but the conceptual error is with our understanding.

Fixing a Wrong Command. When a command is at fault, we must debug the system, even if we didn't make the system. We will follow the steps outlined in this chapter, but we also need precision in typing and thinking so that we don't create new errors. Introducing new errors simply makes the problem worse, usually much worse, so it is a good idea to rivet our attention on debugging the immediate problem, putting aside distractions and other concerns until later.

{ G R E A T **FIT** M O M E N T S }

Computer Pioneer Grace Hopper > >

Rear Admiral Grace Murray Hopper, a computer pioneer, coined the term bug for a glitch in a computer system while she was working on the Harvard Mark I in the 1940s. When the Mark II computer got a moth jammed in one of its relays (electro-mechanical switches), bringing the machine down, technicians taped the bug into the machine's logbook (Figure 7.1).

Hopper was one of the inventors of a kind of software known as a compiler, which translates a programming language into machine instructions (see Chapter 9), and she greatly influenced the development of the programming language Cobol. Conscious of the physical limitations on computing, Hopper used a length of copper wire (approximately one foot long) to illustrate a "nanosecond" ($1/1,000,000,000$th of a second), because it is the distance electricity can travel in that time.

A Navy ship was named in her honor.

FITBYTE

A Bug's Life. What insect was jokingly called the first bug? On a recent TV game show, answering this question correctly was worth $1 million. The answer? A moth.

Figure 7.1. *The Harvard Mark II logbook noting "First actual case of bug being found," from the Smithsonian Institution.*

Using the Computer to Debug

Finally, not only is the computer unable to debug itself, we can't debug it directly, either. That is, the error is internal to the computer, either in the data stored or in the logic of the software. To get information about the error, we have to ask the computer to tell us what data it has stored, to run the faulty software, and so forth. We are one step removed from the failure and what's causing it, and we need the computer to help us find the problem.

A modern version of the 1960s slogan "If you're not part of the solution, you're part of the problem" is: "If it's not part of the solution, it can't be part of the problem." That is, if you can find a solution without using a problem (faulty) part of the system, you've achieved your goal. This idea of bypassing an error with an alternative approach is called a **workaround**. Workarounds are essential when you are using commercial software. Bugs in commercial systems are usually not fixed until the next version, so we have to work around them until then.

A DIALOG ABOUT DEBUGGING

Consider the following scenario:

You and your friends have made a video spoofing college life. You showed it to your cluster in the dorm, and everyone thought it was hilariously funny. You sent a copy to your parents, hardly able to wait to hear their praise of your cleverness, but you heard nothing. Eventually you phoned them to ask if they got the tape, and they replied, "Yes. We tried it in the VCR player, but something's wrong." Your impulse is to say, "Fix it!" but you ask brightly, "What's wrong?"

You are about to debug your parents' VCR. What you know is that your parents have tried the videotape in their VCR player—which you're very familiar with, having spent most of last vacation watching movies on it—and it didn't play the tape. That's all the information you have, and it's typical.

Debugging is solving a mystery, and just as we watch detectives solve mysteries in whodunits, we should watch ourselves solving the mystery when debugging. Why? Because this approach will probably get us to a solution faster than if we aimlessly "try stuff." By purposely asking questions such as, "Do I need more clues (inputs)?"; "Are my clues reliable?"; and "What is the theory to explain the problem?" we will focus better and discover a solution faster.

The first step in debugging is to check that the error is reproducible. Computers are deterministic, which means that they will do exactly the same thing every time if given the same input. But there is a tiny possibility that a one-time transient glitch caused the problem, so start by trying to re-create the problem.

You ask your folks,

"Can you try the tape again?"

And, as the scenario unfolds, your parents report that there is nothing showing on the TV.

The next step is to be sure that you know exactly what the problem is. Mystery novels usually have a dead body, making the problem clear. The mystery is who murdered the person, not why the dead person failed to show up for work the next morning. But in information technology, the computer may perform a sequence of operations *after* an error, and they must be eliminated first as the focal point of the debugging. For example, the reason there are no mailing labels coming out of the printer may be due to a printer problem, but it could be a problem with the word processor or database that is sending the labels to the printer, or it could be that the file containing the addresses is empty; that is, there are no addresses to print. We don't want to be debugging the printer when the problem is an empty file. So, finding out what exactly is the problem is critical.

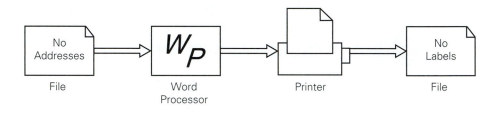

Your parents should be a little more specific about the problem. You patiently ask,

> "What's on the screen?"
>
> "Nothing."
>
> "Is it black nothing, blue nothing, or snow nothing?"
>
> "Snow."

A standard next step is to check all of the "obvious" sources of error. Of course, if the error were all that obvious, you wouldn't be debugging—you'd have fixed the problem and be on your way. What kinds of errors are obvious depends on the problem being debugged, naturally, but checking inputs, connections, links, and so on is standard.

Ask your parents to check all of the obvious causes:

> "Is there power to the VCR?" (The TV obviously has power.)
>
> "Yes."
>
> "Is the tape in the machine?" (It couldn't be upside down because the drive mechanism doesn't allow that.)
>
> "Yes."
>
> "Is the tape rewound?"

"Yes."

"Have you clicked Play?"

"Yes."

"Is the tape advancing?"

"Sounds like it."

"What happens?"

"Snow reigns."

Clearly the VCR is pretty much as you left it. Except it isn't playing your hilarious tape.

It's now time to apply a basic strategy of debugging: isolate the problem by dividing the operation into those parts that are working and those that are not. This means coming up with a theory about where the problem is located, and possibly gathering more information. At this point you should take nothing for granted. Limit the number of untested assumptions you make. The error could be anywhere. The goal is to eliminate as many possibilities as you can, or to focus in on the failing part.

In the case of your parents' VCR, the system has two basic units, the TV and the VCR player. The data, which is on the tape, is read by the player and sent to the TV for display. You ask yourself, can either of them be eliminated from consideration? If the VCR were OK and the TV were faulty, the TV probably wouldn't show regular programs. You ask your parents:

"Do you get normal TV programs?"

"Define normal."

"You know what I mean . . . ABC?"

"Yes."

So, if the TV is OK, the VCR must be broken, though it seems from the earlier conversation that it is working mechanically; that is, the videotape is running through it. So, if it's OK, what other parts are there? There's the cable connecting the VCR to the TV.

"Are the TV and VCR connected?"

"Didn't look, but it's the way it's always been."

So, they're connected as you left them when you left for college. And there are no other parts.

Everything seems to check out. This is a common situation in debugging. You analyze the problem, perhaps getting more data, and conclude that everything is OK. Except it's not. There is a bug somewhere. Though it is natural to become frustrated, the best response is to review your analysis. You've made some assumptions, gathered data, made some tests, interpreted the results, and made some deductions. Ask yourself, "Is there a wrong assumption?" "Am I misunderstanding what the data mean?" "Did I make a wrong deduction?" It's important at this point to think objectively about the process. *A good approach is to step through the process from beginning to end, comparing what should be happening with what is happening.*

So, starting from the beginning, you ask your parents to put in a different tape.

"OK, we put in the tape of your sister's wedding, but it's the same thing. Snow."

You know that tape works. You had to sit through the whole two tedious hours of it last summer.

"Is it rewound?"

"Yes. Just did it."

"When you clicked on Rewind, was the screen blue and the letters R-E-W displayed?"

This is a prediction you make about how the TV/VCR system is supposed to operate based on your knowledge or experience with it.

"No, it's still snow."

At this point you have a prediction that doesn't match the facts. That's what you're looking for. Why would the VCR not be telling the TV that it is rewinding the tape? Maybe because they're not connected.

"Can you check if the cable from the VCR is plugged into the back of the TV?"

And now you know the problem. As you're waiting for your parents to verify that the cable is not connected to the back of the TV, you recall last summer when the Women's World Cup Soccer final was on and how a bunch of your friends came over to watch the game and you carried the TV out to the patio. Everyone sat around eating pizza and cheering. It was late when you carried the TV back into the house, and you postponed plugging in the VCR cable until morning. And forgot. When you left for college they were still unconnected.

"Nope, the cable wasn't plugged into the TV. It's working now. How'd you figure that out?"

"Got lucky, I guess. Hope you like the video."

DEBUGGING RECAP

The key point of the debugging illustration is not that debugging occasionally reveals embarrassing errors, but rather that there is a semi-organized process to follow to find out what's wrong. The key points were

> Make sure that you can reproduce the error.

> Determine exactly what the problem is.

> Eliminate the "obvious" causes.

> Divide the process, separating out the parts that work from the part that does not.

> When you reach a dead end, reassess your information, asking where you may be making wrong assumptions or conclusions; then step through the process again.

> As you work through the process from start to finish, make predictions about what should happen and verify that the predictions are fulfilled.

This is not a recipe, but it is a useful set of guidelines. Debugging requires tough, logical reasoning to figure out what's wrong. But, it's possible to do, and though it is not as entertaining as deducing whodunit from the few clues in a mystery novel, there is a certain satisfaction to figuring it out

FITBYTE

Closer Examination. Watching yourself debug as though you were a mystery detective is important. It helps you be more objective—is the debugger (you) chasing the wrong lead?—and it helps you separate yourself from the process, reducing frustration. Thinking about what you are doing is a good idea generally, of course. After all, Socrates said, "The unexamined life is not worth leading."

BUTTERFLIES AND BUGS: A CASE STUDY

To illustrate the debugging principles in action, we develop a small table in HTML. Our goal page is shown in Figure 7.2. The HTML code we've written is shown in Figure 7.3, together with the Netscape browser's interpretation of it. Obviously, there is an error somewhere. We could study the HTML very, very closely and "brain out" where the error is, or we could use the debugging strategy. Follow along online; the file is at www.aw.com/snyder.

Butterflies Only -- No Bugs

Food 'n' Foto

Name	Larval Diet	Picture
Behr's Metalmark	Buckwheat	
Bog Copper	Cranberries	
Satyr Comma	Nettles	

Figure 7.2. The intended HTML table.

```
<html>
 <head>
  <title>Butterflies</title>
 </head>
<body>
<h1> Butterflies Only — No Bugs</h1>

 <table border width="50%">
 <caption><b>Food 'n' Foto</b></caption>
  <tr bgcolor="silver">
    <td> Name </td>
    <td> Larval Diet</td>
    <td> Picture </td> </tr>

    <td>Behr's Metalmark</td>
    <td>Buckwheat</td>
    <td align="center"> <img src="butterflies/Apodvirg.jpg
       width="80" height="60"></td>

    <td>Bog Copper</td>
    <td>Cranberries</td>
    <td align="center"> <img src="butterflies/Bog.jpg
       width="80" height="60"></td>

    <td>Satyr Comma</td>
    <td>Nettles</td>
    <td align="center"> <img src="butterflies/Satyr.ipg"
       width="80" height="60"></td>
  </tr>
 </table>
</body>
</html>
```

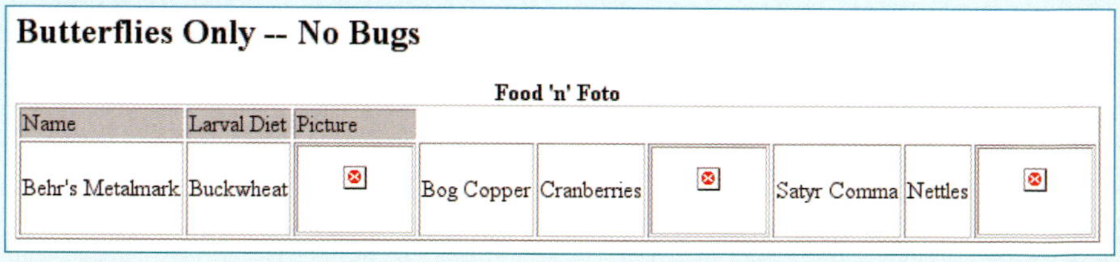

Butterflies Only -- No Bugs								
				Food 'n' Foto				
Name	Larval Diet	Picture						
Behr's Metalmark	Buckwheat	⊠	Bog Copper	Cranberries	⊠	Satyr Comma	Nettles	⊠

Figure 7.3. Faulty HTML text and its rendering in the browser.

Applying the Steps in Debugging HTML

As we begin, watching ourselves debugging the HTML, we recall that the first step is to be sure we can re-create the error.

Reproduce the Error. So, we close Netscape and reopen our file using a "fresh" copy of that browser. Unfortunately the results are the same. In fact, Internet Explorer produces the same result, so it is definitely a problem with our HTML.

Determine the Problem Exactly. The next step is to determine the problem exactly. In the case of debugging HTML, identifying the problem is simple: just look at the page. We have a table with no pictures and nine columns, so there seem to be two bugs here. There could be more, but we focus on these, guessing that problems like the caption that is supposed to be centered over the table, and is now centered over the broken table, will be in the right place when the table is right. So, we focus on the two problems: too many columns and missing images.

Eliminate the Obvious. Once we know what the problem is, we look for the "obvious" errors. The most obvious HTML error is to forget to close a tag; that is, to forget the matching "slash-tag." Checking the HTML, we see that every tag is matched. However, we do get lucky. In reading the HTML text, we notice that our triples of cell data are not all surrounded by the row tags, `<tr>` and `</tr>`. We have row tags around the heading row—the silver background of the heading proves that—but not around the others. Surrounding them with row tags produces the result in Figure 7.4, a definite improvement. As we predicted, the caption is now centered over the table. Notice that although we described the problem as too many columns, the actual bug was too few rows.

Butterflies Only -- No Bugs

Food 'n' Foto

Name	Larval Diet	Picture
Behr's Metalmark	Buckwheat	⊗
Bog Copper	Cranberries	⊗
Satyr Comma	Nettles	⊗

Figure 7.4. Page with row tags added.

With one bug swatted, we focus on why there are no pictures. Another obvious error in HTML is to get the relative pathnames wrong, and when checking our **butterflies** directory (see Figure 7.5), we notice that we indeed have an inconsistency.

Figure 7.5. Files in the butterflies *folder.*

The names are capitalized in the HTML and they are lowercase in the directory. Though we may not know whether case matters for this computer, we make the change anyway. And when we try out the revised page, it looks no different from Figure 7.4. Apparently the change didn't hurt the program, but it didn't help either. There must be a different error. Because the relative pathname directs the browser into a directory to find the file, it could still be wrong. Removing the indirection—that is, the use of the subdirectory to store the images—may help. So, we move the butterfly images into the same directory as the HTML for our page, and rewrite the `<img...>` tags to remove the **butterflies/** directory level. The table data for the Metalmark becomes

```
<td align="center"> <img src="apodvirg.jpg width="80"
    height="60"></td>
```

But there is no improvement. What else is there to check?

Divide Up the Process. Having run out of obvious errors and with everything checking out, we move on to the next step of debugging, which is to divide the system to focus on the faulty parts. Again, HTML is relatively easy because the page shows visually where the error must be. It almost certainly must be in the `<img...>` tags. Ignoring the rest of the HTML, we carefully analyze that text, using the **View > Page Source** feature of the Web browser. The source display shows, using color and different fonts, how the browser interprets our HTML. Netscape displays the line as

```
<td align="center"> <img src="apodvirg.jpg width="80"
    height="60"></td>
```

whereas Internet Explorer shows it as

```
<td align="center"> <img src="apodvirg.jpg width="80"
    height="60"></td>
```

Our simplified relative pathname attribute is displayed, but its coloring is strange. The browser shows that the blue file name includes the word `width`, which is wrong. We then notice that there is no closing quote mark after the file name. With no closed quote, the pathname spills into the `width` specification. Fixing only this line produces the result shown in Figure 7.6.

The fact that this row is improved indicates that this is the fix, so we change the other two lines, producing the result shown in Figure 7.7. Focusing our attention on the `<img...>` tags has helped, but apparently not quite enough.

Although adding a closed quote didn't display the Satyr Comma's image, it did change the spacing. So, the quote was the problem, and we infer that perhaps there is something wrong with the file. We can see the thumbnail image (Figure 7.5), but that doesn't mean there isn't a problem. Sometimes, derived data (thumbnail) is OK, but the file has some other error. One debugging strategy is to run an experiment, so we try to use the `satyr.jpg` file in another application. And it works fine. What can the problem be?

Figure 7.6. The result of revising one row of HTML.

Figure 7.7. The result of including quotes after all pathnames.

Assess, then Step through the Process. Let's review our progress so far: We have corrected the capitalization, so that can't be a problem. We have changed the relative pathnames so that they don't involve the directory **butterflies**, and that works, which we know because two pictures do display. We have fixed the quote, so now the table cells match in all cases. We have checked the Satyr Comma image file and it works in another application. Basically, the HTML should work. We must be making a wrong assumption or misunderstanding the evidence.

Focusing on the `<img...>` tag must be the right strategy. We assumed that the "quotation mark fix" corrected the names for each file. That's certainly right for the first two butterflies, and we thought it was right for the Satyr Comma, based on the fact that it fixed the table spacing. But maybe not. Reviewing the third image tag using the browser's **Source View** again,

```
<td align="center"> <img src="satyr.ipg" width="80"
    height="60"> </td>
```

we see that indeed all of the parameters to the attributes (blue) are interpreted correctly. However, there is one tiny mistake: the file extension has been written `ipg` rather than `jpg`. It's not particularly visible in Figure 7.3, but it's there. So, we had jumped to conclusions about the "quotation mark fix." It helped, but it didn't eliminate the third `<img...>` tag from consideration. When we correct the extension, the result is as shown in Figure 7.8. This solves the problem, but when we compare it to the goal page, we notice there is still a small difference.

The column headings are not correct. Reviewing the figures, we see that it's obvious this has been a problem the whole time. It just wasn't particularly noticeable, given the other problems. And thinking about it, it's clear what the problem is. Tables in HTML should have a **table heading** tag, `<th>` and `</th>`, rather than a table data tag. Correcting that detail gives the goal page, completing the debugging task. The column headings are now bold and centered. We revise the text to restore the relative pathnames to use the `butterflies` subdirectory, as we originally intended.

Figure 7.8. *The corrected file extension page, left, and the goal page, right.*

Butterflies and Bugs Postmortem

The bugs in the HTML text have been crushed. In the process we made a series of conjectures, tried different changes to the program, ran a couple of experiments, and drew conclusions. How did we do? Certainly the result turned out fine.

Changes Made. For the record, we made the following changes to the HTML during the debugging process:

1. Enclosed the table rows with `<tr>` `</tr>` tags.

2. Corrected the capitalization of the file names.

3. Simplified the pathnames to avoid referring to the `butterflies` subdirectory.

4. Corrected the quotation mark problem.

5. Corrected the file extension problem for the Satyr Comma.

6. Fixed the `<th>` `</th>` tags for the first row.

7. Restored the pathnames to allow the images to be kept in the `butterflies` directory.

Unnecessary Changes. Of these seven changes, only 1, 4, 5, and 6 were necessary to fix the program. The other changes were not needed: change 2 was not needed because the file names are not case sensitive; change 3 was not needed because there was no problem with the relative pathnames; and change 7 reversed change 3. The unnecessary changes were introduced when we made wrong conjectures about the cause of the error. Making changes that are unnecessary is quite typical, because making incorrect conjectures is also quite typical. Luckily these changes didn't make the situation worse, but it is possible to introduce new errors when following the wrong logical path.

Hiding Other Errors. When we first described the errors, we thought we had two: too many columns and no pictures. In fact, we had four errors:

1. Too many columns, which was actually not enough rows.

2. No pictures, because of a consistent error of leaving out the closing quote.

3. No Satyr Comma picture, because of a mistyped extension.

4. Wrong heading tags.

Error 3 was hidden by error 2, and we simply didn't notice error 4 at first. One error hidden by another is also typical. Though this hidden error didn't have any effect on the other errors here, hidden errors often do have an effect, which can make bugs hard to find. Interacting errors can be very difficult to track down because they can make the data seem very confusing. For that reason, we must always remember that more than one error could be causing the observed problems.

Viewing the Source. Notice that the most effective technique in our debugging exercise was to use the browser's **Source View** feature. Seeing the color- and font-coded HTML source told us how the browser interpreted our page. This revealed an error and then confirmed that it had been corrected. In general, one of the most powerful debugging techniques is to find ways for the computer to tell us the meaning of the information it stores or the effects of the commands it executes. Having the computer say how it's interpreting the instructions can separate the case in which we tell it to do the wrong thing from the case in which we command it correctly but the computer is doing it wrong. This is an important difference for finding a bug.

Little Errors, Big Problems. Finally, the errors in the HTML code were—with the exception of forgetting the row tags—quite tiny: three missing quotation marks, a wrong character in the file extension, and a wrong character in table heading tags. Of the 582 non-space characters in the original file, the 27 row tags (27=3(4 + 5)) and three quotes represent a 5 percent addition. The four character corrections are less than 1 percent. But, as we've seen, a single missing or erroneous character can ruin the HTML source. The conclusion: We must be extremely precise.

NO PRINTER OUTPUT: A CLASSIC SCENARIO

Though debugging HTML is possible because we know and write HTML, we don't create most computer systems, and they are extremely complex, way beyond our understanding. A standard personal computer and its software are more complex in several ways than the (noncomputer parts of the) space shuttle. As users, we have no idea how something so complex works, so how is it possible to troubleshoot a system we do not understand?

Of course, we cannot debug software and information systems at the detailed level used by programmers or engineers. If there is a basic, conceptual error in the system, users probably won't find it. But we don't have to. Before we ever come in contact with a system, it has been extensively tested. This testing doesn't eliminate all errors, but it probably means that the "standard operations" used by "average" users have been run through their paces many times. They should be bug-free, and we should be able to depend on the software.

FITBYTE

> **Putting It to the Test.** As noted in Chapter 2, "getting out and getting back in" often works when an application is not operating correctly. The reason this tends to work is related to how software is tested. Beginning with a fresh configuration, the testing proceeds "forward" into the application, with the common operations getting the most attention. So the most stable part of a system is the part that is reachable from an initial configuration—the part you first meet when you're "getting back in."

To illustrate debugging a system without understanding it, consider a classic debugging scenario: You try to print a document and nothing comes out of the printer. This problem happens often to all users. In many ways this situation is like our videotape example. Like the TV/VCR system, the computer/printer system is connected by a cable, part of the system is mechanical, the flow of information is from one device to the other, and the system has worked in the past.

Applying the Debugging Strategy

The printing problem is solved just as the videotape problem was solved: *reproduce the error, understand the problem, and check the obvious causes.* These steps include checking the printer's control panel, the paper, the cartridges, the cable connections, the file to be printed, the installation of the printer driver (the correct printer dialog box comes up when the print command is issued), whether others can print if this is a shared printer, and whether you can print a different document. If all this has not solved the problem, you may think it's time to ask for help. You've already gone further than most users, so this wouldn't be embarrassing, but you can do more.

Pressing On

You can take the next step in the debugging strategy: *try to isolate the problem*. But this is daunting because you don't really understand how printing works. Not to worry. It's still possible to make progress.

Because you have printed before, you know your computer is configured correctly. You try printing a simple document like a text file, but it's the same story: The printer driver's dialog box comes up, asking how many copies you want, and so forth—you reply 1, click **Print**, and the machine appears to compute for a moment, but when you check the printer, nothing's there. What could be happening to your output?

Thinking through what you imagine to be the process, you guess that when you click **Print**, the printer driver must convert the file into the form suitable for the printer. Because the computer runs briefly after you click **Print**, it's a safe bet that it's doing something like a conversion. Then your computer must send the converted file to the printer. Does it go? Surely, if the computer tried to send the file to the printer and the printer didn't acknowledge getting it, the computer would tell you to plug in the printer. Or would it? Suppose you unplugged the printer from the computer and tried again to print. You run this experiment and the same thing happens! The printer couldn't even receive the converted file, and there were no complaints. What's happening? Where is the file?

Perhaps the computer is saving the converted file. Why? Shouldn't it print if it's told to print? This is a little odd, because it's not asking you to plug in the printer. Could the other files you tried to print be waiting too, even though the printer was plugged in earlier? So, you start looking around for the stranded file(s). You locate the printer driver's printing monitor (**Start > Settings > Printers** on the PC; among the active programs on the Mac). When you open up this monitor, what you find is a list of all the files you've tried to print recently. They're not printing—they're just listed. (See Figure 7.9.)

The Print Queue

What you have discovered is the "print queue" for your machine. You didn't even know that computers *have* print queues, but they apparently do. Not being a computer scientist, you don't know why they have them, either. But it's obvious that your printing is stalled in the queue. As described in Chapter 2 under "Clicking Around," you explore the monitor application, discovering that the queue is "turned off" or possibly "wedged." (The actual description for "turned off" varies from system to system; for the PC it is **Use Printer Offline**, which is set under **File**; for Macs the Print Queue button is configured to **Start Print Queue**; shared printers are different still.) Though machines are different, the situation is the same: The computer's settings tell it to queue your converted files rather than print them immediately. How it got into this state you may never know. The best approach is to cancel or trash all of the jobs in the queue, because there are probably many duplicates, and restart the queue. That is, configure it so that it tries to print your files rather than queuing them. Your printing problem may be solved! Or have you forgotten to recable your printer?

> **FITBYTE**
>
> **Sleep on It.** One fact that professionals know about debugging is that when they can't solve a bug, it's good to take a break. Whether your mind keeps working on the problem subconsciously or returning to the problem refreshed just clears your thinking, briefly getting away helps.

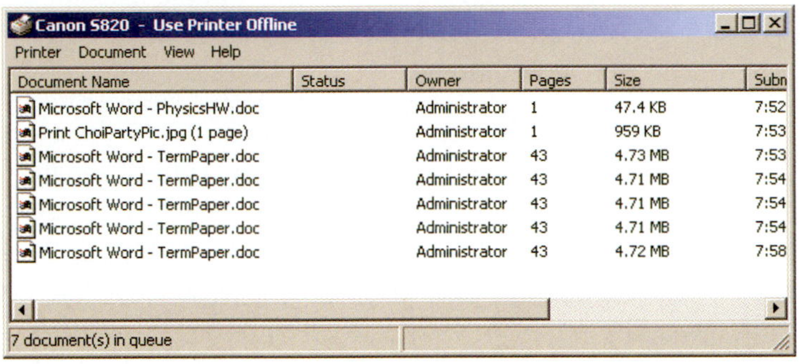

(a)

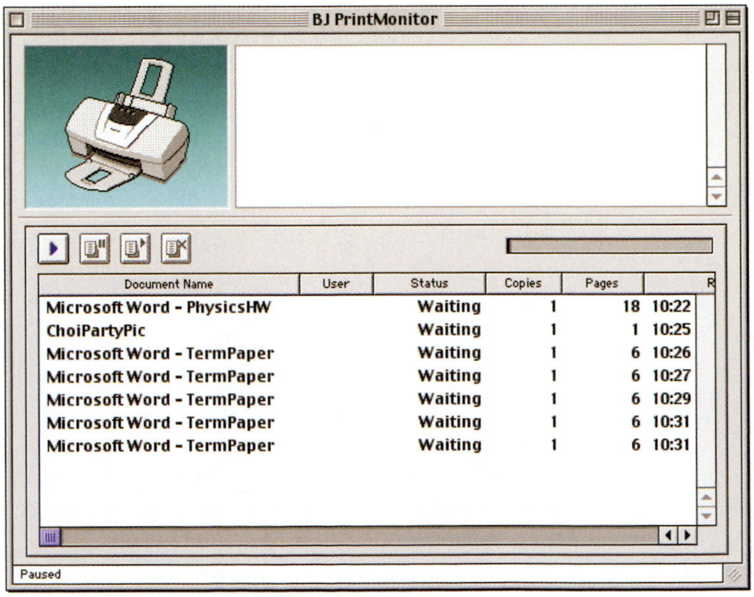

(b)

Figure 7.9. Printer queues for Windows (a), and Mac operating systems (b).

Calling Tech Support?

Summarizing the situation, you have debugged the printing operation in spite of the fact that it's complicated and you know almost nothing about how computers print. A key assumption was that the software is correct. You discovered that computers use a print queue, though it's a mystery why. The queue can become stopped or stalled, but by using the print monitor you can restart it. Locating the problem was just the standard debugging strategy applied with courage and common sense. The results were successful. Though there are obviously many problems that will not be solved by this approach—that actually require some technical knowledge—you should always assume that the standard debugging strategy will work. When you've applied it without success, it's time to call Tech Support.

SUMMARY

This chapter began by emphasizing why being precise is so important when using computers. The standard of precision is higher than in most other situations, so being careful and exact makes using computers easier. Next we looked at what debugging is and why we need to know how to do it. Then we introduced the basic strategy of debugging by helping virtual parents watch their college student's video spoof. That let us discuss the whys and hows of debugging. The principles that form the debugging strategy were abstracted into a tidy list to prepare for using them in debugging a Web page. We debugged a Web page, thanks in part to the **Source** view of the document that showed how the computer was interpreting the HTML. Analyzing our performance, we noted that debugging involves both correct and incorrect conjectures about the cause of a problem. Acting on incorrect guesses can result in unnecessary changes or, worse, harmful changes. Finally, we emphasized that it is possible to debug a sophisticated system like a computer's printing facility with little more than a vague idea of how it works, using our standard debugging strategy, applied with common sense and courage.

EXERCISES

Multiple Choice

1. An example of an understanding error is a:
   A. memory error
   B. data entry error
   C. design error
   D. none of the above

2. The best way to solve an understanding error is to:
   A. restart the system
   B. change software
   C. try again
   D. all of the above

3. The first step in debugging is to:
   A. check for obvious errors
   B. try to reproduce the problem
   C. isolate the problem
   D. find exactly what the problem is

4. The debugging process can be described as a:
   A. recipe
   B. road map
   C. set of guidelines
   D. list

5. The last step in the debugging process is to:
   A. look again to identify the mistake
   B. re-create the problem
   C. divide up the process
   D. determine the exact problem

Short Answer

1. _____ are information that is entered into boxes on a form.

2. A _____ is a set of rules that determine what is legal for field input.

3. Use a _____ to represent a space on the computer.

4. _____ and debugging mean essentially the same thing.

5. A glitch in a computer system is called a(n) _____.

6. A(n) _____ is an error in the way a system was developed.

7. An alternative approach to get around a problems is called a(n) _____.

Exercises

1. You walk into a room and flip the light switch. Nothing happens. Describe the debugging process you use to solve the problem.

2. What advantages does an organized approach have over a trial and error approach?

3. Draw a schematic of the debugging process. Apply this to the debugging process for question 1.

4. How would you say "Room 309"? Did you say "zero" or "oh"? How about a ZIP code? Try 57026.

5. What is the lexical structure for entering dates into the computer? Use the standard American format for a two-digit month, a separator, a two-digit day, a separator, and a four-digit year.

6. Devise a lexical structure for entering a phone number into the computer. What characters are allowed and when? Do the same thing for ZIP codes.

7. Think "outside the box" to solve a problem. You have a quiz in an hour and you're stranded. You must contact the professor before the quiz or you'll get a zero. How do you contact the professor? List multiple alternatives.

8. You've been doing debugging since you learned how to check your math back in grade school. Check the math on this problem.

    $N = -((12 + 6) - 7 \times 4 + ((9 - 2) \times 3) / 7)$
    $N = 18 - 7 \times 4 + 7 \times 3 / 7$
    $N = 11 \times 4 + 21 / 7$
    $N = 44 + 25 / 7$
    $N = 49 / 7$
    $N = 7$

9. Design several workarounds for the computer printing error. Pretend it's your term paper and it has to be printed. How would you get around the problem that that computer and the printer aren't printing?

10. Here is the HTML for a simple Web page. Find the errors in it and get the page to display properly. Test the page to be sure it works properly.

```
<html>
<head>
<title>My Favorites</title>
</head>
<body>
<ol>
    <li>Movies</li>
</ol>
<ul>
    <li><i>Grease</i></li>
    <li><i>Road to Perdition</i></li>
    <li><i>Titanic</i></li>
```

```
</ul>
<ol>
    <li>Shows</li>
    <li><i>Survivor</i></li>
    <li><i>American Idol</i></li>
    <li><i>Everybody Loves Raymond</i></li>
    <li>Stars</li>
</ol>
<ol>
    <li>Matt Damon</li>
    <li>Kate Hudson</li>
    <li>Lucy Lui</li>
</ol>
</body>
</html>
```

BITS AND THE "WHY" OF BYTES

Representing Information Digitally

Before heaven and earth had taken form all was vague and amorphous. Therefore, it was called the Great Beginning. The Great Beginning produced emptiness and emptiness produced the universe. . . . The combined essences of heaven and earth became the yin and yang, the concentrated essences of the yin and yang became the four seasons, and the scattered essences of the four seasons became the myriad creatures of the world.

—HUAI-NAN TSU, 2ND CENTURY, B.C.

MOST PEOPLE know that computers and networks record and transmit information in *bits* and *bytes*. From basic English, you can guess that whatever bits are, they probably represent little pieces of information. But what are bytes? And why is "byte" spelled with a y? In this chapter we confirm that bits do represent little pieces of information, we define what bytes are, and, by the very end, we explain the mysterious *y*. But the chapter is much more fundamental than even these basic concepts. It describes how bits and bytes—the atoms and molecules of information—combine to form our virtual world of computation, information, and communication. (Multimedia is covered in Chapter 11.) We even explain how information exists when there is nothing, as when Sherlock Holmes solves the mystery using the information that "the dog didn't bark in the night."

The first goal of this chapter is to establish that digitizing doesn't require digits—any set of symbols will do. We explore encoding information using dice, learn how pattern sequences can create symbols, and discover that symbols can represent information. Our next goal is to learn the fundamental patterns on which all information technology is built: the presence and absence of a phenomenon. Called PandA encoding here, this meeting of the physical and logical worlds forms the foundation of information technology. We then define bits, bytes, and ASCII. And, finally, we describe the digitization of the *Oxford English Dictionary* (*OED*) to show how metadata is added to content so the computer can help us use it.

DIGITIZING DISCRETE INFORMATION

The dictionary definition of *digitize* is to represent information with digits. In normal conversation, *digit* means the ten Arabic numerals 0 through 9. Thus digitizing uses whole numbers to stand for things. This familiar process represents Americans by Social Security numbers, telephone accounts by phone numbers, and books as ISBN numbers. Such digital representations have probably been used since numerals were invented. But this sense of *digitize* is much too narrow for the digital world of information technology.

> **Digital Man.** The first person to apply the term digital to computers was George Stibitz, a Bell Labs mathematician. While consulting for the U.S. military, he observed that "pulsed" computing devices would be better described as digital because they represent information in discrete (that is, separate) units.

Limitation of Digits

A limitation of the dictionary definition of *digitize* is that it calls for the use of the ten digits, which produces a whole number. But in many cases the property of being numeric is unimportant and of little use. The benefit of numbers is that they quantify things and they enable us to do arithmetic. But Social Security numbers, phone numbers, and ISBN numbers are not quantities. You are not better than someone else is if you have a larger telephone number. And it doesn't make sense to multiply two ISBN numbers together. So, when we don't need numbers, we don't need to use the digits. But what else can we use to digitize?

Alternative Representations

Digitizing in information technology can use almost any symbols. For example, the North American telephone number `888 555 1212` could be represented as `*** %%% !@!@`. This encoding, rather than using {1, 2, 3, 4, 5, 6, 7, 8, 9, 0}, uses the symbol set {!, @, #, $, %, ^, &, *, (,)}. These symbols are simply the uppercase digit characters on a keyboard. If we use the symbol set { ▶, ▼, ◀, ▶▶, ■, ◀◀, ▶▶|, ▲, |◀◀, || } the phone number is represented as: ▲ ▲ ▲ ■ ■ ■   ▶ ▼ ▶ ▼ . This could be called **player encoding** because it uses the standard symbols from tape and disc players. These symbols work just as well as the digits as long as the telephone keypad is relabeled, as shown in Figure 8.1. The reason the encoding works is that a phone number's digits just tell us which sequence of keys to press. Any ten distinct symbols will work as long as the keypad is labeled properly.

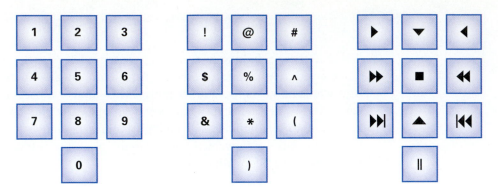

Figure 8.1. *Three symbol assignments for a telephone keypad.*

Symbols, Briefly

One practical advantage of digits over other less familiar symbols is that digits have short names. Imagine speaking your phone number as "asterisk asterisk exclamation point closing parenthesis exclamation point. . . ." In fact, as information technology has adopted these symbols, they are getting shorter names. For example, computer professionals often say exclamation point as *bang* and asterisk as *star*. Instead of saying "eight eight eight five five five one two one two" we could say "star star star per per per bang at bang at," which is just as brief. So, the advantage of brevity is not limited to digits.

Ordering Symbols

One other advantage of digits for encoding information like telephone numbers is that the items can be listed in numerical order. This feature is rarely used for the kinds of information discussed here; for example, telephone books are ordered by the name of the person rather than by the number. But, sometimes ordering items is useful.

To place information in order by using symbols (other than digits), we need to agree on an ordering for the basic symbols. This is called a **collating sequence**. In the same way that the digits are ordered

0 < 1 < 2 < 3 < 4 < 5 < 6 < 7 < 8 < 9

the player symbols could be ordered

‖ < ▶ < ▼ < ◀ < ⏩ < ■ < ⏪ < ⏭ < ▲ < ⏮

Then, two coded phone numbers can be ordered based on which has the smaller first symbol, or if the first symbol matches, then on which has the smaller second symbol, or if the first two symbols match, which has the smaller third symbol, and so on. For example,

▲ ‖ ‖ ■ ■ ■ ▶ ▼ ▶ ▼ < ▲ ▲ ▲ ■ ■ ■ ▶ ▼ ▶ ▼

Today, digitizing means *representing information by symbols*—not just the ten digit symbols. But which symbols would be best? Before answering that question, we should consider how the choice of symbols interacts with the things being encoded.

ENCODING WITH DICE

Because information can be digitized using any symbols, consider a representation based on dice. A single die has six sides, and the patterns on the sides of the dice can be used for this digital representation. (The patterns can be interpreted as numbers, of course, but for the moment we ignore that property.)

Consider representing the Roman alphabet with dice.

With 26 letters in the Roman alphabet, but only six different patterns on a die, there are more letters to represent than there are patterns available. This is a typical problem in encoding. So we use multiple patterns to represent each letter. How many will be required? Two dice patterns together produce $6 \times 6 = 36$ different pattern sequences because each of the six patterns of one die can be paired with each of the six different patterns of the other die (see Figure 8.2). Three dice can define $6 \times 6 \times 6 = 216$ different pattern sequences because there are six choices for the first position, six for the second position, and six for the last. More generally, n dice together can produce 6^n different pattern sequences. If instead of six there is some other number, p, of basic patterns, a sequence of n of them produces p^n different pattern sequences. (Recall that p^n means $p \times p \times \ldots \times p$; that is, n copies of p multiplied together.)

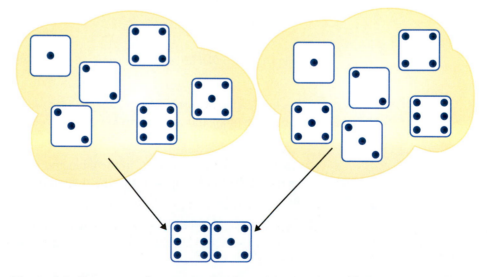

Figure 8.2. Pairing two dice patterns results in $36 = 6 \times 6$ possible pattern sequences.

Returning to the problem of digitizing the alphabet, we can agree to call each of the pattern sequences produced by pairing two dice a symbol. Then we can associate these dice-pair symbols with the letters simply by listing them.

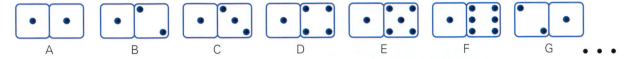

It helps to be systematic when associating the letters with the symbols to make the encoding easier to remember. In fact, because two dice form the symbols, the simplest way to present the association between the symbols and the values they encode (letters) is a table, as illustrated in Figure 8.3.

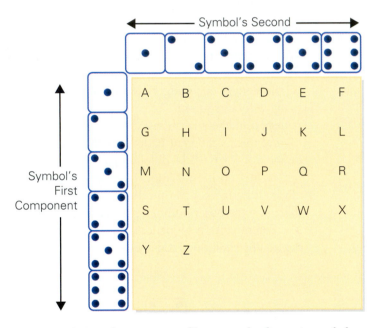

Figure 8.3. Initial assignment of letters to the dice-pair symbols.

The table is organized so that the pattern along the left side of the table is the first component of the symbol and the pattern along the top is the second. This makes the digitizing process easy.

> *Encode a letter.* Find the letter in the table and use the pattern of the row as the left half of the symbol and the pattern of the column as the right half.

> *Decode a symbol.* Find the row for the left half of the symbol and the column for the right half; the letter is at the intersection of the row and column.

Use the table (Figure 8.3) to find out what word (acronym) is represented by the three symbols shown.

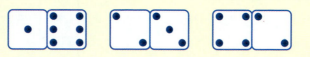

Did you come up with "FIT"?

Extending the Encoding

The representation has associated 26 of the symbols with the Roman letters, leaving ten positions unassigned. If the information to be digitized only uses letters, we're done, because a symbol is associated with each letter. But this rarely happens. A more common situation is that the information uses letters and numerals; many automobile license plates use those 36 characters. In such cases, associating the Arabic numerals to the unassigned symbols of Figure 8.3 would then complete the digitization, as shown in Figure 8.4(a).

But usually the textual information to be digitized includes more than letters and numerals; it also includes punctuation. Including punctuation complicates the dice-pair representation because we need more symbols than we have pairs of dice. Anyone inventing a digitization faces the problem of deciding which items are the most important to represent.

Perhaps the most important character is the space character, because we use it to *delimit* letter sequences, that is, separate words. We cannot use spacing in the digitization (that is, separations in our arrangement of dice-pairs) to indicate word separations in the text because we have no control over how the digital form will be used. For example, using the Figure 8.4(a) digitization, two people could communicate in a noisy environment with a single pair of dice by spelling out words one letter at a time. But with only one pair of dice, there is no way to "separate the pairs" to indicate the end of a word. The point is that the digitization must encode all the information, and the spaces separating words are part of the information. So space must be assigned to some symbol. After that the nine remaining symbols are not enough to represent the digits, so we'll use them for more punctuation. A representation of this type is shown in Figure 8.4(b).

Figure 8.4(b) has the advantage of representing space and other punctuation, but it doesn't represent the numerals. In some cases, this might not be a serious problem because we can find other ways to represent these characters. For example, the two people communicating in a noisy environment with a pair of dice might simply spell out each numeral. There would be no single symbol for zero, for example, but it could be presented as

Z   E   R   O

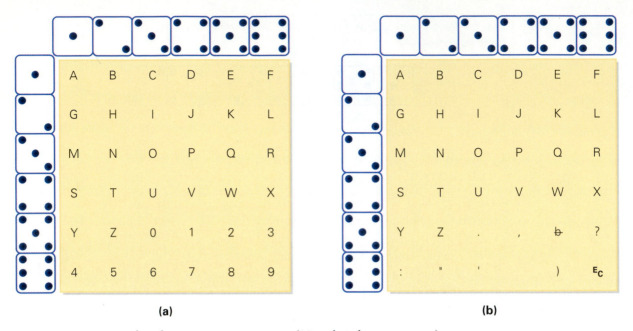

(a)   **(b)**

Figure 8.4. *Two complete dice-pair representations.* (*Note:* ␢ *indicates a space.*)

But spelling out numerals limits how this digital representation can be used, and we want to avoid limitations if we possibly can. Though it appears that we need to use dice triples, there is an alternative.

The Escape: Creating More Symbols

In Figure 8.4(b) the "boxcars" symbol (double sixes) has been associated with an unfamiliar character, E_C. This character, which is not a letter, numeral, or punctuation character, will be called *escape*. It has been included to illustrate how to extend a representation. Because escape does not match any legal character, we will never need it in the normal process of digitizing text. So we can use it to indicate that the digitization is "escaping from the basic representation" and applying a secondary representation. In this way, more symbols can be represented because pairing escape with another symbol doubles the number of representations, though the new symbols are twice as long.

To illustrate the idea, let's encode the numerals by pairing the escape symbol with each of the first ten symbols of the encoding, that is, those assigned to A through J. Each symbol pair, that is, four dice, is assigned to a numeral in order. Thus the symbol pair

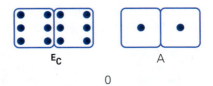

E_C A

0

which is escape-A, represents 0. Escape-B represents 1, and so on. Notice that the escape symbol precedes the letter. So, 10 is represented as

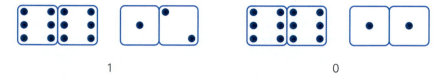

        1   0

There can be no "group discount" here: We can't place escape before the first of a whole string of digits because the decoder would not know when the string ended and the base encoding (non-escape characters) resumed. So, a ten-digit number needs 20 symbols in this dice-pair encoding extended by escape.

> **Shifty.** The escape technique is familiar. The Shift keys are used as an escape for the keyboard; they double the encoding, giving uppercase characters. Control works this way, too.

Double Escape

Using this escape gives 35 basic symbol assignments because the E_C takes up the boxcars symbol. But, escape gives an equal number of two-symbol assignments. These secondary assignments should probably be associated with the less frequently used values because the encoding is less efficient. Of course, the idea can be continued because we could use E_C E_C as another escape for yet another alternate set of symbols. But there are other, more sophisticated ways to use the escape symbol. The point is that in digitizing information, do not associate all symbols with legal information, as was done in Figure 8.4(a), but rather reserve one symbol as an escape, as shown in Figure 8.4(b). The escape gives flexibility to a representation.

Notice that when the 36 symbols created from two dice weren't enough for the letters, numerals, and punctuation, we could have used three dice pattern sequences. That would have given $6^3 = 216$ symbols. The advantage is that numerals would have been encoded with three dice rather than four. The disadvantage is that the letters and punctuation would have been encoded with three dice rather than two. If numerals make up less than half of the values we wish to encode, our "two plus escape" uses fewer dice than the "triples" solution.

To summarize, digitizing involves associating symbols with values, which in the case of text are the keyboard characters. The method of constructing symbols—combining base patterns—creates a fixed-size set of symbols. The symbol set must be large enough to represent each value. Saving one symbol for escape allows the encoding to be extended.

THE FUNDAMENTAL REPRESENTATION OF INFORMATION

The six base patterns of a die are familiar, but not fundamental. The fundamental patterns used in information technology come when the physical world meets the logical world. In the physical world, the most fundamental form of information is the presence or absence of a physical phenomenon:

> Does matter occupy a particular place in space and time, or not?

> Is light detected at a particular place and time, or not?

> Is magnetism sensed at a particular place and time, or not?

The same goes for pressure, charge, flow, and so on. In many cases, the phenomena have a continuous range of values. For example, light and color have a smooth range of intensities

while others like clicking and drumming are discrete

(The continuous case is discussed in Chapter 11.) From a digital information point of view, the amount of a phenomenon is not important as long as it is reliably detected—whether there is some information or none; whether it is present or absent.

In the logical world, which is the world of thinking and reasoning, the concepts of *true* and *false* are all important. Propositions such as "Rain implies wet streets" can be expressed and combined with other propositions such as "The streets are not wet" to draw conclusions such as "It is not raining." Logic is the foundation of reasoning, and it is also the foundation of computing. *By associating true with the presence of a phenomenon and false with its absence, we can use the physical world to implement the logical world. This produces information technology.* In this section, we make that association.

The PandA Representation

PandA is the name we use for the two fundamental patterns of digital information based on the presence and absence of a phenomenon. PandA is mnemonic for "presence and absence." A key property of the PandA representation is that it is black and white; that is, the phenomenon is either present or it is not; the logic is either *true* or *false*. Such a formulation is said to be *discrete*, meaning "distinct" or "separable"; it is not possible to transform one value into the other by continuous gradations. There is no gray.

A Binary System. The PandA encoding has just two basic patterns— Present and Absent—making it a **binary system**. The names Present and Absent are not essential to our use in digitization, so we often use other words that suggest the discrete, black-and-white nature of the two patterns (see Table 8.1). The assignment of these names to the two patterns is also arbitrary. There is no law that says that in all cases and forever and ever *On* means "Present" and *Off* means "Absent." We could agree to assign the names the other way around, and engineers deep into a design often do. As long as all of the information encoders and decoders agree, any assignment works. The associations given in the table seem reasonable, however, and they are probably the most common. But the entries are only names for the two fundamental patterns.

Table 8.1. *Possible interpretations of the two PandA patterns*

Present	Absent
True	False
1	0
On	Off
Yes	No
+	–
Black	White
For	Against
Yang	Yin
Lisa	Bart
...	...

Bits Form Symbols. The unit that can assume the different patterns can vary. In the dice representation, the unit was the top of a single die. This unit could be set to any of six patterns to encode letters. In the same way, in the PandA representation the unit is a specific place (in space and time), where the presence or absence of the phenomenon can be set and detected. The PandA unit is known as a *bit*, which can assume either of the two PandA patterns, Present or Absent. *Bit* is a contraction for "binary digit." (The term *bit* was originally adopted because early computer designers interpreted the two patterns as 1 and 0, the digits of the binary number system.) Though bit sequences can be interpreted as binary numbers, the key idea is that bits form *symbols*. Encoding numbers is a particularly useful application of symbols, but the idea is more general.

Bits in Magnetic Media

The two patterns are called the **states** of the bit when they are part of a storage medium. To illustrate bits in the physical world, consider the magnetic encoding of information as might be used on tapes, floppy disks, or hard disks. Like audiocassette tapes, these media are made out of a material containing iron that can be magnetized. Figure 8.5 shows a sequence of positions, some of which are positively magnetized and some of which are not.

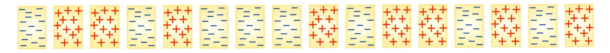

Figure 8.5. Schematic diagram of a sequence of bit positions on a magnetic medium. The boxes illustrate a position where magnetism may be set and sensed; pluses (red) indicate magnetism of positive polarity, interpreted as "present" and minuses (blue) indicate magnetism of negative polarity, interpreted as "absent."

Each position can represent a bit because it can be configured into both states, positively magnetized or not—that is, the two PandA patterns. For example, the 16 positions shown in Figure 8.5 encode the 16 bits.

> absent-present-present-absent-present-absent-absent-absent-
> present-absent-present-present-absent-present-absent-present

or, more briefly,

> 0110 1000 1011 0101

It is obvious why computer scientists and engineers prefer the names 1 and 0 to Present and Absent, even when the information is not numbers. Ones and zeros are simpler to read, write, and say.

Bits in Computer Memory

Inside the computer the memory is arranged in a very long sequence of bits. That is, places where a phenomenon can be set and detected.

Analogy: Sidewalk Memory. To illustrate how memory works, imagine a sidewalk made of a strip of concrete with lines (expansion joints) across it forming squares, and suppose it has been swept clean. We agree that a stone on a sidewalk square corresponds to 1 and the absence of a stone corresponds to 0. This makes the sidewalk a sequence of bits. (Figure 8.6.) Sidewalk memory can encode information just like computer memory. But, it is not as economical of space!

Figure 8.6. Sidewalk sections as a sequence of bits (1010 0010).

The bits can be set to write information into the memory, and they can be sensed to read the information out of the memory. To write a 1 the phenomenon must be made to be present; for example, put a stone on a sidewalk square. To write a 0, the phenomenon must be made to be absent; for example, sweep the sidewalk square clean. To determine what information is stored at a specific position, sense whether the phenomenon is present or absent. So, if a stone is on a square, the phenomenon is present (1); otherwise, it is absent (0).

Alternative PandA Encodings. There is no limit to the number of ways to encode two states using physical phenomena, of course. Remaining just in the world of sidewalks, we could use stones on all squares but use white stones and black stones for the two states. Black could be chosen as present and not black as absent. Or, we could use multiple stones of two colors per square, saying that more white stones than black means 1 and more black stones than white means 0. (We must take care that the total number of stones on each sidewalk square is always odd.) Or we could place a stone in the center of the square for one state and off center for the other state. And so forth. These are all PandA encodings, provided the "phenomenon" is chosen properly: presence of black, presence of majority of white, presence of a centered stone.

FITBYTE

No Barking. Sherlock Holmes used one bit of information to solve the disappearance of a prize racehorse in the story "Silver Blaze." In the vicinity of the stable during the night [place and time], the phenomenon [barking watchdog] was not detected [absent], implying to Holmes the dog knew the thief, which meant the thief had to be Simpson, the owner. Holmes's deduction used information [perpetrator known to the household] represented by the absence of a phenomenon, that is, the dog was *not* barking.

Combining Bit Patterns. Like the sides of a die, the two bit patterns alone only give us a limited resource for digitizing information. If the information has only two alternative values—that is, it's binary information, such as votes (*aye, nay*), personality types (*A, B*), Mariners baseball games (*won, loss*)—one bit is enough. But usually the two patterns must be combined into sequences to create the necessary symbols. As we learned in the last section, if there are $p = 2$ patterns, as in the PandA representation, arranged into n-length sequences, we can create 2^n symbols. Table 8.2 relates the length of the bit sequence to the number of possible symbols.

Table 8.2. Number of symbols when the number of possible patterns is two

n	2^n	Symbols
1	2^1	2
2	2^2	4
3	2^3	8
4	2^4	16
5	2^5	32
6	2^6	64
7	2^7	128
8	2^8	256
9	2^9	512
10	2^{10}	1024

The 16 symbols of $n = 4$ length bit sequences are shown in Table 8.3.

The PandA encoding is the fundamental representation of information. By grouping bits together, we can produce enough symbols to represent any number of values. By creating symbols using the two PandA patterns, we can record and transform information using resources from the physical world. Information and computation are abstract without physical form, but the miracle of information technology is that they can be made real. With machines and networks doing the work, our lives are simplified.

HEX EXPLAINED

Before using PandA to represent text, let's solve a mystery from Chapter 4. Recall that when we specified custom colors in HTML—`<font color="#FF8E2A">` as shown in Figure 4.2—we used **hex digits**, short for hexadecimal digits, or base-16. We didn't explain hex at the time but simply presented Table 4.4, so we could convert back and forth between decimal and hexadecimal.

Table 8.3. *The basic PandA encoding of length four symbols and the associated bits*

Sixteen Symbols of the 4-Bit PandA Representation

Symbol	Binary	Physical Bits	Hex	Symbol	Binary	Physical Bits	Hex
AAAA	0000		0	PAAA	1000		8
AAAP	0001		1	PAAP	1001		9
AAPA	0010		2	PAPA	1010		A
AAPP	0011		3	PAPP	1011		B
APAA	0100		4	PPAA	1100		C
APAP	0101		5	PPAP	1101		D
APPA	0110		6	PPPA	1110		E
APPP	0111		7	PPPP	1111		F

The reason for using hexadecimal is as follows. When we specify an RGB color or other encoding using bits, we must give the bits in order. The bit sequence might be given in 0's and 1's,

`<font color="#1111111100110001110000101010">` *Illegal HTML tag*

but writing so many 0's and 1's is tedious and error prone. Computer professionals long ago realized that they needed a better way to write bit sequences, and so began using hexadecimal digits.

The 16 Hex Digits

The digits of hex are `0`, `1`, . . . , `9`, `A`, `B`, `C`, `D`, `E`, `F`. Because there are 16 digits, they can be represented perfectly by the 16 symbols of 4-bit sequences. In Table 8.3, the binary column is associated with the hex column. So bit sequence 0000 is hex 0, bit sequence 0001 is hex 1, and so forth, up to the bit sequence 1111, which is hex F. (This is simply a numeric interpretation of the bits, which will be explained in Chapter 11.)

Changing Hex Digits to Bits and Back Again

Because each hex digit corresponds to a 4-bit sequence, and vice versa, we can translate between hex and bits easily: given hex, write down the associated groups of 4 bits. Given a sequence of bits, group them into sequences of four, and write down the corresponding hex digit. Thus,

`0010 1011 1010 1101 = 2BAD`

and

`1B40 = 0001 1011 0100 0000`

So, in HTML when we specify the color white as `"#FFFFFF"`, we are effectively setting each bit of the RGB specification bits to 1.

TRY IT

> What is ABE8 BEEF as a bit sequence? To find the answer, check Table 8.3. Find each letter in the hex column, and write down the corresponding 4-bit sequence from the binary column. For example, A is in the second column and corresponds to the bits: 1010.
>
> *Answer:* 1010 1011 1110 1000 1011 1110 1110 1111

DIGITIZING TEXT

The two earliest uses of the PandA representation were to encode numbers and keyboard characters. These two applications are still extremely important, though now representations for sound, images, video, and other types of information are almost as important. In this section we talk about how the text is encoded; we discuss how numbers are encoded in Chapter 11.

Remember that the number of bits determines the number of symbols available for representing values: n bits in sequence yield 2^n symbols. And, as we've learned, the more characters we want encoded, the more symbols we need. Roman letters, Arabic numerals, and about a dozen punctuation characters are about the minimum needed to digitize English text. We would also like to have uppercase and lowercase letters, and the basic arithmetic symbols like +, −, *, /, and =. But, where should the line be drawn? Should characters not required for English but useful in other languages like German (ö), French (é), Spanish (ñ), and Norwegian (ø) be included? What about Czech, Greek, Arabic, Thai, or Cantonese? Should other languages' punctuation be included, like French (« ») and Spanish (¿)? Should arithmetic symbols include degrees (°), pi (π), relational symbols (≤), equivalence (≡), for all (∀)? What about business symbols: ¢, £, ¥, ©, and ®? What about unprintable characters like backspace and new-line? Should there be a symbol for smiley faces (☺)? Some of these questions are easier to answer than others. Though we want to keep the list small so that we use fewer bits, not being able to represent critical characters would be a mistake.

Assigning Symbols

The 26 uppercase and 26 lowercase Roman letters, the 10 Arabic numerals, a basic set of 20 punctuation characters (including blank), 10 useful arithmetic characters, and 3 nonprintable characters (new-line, tab, backspace) can be represented with 95 symbols. Such a set would be enough for English and the keys on a basic computer keyboard. To represent 95 distinct symbols, we need 7 bits because 6 bits gives only $2^6 = 64$ symbols. Seven bits give $2^7 = 128$ symbols, which is more than we need for the 95 different symbols. Some special control characters must also be represented. These control characters are used for data transmission and other engineering purposes. They are assigned to the remaining 33 of the 7-bit symbols.

An early and still widely used 7-bit code for the characters is **ASCII**, pronounced *AS·key*. ASCII stands for American Standard Code for Information Interchange. The advantages of a "standard" are many: computer parts built by different manufacturers can connect together; programs can create data and store it so that different programs can process it later; and so forth. In all cases, there must be an agreement as to which character is associated with which symbol (bit sequence).

Extended ASCII: An 8-bit Code

As the name implies, ASCII was developed in the United States. But by the mid-1960s, it became clear that 7-bit ASCII was not enough because it could not fully represent text from languages other than English. So IBM, the dominant computer manufacturer at the time, decided to use the next larger set of symbols, the 8-bit symbols, as the standard for character representation. Eight bits produce $2^8 = 256$ symbols, enough to encode English and the Western European languages, their punctuation characters, and a large set of other useful characters. The larger, improved encoding was called **Extended ASCII**, shown in Figure 8.7. The original ASCII is the "first half" of Extended ASCII; that is, 7-bit ASCII is the 8-bit ASCII representation with the leftmost bit set to 0. Though Extended ASCII does not handle all natural languages, it does handle many languages that derived from the Latin alphabet. Handling other languages is solved in two ways: recoding the second half of Extended ASCII for the language's other characters; and using the escape mechanism mentioned earlier.

ASCII	0000	0001	0010	0011	0100	0101	0110	0111	1000	1001	1010	1011	1100	1101	1110	1111
0000	N_U	S_H	S_X	E_X	E_T	E_Q	A_K	B_L	B_S	H_T	L_F	V_T	F_F	C_R	S_O	S_I
0001	D_L	D_1	D_2	D_3	D_4	N_K	S_Y	E_Σ	C_N	E_M	S_B	E_C	F_S	G_S	R_S	U_S
0010		!	"	#	$	%	&	'	(	)	*	+	,	-	.	/
0011	0	1	2	3	4	5	6	7	8	9	:	;	<	=	>	?
0100	@	A	B	C	D	E	F	G	H	I	J	K	L	M	N	O
0101	P	Q	R	S	T	U	V	W	X	Y	Z	[	\	]	^	_
0110	`	a	b	c	d	e	f	g	h	i	j	k	l	m	n	o
0111	p	q	r	s	t	u	v	w	x	y	z	{			}	~	D_T
1000	8_0	8_1	8_2	8_3	I_N	N_L	S_S	E_S	H_S	H_J	V_S	P_D	P_V	R_I	S_2	S_3
1001	D_C	P_1	P_Z	S_E	C_C	M_M	S_P	E_P	Q_8	Q_Q	Q_A	C_S	S_T	O_S	P_M	A_P
1010	A_O	¡	¢	£		¥	¦	§	¨	©	♀	«	¬	-	®	¯
1011	°	±	²	³	´	µ	¶	·	¸	¹	♂	»	¼	½	¾	¿
1100	À	Á	Â	Ã	Ä	Å	Æ	Ç	È	É	Ê	Ë	Ì	Í	Î	Ï
1101	Ð	Ñ	Ò	Ó	Ô	Õ	Ö	×	Ø	Ù	Ú	Û	Ü	Ý	Þ	ß
1110	à	á	â	ã	ä	å	æ	ç	è	é	ê	ë	ì	í	î	ï
1111	ð	ñ	ò	ó	ô	õ	ö	÷	ø	ù	ú	û	ü	ý	þ	ÿ

Figure 8.7 *ASCII, The American Standard Code for Information Interchange*

Note: The original 7-bit ASCII is the top half of the table; the whole table is known as Extended ASCII (ISO/IEC8859-1). The 8-bit symbol for a letter is the four row bits followed by the four column bits (e.g., female (♀) = 10101010, while male(♂) = 10111010). Characters shown as two small letters are control symbols used to encode nonprintable information (e.g., B_S = 00001000 is backspace). The bottom half of the table represents characters needed by Western European languages, such as Icelandic's eth (ð) and thorn (Þ).

IBM's move to 8 bits was bold because it added the extra bit at a time when computer memory and storage were extremely expensive. IBM gave 8-bit sequences a special name, **byte**, and adopted it as a standard unit for computer memory. Bytes are still the standard unit of memory, and their "8-ness" is noticeable in many places. For example, recent computers have been "32-bit machines," meaning their datapath widths (the size of information processed by most instructions) are 4 bytes.

FITBYTE

> **The Ultimate.** Though ASCII and its variations are widely used, the more complete solution is a 16-bit representation, called *Unicode*. With 65,536 symbols, Unicode can handle *all* languages.

ASCII Coding of Phone Numbers

Let's return to the phone number, `888 555 1212`, whose representation concerned us at the start of the chapter. How would a computer represent this phone number in its memory? Remember, this is not really a number, but rather, it is a keying sequence for a telephone's keypad represented by numerals; it is not necessary, or even desirable, to represent the phone number as a numerical quantity. Because each of the numerals has a representation in Extended ASCII, we can express the phone number by encoding each digit. The encoding is easy: Find each numeral in Figure 8.7, and write down the bit sequence from its row, followed by the bit sequence from its column. So the phone number 888 555 1212 in ASCII is

```
0011 1000   0011 1000   0011 1000   0011 0101   0011 0101   0011 0101
0011 0001   0011 0010   0011 0001   0011 0010
```

You can use Figure 8.7 to check this encoding. This is exactly how computers represent phone numbers. The encoding seems somewhat redundant because each byte has the same left half: 0011. The left halves are repeated because all of the numerals are located on the 0011 row of the ASCII table. If only phone numbers were to be represented, fewer bits could be used, of course. But there is little reason to be so economical, so we adopt the standard ASCII.

FITBYTE

> **Two bits, four bits . . .** The term *byte* has motivated some people to call 4 bits—that is, half a byte—a *nibble*.

Notice that we have run all of the digits of the phone number together, even though when we write them for ourselves we usually put spaces between the area code and exchange code, and between the exchange code and the number. The computer doesn't care, but it might matter to users. However, it is easy to add these spaces and other punctuation.

TRY IT

> Encode the phone number (888) 555-1212 in Extended ASCII, that is, insert the punctuation. (Notice that there is a space before the first 5.)
>
> To find the answer, locate each character in Figure 8.7 and write down the four bits at the left of the row and the four bits at the top of the column. For example, the open parenthesis (is in the third row and corresponds to `0010 1000`.
>
> *Answer:*
> ```
> 0010 1000   0011 1000   0011 1000   0011 1000   0010 1001
> 0010 0000   0011 0101   0011 0101   0011 0101   0010 1101
> 0011 0001   0011 0010   0011 0001   0011 0010
> ```

NATO Broadcast Alphabet

Finally, although we usually try to be efficient (use shortest symbol sequences) to minimize the amount of memory needed to store and transmit information, not all letter representations should be short. The code for the letters used in radio communication is purposely inefficient in this sense, so they are distinctive when spoken amid noise. The NATO broadcast alphabet, shown in Table 8.5, encodes letters as words; that is, the words are the symbols, replacing the standard spoken names. For example, *Mike* and *November* replace "em" and "en," which can be hard to tell apart. This longer encoding improves the chances letters will be recognized when spoken under less-than-ideal conditions. The digits keep their usual names, except nine, which is frequently replaced by *niner*.

Table 8.5. *NATO broadcast alphabet designed not to be minimal*

A	Alpha	G	Golf	M	Mike	S	Sierra	Y	Yankee
B	Bravo	H	Hotel	N	November	T	Tango	Z	Zulu
C	Charlie	I	India	O	Oscar	U	Uniform		
D	Delta	J	Juliet	P	Papa	V	Victor		
E	Echo	K	Kilo	Q	Quebec	W	Whiskey		
F	Foxtrot	L	Lima	R	Romeo	X	X-ray		

FITBYTE

It's Greek to Me. There are dozens of phonetic alphabets for English and many other languages. The NATO alphabet, used for air traffic control, begins with "alpha," raising the question, "What is the first letter of the Greek phonetic alphabet?" Alexandros.

THE *OXFORD ENGLISH DICTIONARY*

Representations like Extended ASCII encode text directly, 8 bits per letter, with more characters available using the escape technique. But most documents have more than just text. For example, one might need to format information, such as font, font size, justification, etc. We could add formatting characters to ASCII—for example, Escape A might represent the Times Roman font—but this is a poor idea for several reasons. The most serious problem is that it mixes the content (i.e., the text) with the description of its form. The descriptive information—it's called **metadata**—specifies the content's formatting or structure, and should be kept separate from the text. So, we specify metadata by using tags, as we have seen in the searching discussion (Chapter 2) and HTML (Chapter 4). Tags use the same character representation as the content itself, which simplifies the encoding, and they are much more versatile. In this section we illustrate how tags encode the structure of a document, by describing the digitization of the *Oxford English Dictionary*.

{ FITLINK }

Encoding Bits on a CD ROM > >

The compact disc read-only memory (CD-ROM) is the technology of the familiar audio CD applied to storing programs and data. Developed jointly by the Phillips and Sony Corporations, the CD was originally intended only for recorded audio and video. But the two companies engineered the technology so cleverly that CDs are almost error free, making them perfect for storing data and software. Here's how CDs work.

CDs are made of clear plastic that is forced into a round mold, something like a round waffle iron, having a smooth bottom and a bumpy top. When the plastic has hardened and been removed from the mold, the topside bumpy pattern is covered with aluminum to make it shiny. A protective layer is put over the aluminum and the "label" is printed on the top.

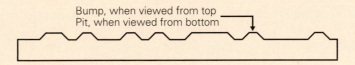

Bump, when viewed from top
Pit, when viewed from bottom

The bumps encode the information. But because they are read from the bottom of the CD, the bumps are called *pits*. The region between the pits is called the *land*. A laser beam is focused up through the CD onto the pitted surface. The beam reflects off of the aluminum and back to a sensor that can detect whether the beam is striking a pit, a land or a diagonal in between.

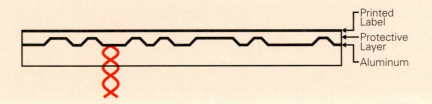

Printed Label
Protective Layer
Aluminum

The pits are arranged in a line that begins at the *inner* edge of the CD and spirals out to the *outer* edge. (Notice that inside-out is the opposite of vinyl records.) The first part of the spiral is used for calibrating the laser reading device; then comes an index (track list) for locating specific positions on the CD; and finally the actual information (music or software) in binary.

In addition to CD ROMs, which are manufactured with the information already stored on them, there are CD Recordable (CR-R) discs and CD ReWriteable (CD-RW) discs. Both types are blank to begin with and use somewhat different materials. CD-R disks can be written once and read thereafter; CD-RW disks can be written and rewritten.

Using Tags to Encode

The *Oxford English Dictionary* is the definitive reference for every English word's meaning, etymology, and usage. Because it is so comprehensive, the OED is truly monumental. The printed version is 20 volumes, weighs 150 pounds, and fills 4 feet of shelf space. In 1857, the Philological Society of London set the goal of producing a complete listing of all English words. They expected that the completed dictionary would have 6400 pages in four volumes. By 1884, with the list completed only up to *ant*, it became clear to James Murray, the lexicographer in charge, that the effort was much more ambitious than originally thought. The first edition, completed in 1928, long after Murray's death, filled 15,490 pages and contained 252,200 entries. In 1984, the conversion of the *OED* to digital form began.

Now imagine that you have typed in the entire *OED* as a long sequence of ASCII characters from A through the end of the definition for *Zyxt*, the last word in English. That would take one person about 120 years. Once the dictionary is digitized, however, we expect the computer to help us use it. Can it help?

Suppose you want to find the definition for the verb *set*, which has the longest entry in the *OED*. The searching software—as described in Chapter 2—would look for *s-e-t* and find it thousands of times. This is because *set* is part of many words, like be*set*, cas*set*te, and *set*tle, and *set* is used in many definitions; for example, "*match-point* in tennis is the final score ending the present game, *set* and match."

We can solve the first problem—avoiding *s-e-t* within words—by ignoring all occurrences that do not have a punctuation character or space before and after the *s-e-t*. The software can do that. But how does it find the definition for *set* among the thousands of true occurrences of the word *set* in other definitions? The software processing the text file, unable to understand the dictionary's contents, would have no clue which one that is.

People use a number of cues to find information in the dictionary, such as alphabetic order and the fact that a new definition begins on a new line, and the defined word is set in bold. Though we could insert HTML-like tags for new lines or boldface type, a better solution is to use the tags to describe the *structure* of the dictionary's content.

Structure Tags

For specifying the *OED*'s **structure**, a special set of tags was developed. For example, `<hw>` is the *OED*'s tag for a *headword*, the word being defined. As usual, because tags surround the text like parentheses, there is a closing *headword* tag, `</hw>`. Thus, the place in the *OED* where the verb *set* is defined appears in the tagged text file of the dictionary as

```
<hw>set</hw>
```

Other tags label the pronunciation `<pr>`, phonetic notations `<ph>`, the parts of speech `<ps>`, the homonym number `<hm>` for headwords that sound the same, and so forth. There are also tags to group items, such as `<e>` to surround an entire entry and `<hg>` to surround a head group (that is, all of the information at the start of a definition). In the *OED* the first entry for the verb set begins

set (sɛt), *v.*[1]

giving the word being defined, the pronunciation, the part of speech (verb), and the homonym number (1). We expect it must be tagged as

`<e><hg><hw>set</hw> <pr><ph>s&epsilont</ph></pr>, <ps>v</ps>.`
`<hm>1</hm></hg>`

Notice the use of the escape code (`&epsilon`) for the epsilon character in the pronunciation. Also, the `</e>` is not shown because it must be at the very end of the entry.

With the structure tags in the dictionary, software can find the definition of the verb *set* easily: Search for occurrences of `<hw>set</hw>`, which indicate a definition for set, check within its head group for `<ps>v</ps>`, which indicates that it is a verb form of set being defined, and then print out (formatted) all of the text within the `<e>`, `</e>` tags.

Of course, the tags are not printed. They are included only to specify the structure, so the computer knows what part of the dictionary it is looking at. But in fact, structure tags are very useful for formatting. For example, the boldface type used for headwords can be automatically applied when the dictionary is printed based on the `<hw>` tag. In a similar way, italics typeface can be applied in the part of speech. The parentheses surrounding the pronunciation and the superscript for the homonym number are also generated automatically. Thus, knowing the structure makes it possible to generate the formatting information.

The opposite is not true. That is, formatting tags do not usually tell us enough about a document to allow us to guess its structure. In the *OED* example, though boldface is used for headwords, it is also used for other purposes, meaning that just because a word is boldface does not mean it is a headword. In fact, because some formatting information, like italics, has both structural and nonstructural occurrences, the *OED* digitization includes some formatting information with the structural information. Thus, structure is more important, but most complex documents use both types of tags. (We discuss structure tags further in the XML discussion of Chapter 16.)

Sample OED Entry

Figure 8.8 shows the entry for *byte*, together with its representation, as it actually appears in the file of the online *OED*. At first the form looks very cluttered, but if you compare it with the printed form, you can make sense out of the tags. The tags specify the role of each word of the dictionary. So, for example, to find the first time the word byte was used in print, the software will search for `<hw>byte</hw>`, then look for the quote date tags, `<qd>,</qd>`, to find that the first use was 1964. Structure tags help the software help the user.

---

byte (baIt). *Computers.* [Arbitrary, prob. influenced by <u>bit</u> sb.[4] and <u>bite</u> sb.] A group of eight consecutive bits operated on as a unit in a computer.

1964 *Blaauw* & *Brooks* in *IBM Systems Jrnl.* III. 122 An 8-bit unit of information is fundamental to most of the formats [of the System/360]. A consecutive group of *n* such units constitutes a field of length *n*. Fixed-length fields of length one, two, four, and eight are termed bytes, halfwords, words, and double words respectively. **1964** *IBM Jrnl. Res. & Developm.* VIII. 97/1 When a byte of data appears from an I/O device, the CPU is seized, dumped, used and restored. **1967 *P. A. Stark*** *Digital Computer Programming* xix. 351 The normal operations in fixed point are done on four bytes at a time. **1968** *Dataweek* 24 Jan. 1/1 Tape reading and writing is at from 34,160 to 192,000 bytes per second.

```
<e><hg><hw>byte</hw> <pr><ph>baIt</ph></pr></hg>. <la>Computers
</la>. <etym>Arbitrary, prob. influenced by <xr><x>bit</x></xr>
 <ps>n.<hm>4</hm></ps>and <xr><x>bite</x> <ps>n.</ps></xr></ety
m> <s4>A group of eight consecutive bits operated on as a unit
 in a computer.</s4> <qp><q><qd>1964</qd><a>Blaauw</a> &amp. <
a>Brooks</a> <bib>in</bib> <w>IBM Systems Jrnl.</w> <lc>III. 1
22</lc> <qt>An 8-bit unit of information is fundamental to most
 of the formats <ed>of the System/360</ed>.&es.A consecutive gr
oup of <i>n</i> such units constitutes a field of length <i>n</
i>.&es.Fixed-length fields of length one, two, four, and eight
are termed bytes, halfwords, words, and double words respective
ly. </qt></q><q><qd>1964</qd> <w>IBM Jrnl. Res. &amp. Developm.
</w> <lc>VIII. 97/1</lc> <qt>When a byte of data appears from a
n I/O device, the CPU is seized, dumped, used and restored.</qt
></q> <q><qd>1967</qd> <a>P. A. Stark</a> <w>Digital Computer P
rogramming</w> <lc>xix. 351</lc> <qt>The normal operations in f
ixed point are done on four bytes at a time.</qt></q><q><qd>
1968</qd> <w>Dataweek</w> <lc>24 Jan. 1/1</lc> <qt>Tape reading
and writing is at from 34,160 to 192,000 bytes persecond.</qt>
</q></qp></e>
```

Figure 8.8. The OED entry for the word byte, *together with the representation of the entry in its digitized form with tags.*

Because the tag characters are included with the content characters, they increase the size of the file compared with plain text. The entry for *byte* is 841 characters, but the tagged code is 1204 characters, an almost 50 percent increase.

Why "Byte"?

As informative as the OED definition is, it doesn't answer that nagging question: Why is *byte* spelled with a *y*? To understand the charming nature of the answer, we need to know that computer memory is subject to errors (a zero changing to a one, or a one to a zero), caused by such things as cosmic rays. Really. It doesn't happen often, but often enough to worry computer engineers, who build special circuitry to detect and correct memory errors. They often add extra bits to the memory to help detect errors—for example, a ninth bit per byte can detect errors using parity.

Parity refers to whether a number is even or odd. To encode bytes using **even parity**, use the normal byte encoding and then count the number of 1's in the byte; if there is an even number of 1's, set the ninth bit to 0; if there is an odd number, set the ninth bit to 1. The result is that all 9-bit groups will have even parity, either because they were even to begin with and the 0 didn't change that, or they were odd to begin with, but the 1 made them even. Any single bit error in a group causes its parity to become odd, allowing the hardware to detect that an error occurred, though not which bit is wrong.

So, why is *byte* spelled with a *y*? The answer comes from Werner Buchholz, the inventor of the word and the concept. In the late 1950s, Buchholz was the project manager and architect for the IBM supercomputer, called Stretch. For that machine, he explained to me, "We needed a word for a quantity of memory between a bit and a word." (A "word" of computer memory is typically the amount required to represent computer instructions and the "usual" integer numbers. On modern computers, a word is 32 bits.) Buchholz continued, "It seemed that after 'bit' comes 'bite.' But we changed the 'i' to a 'y' so that a typist couldn't accidentally change 'byte' into 'bit' by the single error of dropping the 'e'. " No single letter change to *byte* can create *bit*, and vice versa. Buchholz and his engineers were so concerned with memory errors that he invented an error-detecting *name* for the memory unit!

SUMMARY

We began by learning that digitizing doesn't require digits—any symbols will do. Using dice as a source of patterns, we considered problems of encoding keyboard characters. We solved these problems by using sequences of dice, by assigning a special escape symbol, and by deciding not to encode certain characters. Then we introduced PandA encoding, the fundamental representation of information, which is based on the Presence and Absence of a physical phenomenon. PandA patterns are discrete; that is, they form the basic unit of a bit. And their names—most often 1 and 0—could be any pair of opposite terms. The term bit is a contraction for binary digit, but bits are used for more than just representing numbers. Next, we learned about 7-bit ASCII, an early, and still useful, assignment of bit sequences (symbols) to keyboard characters. Extended ASCII is now the standard. Once there is an encoding for keyboard characters, documents like the *Oxford English Dictionary* can be encoded. There, we learned that tags associate metadata with every part of the OED. Using that data, a computer can easily help us find words and other information, because every part of every entry has been identified. Finally, we resolved the mystery of the *y* in *byte*.

EXERCISES

Multiple Choice

1. Without an escape sequence, a pair of dice can encode _____ symbols and three dice can encode _____ symbols.
   A. 36, 72
   B. 36, 256
   C. 36, 216
   D. 72, 216

2. How many characters could be represented by two eight-sided dice?
   A. 16
   B. 36
   C. 64
   D. 256

3. Which of the following is not an example of an escape key?
   A. Control
   B. Alt
   C. Shift
   D. Tab

4. Using just the letter keys and the Shift, Alt, and Control modifier keys, how many possible combinations are there?
   A. 29
   B. 78
   C. 104
   D. 256

5. Which of these is not digital?
   A. a clock with hands
   B. a calendar
   C. a checkbook balance
   D. a television channel

6. PandA is a combination of:
   A. true and false
   B. on and off
   C. yes and no
   D. all of the above

7. Finish this: I like cats. Fluffy is a cat. Therefore:
   A. Fluffy is not a dog.
   B. I don't like dogs.
   C. Cats don't like dogs.
   D. I like Fluffy.

8. A binary system:
   A. consists of only two possible items
   B. uses discrete data
   C. can be represented by PandA
   D. all of the above

9. The medium used for storing data on a disk is made from:
   A. iron
   B. plastic
   C. magnetism
   D. light

10. On the computer, PandA is represented by:
   A. 1 and 0
   B. 0 and 1
   C. bits and bytes
   D. off and on

Short Answer

1. If bits are to atoms, bytes are to _____.
2. To _____ is to represent information with digits.
3. PandA is short for _____.
4. When data are _____, they are separate and distinct and cannot be transformed into another value by gradations.
5. A(n) _____ is an agreed upon order for basic symbols.
6. A(n) _____ is another name for a separator.
7. A(n) _____ is a character that is not a letter or numeral or punctuation character.
8. All the values in a PandA formulation are _____.
9. _____ is short for binary digit.
10. The _____ of a bit is its storage pattern in the physical world.
11. _____ is short for hexadecimal.
12. Base-16 is also called _____.
13. Letters, numbers, and symbols are represented on the computer using the _____.
14. All computer systems share a _____ set of symbols used to represent characters.

Exercises

1. Make a list of the numbers you use that are not treated as numbers. (For example, you do not perform math on them.)

2. What is a bit and how was the word created?

3. What does PandA stand for and what does PandA name?

4. Come up with a list of ten different PandA items.

5. What North American telephone number is: ▲ ‖ ‖ ◀ ◀ ■ ▲ ◀◀ ‖ ‖ ?

6. Encode (888) 555-1212 in Extended ASCII, including punctuation.

7. You bought a mosaic coffee table in Santorini, Greece, last summer called "Animals of Atlantis." While listening to a boring story about your friend's visit home, you notice the table is eight tiles across, which could be the bits of a byte. What ASCII message did the Greeks encode, using the obvious PandA encoding?

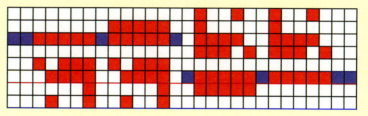

8. The Hawaiian alphabet has 18 symbols. Discuss the symbols you would use for their character set and how many bits would be needed for it.

9. Translate the following hexadecimal into binary and then into English.

    68   65   78   61   64   65   63   69   6D   61   6C

10. Change the letters of the sentence "THE APPLE LOGO HAS A BYTE MISSING" into NATO broadcast code (ignore spaces in all cases) and then represent the result with ASCII. How many bytes are required for each?

FOLLOWING INSTRUCTIONS

Principles of Computer Operation

learning | *objectives*

> Describe how the Fetch/Execute Cycle
  works

  - List the five steps

  - Give an example (from the Ice Classic
    analogy) of each of the five steps

> Explain the function of the memory, control
  unit, ALU, input unit and output unit,
  program counter

> Explain why integration and
  photolithography are important in
  integrated circuits

> Discuss the purpose of an operating system

> Describe how large tasks are performed
  with simple instructions

Worthless.

—REPLY BY THE BRITISH ASTRONOMER ROYAL, SIR GEORGE BIDDELL AIRY, 1842, RESPONDING TO A QUERY BY THE CHANCELLOR OF THE EXCHEQUER, WHO WAS CONSIDERING FUNDING CHARLES BABBAGE'S ANALYTICAL ENGINE, A MECHANICAL CALCULATOR AND PREDECESSOR OF MODERN DIGITAL COMPUTERS.

Where . . . ENIAC is equipped with 18,000 vacuum tubes and weighs 30 tons, computers in the future may have 1,000 vacuum tubes and perhaps weigh just one-half ton.

— POPULAR MECHANICS, 1949

There is no reason why anyone would want to have a computer in their home.

—KEN OLSEN, PRESIDENT OF DIGITAL EQUIPMENT CORPORATION, 1977

THIS CHAPTER introduces two key inventions in information technology that rank among the top technological achievements of all time: computers and integrated circuits (ICs). Naturally they are both complex and sophisticated topics, so specialized in fact that a Ph.D. degree is not enough training to understand current practice fully. Making today's computers and chips each requires large teams of specialists. If an expert can't completely understand computers and integrated circuits, is there hope for the rest of us?

Both topics are based on easy-to-understand ideas. What makes the technology so sophisticated and complex is pushing the basic ideas to their limit, and that is definitely beyond our needs. But we should learn the main ideas, because the same basic processes of instruction execution used by computers come up often in information technology. Web browsers process Web pages using instruction execution that is just like computer operation. Spreadsheets use the same ideas. You are even an instruction executer when you prepare your income taxes. This idea is fundamental to processing information and a key concept of IT.

First, we discuss the Fetch/Execute Cycle. Next, we describe the parts of a computer, how they're connected, and briefly what each does. We then outline how these parts can execute instructions. We give a detailed example that shows that computers operate in a straightforward way. Next, we discuss software and operating systems to explain how a computer's primitive abilities can achieve such impressive results. Finally, we explain the "big ideas" behind integrated circuits and how semiconductor technology works.

World Domination. During the 1950s and 1960s, as computers were leaving the lab and entering business, there was concern in the popular press about "computers taking over the world." People worried because computers could do some tasks amazingly well, for example, adding 100,000 numbers in a second. There were grim stories of tyrannical computers enslaving people. When it finally happened—when life as most people knew it *depended* on computers—no one apparently noticed.

INSTRUCTION EXECUTION ENGINES

Before dissecting a computer, consider what a computer actually does. The obvious answer, "It computes," does not say very much to those of us who use modern information processing applications. These applications—Web searching, downloading MP3 tunes, word processing—are very complex and sophisticated. They work by piling layers and layers of powerful software on the basic processing capabilities of the computer's hardware, hiding its fundamental characteristics. Beneath all of this software is the basic computer. What is it doing?

What Computers Can Do

As a definition, **computers** deterministically perform or execute instructions to process information. Another term for *computer* would be "instruction execution engine." The most important aspect of this definition is that the computer is doing what it is told—following instructions—so obviously someone or something else must have decided what those instructions should do. Programmers do that, of course. So, if the instructions don't do what we want them to do, it's certainly not the computer's fault. It's just following instructions.

What Computers Can't Do

A key feature of the definition is the term *deterministically*. This means that when it comes time for the computer to determine which instruction to execute next, it is required by its construction to execute a specific instruction based only on the program and the data that it has been given. It has no options. As compared to people, computers are very methodical:

> Computers have no imagination or creativity.

> Computers have no intuition.

{ G R E A T **FIT** M O M E N T S }

No. 1 Computer > >

Credit for inventing the first electronic computer is in dispute, but most people give the credit to J. Presper Eckert and John Mauchley of the University of Pennsylvania. Named **ENIAC** for Electronic Numerical Integrator And Calculator, the Eckert/Mauchley machine was built for the U.S. Army in 1946. ENIAC is in many ways the intellectual antecedent of present day computers. Another academic, John V. Atanasoff of Iowa State University, developed ideas used by Eckert and Mauchley, and at about the same time built the **ABC**, Atanasoff Berry Computer, with graduate student Clifford E. Berry. In an epic patent infringement lawsuit, Judge Earl Larson decided on October 19, 1973 that Atanasoff's prior invention invalidated the Eckert/Mauchley patent on the computer.

Clockwise from top left: J. Presper Eckert and John Mauchley, John V. Atanasoff, Clifford E. Berry, the ENIAC with operator.

> Computers are literal, with no sense of irony, subtlety, proportion, or decorum.

> Computers don't joke or have a sense of humor.

> Computers are not vindictive or cruel. (Admittedly some frustrated users will find these assertions far-fetched.)

> Computers are not purposeful.

> Computers have no free will.

They only execute instructions. Deterministically. One result of determinism is that rerunning a program with the same data produces exactly the same result every time.

THE FETCH/EXECUTE CYCLE

Calling a computer an "instruction execution engine" suggests the idea of a machine cycling through a series of operations, performing an instruction on each round. And that's pretty much the idea. Computers implement in hardware a process called the **Fetch/Execute Cycle**. The Fetch/Execute Cycle consists of getting the next instruction, figuring out what to do, gathering the data needed to do it, doing it, saving the result, and repeating. It's a simple process, but repeating it billions of times a second can accomplish a lot.

A Five-Step Cycle

The five steps of the Fetch/Execute Cycle have standard names, and because these operations are repeated in a never-ending sequence, they are often written with an arrow from the last step to the first showing the cycle (see Figure 9.1). The step names suggest the operations described in the previous paragraph. But the Fetch/Execute Cycle is a little more complicated than that. What is an instruction like? How is the next instruction located? When instructions and data are fetched, where are they fetched from, and where do they go?

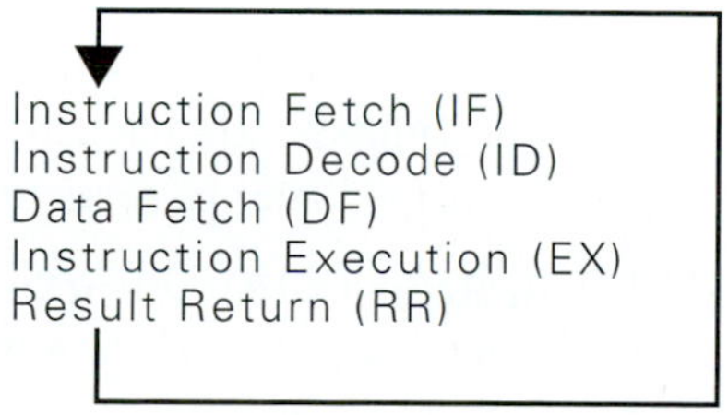

```
    ┌─────────────────────┐
    ▼                     │
Instruction Fetch (IF)    │
Instruction Decode (ID)   │
Data Fetch (DF)           │
Instruction Execution (EX)│
Result Return (RR)        │
    └─────────────────────┘
```

Figure 9.1. The fetch/execute cycle.

The Ice Classic Analogy

To help answer these questions, consider an analogy based on the person who opens the mail at the Nenana Ice Classic, a lottery run by the town of Nenana, Alaska (pop. 449). People worldwide buy $2 tickets to guess the exact minute in springtime when the ice will break up on the town's river, the Tananah, and flow downstream. In 2001, breakup was exactly 1:00 P.M., May 8, and the jackpot, split among eight winners, was $308,500. After competition is closed, but before breakup, the town publishes a thick book listing the names of all the contestants organized by the date and time of their guesses. The process of compiling the data for this book is like the Fetch/Execute Cycle.

Imagine in the office at Ice Classic Headquarters a table with trays containing a few thousand 3 × 5 cards, each labeled with a month, day, hour, and minute. The card records the names of contestants guessing that time. For example, the 2001 winners' names would have been listed on the card labeled 5/08-13:00. The cards are filed in time order in several long trays so the card for each date and time can be easily found. Also, imagine a tray of unopened envelopes.

The Ice Classic volunteer, a human version of the Fetch/Execute Cycle, proceeds as follows:

> **Instruction Fetch (IF)** He or she *fetches* the first envelope, opens it, and removes its contents, setting aside the $2 fee in the cash drawer. What comes out of the envelope is an instruction to the volunteer to enter the contestant's guess of a particular date and time.

> **Instruction Decode (ID)** The volunteer *decodes* the instruction, finding the contestant's name and the day, hour, and minute that the contestant predicts for the ice breakup. The key part of the decoding operation is finding the day and time guessed, because together they determine which card is needed.

> **Data Fetch (DF)** The volunteer then *fetches* the proper card. This Data Fetch retrieves the list of the other people, if any, who have already guessed that same day and time.

> **Instruction Execute (EX)** The volunteer then *executes* the instruction by entering the person's name and address on the card. If the space is full, the volunteer simply stores the card in a safe place, gets a blank card, labels it with the same month, day, hour, and minute, and begins using it; the cards will be merged later to create the contestants book.

> **Result Return (RR)** When the entry has been made, the volunteer *returns* the card to its proper place in the tray, which is the human version of the Result Return step of the Fetch/Execute Cycle.

The tireless volunteer then picks up another envelope and repeats the process.

The Ice Classic analogy helps us understand the steps of the Fetch/Execute Cycle. We will refer back to it as we explain how a computer is organized.

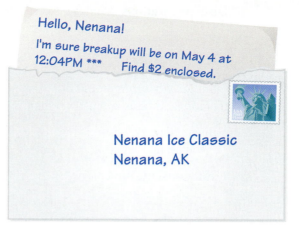

Hello, Nenana!

I'm sure breakup will be on May 4 at 12:04PM *** Find $2 enclosed.

Nenana Ice Classic
Nenana, AK

ANATOMY OF A COMPUTER

Now that we know how the Fetch/Execute Cycle works, we need to know how a computer's parts are arranged to fetch and execute instructions. All computers, regardless of their implementing technology, have five basic parts or subsystems: memory, control unit, arithmetic/logic unit (ALU), input unit, and output unit. These are arranged as shown in Figure 9.2. *Caution:* It is just a coincidence that there are five steps to the Fetch/Execute Cycle and five subsystems to a computer—they're related, of course, but not one-to-one.

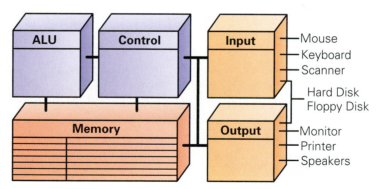

Figure 9.2. The principal components of a computer.

The five parts of a computer have the following characteristics.

Memory

Memory stores both the program, while it is running, and the data on which the program operates. In the Ice Classic analogy, the instruction memory is the tray of envelops, and the data memory is the sequence of cards on which the names are written. Memory has the following characteristics:

> **Discrete locations.** Memory is organized as a sequence of discrete locations, like the cards in the Ice Classic analogy. In modern memories, each location is composed of 1 byte (that is, a sequence of 8 bits).

> **Addresses.** Every memory location has an address, like the month/day/hour/minute card labels in the analogy, although computer memory addresses are just whole numbers starting at 0.

> **Values.** Memory locations record or store values, like the cards that record the contestants' names.

> **Finite capacity.** A memory location has finite capacity—limited size—like the cards in the tray. So programmers must keep in mind that the data may not "fit" in the memory location.

Byte-Size Memory Location. These characteristics motivate a commonly used diagram of computer memory (see Figure 9.3). The discrete locations are represented as boxes. The address of each location is displayed above the box. The value or contents of the memory locations are shown in the boxes.

0	1	2	3	4	5	6	7	8	9	10	11
100	T	h	a	N	K	$	*	4	~~b~~	d	a	...

Figure 9.3. Diagram of computer memory illustrating its key properties.

The 1-byte size of a memory location is enough to store one ASCII character (letter or numeral or punctuation symbol) or a number less than 256. Obviously a single computer memory location, unlike the 3 × 5 cards in our analogy, would not be large enough to store the names of several contestants. To overcome the small capacity of computer memory locations, a programmer simply uses a sequence of memory locations and ignores the fact that they all have separate addresses; that is, the programmer treats the address of the first location as if it were the address of the whole block of memory.

Random Access Memory. Computer memory is often called **random access memory** (RAM). The modifier "random access" is out-of-date and simply means that the computer can refer to the memory locations in any order. RAM is most often measured in megabytes, abbreviated MB. A large memory is generally preferable to a small memory because there is more space for programs and data.

FITBYTE

Free Memory. *Mega-* is the prefix for "million," so a megabyte should be 1,000,000 bytes of memory. In fact, a megabyte is 1,048,576 bytes. Why such a weird number? Computers need to associate a byte of memory with every address. A million addresses require 20 bits. But with 20 bits, 2^{20} = 1,048,576 addresses are possible with binary counting. So, to ensure that every 20-bit address has its byte of memory, the extra 48,576 bytes are included "free."

In summary, memory is like a sequence of labeled containers known as locations: The address is the location's number in sequence; the value or the information stored at the location is the container's contents; only so much can fit in each container.

Control Unit

The **control unit** of a computer is the hardware implementation of the Fetch/Execute Cycle. Its circuitry fetches an instruction from memory and performs the other operations of the Fetch/Execute Cycle on it. In the Ice Classic analogy, the tireless volunteer is the control.

Computer instructions are more primitive than the "Enter my name . . ." instructions of the Ice Classic analogy. A typical machine instruction has the form

```
ADD 2000, 2080, 4000
```

which appears to be commanding that three numbers, 2000, 2080, and 4000, be added together, *but it does not*. Rather, the instruction asks that the two numbers stored in the memory locations 2000 and 2080 be added together, and that the result be stored in the memory location 4000. So the Data Fetch step of the Fetch/Execute Cycle must get the two values at memory locations 2000 and 2080, and after they are added, the Result Return step will store the answer in memory location 4000.

We must emphasize a fundamental property of computer instructions. The instruction `ADD 2000, 2080, 4000` does not command the computer to add together the numbers 2000 and 2080—the answer is 4080 and it is pointless to program a computer to do a task we know the answer to. Rather, the instruction commands the computer to add together the numbers *stored in memory locations* 2000 and 2080, whatever those numbers may be. Because different values can be in those memory locations each time the computer executes the instruction, a different result can be computed each time. The concept is that computer instructions encode the memory addresses of the numbers to be added (or subtracted or whatever), not the numbers themselves, and so refer to the values *indirectly*. The indirection means that a single instruction can combine any two numbers simply by placing them in the referenced memory locations (see Figure 9.4). Referring to a value by referring to the address in memory where it is stored is fundamental to a computer's versatilitiy.

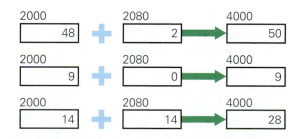

Figure 9.4. *Illustration of a single ADD instruction producing different results depending on the contents of the memory locations referenced in the instruction.*

Arithmetic/Logic Unit (ALU)

As its name suggests, the arithmetic/logic unit (ALU) performs the "math." The ALU is the part of the computer that generally does the work during the Instruction Execute step of the Fetch/Execute Cycle. So, for the example instruction `ADD 2000, 2080, 4000`, the ALU does the actual addition. A circuit in the ALU can add two numbers—an amazing capability when you think about it. There are also circuits for multiplying two numbers, circuits for comparing two numbers, and so on. You can think of an ALU as carrying out each machine instruction with a separate circuit, though modern computers are so sophisticated that they can combine several operations into one circuit.

In the Ice Classic analogy, the ALU corresponds to the office calculator. The instruction execution in the analogy didn't require any arithmetic, just writing names on the card. The calculator (the ALU) doesn't come into the process until the volunteer performs the instruction "Add the amount in the cash drawer to the amount previously received to compute the total receipts." This is true for computers, too: Some instructions use the ALU and others do not. Computers sometimes **transform** information (using the ALU) and sometimes **transfer** information. Both transforming and transferring are included in the term **information processing**.

For instructions that use the ALU, it is now clear what the Data Fetch and Result Return steps of the Fetch/Execute Cycle must do. Data Fetch gets the values from memory that the ALU needs to perform operations like `ADD` and `MULTIPLY`. These values are called **operands**. The instruction includes the addresses where the data is to be found. The Data Fetch step delivers these values to the ALU. When the ALU completes the operation, producing a sum or product or other value, the Result Return step moves that answer from the ALU to the memory at the address specified in the instruction.

Input Unit and Output Unit

These two components, which are inverses of each other, and so can easily be discussed together, are the wires and circuits through which information moves into and out of a computer. A computer without input or output—that is, the memory, control, and ALU sealed in a box—is useless. Indeed, from a philosophical perspective, we might question whether it can even be said to "compute."

The Peripherals. As shown in Figure 9.2, many kinds of devices—called **peripherals**—connect to the computer **input/output (I/O)** ports, providing it with input or receiving its output. The *peripherals* are not considered part of the computer, but rather they are specialized gadgets that encode or decode information between the computer and the physical world. The keyboard encodes the keystrokes we type into binary form for the computer. The monitor decodes information from the computer's memory, displaying it on a lighted, color screen. In general, the peripherals handle the physical part of the operation, sending or receiving the binary information the computer uses.

The cable from the peripheral to the computer connects to the input unit or the output unit. These units handle the communication protocol with the peripherals. As a general rule, think of the input unit as moving information from the peripheral into the memory, and the output unit as moving information from the memory and delivering it to the outside world. (The real details are much more complicated.)

Floppy Disks and Hard Drives. Some peripherals, such as floppy disks and hard disks, are used by computers for both input and output. That makes them storage devices, places where the computer files away information when it is not needed (an output operation) and where it gets information when it needs it again (an input operation). The hard disk is the *alpha-peripheral,* being the most aggressively engineered and the device most tightly linked to the computer. Why? Because although programs and their data must reside in the computer's memory when programs run, they reside on the hard disk the rest of the time because that's where there is more permanent space. In that sense, the hard disk is an extension of the computer's memory, but typically it is a hundred times larger and several thousand times slower.

A Device Driver for Every Peripheral. Most peripheral devices are "dumb" in that all they provide is basic physical translation to or from binary signals. They rely on the computer for any further processing, which is almost always required to make the peripheral operate in an "intelligent way." So, as I type the letters of this sentence, signals are sent from the keyboard to the computer indicating which keys my fingers depress. When the computer receives information that I've pressed the *w* and the *Shift* key at the same time, the computer—not the keyboard—converts the *w* keystroke to a capital *W.* Similarly, keys like *Ctrl* and *Backspace* are just keys to the keyboard. It is the added processing by a piece of software called a **device driver** that gives the keyboard its standard meaning and behavior. Every device needs a device driver to provide this added processing. Naturally, because the peripheral device may have unique characteristics, a device driver will be specialized to only one device.

FITTIP

New Toys. Many users are excited about getting a new peripheral such as a printer, scanner, or CD-ROM. They plug it into their computer, but forget that it needs a device driver before it can run. This is partly because computers often come loaded with standardized or popular device drivers, and so users don't know that peripherals need them, or they forget. A floppy disk or a CD containing the device driver(s) should come with the peripheral, or the driver can be downloaded from the manufacturer's Web site.

Ice Classic Analogy: Input and Output. In the Ice Classic analogy, the output device is the printing company in Fairbanks that prints and binds the list of contestants. When all of the entries have been received, the data for the list will have been recorded in the memory (3 × 5 cards), once all of the filled-up cards are merged back in the tray in the right order. Of course, the printing company doesn't want to deal with trays of cards, so the tireless volunteer becomes the device driver, converting the information on the cards into the right form for the printing company. This might mean putting 6–8 cards on the copier glass, and photocopying them to create a page that the printer can use, maybe including cards with headings for each day. The copier is like the output unit, because it takes the data from memory (the cards) and prepares it for the output device, the printer. When the pages are done, they are transmitted to the company in Fairbanks to produce the user-readable output: the list of contestants.

THE PROGRAM COUNTER: THE PC'S PC

The final question is how a computer determines which instruction to execute next. In the Ice Classic analogy, the volunteer simply removes letters from a tray of mail to get the next "instruction." The order doesn't matter with mail, so any letter will do. In computers, the order in which instructions are executed is critical.

Address of the Next Instruction

Recall that when the Fetch/Execute Cycle is executing a program, the instructions are stored in the memory. That means every instruction has an address, which is the address of the memory location of the first byte of the instruction. (Instructions of present-day computers use 4 bytes.) Naturally, computers keep track of which instruction to execute next by its address. This address, stored in the control part of the computer, should probably be called the *next instruction address,* but for historic reasons it is actually known by the curious term, **program counter**, abbreviated PC. *(For the rest of the chapter PC will mean program counter, not personal computer.)*

The Instruction Fetch step of the Fetch/Execute Cycle transfers the instruction from memory at the address specified by the program counter to the decoder part of the control unit. Once the instruction has been fetched, and while it is being processed by the remaining steps of the F/E Cycle, the computer prepares to process the next instruction. The next instruction is assumed to be the next instruction in sequence. Because instructions use 4 bytes of memory, the next instruction must be at the memory address PC + 4, that is, 4 bytes further along in sequence. Therefore, the computer adds four to the PC, so that when the F/E Cycle gets around to the Instruction Fetch step again, the PC is "pointing at" the new instruction.

Branch and Jump Instructions

This scheme of executing instructions in sequence seems flawed: Won't the Fetch/Execute Cycle blaze through the memory executing all the instructions, get to the last instruction in memory, and "fall off the end of memory," having used up all of the instructions? This won't happen unless the program has a bug in it. The reason is that computers come with instructions called *branch* and *jump* that change the PC. After the control unit has prepared for the next instruction in sequence by adding four to the PC, the Instruction Execute step of the current (branch or jump) instruction can reset the PC to a new value. This overrides the selection of the next instruction in sequence and makes the PC address some other instruction in memory. The next instruction will be fetched from this memory location on the next round of the Fetch/Execute Cycle.

INSTRUCTION INTERPRETATION

The process of executing a program is also called **instruction interpretation**. The term comes from the idea that the computer is interpreting our commands, but in its own language.

To illustrate the idea of interpreting instructions, let's follow the execution of a typical **ADD** instruction. Figure 9.5 shows the situation before the Fetch/Execute Cycle starts the next instruction. Notice that some of the memory locations and the program counter (PC) are visible in the control unit.

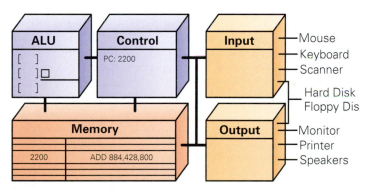

Figure 9.5. Computer before executing an ADD instruction.

Instruction execution begins by moving the instruction at the address given by the PC from the memory unit to the control unit. (See Figure 9.6, where the instruction address is 2200 and the example instruction is `ADD 884, 428, 800` .) The bits of the instruction are placed into the decoder circuit of the control unit. Once the instruction is fetched, the PC can be readied for fetching the next instruction. For present-day computers whose instructions are 4 bytes long, 4 is added to the PC. (The updated PC value will be visible in the Data Fetch configuration shown in Figure 9.8 and those that follow.)

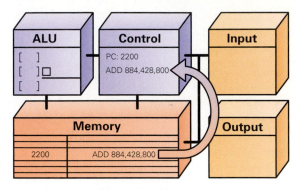

Figure 9.6. *Instruction Fetch: Move instruction from memory to the control unit.*

Figure 9.7 shows the Instruction Decode step, in which the ALU is set up for the operation in the Instruction Execute step. Among the bits of the instruction, the decoder will find the memory addresses of the instruction's data, the *source operands*. Like **ADD**, most instructions operate on two data values stored in memory, so most instructions have addresses for two source operands. These two addresses (**884**, **428**) are passed to the circuit that will fetch the operand values from memory during the next (Data Fetch) step. Simultaneously, the decoder finds the *destination address,* the place in memory where the answer is to be sent during the Result Return step. That address (**800**) is placed in the RR circuit. Finally, the decoder will figure out what operation the ALU should perform on the data values (**ADD**), and set up the ALU appropriately for that operation.

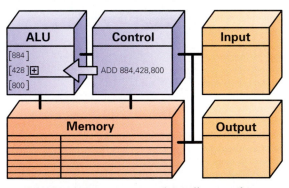

Figure 9.7. *Instruction Decode: Pull apart the instruction, set up the operation in the ALU, and compute the source and destination operand addresses.*

Figure 9.8 shows the Data Fetch step. The data values for the two source operands are moved from the memory into the ALU. These values (**12**, **42**) are the data that the instruction will work on in the next (Execute) step.

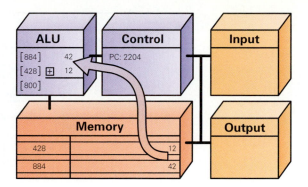

Figure 9.8. *Data Fetch: Move the operands from memory to the ALU.*

Instruction Execution is illustrated in Figure 9.9. The operation—set up during the Instruction Decode step—performs the computation. In the present case, the addition circuit adds the two source operand values together to produce their sum (54). This is the actual computation.

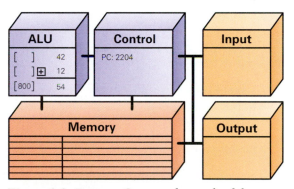

Figure 9.9. *Execute: Compute the result of the operation in the ALU.*

FITBYTE

Micro Computer. In our presentation, Instruction Execution—the "compute" part of the Fetch/Execute Cycle—accounts for only 20 percent of the time spent executing an instruction; it averages even less on real computers. Measured by silicon area, the ALU—the circuitry that does the computing—takes up less than 5 percent of a typical processor chip.

Finally, the Result Return step, shown in Figure 9.10, returns the result of Instruction Execution (54) to the memory location specified by the destination address (800) and set up during Instruction Decode. Once the result is returned, the cycle begins all over again.

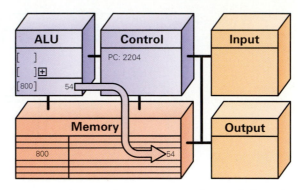

Figure 9.10. *Result Return: Store the result from the ALU into the memory at the destination address.*

FITBYTE

Stop! If the Fetch/Execute Cycle is an infinite loop, how does a computer stop? Early computers actually had Start and Stop buttons, but modern computers simply execute an "idle loop" when there's nothing to do. The instructions keep checking to see if there's anything to do, like process a mouse click or keystroke.

CYCLING THE F/E CYCLE

Using **ADD**, we have illustrated how a computer is able to execute instructions. **ADD** is representative of the complexity of computer instructions—some are slightly simpler, some slightly more complex. There are no instructions like

```
Check_spelling_of_the_document_beginning_at_location 884
```

So, with such primitive instructions, it is surprising that computers can do anything at all. They get their impressive capabilities by executing many of these simple instructions per second, and by programmers translating complex tasks into simple instructions.

The Computer Clock

Computers are instruction execution engines. We have just studied in detail how the Fetch/Execute Cycle carries out one **ADD** instruction. Since the computer does one instruction per cycle, the speed of a computer—the number of instructions executed in a second—depends on the number of Fetch/Execute Cycles it does in a second. The rate of the Fetch/Execute Cycle is determined by the computer's **clock**, and it is measured in **megahertz**, or millions (mega) of cycles per second (hertz). Computer clock speeds have increased dramatically in recent years, resulting in speeds of 1000 MHz or more. A 1000 MHz clock ticks a billion (in American

English) times per second, which is one gigahertz (1 GHz) in any language. (See Figure 9.11 for terms; "giga" is pronounced with hard g's.) Clock speeds are a common feature of computer advertisements, but how important are they?

1000^1	kilo-	$1024^1 = 2^{10} = 1,024$	milli-	1000^{-1}
1000^2	mega-	$1024^2 = 2^{20} = 1,048,576$	micro-	1000^{-2}
1000^3	giga-	$1024^3 = 2^{30} = 1,073,741,824$	nano-	1000^{-3}
1000^4	tera-	$1024^4 = 2^{40} = 1,099,511,627,776$	pico-	1000^{-4}
1000^5	peta-	$1024^5 = 2^{50} = 1,125,899,906,842,624$	femto-	1000^{-5}
1000^6	exa-	$1024^6 = 2^{60} = 1,152,921,504,606,876,976$	atto-	1000^{-6}
1000^7	zetta-	$1024^7 = 2^{70} = 1,180,591,620,717,411,303,424$	zepto-	1000^{-7}
1000^8	yotta-	$1024^8 = 2^{80} = 1,208,925,819,614,629,174,706,176$	yocto-	1000^{-8}

Figure 9.11. *Standard prefixes from the Système International (SI) convention on scientific measurements. Generally a prefix refers to a power of 1000, except when the quantity (for example, memory) is counted in binary; for binary quantities the prefix refers to a power of 1024, which is 2^{10}.*

FITTIP

Beauty of Prefixes. Prefixes "change the units" so that very large or small quantities can be expressed with numbers of a reasonable size. A well-known humorous example concerns Helen of Troy from Greek myth "whose face launched 1000 ships." The beauty needed to launch one ship is one-thousandth of Helen's, that is, 0.001 Helen, or 1 MilliHelen.

One Cycle per Clock Tick

A computer with a 1 GHz clock has one billionth of a second—one nanosecond—between clock ticks to run the Fetch/Execute Cycle. In that short time, light can travel only about a foot (30 cm). Is it really possible to add or multiply that fast? No. In truth, modern computers try to *start* an instruction on each clock tick. They pass off finishing the instruction to other circuitry, like a worker on an assembly line. This process, called *pipelining*, frees the fetch unit to start the next instruction before the last one is done. As shown in Figure 9.12, if the five steps of the Fetch/Execute Cycle take a nanosecond *each*—which is still extremely fast—it is possible to finish one instruction on each clock tick as long as there is enough circuitry for five instructions to be "in process" at the same time. That way the computer finishes instructions at the starting rate of one per tick. Of course, to execute 1000 instructions in a five-stage pipeline takes 1004 clock cycles—1000 to start each instruction, and 4 more for the last four steps of the last instruction. So it is not quite true that 1000 instructions are executed in 1000 ticks. But that's probably close enough.

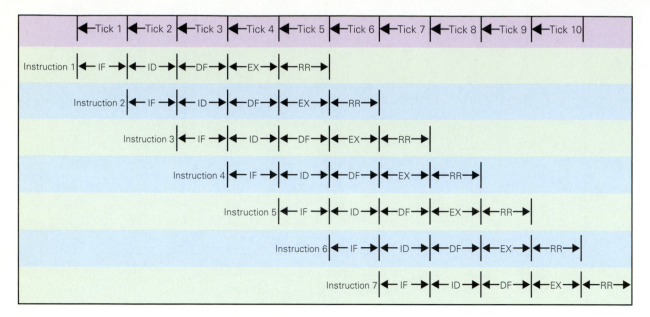

Figure 9.12. *Schematic diagram of a pipelined Fetch/Execute Cycle. On each tick, the IF circuit starts a new instruction, and before the time runs out, it passes it along to the ID (Instruction Decode) unit; the ID unit works on the instruction it receives, finishing just in time to pass it along to the DF (Data Fetch) circuit, and so on. When the pipeline is filled, five instructions are in progress, and one instruction is finished on each clock tick, making the computer appear to be running one instruction per clock tick.*

A Billion Instructions per Second?

So, does a computer with a 1 GHz clock execute a billion instructions per second? Computer salespeople would like you to believe it's true, but it's not. We said that computers *try* to start an instruction on each clock tick, but there is a long list of reasons why it's not always possible. If the computer cannot start instructions on each clock tick, its execution rate falls *below* one billion instructions per second. But the situation is even more complicated. Computer engineers have figured out how to start more than one instruction at a time, even though instructions are supposed to be executed sequentially—that is, the next one isn't started until the current one is finished. If several instructions can be started at the same time often enough, they can make up for not starting instructions at other times. Thus the rate could be *above* one billion per second. It is extremely difficult—even for experts—to figure out how fast a modern computer runs. As a result, the one-instruction-per-cycle guideline—which was once dependable—is no longer correct.

FITBYTE

Speed of Fluency. This book was written on two new laptops with different processors that were the same in most ways except clock speed: one machine's clock was twice as fast as the other's. However, the "slower machine" regularly ran applications faster than the "faster machine," because performance depends on many features: instruction set, memory size and design, other system components like cache, software quality, and so on. The lesson: Clock speed alone doesn't tell you how fast a computer runs.

MANY, MANY SIMPLE OPERATIONS

Computers "know" very few instructions. That is, the decoder hardware in the controller recognizes, and the ALU can perform, only about 100 or so different instructions. And there is a lot of duplication. For example, different types of data usually have different kinds of **ADD** instructions, one for adding bytes, one for adding whole numbers, one for adding "decimal" numbers, and so on. *Everything* that computers do must be reduced to one of these primitive, hardwired instructions. They can't do anything else. We return to this idea in Chapter 23.

The **ADD** instruction has about average complexity, and **MULT** (multiply) and **DIV** (divide) are at the screaming limit of complexity. Examples of other instructions include:

> Shift the bits of a word (4 bytes) to the left or right, filling the emptied places with zeros and throwing away the bits that fall off the end. (Where do they go?)

> Compute the logical **AND**, which tests if pairs of bits are both true (1), and the logical **OR**, which tests if at least one of two bits is true.

> Test if a bit is zero or nonzero, and jump to a new set of instructions based on the outcome.

> Move information around in memory.

> Sense the signals from input/output devices.

Computer instructions are very primitive. There is no DRAW_A_BUTTON or SPELL_CHECK.

Converting Complicated Tasks into Simple Instructions

Computers tirelessly perform their simple instructions very fast, and that is the secret of getting them to do tasks that are more interesting than adding two numbers together. If we can figure out how to describe a more complex operation as a sequence of the primitive hardwired instructions, each time we want the more complex operation done, we simply instruct the computer to follow the sequence. It will *appear* that the computer knows the more complex operation, especially if it does the sequence blazingly fast. Once we have instructed the computer to do more complex operations, we can use them to describe still more complex operations and whole tasks. This is *programming*, of course, and it is key to expanding a computer's abilities. In later chapters, we describe how to build more complex operations from simpler ones.

Think of writing a term paper with a word processor and the thousands of operations that a computer does for you, from recognizing which keyboard key you pressed to spell checking. In order for the computer to do all these things, each

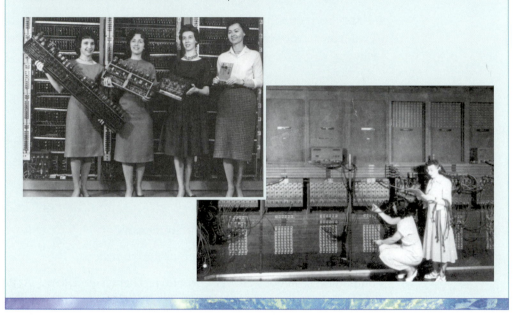

{ GREAT **FIT** MOMENTS }

Programming Pioneers >>

Programming Pioneers. The first programmers, who wrote and ran the programs on the ENIAC, were all women: Kathleen McNulty Mauchley Antonelli, Jean Jennings Bartik, Frances Snyder Holberton, Marlyn Wescoff Meltzer, Frances Bilas Spence, and Ruth Lichterman Teitelbaum. They were recruited from the ranks of "computers," humans who used mechanical calculators to solve complex mathematical problems before the invention of electronic computers.

task had to be converted into a sequence of the primitive hardwired instructions—machine instructions—because none of these word processing operations is primitive. This is programming, but the programmer's job would be tediously boring if the translation to primitive instructions had to be done by hand. If that were the case, no one would be a programmer no matter how much he or she was paid.

Fortunately, one "complex" task that computers can be programmed to do is translate complicated operations into the simpler primitive instructions that they understand. Of course, some programmer had to tell the computer how to do this the first time, but after that the computer can do the translation for itself. This automatic translation—there are actually several levels of translation—helps keep programming interesting. The only role for the programmer is to figure out how to do a complex task in a high-level programming language. High-level languages are expressive, meaning it takes fewer commands to write a complex program. That specification is the *program*. From then on, the computer does the rest.

Forms of Translation: Compiling and Assembling

Computers only understand instructions written in binary digits. Writing a string of 32 or more 0's and 1's is so tedious that the earliest computer builders developed a more convenient form for instructions called **assembly language**. The ADD instruction `ADD 2000, 2080, 4000` is an example of *assembly language, because it is a machine instruction written using letters and numerals rather than binary*. The process of converting from assembly instructions to binary machine instructions is called **assembling**. But these instructions are still too primitive to be of much use to humans. So, computer scientists invented high-level programming languages like Fortran (1958) and Basic (1965) to help programmers express complex tasks more easily. Still more expressive languages such as C, Smalltalk, C++, and Java can do even more than these early programming languages. The translation process from a programming language to an assembly language is called *compilation*. Because the languages are expressive, a single statement in one of these programming languages may convert into dozens of assembly instructions, which are then converted into binary machine instructions. Figure 9.13 summarizes the process.

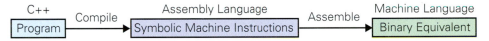

Figure 9.13. *The translation from high-level language to machine instructions.*

Many programmers work in development environments such as Visual C++ in which they simply combine already-written programs, possibly with small amounts of their own code written in the programming language. This is an even more powerful way to instruct a computer.

The Operating System

None of the operations that a computer needs to start up and keep running are hardwired primitive instructions. Because processors are so primitive, programmers must develop a large set of small but complicated procedures to get the computer to start and perform useful work. The result is an operating system. An **operating system (OS)** is software that extends the hardwired operations of a processor with general-purpose facilities to start up (**boot**), manage its memory and applications, and interact with its peripheral devices. These are general-purpose facilities that are performed for applications when needed. For example, device drivers are considered operating system software, so when your word processor prints your term paper, it invokes (runs) the print driver and other parts of the operating system to send your crisp prose from the computer memory onto paper.

The three most common operating systems are Windows, MacOS, and UNIX (including Linux). Each system has several variations. Dozens of others have been created, but these three are the state of the art. The question is not which one is best—they all have their technical triumphs and tragedies—but why do we have them at all? The answer can be found in the list of primitive instructions that are hardwired into computers.

Memory Management.   Memory management is a basic service of operating systems. When you begin to write your term paper, the word processor program is on the hard disk where the operating system put it when the application was installed. The operating system gives you a way to start the word processor— double clicking on the application's icon, perhaps. The OS locates the start of the program on the hard disk, loads the first part of it into memory, and starts it executing. Most modern computers use virtual memory and demand paging, so that it doesn't much matter where in the memory the OS puts the first part of the program or how much it loads. The computer executes the instructions that are available in memory, and when it tries to execute instructions that are still on the disk, it **page faults**, meaning it stops, waiting for the next page of instructions. A page fault is a hardware "wake up," called an **interrupt**, to the operating system, which may not have been active while the word processing application was running. The OS finds the needed page on the disk, loads it, and tells the computer to resume executing your application. And so it goes, the computer faulting when the next page of instructions or data is not in the memory, the OS finding them and loading them in. It happens so fast that we don't even notice that the program keeps stopping and starting.

Other OS Services.   Printing and managing memory are not the only help your word processor application is getting from the OS. There's also everything happening on the monitor—menus, scroll bars, and so on. The OS manages the mouse and creates the mouse pointer fiction. When you click on **Save**, the application asks the OS to write your term paper to the hard disk. In fact, the OS does all sorts of tasks like this, so they don't have to be programmed for each application.

FITBYTE

No Fault. How often have we heard "It was a computer error," as an explanation for a billing or other mistake? As we've often said, true computer errors are extremely rare. A better explanation would be "There was a billing system error caused perhaps by one of the many people who worked on the application software or OS, installed and configured the system, entered the data, or modified or configured the database system; it could be the result of fraud, data transmission or network errors, or failed checkpoint recovery; oh, . . . and there's a tiny chance it was a computer error." In other words, "It probably wasn't a computer error, but an problem with some other part of this complex system."

INTEGRATED CIRCUITS

Integrated circuits (**ICs**) are important because the technology allows extremely complex devices to be made cheaply and reliably. Two characteristics of ICs make this possible: integration and photolithography. Oh, yes. Integrated circuits are also very small.

Miniaturization

One reason that modern computer clocks can run at GHz rates is that the processor chips are so tiny. The farthest electrical signals can travel in a nanosecond is about 1 foot, and in a computer much more has to happen to the signals than simply being transmitted. One reason early computers, which filled whole rooms, could never have run as fast as modern computers is that their components were farther apart than a foot. Making everything smaller has made computers faster by allowing for faster clock rates.

Integration

But the real achievement of microchip technology is not miniaturization, but **integration**. It is impossible to overstate its significance. T. R. Reid in his book *The Chip* called the invention "a seminal event of postwar science: one of those rare demonstrations that changes everything."

To appreciate how profound the invention of integrated circuitry is, understand that before integration, computers were made from separate parts (discrete components) wired together by hand. The three wires coming out of each transistor, the two wires from each resistor, the two wires from each capacitor, and so on, had to be connected to the wires of some other transistor, resistor, or capacitor. It was very tedious work. Even for printed circuit boards in which the "wiring" is printed metallic strips, a person or machine had to "populate" the board with the discrete components one at a time. A serious computer system would have hundreds of thousands or millions of these parts and at least twice as many connections, which are expensive and time consuming to make, error prone, and unreliable. If computers still had to be built this way, they would still be rare.

FITBYTE

Cray's Limit. Seymour Cray, who designed and built more huge computers than anyone else, once said that there is a "manufacturing complexity limit" of about six million connections. Beyond that a system becomes too complicated to produce, test, and maintain. The fact that the Space Shuttle has (approximately) six million parts is probably independent verification of Cray's limit.

The "big idea" behind integrated circuits is really two ideas working together. The first idea is that the active components—transistors, capacitors, and so forth—and the wires that connect them are all made together of similar materials by a single (multistep) process. So, rather than making two transistors and later connecting them by soldering a pair of their wires together, IC technology places them side by side in the silicon and at some stage in the fabrication process—perhaps while some of the transistor's internal parts are still being built—a wire connecting the two is placed in position. The crux of integration is that the active and connective parts of a circuit are built together. Integration saves space (promoting speed), but its greatest advantage is to produce a single monolithic part for the whole system all at once without hand wiring. The resulting "block" of electronics is extremely reliable.

{GREAT FIT MOMENTS}

IC Man > >

Jack Kilby shared the 2000 Nobel Prize in Physics for inventing the integrated circuit. Kilby worked for the electronics firm Texas Instruments. New to the staff, Kilby hadn't accrued summer vacation time, so while the other employees were away on their holidays, he invented integrated circuits.

Using borrowed and improvised equipment, he conceived of and built the first electronic circuit in which all of the components, both active and connective, were fabricated in a single piece of semiconductor material. On September 12, 1958, he successfully demonstrated in his laboratory the first simple microchip, which was about half the size of a paper clip. Kilby went on to pioneer applications of microchip technology. He later co-invented both the hand-held calculator and a thermal printer used in portable data terminals.

For perspective, the worldwide integrated circuit market in 2000 had sales of $177 billion.

Photolithography

The second idea behind integrated circuits is that they are made with **photolithography**, a printing process. Here's how it works. Making a chip is like making a sandwich. Start with a layer of silicon and add layers of materials to build up the transistors, capacitors, wires, and other features of a chip. For example, wires might be made of a layer of aluminum. But the aluminum cannot be smeared over the chip like mayonnaise covers a sandwich; the wires must be electrically separated from each other and must connect to specific places. This is where photolithography comes in.

The aluminum smear is covered with a layer of light-sensitive material called a *photoresist*. A mask is placed on the chip. The mask—it's like a photographic negative—shows the pattern of the wires. When (ultraviolet) light shines on the mask, it passes through at places to react with the photoresist (see Figure 9.14). The mask is then removed and the changed-by-light resist—and the aluminum it covers—are etched away. Next, the remaining photoresist, but not the aluminum beneath it, is etched away (see Figure 9.15). What remains is the pattern of aluminum that matches the dark pattern on the mask—that is, the wires!

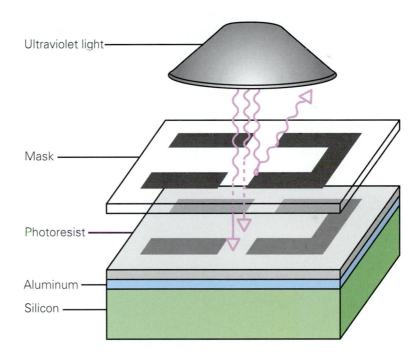

Figure 9.14. *A step in the fabrication of silicon chips. Aluminum for wires is deposited onto the silicon and covered with a layer of photoresist. A mask with the wire pattern is placed over the photoresist. Ultraviolet light passes through light areas of the mask reacting with the photoresist.*

The key aspect of photolithography is that regardless of how complicated the wiring is, the cost and amount of work involved are the same. Like a page of a newspaper, which costs the same to print whether it has 5 words or 5000 words, the cost of making integrated circuits is not related to how complicated they are. Thanks to the photolithographic process, computers and other electronics can be as complicated as we wish.

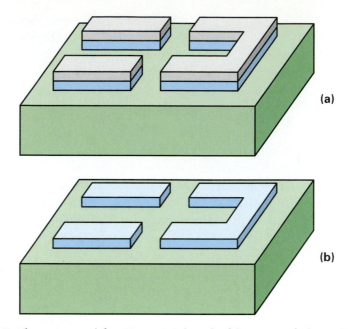

Figure 9.15. *The next step (after Figure 9.14) in the fabrication of silicon chips. The changed-by-light photoresist and its underlying aluminum are etched away, leaving a resist/aluminum pattern corresponding to the dark places on the mask. The remaining resist is removed, leaving the pattern of wires.*

HOW SEMICONDUCTOR TECHNOLOGY WORKS

Silicon is a **semiconductor**, meaning just what its name implies—it sometimes conducts electricity and sometimes does not. The ability to control when semiconductors do and don't conduct electricity is the main tool in constructing computers. To make this point clear, consider an example.

In Chapter 5 we used the **AND** operation when searching for Thai restaurants. The Web pages we wanted had to have both keywords. Inside the Google computer, a test was made to see if "Thai" was on a given page and a test was made to see if "restaurants" was on the same page. When the results of the two tests were known, an instruction in the Google computer **AND**ed them together. How could that be done with electricity?

The On-Again, Off-Again Behavior of Silicon

Imagine that we have a wire with two gaps in it. We fill each gap with specially treated semiconducting material (see Figure 9.16). We send an electrical signal along the wire, which we will interpret as yes, both "Thai" and "restaurants" appear on the page. At the other end of the wire we detect whether the "yes" is present, an application of the PandA encoding from Chapter 8. In between we control (details below) the conductivity of the semiconducting material using the outcomes of the two tests. We make the material in the first gap conduct if "Thai" was found, and the material in the second gap conduct if "restaurants" was found. If the material conducts electricity, the signal can pass to the other end of the wire. So, if "yes" is detected at the output end, both gaps must be conducting; that is, both outcomes are true. If "yes" is not detected, then one or the other (or possibly both) of the two semiconducting points must not be conducting, which means "Thai" and "restaurants" were not both found.

This simple principle—the setting up of a situation in which the conductivity of a wire can be controlled to create the logical conclusion needed—is the basis of all of the instructions and operations of a computer. In the hardware of the computer where this test was done, the two semiconducting points of the **AND** circuit are not limited to the specific question of whether "Thai" **AND** "restaurants" is true; instead the circuit computes *x* **AND** *y* for any logical values *x* and *y*. Such a circuit is part of the ALU of Google's computer (and yours), and it performs the Execute step of all of the **AND** instructions.

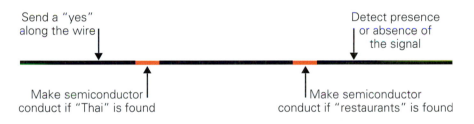

Figure 9.16. Computing `Thai AND restaurants` *using a semiconducting material.*

The Field Effect

So how do we control the conductivity of a semiconductor? The answer is we use the field effect. As we all know from combing our hair with a nylon comb on a dry day, objects can become charged positively or negatively. The comb strips off electrons from our hair, leaving the comb with too many electrons and the hair with too few. Because like-charges repel, our hair "stands on end" as each hair pushes away from its neighbors; but opposites attract, so the comb pulls the hair toward it. This effect that charged objects have on each other without actually touching is the field effect. We can use the field effect to control a semiconductor.

Here's how to control a semiconductor using the field effect. The gap between two wires is specially treated to improve its conducting and nonconducting properties, that is, when it conducts it conducts better than pure silicon (see Figure 9.17). This part of the semiconductor is called a *channel,* because it makes a path for electricity to travel along between the two wires. An insulator such as glass, silicon dioxide, covers the channel. Passing over the insulator (at right angles) is a third wire called the *gate*. The gate is separated from the semiconductor by the insulator, so it does not make contact with the two wires or the channel. Thus, electricity cannot be conducted between the two wires unless the channel is conducting. But how does the channel conduct?

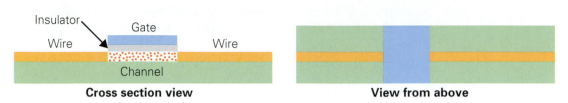

Figure 9.17. *A field-effect transistor. The channel is specially treated to improve its conducting/nonconducting properties.*

Because it has been specially treated, the silicon in the channel can conduct electricity when it is in a charged field. The conductivity is the result of electrons being attracted or repelled in the silicon material, depending on the type of treatment (see Figure 9.18). So, by charging the gate positively we create a field over the channel; electrons are attracted from the silicon material into the channel causing it to conduct electricity between the two wires. If the field is removed, the electrons disperse into the silicon, the channel doesn't conduct, and the two wires are isolated. Of course, the gate is simply another wire, which is or is not conducting (charged) under the control of other gates, and so on.

Transistors

Our example illustrates a **field effect transistor**. A **transistor** is simply a connector between two wires that controls whether or not they are electrically connected. The transistor described is an MOS transistor, where **MOS** stands for **metal, oxide, semiconductor**. Those three terms refer to the materials in the cross-section of the transistor from top to bottom: the gate is metal, the glass insulator is oxide, and the channel is the semiconductor. Modern computers are made out of **CMOS** technology, which stands for "complementary MOS" and means two different, but complementary, treatments for the channels.

Figure 9.18. *Field effect transistor (a) with the gate at neutral causing the channel not to conduct, isolating the wires, and (b) with the gate charged, causing the channel to conduct, connecting the wires.*

COMBINING THE IDEAS

Let's put these ideas all together. We start with an information-processing task. The task will be performed by an application implemented as a large program written by a programmer in a programming language like C or Java. The program performs the specific operations of the application, but for standard operations like **Print** or **Save**, the application program uses the OS. The program's commands, written in the programming language, are compiled into many simple assembly language instructions. The assembly instructions are then translated into more primitive binary form, the machine instructions, that the computer understands directly.

The application program's binary instructions are stored on the hard disk. When we click on the application's icon, the OS brings the first few pages of the program's instructions into the computer's memory and tells the computer to begin executing them. When more instructions are needed, the OS brings in more pages.

The Fetch/Execute Cycle, a hardwired sequence of five steps that are repeated over and over, executes the instructions:

1. (IF) Fetch the instruction stored at the memory location specified by the PC and place it in the control part of the computer. The PC is advanced to reference the next instruction after the fetch.

2. (ID) Decode the instruction. That is, decide what the operation is, where the data values (operands) are, and where the result should go.

3. (DF) Fetch the data from memory while the arithmetic/logic unit is set up to perform the operation.

4. (EX) The ALU performs the operation on the data values.

5. (RR) Store the result back in memory.

The cycle is repeated endlessly.

Instruction Fetch (IF)
Instruction Decode (ID)
Data Fetch (DF)
Instruction Execution (EX)
Result Return (RR)

All of the computer's instructions are performed by the ALU circuits. The **AND** instruction, for example, is implemented with MOS technology by breaking a wire in two places and filling the gaps with the semiconducting material of a field effect transistor forming channels connecting the wires. An oxide insulator and a metal gate cover each semiconductor channel. If, for example, the instruction is `AND 4040, 4280, 2020`, then the data value fetched from memory location

4040 would control the gate on the first MOS transistor, and the data value fetched from memory location 4280 would control the gate on the second MOS transistor. A true operand value creates a field, causing the channel to conduct, and a false operand value is neutral, preventing the channel from conducting. An electrical signal interpreted as "yes" is sent down the wire. If the "yes" is detected at the output end of the wire, both transistors are conducting, and the result is true; otherwise the result is false. Either way, the result is returned to memory location 2020.

That's it, from applications to electrons. It is a sequence of interesting and straightforward ideas working together to create computation. No single idea is *the* key idea. They all contribute. The power comes from applying the ideas in quantity: Application programs and operating systems are composed of millions of machine instructions, the control unit executes billions of cycles per second, memories contain billions of bits, processors have hundreds of millions of MOS transistors, and so on in an impressive process.

Ours has been a simple, but accurate description of a computer. This description mirrors the design and operation of many early computers built in the days before silicon technology had advanced to the microprocessor stage; that is, before everything in Figure 9.2 fit on a chip. Once silicon technology had matured to that stage, computer architects—the engineers that design computers—became very aggressive. By applying integrated circuitry to its fullest, they have optimized the Fetch/Execute Cycle and the simple structure of Figure 9.2 almost beyond recognition. To achieve their impressive speeds, today's computers are dramatically more complex than explained here. But the abstraction—the logical idea of how a computer is organized and operates—is as presented

SUMMARY

We began by describing the Fetch/Execute Cycle, the instruction interpretation engine of a computer system. The process, repeated over and over, is one of fetching the next instruction (indicated by the PC), decoding the operation to be performed and on what data, getting the data, doing the operation, and storing the result back into the memory. This process is hardwired into the control subsystem, one of the five components of a processor. The memory, a very long sequence of bytes, each with an address, stores the program and data while the program is running. The ALU does the actual computing. The input and output units are the interfaces for the peripheral devices attached to the computer.

A key point about machine instructions is that they do not refer to the data (operands) directly, but rather indirectly. Thus, different computations can be done with only one instruction, just by changing the data in the referenced memory locations. Because the instructions are so few and so simple, programmers must create complex computations by software layers, building up simple operations from the base instructions, more complex operations from the simple ones, and so forth. Programmers use sophisticated programming languages to create operating systems as well as the complex applications software.

Finally, the basic ideas of integrated circuits—integrating active and connective components, fabrication by photolithography, controlling conductivity through the field effect—were explained in detail.

EXERCISES

Multiple Choice

1. Which of the following is a characteristic of a computer?
   A. literal
   B. free will
   C. creativity
   D. intuition

2. There are _____ steps in the Fetch/Execute Cycle.
   A. 3
   B. 4
   C. 5
   D. 6

3. The Fetch/Execute Cycle operates:
   A. once a second
   B. thousands of times a second
   C. hundreds of thousands of times a second
   D. hundreds of millions of times a second

4. One byte of memory can store:
   A. any number
   B. one word
   C. one character
   D. one block

5. The ALU is used in the:
   A. Instruction Fetch, Instruction Execution, and Result Return steps
   B. Instruction Fetch, Instruction Execution, and Data Fetch steps
   C. Instruction Execution and Result Return steps
   D. Instruction Decode and Instruction Execution steps

6. Which of the following is used for input and output?
   A. keyboard
   B. hard disk
   C. mouse
   D. printer

7. The program counter is changed by instructions called:
   A. Fetch and Execute
   B. Branch and Jump
   C. Input and Output
   D. Now and Next

8. When there are no instructions for the Fetch/Execute Cycle, the computer:
   A. crashes
   B. executes an idle loop
   C. sends an empty instruction to processing
   D. always has instructions to execute

9. From smallest to largest, the correct order is:
   A. giga, kilo, mega, tera
   B. kilo, mega, giga, tera
   C. terra, kilo, mega, giga
   D. kilo, mega, terra, giga

10. Modern computers know:
    A. only a handful of instructions
    B. a couple of dozen instructions
    C. about a hundred instructions
    D. thousands of instructions

Short Answer

1. _____ deterministically perform or execute instructions to process information.

2. Computers operate under a set of operations called the _____.

3. _____ is an acronym for the name of the location where computer programs run and data is stored.

4. The _____ part of the computer is the hardware part of the Fetch/Execute Cycle.

5. Computers operate _____, that is, they follow instructions exactly based on the program and data they have been given.

6. The math in the computer is done by the _____.

7. Transferring and transforming information is called _____.

8. _____ are the devices that connect to the computer.

9. The _____ encodes keystrokes into binary form for the computer.

10. The computer's clock is measured in _____.

11. _____ is the task of creating complex instructions for the computer to follow from a set of simple instructions.

12. Computers keep track of the next instruction to execute by its _____.

13. _____ is the technical term for the process of executing a program.

14. A(n) _____ sometimes conducts electricity and sometimes doesn't.

15. The flow of electricity in a channel in a semiconductor is controlled by a(n) _____.

Exercises

1. Break the process of brushing your teeth into separate steps. Be as specific as possible.

2. How many bits in a kilobyte? megabyte? terabyte?

3.   Find out how much memory your computer has. Calculate exactly how many bytes it has.

4. If a 1 GHz computer can start four instructions per cycle and can start a new instruction on 80 percent of its cycles, how many instructions can it complete in a second? in a minute?

5. If the mouse cable is five feet long, how long does it take the current generated by a mouse click to travel from the mouse to the computer?

6. If the cable connecting the hard disk to the computer is six inches long, what effect would it have on performance if the length was cut in half? doubled?

7. Explain why the keyboard and the mouse are input devices and the monitor is an output device.

8. Explain how a complicated process like driving can be accomplished as a series of simple steps.

9. Explain how a system that can do only a limited number of very simple tasks can accomplish an almost unlimited number of complicated tasks.

10. Do an online search to find an explanation of how computer circuits are made.

11. Locate a computer circuit and take a close look at it. Describe what it looks like.

12. Using the Fetch/Execute Cycle, describe how you'd answer a true/false question.

10

WHAT'S THE PLAN?

Algorithmic Thinking

learning objectives

> List the five essential properties of an algorithm

> Describe the difference between an algorithm and a program

> Use the *Alphabetize CDs* algorithm to illustrate algorithmic thinking:

 • Follow the flow of the instruction execution

 • Follow an analysis to pinpoint assumptions

 • Explain the function of loops and tests

> Demonstrate algorithmic thinking by being able to:

 • Explain what the *Beta* sweep abstraction does

 • Explain what the *Alpha* sweep abstraction does

The process of preparing programs for a digital computer is especially attractive, not only because it can be economically and scientifically rewarding, but also because it can be an aesthetic experience much like composing poetry or music.

—DONALD E. KNUTH, 1970

Solving a problem means finding a way out of a difficulty, a way around an obstacle, attaining an aim which was not immediately attainable. Solving problems is the specific achievement of intelligence, and intelligence is the specific gift of mankind: solving problems can be regarded as the most characteristically human activity.

—GEORGE POLYA, 1981

The most beautiful thing we can experience is the mysterious. It is the source of all true art and science.

—ALBERT EINSTEIN, 1930

AN ALGORITHM is a precise, systematic method for producing a specified result. We know algorithms as recipes, assembly instructions, driving directions, business processes, nominating procedures, and so on. Algorithms are key to processing information, of course, and we've already met several in this book. There are three main reasons to learn more about algorithms. First, we must create algorithms so that other people or computers can help us achieve our goals. If they are to be successful, the algorithms must "work." This chapter explains how to create effective algorithms. Second, we will find ourselves following algorithms created by others. If we know the "dos" and "don'ts" of algorithm design, we can pay better attention to the details and be alert to errors in other people's instructions. Finally, learning about algorithms will complete the picture begun in Chapter 8 of how computers solve problems. Understanding this process will make us better computer users, better debuggers, and better problem solvers—that is, more Fluent.

The goals of this chapter are to understand what algorithms are and to learn to think algorithmically. We begin by looking at everyday algorithms. Next, we introduce and illustrate the five fundamental properties of algorithms. We explain the role of *language* in specifying algorithms and the value of a formal language. Next, we discuss the relationship between algorithms and programs. Guidelines—useful for writing out driving directions—help us understand the role of context in executing algorithms. We create an algorithm for alphabetizing our audio CD collection, which helps us discover how and why algorithms are structured as they are. We execute the algorithm; that is, we sort a five-slot rack of our favorite CDs, watching the progress of the algorithm. Then, perhaps most important, we analyze the algorithm to extract key concepts in algorithmic thinking.

FITBYTE

Weird Word. *Algorithm* seems to be an anagram of logarithm, but it comes from the name of a famous Arabic textbook author, Abu Ja'far Mohammed ibn Mûsâ al-Khowârizmî, who lived about AD 825. The end of his name, al-Khowârizmî, means *native of Khowârism* (today Khiva, Uzbekistan). It has been corrupted over the centuries into *algorithm*.

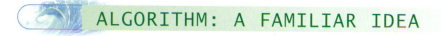

ALGORITHM: A FAMILIAR IDEA

In Chapter 1 we defined an algorithm as a precise and systematic method for producing a specified result. Algorithms are familiar—we've already seen several of them so far in this book:

> **Recognition of a button click.** In Chapter 1, after describing how computers draw buttons on the screen, we explained how the button is "clicked." The systematic method described how, when the mouse is clicked, the computer can look through the list of buttons it has drawn on the screen, and for each button, check to see if the cursor is inside the square defining the button.

> **Placeholder technique.** In Chapter 2 we described a three-step process to eliminate short letter sequences (for example, new-lines), which can also be parts of longer strings (for example, double new-lines), without also eliminating them in the longer strings.

> **Hex to bits.** In Chapter 8 we used algorithms to convert back and forth between hexadecimal digits and bits.

We use algorithms every day. The arithmetic operations—addition, subtraction, multiplication, division—we learned in elementary school are algorithms. Making change is an algorithm, as are looking up a number in a telephone book, sending a greeting card to our parents, and balancing a checkbook. Changing a tire is algorithmic, too, because it is a systematic method to solve a problem (replace a flat tire). Usually, though, *algorithm* means a precise method in information processing.

Algorithms in Everyday Life

Most of the algorithms that we know, like arithmetic, we learned from a patient teacher or we figured out for ourselves, like how to look up a phone number. Because we are the ones performing the operations, we don't think much about algorithms as an explicit sequence of instructions. We simply *know* what to do. Other algorithms—recipes, assembly instructions for a bicycle, driving directions to a party, or income tax filing rules—are written out for us. Written algorithms are of interest here because we want to be able to think up an algorithm, write it out, and have some other agent—another person or a computer—perform its instructions successfully. It's not a matter to be taken lightly.

The specification of an algorithm must be "precise." The algorithms just mentioned from the earlier chapters, though possibly clear enough for a person to follow, were not precise enough for a computer. Computers, as we saw in Chapters 7 and 9, are so clueless and literal that every part of a task must be spelled out in detail. To write a precise algorithm, we need to pay attention to three things:

> **Capability.** Make sure that the computer knows what and how to do the operations.

> **Language.** Ensure that the description is unambiguous—that is, it can only be read and understood one way.

> **Context.** Make few assumptions about the input or execution setting.

These issues are not only crucial when our algorithms are for computers; they're just as important when we're writing for other people. Though we expect people to use their heads and make up for any weaknesses in our descriptions, sometimes they can be clueless and literal, too, especially when dealing with unfamiliar situations. So, it's always in our best interest to make our instructions precise, avoid ambiguity, be sure they know what to do, and minimize assumptions no matter who performs the algorithm.

Five Essential Properties of Algorithms

To write algorithms that are specified well enough for a computer to follow, make sure every algorithm has five essential properties:

> Inputs specified

> Outputs specified

> Definiteness

> Effectiveness

> Finiteness

Inputs specified. The **inputs** are the data that will be transformed during the computation to produce the output. We must specify the type of the data, the amount of data, and the form that the data will take. Suppose the algorithm is a recipe. We must list the ingredients (type of inputs), their quantities (amount of input), and their preparation, if any (form of inputs), as in, "1/4 cup onion, minced."

Outputs specified. The **outputs** are the data resulting from the computation, the intended result. Often the description is given in the name of the algorithm, as in "Algorithm to compute a batting average." As with inputs, we must specify the type, amount, and any form of the outputs. A possible output for some computations is a statement that there can be no output—that is, no solution is possible. Recipes specify their outputs too, giving the type, quantity, and form of food, as in, "3 dozen 3-inch chocolate chip cookies."

Definiteness. Algorithms must specify every step. **Definiteness** means specifying the sequence of operations for transforming the inputs into the outputs. Every detail of each step must be spelled out, including how to handle errors. Definiteness ensures that if the algorithm is performed at different times or by different agents (people or computers) using the same data, the output will be the same. Similarly, recipes should be definite, but because they often rely on the judgment, practicality, and experience of the cook, they can be much less definite than computer algorithms and still be successful. And where they are not definite—"salt and pepper to taste"—it's usually a good thing.

Effectiveness. It must be possible for the agent to execute the algorithm mechanically without any further inputs, special talent, clairvoyance, creativity, help from Superman, and so on. Whereas definiteness specifies which operations to do, **effectiveness** means that they are doable. Examples of ineffectiveness abound: "Enter the amount of income you would have received this year had you worked harder," and "Print the length of the longest run of 9s in the decimal expansion of π."

Finiteness. An algorithm must have **finiteness**; it must eventually stop, either with the right output or with a statement that no solution is possible. If no answer comes back, we can't tell whether the algorithm is still working on an answer or is just plain "stuck." Finiteness is not usually an issue for noncomputer algorithms because they typically don't repeat instructions. But, as we shall see, computer algorithms often repeat instructions with different data. Finiteness becomes an issue because if the algorithm doesn't specify when to stop the repetition, the computer will continue to repeat the instructions forever.

Any process having these five properties will be called an algorithm.

FITBYTE

Work Without End. "Long" division is an algorithm in which finiteness is important. For example, divide 3 into 10. As we add each new digit (3) to the quotient, the computation returns to a situation—call it a *state*—that it has been in before. When should the algorithm stop?

$$
\begin{array}{r}
3.33 \\
3\overline{)10.00} \\
9 \\
\hline
1.00 \\
9 \\
\hline
10 \\
\cdots
\end{array}
$$

Language in Algorithms

Because algorithms are developed by people, but executed by some other agent, they must be written in some language. The most important requirement of the language is that the person who creates the instructions and the agent that performs them both interpret the instructions the same way.

Natural Language.
If the agent is a person, we use a natural language, such as English. Although we usually assume all speakers understand every sentence of a language alike, it's not true. In fact, it's probable that no two people understand a language exactly the same way. So, an instruction may mean one thing to the writer and something else to the agent. Ambiguity is very common in natural languages, of course, but ambiguity is not so much the problem as the fact that natural languages are not very precise. So, for example, recipe writers must choose their words carefully to guide the cook—rather than stir they choose *fold in* or *beat*—but there are only a few terms to control how to mix ingredients. Generally, a natural language is an extremely difficult medium in which to express algorithms.

Programming Language.
Since natural languages don't work well, we use a programming language when the executing agent is a computer. Programming languages are **formal languages**, and they are called synthetic instead of natural because they were designed just to express algorithms. They are precisely defined. Programming languages are rarely ambiguous, and the precise definition ensures that the programmer and the computer agree on what each instruction means. So, programmers know that what they tell the computer to do is exactly what it will do. Of course, programmers may make mistakes, but at least they can be sure that if the computer does something wrong, the problem is with their design of the algorithm, not with the way the computer interprets the algorithm.

The Difference between an Algorithm and a Program

A program is an algorithm that has been customized to solve a specific task under a specific set of circumstances in a specific language. Making change—subtracting an amount of money, *x,* from a larger amount paid, *y,* and returning the result as coins and currency—is an *algorithm,* but making change in U.S. dollars is a *program.* The program uses the "making change" algorithm specialized to the denominations of coins (1¢, 5¢, 10¢, 25¢, 50¢, $1) and paper currency ($1, $2, $5, $10, . . .) of the United States. Making change in New Zealand dollars is a different program; it also uses the making change algorithm but with the New Zealand coins (5¢, 10¢, 20¢, 50¢, $1, $2) and paper currency ($5, $10 $20, . . .). From our point of view, whether the method is general (algorithm) or specialized (program) makes no difference. The issues are the same.

The Context of a Program

A program can fulfill the five properties of an algorithm (inputs specified, outputs specified, definiteness, effectiveness, and finiteness), and be unambiguous, and still not work right because it is executed in the wrong **context** (the assumptions of the program are not fulfilled). For example, a form that asks you for your *Last Name* may mean your family name or surname, as is the case for Western names. The request has the right result in the United States, but perhaps not in countries like China where the family name is given first. Good algorithm designers reduce the dependence on context by asking for *Family Name* rather than *Last Name,* and *Given Name* rather than *First Name.*

Context Matters: Driving Instructions. Consider driving directions, another example where context matters. For example, the instruction

> From the Limmat River go to Bahnhof Strasse and turn right.

seems reliable, but it may not be. The "turn right" instruction assumes that you are traveling in a specific direction. If you are traveling east, the instruction works, because you are in the context the instruction writer assumed. But if you are traveling west, you will need to turn left on Bahnhof Strasse and the instruction doesn't work (see Figure 10.1). You are following the instructions in a context the writer didn't expect. Turning right will send you north if you approach from one direction and send you south if you approach from the other direction.

The context in which to apply the algorithm—the point of departure in this case—must be considered. Such conditions can be written as input conditions or they can simply be avoided. The best solution is not to use words like *right* that depend on orientation until you've specified it. Terms like *north* that are orientation independent are better.

When you develop algorithms and programs, you need to think ahead to make sure your algorithm works in any context.

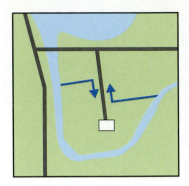

Figure 10.1. Diagram of approaching a street (Bahnhof Strasse) from different directions, resulting in the instruction "turn right" having different meanings.

Travel Directions: To give better travel directions, follow these rules to reduce the dependence on context.

- ✔ *Give the* starting point, *"From Place de la Concorde. . . ."*

- ✔ *State the* direction *of travel, "Going west on Route 66. . . ."*

- ✔ *Give* landmarks, *especially when turning, "Turn left; you'll see a temple (Todai-ji) on your right. . . ."*

- ✔ *Give* measured distances *(2.3 miles) instead of blocks, cross streets, or traffic lights, which can be ambiguous.*

- ✔ *Include an* "overshot" test, *"If you cross Via Giuseppi Verdi, you've gone too far."*

AN ALGORITHM: *ALPHABETIZE CDS*

It's time for an example algorithm. Though most of the algorithms in later chapters use a programming language to ensure precision, our first algorithms will be written in English.

Imagine that your audio CD collection, which fills a large, slotted rack, is completely disorganized. You've decided that it's time to get your CDs in order, and you want to alphabetize them by the name of the group, the performing musician, or perhaps the composer. How would you go about solving this problem?

Here is an algorithm for alphabetizing CDs:

ALPHABETIZE CDS

Input: An unordered sequence of CDs filling a slotted rack
Output: The same CDs in the rack in alphabetical order
Instructions:

1. Use the term *Artist_Of* to refer to the name of the group or musician or composer on a CD.

> **2.** Decide which end of the rack is to be the beginning of the alphabetic sequence and call the slot at that end the *Alpha* slot.
>
> **3.** Call the slot next to the *Alpha* slot the *Beta* slot.
>
> **4.** If the *Artist_Of* the CD in the *Alpha* slot comes later in the alphabet than the *Artist_Of* the CD in the *Beta* slot, swap the CDs; otherwise, continue on.
>
> **5.** If there is a slot following the *Beta* slot, begin calling it the *Beta* slot and go to Instruction 4; otherwise, continue on.
>
> **6.** If there are two or more slots following the *Alpha* slot, begin calling the slot following the *Alpha* slot *Alpha* and begin calling the slot following it the *Beta* slot, and go to Instruction 4; otherwise, stop.

In the next sections, we'll check to see that the properties of definitiveness, effectiveness, and finiteness hold true; in other words, we'll check that we truly have an algorithm.

How does this algorithm work? Follow Figure 10.2 as we go through the process.

Instruction 1. *Use the term* Artist_Of *to refer to the name of the group or musician or composer on a given CD.* This instruction gives a name to the operation of locating the name used for alphabetizing. (*Artist_Of* is shorthand for extracting the name of the performer, simplifying Instruction 4; it could be eliminated at the expense of a wordier Instruction 4.)

Instruction 2. *Decide which end of the rack is to be the beginning of the alphabetic sequence and call the slot at that end the* Alpha *slot.* The purpose of this instruction is to give the process a starting point. It also gives the initial meaning to the word *Alpha*. In the algorithm, *Alpha* refers to slots in the rack. At the start, *Alpha* refers to the first slot in the alphabetic sequence. As the algorithm progresses, it refers to successive slots in the rack.

Instruction 3. *Call the slot next to the* Alpha *slot the* Beta *slot.* This instruction gives the word *Beta* its initial meaning. The names *Alpha* and *Beta* have no inherent meaning; the programmer needs to name slots in the rack and just chose these two words.

Instruction 4. *If the* Artist_Of *the CD in the* Alpha *slot comes later in the alphabet than the* Artist_Of *the CD in the* Beta *slot, swap the CDs.* This is the workhorse instruction of the algorithm. It compares the names of the recording artists of the CDs in the slots *Alpha* and *Beta* and, if necessary, exchanges them so that they are in the proper order. It may not be necessary to swap if the CDs are already positioned properly. But either way, the alphabetically earlier CD is in the *Alpha* slot when this instruction is done.

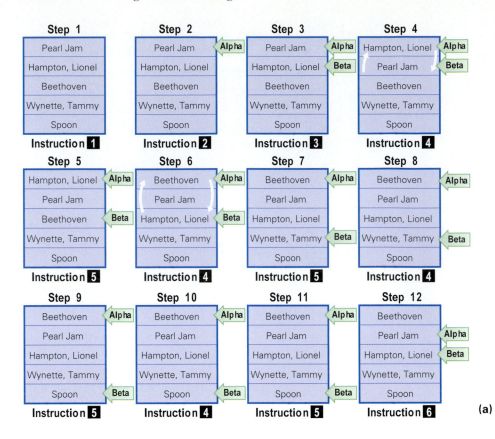

(a)

Figure 10.2. The steps of Alphabetize CDs. A snapshot of the CD rack is shown at the completion of each instruction. The numbers in the boxes give the instruction from the algorithm and step in the overall execution just completed. For example, Step 9 Instruction 5 means "the ninth step of the computation is to perform instruction 5 of the algorithm." Notice how Beta sweeps through all of the slots following Alpha. After the first 11 steps, the alphabetically earliest CD, Beethoven, is in the Alpha slot.

Instruction 5. *If there is a slot following the Beta slot, begin calling it the Beta slot and go to Instruction 4; otherwise, continue on.* This instruction gives a new definition for the *Beta* slot so that it refers to the next slot in the sequence, if there is one. With this new definition of *Beta*, Instruction 4 can be executed again, comparing a different pair of CDs. One of the pair, the CD in the *Alpha* slot, was compared the last time Instruction 4 was executed, but because *Beta* refers to a new slot, the pair of CDs is "new." If all slots have been considered—that is, there is no next slot for *Beta* to refer to—the algorithm continues on to Instruction 6 instead of returning to Instruction 4.

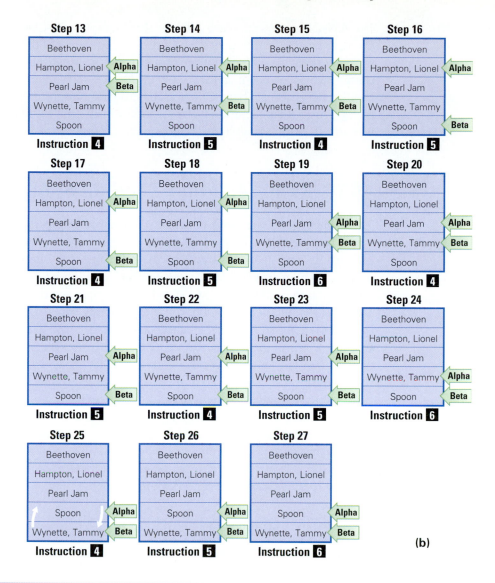

(b)

Instruction 6. *If there are two or more slots following the* Alpha *slot, begin calling the slot following the* Alpha *slot* Alpha *and the slot following it the* Beta *slot, and go to Instruction 4; otherwise, stop.* By the time we get to this instruction, the alphabetically earliest CD is in the *Alpha* slot, thanks to the combination of Instructions 4 and 5. The idea now is to advance *Alpha* to the next slot and to sweep through the last of the rack again locating the alphabetically next-earliest CD with the Instruction 4–5 combination. Then *Alpha* moves again, the Instruction 4–5 combination is repeated again, and so on. Each time, the CDs in slots up to and including *Alpha* will be alphabetized. When there are no longer enough slots to call one *Alpha* and the next one *Beta*, the whole rack has been alphabetized and the algorithm stops.

The *Alphabetize CDs* approach is better than dumping the CDs on the floor, and trying to return them to the rack in order. Though it keeps the CDs in the rack while it orders them, that's not the property that makes *Alphabetize CDs* an algorithm. It could be rewritten to work with the CDs spread out on the floor. Rather, it is the fact that *Alphabetize CDs* uses a method to find the alphabetically first CD, then the next, then the next after that, and so forth until the alphabetically last CD is found. That is, *Alphabetize CDs* is systematic.

ANALYZING *ALPHABETIZE CDS* ALGORITHM

The *Alphabetize CDs* example illustrates the five basic properties of algorithms. The inputs and outputs were listed. Each instruction was described precisely—or as precisely as English allows—fulfilling the definiteness requirement. The operations of the algorithm are effective because actions like selecting the next slot and counting to see if there are at least two slots left are simple and doable mechanically. The most complicated operation, deciding which of two artists' names is earlier in the alphabet, is also a completely mechanical process. We need only compare the first two letters of the names, and the one closer to *A* is the earlier; if the two letters are the same letter, we compare the second letters, and so forth. So, our algorithm has the effectiveness property. Finally, the algorithm is finite. Because Instructions 4, 5, and 6 are repeated, this property is not so obvious. However, notice that each time Instruction 4 is repeated, *Alpha* and *Beta* refer to a different pair of slots that has not previously been considered. Because slots can be paired in a rack in only a finite number of *different* ways, Instruction 4 cannot be repeated forever. Instructions 5 and 6 cannot be repeated forever without repeating Instruction 4 forever. Hence, the program satisfies the finiteness property.

A Deeper Analysis

We have shown that *Alphabetize CDs* meets the requirements of an algorithm, but there are other, more interesting aspects to discover.

Structural Features. The algorithm has two instructions, 5 and 6, in which the agent is directed to go back and repeat instructions. Such instructions create **loops** in the algorithm. Loops are instruction sequences that repeat, and they are more obvious when the instructions are given in a form other than English. Consider the flowchart in Figure 10.3. Loops are fundamental to algorithms because they cause parts of the computation to be performed as many times as there are data items. So, the loops in the *Alphabetize CDs* algorithm repeat instructions as many times as there are slots, or CDs.

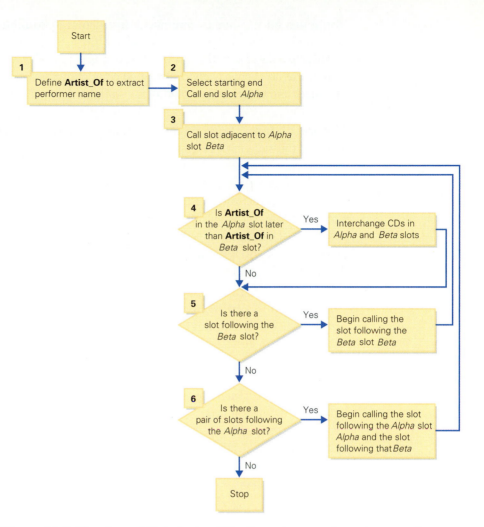

Figure 10.3. *Flowchart of* Alphabetize CDs. *Operations are shown in rectangles; decisions are shown in diamonds. Arrows indicate the sequencing of the operations.*

Loops and Tests. A loop must include a **test** to determine whether the instructions should be repeated one more time. As Figure 10.3 shows *Alphabetize CDs* has two loops. Instruction 5 tests whether there are slots following the *Beta* slot; if so, Instruction 4 will be repeated; if not, that repetition of the inner loop will end. Instruction 6 tests whether there is at least a pair of slots after the *Alpha* slot. If so, Instructions 4 and 5 will be repeated; if not, the outer loop ends. These tests cause the loop to complete and ensure the finiteness property.

FITBYTE

Failed Test. Requiring a test to determine when to stop repeating instructions may seem obvious, but some shampoo directions read "Wet hair, massage in shampoo, rinse, repeat," failing the finiteness test. Does the shampoo run out before the shower's hot water?

Notice that for the loop to continue at Instruction 5, *Beta* must move to the next slot. Similarly, Instruction 6 moves *Alpha* to the next slot and resets *Beta* to follow it. These moves ensure that on the next test *Beta* and *Alpha* refer to different slots. If there are no changes between the two consecutive tests, the outcome must be the same, and so the loop would never stop.

Assumptions. Assumptions are made in specifying *Alphabetize CDs*. First, we assume (and state in the Input specification) that the CD rack is full. This matters because the instructions do not handle the case of empty slots in the rack. (For example, if *Beta* were an empty slot, how would Instruction 4 operate?) The algorithm requires that the *Artist_Of* two CDs be compared, but if one or both of the slots are empty, the agent might not know what to do. The specification is correct because it states that it expects a full CD rack as input. But a better solution would explain what to do if the rack is not full. Then the "full" requirement could be dropped.

"Following" an Assumption. When the *Beta* slot is first set in Instruction 3, only one slot is next to *Alpha* because in Instruction 2 *Alpha* was chosen to be an end slot. This ensures that there is a unique slot *following Alpha* for *Beta* to refer to, and so the specification is effective. There is an assumption in the use of the term *following* in Instructions 5 and 6. Instruction 5 refers to a slot "following" *Beta,* which means a slot further from the end chosen in Instruction 2. Similarly, Instruction 6 refers to a pair of slots "following" *Alpha,* meaning the slots further from the end chosen in Instruction 2. But, nowhere is the term *following* defined. This makes the orientation of the term *following* an assumption. The orientation can be defined—and would have to be for a computer to execute the algorithm—but people know what "following" means.

The Exchange Sort Algorithm

The *Alphabetize CDs* example illustrates a well-known algorithm called **Exchange Sort**. In the *Alphabetize CDs* example, we used the Exchange Sort algorithm to alphabetize CDs based on the names of the musicians. The Exchange Sort algorithm is the idea of comparing pairs of items chosen in a particular way, exchanging them if they are out of order, and continuing to sweep through the items to locate the next minimal item.

A different program based on the Exchange Sort algorithm might alphabetize CDs based on their titles, and another might alphabetize CDs based on the recording company's name (label). The Exchange Sort algorithm can be specialized into programs for alphabetizing books by their authors, ordering books by their ISBNs, ordering canceled checks by date, and so on. When we choose the kind of item (e.g., CDs), the criterion for "order" (e.g., alphabetically ordered by musician's name), and specific names for keeping track of the items (e.g., *Alpha* and *Beta)*, we have created a program based on the algorithm. The algorithm is a systematic process, and the program is that process formulated for a particular situation. An algorithm continues to be an algorithm even when it is specialized into a program.

Are there other ways to alphabetize CDs? Of course. There are dozens of sorting algorithms, and most of them could be the basis of programs for alphabetizing CDs. Why one algorithm might be better than another is the sort of question computer scientists worry about. It need not concern us.

{ GREAT FIT MOMENTS }

Impossible Dream >>

At the start of the twentieth century, German mathematician David Hilbert listed several great problems worthy of study in the new century. His tenth problem was to develop an algorithm to decide whether logical propositions were true or false. Algorithmically testing truth seemed like a great goal. Logicians Bertrand Russell and Alfred North Whitehead began setting down axioms and logic rules for mathematics in their three volume *Principia Mathematica*. But in 1931 Slovak-American logician Kurt Gödel astonished everyone by proving it wasn't going to be possible. Soon American logician Alonzo Church and English mathematician Alan M. Turing extended Gödel's work, proving there can be no algorithm to decide truth and laying the foundations for theoretical computer science.

ABSTRACTION IN ALGORITHMIC THINKING

The *Alphabetize CDs* example seems very complicated when described in so much detail, but it is easier to understand than it may first appear. This is because we can think of parts of the algorithm's behavior as whole units rather than as individual instructions. This is abstraction, as defined in Chapter 1.

Beta Sweep Abstraction

For example, the "*Beta* sweep" of Instructions 4 and 5 can become a single concept in our minds. That is,

> **Beta Sweep:** While *Alpha* points to a fixed slot, *Beta* sweeps through the slots following *Alpha*, in sequence, comparing each slot's CD with the CD in the *Alpha* slot, and swapping them when necessary.

 FIT CAUTION   **Know the Score.** The ideas in this section may be difficult to comprehend by just reading them. They are much easier to understand if, using five of your favorite CDs, you first follow the instructions of *Alphabetize CDs* to sort them.

The idea of treating parts of the algorithm's behavior as a unit—not the instructions themselves, but the behavior the instructions define—is key to algorithmic thinking. We want to discipline ourselves to think about algorithms this way.

The unit of behavior is an *abstraction,* an idea or concept extracted from a specific situation. For example, the *"Beta* sweep" considers in order all CDs following a specific *Alpha.* The sweep process tick-tick-ticks through the following slots, comparing artists, and swapping them when necessary.

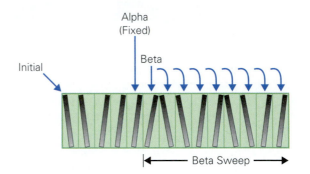

Properties of *Beta* Sweep Abstraction.   When we think of the *Beta* sweep abstraction, we can recognize some of its important properties. The *Beta* sweep is

1. **Exhaustive.** It considers all CDs from the *Alpha* slot to the end of the rack, making sure that none is left out.

2. **Nonredundant.** It considers each slot following *Alpha* only once, and so never considers the same pair of CDs twice, which ensures that the sweep will stop.

3. **Progressive.** At any given time, the alphabetically earliest CD seen so far in this sweep is in the *Alpha* slot.

4. **Goal-achieving.** After the sweep completes, the alphabetically earliest CD among all CDs considered in this sweep (including *Alpha*) is in *Alpha.*

These are not general properties that all algorithms have. These are only specific properties of the *Beta* sweep abstraction of the *Alphabetize CDs* program. (They are also properties of the "inner loop sweep" of the Exchange Sort algorithm if we make them general, so as not to refer to "CDs," "slots," "*Alpha,*" "*Beta,*" etc.).

Where did the four properties of the *Beta* sweep abstraction come from? We noticed them when we analyzed how the *Alphabetize CDs* algorithm works. (They are all mentioned in the discussion in the "Analyzing Alphabetize CDs Algorithm" section.) Though they have been listed here so that we can discuss them, they are examples of the features we should notice about the behavior of an algorithm when we study how it operates. Why? Because these properties (together with the *Alpha* sweep properties below) will convince us that the algorithm actually works, that it achieves its goal of alphabetizing.

To see how the properties of the *Beta* sweep can convince us that the algorithm works, first note that properties 1 through 3 imply property 4. That is, the *Beta* sweep considers all CDs once and keeps the alphabetically earliest in *Alpha* at all times. That behavior after processing all CDs in a sweep ensures that the alphabetically earliest CD is in *Alpha,* which is part of the answer.

Alpha Sweep Abstraction

For the rest of the answer, consider the *Alpha* sweep abstraction:

> **Alpha Sweep:** *Alpha* sweeps from the slot where the alphabetization begins through all slots (except the last) performing the *Beta* sweep instructions each time.

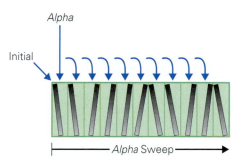

Properties of Alpha Sweep Abstraction.
We can list properties that we notice about the *Alpha* sweep abstraction. The *Alpha* sweep is

1. **Exhaustive.** It considers all CDs from the first to (but not including) the last.

2. **Nonredundant.** No slot is assigned to *Alpha* more than once, so the process stops if the *Beta* sweep stops, and it does by property 2 of the *Beta* sweep abstraction.

3. **Progressive.** At the end of each *Beta* sweep, the alphabetically next earliest CD is in *Alpha.*

4. **Complete.** When the last *Beta* sweep is completed, the CD in the last slot is later in the alphabet than the CD in the next-to-last slot because the last *Beta* sweep involved these last two slots and it is property (3) of the *Beta* sweep. (Refer to Figure 10.2, Step 25.)

5. **Goal-achieving.** The alphabetically earliest CD is in the first slot at the end of the first *Beta* sweep, by its property (4) and the fact that all CDs are considered; and thereafter in every new position for *Alpha,* the *Beta* sweep assigns the next earliest CD. The program alphabetizes.

Property (5) of the *Alpha* sweep says this program works. We stated that it did originally, but by noticing these properties of the two abstractions—*Beta* sweep and *Alpha* sweep—we can see *why* it works. When we create computer solutions, knowing why our solution works is the only way to be sure the solution does work, achieving our IT goal. Algorithmic thinking involves inventing algorithms that achieve our goals, and understanding why they work.

Abstracting for Other Algorithms and Programs

It must be emphasized that the *Alpha* sweep and *Beta* sweep abstractions are *specific* to the Exchange Sort algorithm and to programs like *Alphabetize CDs* derived from it. Other algorithms and programs will exhibit different behaviors and require different abstractions based on the way they solve their problem. Further, those abstractions will have properties different from (but analogous to) the four properties of the *Beta* sweep and the five properties of the *Alpha* sweep. Every situation is different, but the approach—abstracting the behavior and understanding the properties—is always the same.

Looking to the Future

This chapter has introduced many deep ideas. The reward for the reader who has reached this point with an understanding of these concepts is the satisfaction of having seen nearly all of the basic ideas underlying algorithms and programming. With perhaps two exceptions, every programming idea covered in this book appears in this chapter. All that is left is elaborating on these ideas and mastering them. This isn't trivial, of course, but it won't require many more ideas.

Because we have spent a lot of time understanding these complex ideas, it is worth our while to spend a moment naming them, especially since we will run into them again in later chapters:

> **Variables.** *Alpha* and *Beta* are variables in the *Alphabetize CDs* program.

> **Locations.** The slots in the CD rack are like a computer's memory locations.

> **Values.** The CDs are the values stored in the locations.

> **Function.** *Artist_Of* is a function for locating the name of the group or performer on a CD (a value).

> **Initialization.** Instructions 2 and 3 initialize the variables *Alpha* and *Beta,* respectively.

> **Loops.** The Instructions 4 and 5 form a loop; the Instructions 4 through 6 also form a loop.

> **Array.** The rack is a (linear) array.

We will be studying these terms more completely in the future.

SUMMARY

In this chapter we introduced one of the most fundamental forms of thinking. We learned that recipes and other everyday algorithms can be poor because we write them in an imprecise natural language. The five fundamental properties of algorithms were introduced and explained, and then the role of language in making the specification precise was reviewed. A discussion of being sensitive to context followed. We then presented an algorithm for alphabetizing the audio CDs in a filled rack. This was a six-instruction program that named two slots, *Alpha* and *Beta,* and made repeated sweeps over the remaining CDs. Each instruction was explained, as were several of the general properties of the process. We noted that *Alphabetize CDs* is a program built using the Exchange Sort algorithm. Finally, we abstracted the processing of *Alphabetize CDs,* recognizing two interacting behaviors: the *Beta* sweep and the *Alpha* sweep. These two abstractions have several properties, which explain why the algorithm produced an alphabetized sequence. These sorts of abstractions and their properties are the essence of algorithmic thinking. With a little practice, algorithmic thinking can become second nature, making us much more effective problem solvers.

EXERCISES

Multiple Choice

1. An algorithm has _____ basic requirements
   A. three
   B. four
   C. five
   D. seven

2. An algorithm must be:
   A. precise
   B. approximate
   C. concise
   D. general

3. Which of the following does not fit?
   A. natural language
   B. formal language
   C. synthetic language
   D. programming language

4. A computer program must:
   A. complete a specific task
   B. work in a specific set of circumstances
   C. be written in a specific language
   D. all of the above

5. Which instructions are repeated in the Alphabetizing CDs algorithm on pages 283–285?
   A. all of them
   B. 4 and 5
   C. 4 to 6
   D. 3 to 5

6. If you saw a monitor, keyboard, mouse, printer, and CPU, you would assume these parts formed a computer. This is an example of:
   A. abstraction
   B. encapsulation
   C. utilization
   D. algorithm

7. You notice that the only item in alphabetical order after the *Alpha* sweep of Alphabetize CDs is the first item. This is an example of:
   A. abstraction
   B. encapsulation
   C. utilization
   D. algorithm

8. In the Alphabetize CDs:
   A. the *Alpha* sweep points to every slot except the last
   B. the *Beta* sweep points to every slot on every sweep
   C. the *Alpha* points to the first slot of the sweep and the *Beta* points to the rest
   D. the *Alpha* points to the first slot and the *Beta* points to the last slot

9. The differences between the *Alpha* sweep and the *Beta* sweep in Alphabetize CDs include all of the following except:
   A. the *Alpha* sweep must be made first and the *Beta* sweep is made next
   B. the *Beta* sweep is repeated while the *Alpha* sweep is not
   C. the *Beta* sweep organizes every item except the first one, while the *Alpha* sweep organizes just the first item
   D. the *Alpha* sweep organizes one item at a time, while the *Beta* sweep does not

10. Following an *Alpha* sweep, how many items are you sure are in the correct order?
    A. 0
    B. 1
    C. 2
    D. all of them

Short Answer

1. An explicit set of instructions is a(n) _____.

2. A programming language is a(n) _____ language because it is precisely defined.

3. A(n) _____ is a generalized method while a(n) _____ is a specialized solution.

4. The _____ of an algorithm defines the setting for its use.

5. A(n) _____ finds the item in a list that is next in order to the *Alpha* item.

6. In a Beta sweep, the _____ property makes sure every item in the list is considered.

7. In a Beta sweep, the _____ property makes sure the sweep is finite.

8. The *Alpha* and the *Beta* in the *Alphabetize CDs* program are called _____.

9. A(n) _____ is the computer term of a set of instructions that repeat.

10. The memory locations of a computer store items, but the contents of these locations contain the _____ of the items.

Exercises

1. Describe the process for subtracting a four-digit number from a five-digit number.

2. Why aren't natural languages such as English good for programming?

3. Using the *Alphabetize CDs* algorithm, illustrate the five properties of an algorithm.

4. Does the instruction "go downhill" have the same problems as "go right"? Explain.

5. What is the purpose of the *Artist_Of*, Step 1, of the *Alphabetize CDs* algorithm?

6. Given the following artists, write down the instructions and steps to put these in order.

   Newton-John, Olivia
   Hill, Faith
   Incubus
   Chapman, Steven Curtis
   Mendelssohn, Felix

7. What would you need to do to arrange the CDs in reverse order instead of alphabetical order? What would you need to do to arrange them in order by copyright?

8. Discuss what you would need to add to the *Alphabetize CDs* algorithm to alphabetize the CDs of Juice Newton, Wayne Newton, and Olivia Newton-John.

9. Explain why *Alpha* doesn't have to reference the last slot.

10. Write a version of the Exchange Sort algorithm to alphabetize CDs in a slotted rack, from last to first order; that is, that has the same result as *Alphabetize CDs*, but from the back end forward.

SOUND, LIGHT, MAGIC

Representing Multimedia Digitally

learning   objectives

> Explain how RGB color is represented in bytes

> Change an RGB color by binary addition

> Explain the meaning of "computing on a representation"

> Explain concepts related to digitizing sound waves

> Explain the meaning of the Bias-free Universal Medium Principle

> Explain the difference between "bits" and "binary numbers"

Science will never be able to reduce the value of a sunset to arithmetic.
                              —DR. LOUIS ORR, 1960

Blue color is everlastingly appointed by the Deity to be a source of delight.
                              —JOHN RUSKIN, 1853

A TYPICAL DAY at college involves so many forms of digital information that few of us notice any longer: There's email to the folks, maybe with a photo attached, MP3 tunes off the Web, the EKG needed to try out for the swim team, the roommate's new DVD movie, the smart ID card from work, and the ever-popular database called the Library Online Catalog. Though these all seem to be way more complicated than the digital representations we've seen so far—well, maybe not the email—they are not. As we'll see in this chapter, all these common multimedia representations build on the basic ideas we've already learned.

From our earlier discussions we learned that discrete things—things that can be separated from each other—can be represented by bits. We begin this chapter by looking more closely at RGB color, which we've mentioned several times before. We learn how a color is encoded in bits, and how we can make the colors darker or lighter. This process—a basic part of digital photo software—is little more than arithmetic on binary numbers. Changing the color of an image and performing other modifications will illustrate these ideas. Next, we discuss JPEG and MPEG and the need for compression techniques for images and video. We then discuss optical character recognition as a way of emphasizing the advantages of encoding information in digital form. The discussion of virtual reality that follows helps make clear how well computers can create synthetic worlds. And finally, the whole topic of digital representation is summarized in one fundamental principle.

DIGITIZING COLOR

When we discussed the binary encoding of keyboard characters to create the ASCII representation (Chapter 8), we (and the creators) didn't pay much attention to which bit patterns were associated with which characters. It's true that in ASCII the numerals are encoded in numeric order, and the letter sets are roughly in alphabetical order, but the assignment is largely arbitrary. The specifics of the keyboard character encoding don't matter much (as long as everyone agrees on them) because the bytes are used as units. We rarely manipulate the individual bits that make up the pattern for the characters. For other encodings, however, manipulating the individual bits is essential.

RGB Colors: Binary Representation

Recall that giving the intensities for the three constituent colors—red, green, and blue (RGB)—specifies a color on the monitor. Each of the RGB colors is assigned a byte (8 bits) to record the intensity of that color. But the color intensities are not assigned arbitrarily, like the letter characters in ASCII. Instead, color intensity is represented as a quantity, ranging from 0 (none) through 255 (most intense); the higher the number, the more intense the color. When we want to change the intensity, we just add to or subtract from the values, implying that the encoding should make it simple to perform arithmetic on the intensities. So, RGB intensities are encoded as binary numbers.

Binary Numbers Compared with Decimal Numbers. Binary numbers are different from decimal numbers because they are limited to two digits, 0 and 1, rather than the customary ten digits, 0 through 9. But that is really the only difference. The other features distinguishing binary from decimal relate to that one difference.

For example, in decimal numbers, we use a **place value** representation, where each "place" represents the next higher power of 10, starting from the right.

Place Value in a Decimal Number. Recall that to find the value of a decimal number, the digit in a place is multiplied by the place value and the results are added up. So, in Figure 11.1, for example, the result is one thousand ten, found by adding from right to left: the digit in the 1s place (0) is multiplied by its place value (1), plus the digit in the 10s place (1) is multiplied by its place value (10), and so on: $0 \times 1 + 1 \times 10 + 0 \times 100 + 1 \times 1000$.

Place Value in a Binary Representation. Binary works in exactly the same way except that the base of the power is not 10 but 2, because there are only two digits, not ten. As usual if given a binary representation, we can find the (decimal) value if we multiply the digit times the place value and add the results. See Figure 11.2, which shows that 1010 in binary has the value 10 in decimal: $0 \times 1 + 1 \times 2 + 0 \times 4 + 1 \times 8$.

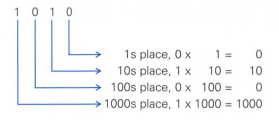

Figure 11.1. Diagram of the decimal number 1010 representing one thousand ten = 10 + 1000.

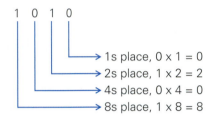

Figure 11.2. Diagram of the binary number 1010, representing the decimal number ten = 2 + 8.

 2nd Base. The "base" of a numbering system, 10 for decimal and 2 for binary, is also called its radix.

Because powers of 2 don't increase as fast as powers of 10, binary numbers need more digits than decimal numbers to represent the same amount. So, for example, representing the decimal number 1010 as a binary number requires ten digits: $0 \times 1 + 1 \times 2 + 0 \times 4 + 0 \times 8 + 1 \times 16 + 1 \times 32 + 1 \times 64 + 1 \times 128 + 1 \times 256 + 1 \times 512$. Compare Figure 11.3 with Figure 11.1.

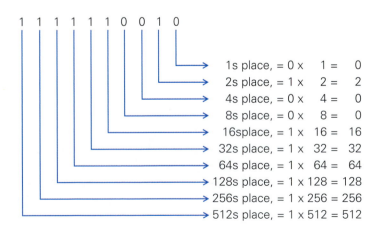

Figure 11.3. Binary representation of the decimal number one thousand ten = 2 + 16 + 32 + 64 + 128 + 256 + 512.

Converting a Binary Number to a Decimal Number. Because the digit is either 0 or 1, the "multiply the digit times the place value" rule is especially easy in binary—a 1 means include the place value and a 0 means "forget it." So, to convert a binary number to its decimal equivalent, just add the place values for the places with 1s. Thus, in Figure 11.3, if we start with the highest place value, we have $512 + 256 + 128 + 64 + 32 + 16 + 2 = 1010$.

FITTIP

Spacing Out. When writing long decimal numbers, North Americans usually separate groups of three digits with a comma for readability. Binary numbers, which are usually even longer, are usually grouped in four-digit units, separated by a *space*.

Black and White Colors

Returning to the representation of color, the fact that a byte—8 bits—is allocated to each of the RGB intensities means that the smallest intensity is 0000 0000, which is 0, of course, and the largest value is 1111 1111. Figuring out what decimal number this is, we add up the place values for the 1s,

$$
\begin{aligned}
1111\ 1111 &= 2^7 + 2^6 + 2^5 + 2^4 + 2^3 + 2^2 + 2^1 + 2^0 \\
&= 128 + 64 + 32 + 16 + 8 + 4 + 2 + 1 \\
&= 255
\end{aligned}
$$

which explains why the range of values is 0 through 255 for each color.

As we learned in Chapter 4, black is no color,

0000 0000	0000 0000	0000 0000	*RGB bit assignment for black*
red byte	green byte	blue byte	

whereas white

1111 1111	1111 1111	1111 1111	*RGB bit assignment for white*
red byte	green byte	blue byte	

has full intensity for each. Between these extremes is a whole range of intensity.

Changing a Decimal Number to a Binary Number

As we've seen, to convert a binary number to decimal representation we add up the powers of 2 corresponding to 1 bits. Converting a decimal number x into a binary representation is only slightly harder. Start by finding the largest power of 2 that is less than or equal to the number. For example, for the number 200, the largest power of 2 less than or equal to 200 is $128 = 2^7$ because $256 = 2^8$ is too large.

If the largest power of 2 is 2^d, there will be $d + 1$ digits in the binary result. To find those digits, follow the simple procedure shown in Figure 11.4.

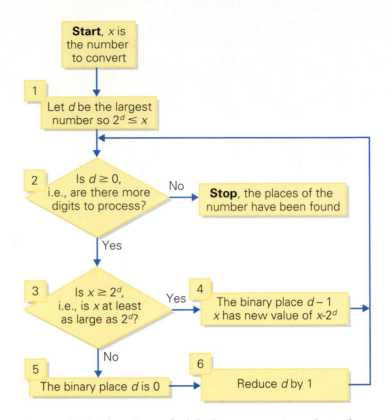

Figure 11.4. *Algorithm to find the bits representing a decimal number x. Begin at Start and follow the operations.*

Build the binary number one place at a time from left to right. At the same time, you are reducing the decimal number by the largest power of 2. The conversion of the decimal number 200 into binary produces the sequence of values shown in Figure 11.5.

Place Number	x	Power of 2	x ≥ 2d	Digit	Comments
7=d	200	$2^7 = 128$	yes	1	Leftmost digit, always 1
6	72	$2^6 = 64$	yes	1	
5	8	$2^5 = 32$	no	0	
4	8	$2^4 = 16$	no	0	
3	8	$2^3 = 8$	yes	1	
2	0	$2^2 = 4$	no	0	
1	0	$2^1 = 2$	no	0	
0	0	$2^0 = 1$	no	0	Rightmost digit

Figure 11.5. *Converting the decimal number 200 into the binary number 1100 1000.*

FITTIP

1 Is First. The algorithm for converting decimal to binary always produces 1 as its first digit. Why? Because we start at the place corresponding to the largest power of 2 less than the decimal number.

Lighten Up: Changing Color by Addition

Returning to our discussion of color representation, the extreme colors of black and white are easy, but what color does the following represent?

1100 1000 1100 1000 1100 1000

    red   green   blue
   byte   byte   byte

First we notice that each byte contains the decimal value 200, which we recognize from the conversion in Figure 11.5. So our mystery color is the color produced by the specification `RGB(200, 200, 200)`. In HTML we write this as `#C8C8C8`. Like black and white, our mystery color has equal amounts of red, green, and blue, and it is closer to white than black. In fact, it is a medium gray ▪. All colors with equal amounts of RGB are gray if they are not black or white. It's just a question of whether they're closer to black or white.

To Increase Intensity: Add in Binary

To make a *lighter* color of gray, we obviously change the common value to be closer to white. Suppose we do this by increasing each of the RGB values by 16—that is, by adding 16 to each byte—as shown in Figure 11.6.

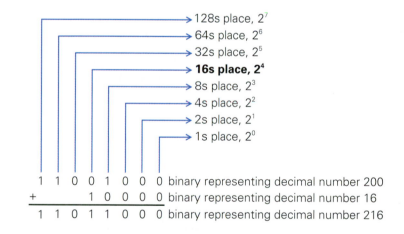

128s place, 2^7
64s place, 2^6
32s place, 2^5
16s place, 2^4
8s place, 2^3
4s place, 2^2
2s place, 2^1
1s place, 2^0

```
  1 1 0 0 1 0 0 0   binary representing decimal number 200
+         1 0 0 0 0 binary representing decimal number 16
  1 1 0 1 1 0 0 0   binary representing decimal number 216
```

Figure 11.6. *Adding 16 to an RGB value.*

The result in Figure 11.6 is found by simply setting the 16s place value—that is, changing it from 0 to 1. The result

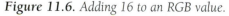

1101 1000 1101 1000 1101 1000

    red   green   blue
   byte   byte   byte

is a lighter shade of gray ▪.

Lighter Still: Adding with Carry Digits

Imagine that we want the color lighter still by another 16 units of intensity for each RGB byte. Adding another 16 isn't quite as easy this time. The 16s position in the binary representation 1101 1000 of 216 is already filled with a 1. So we "carry" to the next higher place. Thus,

```
       1            ← carry digit
   1101 1000        binary representing decimal number        216
 +    1 0000        binary representing decimal number         16
   ─────────                                                  ────
   1110 1000        binary representing decimal number        232
```

So our color intensities are

`1101 1000` `1101 1000` `1101 1000`

red	green	blue
byte	byte	byte

Notice that if we'd simply added 32 to 200 originally, we'd have ended up with the same result, the gray with each intensity set at 232 ▢ .

The process just illustrated is binary addition. As with other aspects of binary, binary addition is similar to decimal addition. We work from right to left, adding corresponding digits in each place position and writing the sum below. Like decimal addition, there are two cases. Sometimes, we can add the two numbers together and the result is expressed as a single digit. That was the case the first time we added in 16 to the RGB byte: we added 1 + 0 in the place and the result was 1. Other times, when we add two digits together their sum is larger than can be expressed by a single digit, so we must carry to the next higher places. That was the case the second time we added in 16 to the RGB byte: we added 1 + 1 in the place and got 0 with a carry to the next higher digit. Because there may be a carry involved, it is best to think of adding as involving three digits in each place: the two digits being added plus (possibly) a carry.

The rules for binary addtion can be learned using an example for each case.

The first example—called the "no carry-in" case—adds A + B when A is the binary number 1100, which is 12 in decimal, and B is 1010, which is 10 in decimal.

```
    ⤓⤓⤓⤓ ──────    Illustrates the "no carry-in" cases
  1  0000    ← Carry, shown explicitly
     1100    ← A
 +   1010    ← B
  ────────
  1  0110    ← Sum
```

The four cases of adding binary digits—all combinations of 0 and 1—are illustrated. In each case there is no *carry-in*—that is, no carry from the previous place. The only interesting case is 1 + 1. Of course, in decimal 1 + 1 = 2. But in binary, there is no 2 digit, only 0 and 1, so the result of 1 + 1 cannot be expressed by a single digit. The decimal number 2 is 10 in binary, so we put down the 0 in the first position and carry the 1 to the next higher position. The carry to the next higher digit is called a *carry-out,* and we notice that the carry-out of one place becomes the carry-in of the next higher place. (Verify that the sum is the binary representation of 22 = 12 + 10.)

The second example, the "carry-in" case, adds A + B when A is 1011, which is 11 in decimal, and 111, which is 7 in decimal. Leading 0's will be shown to complete the picture, and the rightmost place adds 1 + 1 to get the "carrying process" started.

```
  ↓ ↓↓↓          Illustrates the "carry-in" cases
  1 1110   ←  Carry, shown explicitly
  0 1011   ←  A
+ 0 0111   ←  B
  1 0010   ←  Sum
```

The four cases illustrate adding binary digits with a carry-in. Three of the four have the property that the sum of the two digits and the carry are too large to be expressed by a single binary digit, so there is a carry-out to the next higher place. Only the leftmost case, 0 + 0 with a carry-in, can be expressed by a single digit, 1. The new case is the second from right position, which adds 1 + 1 with a carry-in yielding the decimal 3 or binary 11. We write down the 1 in the place and carry-out a 1 to the next higher position. (Verify that the sum is the binary representation of 18 = 11 + 7.)

The rules from the examples are summarized in Table 11.1 We can now apply the rules to add the binary numbers 110 1001 and 110 0011. (What decimal numbers are these?) This time, we follow the usual procedure of showing only the nonzero carries.

```
   11     11     ←  Carry
   110  1001     ←  A
 + 110  0011     ←  B
  1100  1100     ←  Sum
```

Binary addition is so easy, even computers can do it.

Table 11.1. *Summary of the rules for binary addition. The carry-in is added to the two operands, A and B, to give the place digit and the carry-out.*

Carry-in	0	0	0	0	1	1	1	1
A	0	1	0	1	0	1	0	1
B	0	0	1	1	0	0	1	1
Place digit	0	1	1	0	1	0	0	1
Carry-out	0	0	0	1	0	1	1	1

Overflow

Because computers use fixed-size bit sequences (for example, a byte is 8 bits long), an interesting question is what happens when there is a carry-out of the most significant bit—that is, the leftmost bit. For example, 255 + 5 in binary is

```
    1111  1111
+  0000  0101
  1 0000  0100
```

But 260 needs 9 bits, one bit too many to fit into a byte. Such situations are called *overflow exceptions*. Computers report them when the computation they're told to perform overflows, and it is up to the programmer to plan for that. Usually programmers try to avoid the situation by choosing large bit fields.

COMPUTING ON REPRESENTATIONS

Though we have focused on binary representation, conversions between decimal and binary, and binary addition, the previous sections have also introduced another fundamental concept of digital representation—the idea of *computing on a representation*. That is, when we made gray lighter, we were showing how digital information—for example, the RGB settings of a pixel—could be changed through computation because we could have made every shade of gray in the image lighter by the same process. Consider a more involved example, for a better understanding of the idea.

Changing the Colors of a Moon Photo

Imagine that you have scanned into your computer a black-and-white photo you took of the moon, similar to Figure 11.7(a). This is a memento from last weekend when you were out with your friends, and you tried connecting your camera to Jaime's telescope. Unfortunately, you only had black-and-white film loaded, so you missed the gorgeous orange of the close-to-the-horizon moon. In the computer, the pixels of your photo form a long sequence of RGB triples. What values do they have?

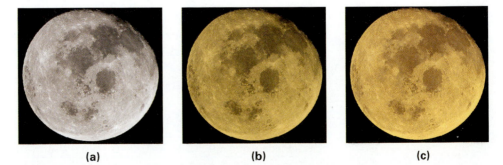

(a)   (b)   (c)

Figure 11.7. Moon photographs. (a) The original black-and-white picture, (b) tinted version of original, (c) with boosted highlights.

Because they are all black, white, or gray, it's easy to guess. There is the (0,0,0) of the black night sky, the (255,255,255) of the brightest part of the moon, some light gray values very close to white—for example, (234,234,234)—of the craters and *marae* of the moon, and some dark gray values very close to black—for example, (28,28,28)—from the smudge left on the glass when someone scanned in a burrito. What you would like to do is email a colorized version of your photo to your friends, similar to Figure 11.7(c).

Removing the Smudges. To create the picture, you must remove the smudges and transform the pixels of the black-and-white image into the colors that you remember. The first task is easy because any value "close" to black can be changed to be true black by replacing it with (0,0,0). But what does *close* mean? The example dark gray value (28,28,28) is represented in binary as

`0001 1100  0001 1100  0001 1100`

Though other dark gray values may be somewhat larger or smaller, it is a safe guess that any dark gray pixel will have the most significant (leftmost) 2 bits of each of its RGB bytes set to 00. That's because, from the binary representation, a byte whose most significant two bits are 00 is less than 64—that is, less than one quarter of the magnitude of full intensity—and any pixel all of whose colors are less than a quarter magnitude must be a darker color.

To change the smudges to pure black, we go through the image looking at each pixel and testing to see if the first 2 bits of each of its bytes are 00. If they are, we set each byte to 0. Recalling our substitution arrow from Chapter 2, we describe this operation as

`00xx xxxx  00xx xxxx  00xx xxxx  ← 0000 0000  0000 0000  0000 0000`

where *x* is a standard symbol for "don't care" or "wildcard"—that is, a symbol matching either 0 or 1. So the substitution statement says "Any three RGB bytes, each of whose first 2 bits are 00, are replaced with all zeros." Making that substitution throughout the image removes the digitized smudge. (Notice that that was an algorithm.)

Making the Moon Orange. Similarly, turning the moon to orange involves changing the white pixels (255,255,255). You decide that the orange of the moon (▮) must be about the color represented by (255,213,132). Changing all of the white pixels to this orange color requires the substitution

`255 255 255 ← 255 213 132`

or, in binary,

`1111 1111  1111 1111  1111 1111  ← 1111 1111  1101 0101  1000 0100`

to produce an orange moon. But it will not change the gray of the craters, because they are not pure white and therefore won't be modified by this replacement. If, like changing the dark gray to black, the very light gray were changed to this orange too, all of the beautiful detail of the craters would be lost. How do we get the white changed to orange and the gray changed to the appropriate orange-tinted gray?

Light Gray into Orange Tint. Though there are many very sophisticated ways to adjust color, the technique that we'll use is to change any light gray into orange in three steps:

> Red byte—leave unchanged

> Green byte—subtract 42 from the green value; that is, reduce the green slightly

> Blue byte—subtract 123 from the blue value; that is, reduce the blue quite a bit

Thus, the light gray color (234,234,234) would be changed into (234,192,111), and the slightly darker light gray (228,228,228) would change into (228,186,105), a slightly grayer orange. These numbers were computed by noting how white (255,255,255) changed into the chosen orange (255,213,132): the red byte was unchanged, the green byte was reduced by 42, and the blue byte was reduced by 123. If all pixels having the most significant bit of each RGB byte equal 1 (that is, the white pixels and all the light gray pixels) are changed by this three-step process, the white areas would become orange and the gray parts would become grayish orange.

You have cleaned up the smudge and colorized the moon, as shown in Figure 11.7(b).

Boosting the Red. Now you inspect your work and decide that the gray parts of the moon are really not as luminous as you remembered. So, you decide to boost the red. If the red in all of the orange pixels is shifted to 255, the moon's craters look too red and "unnatural." But a compromise is to "split the difference." That is, if the current value of the red byte in an orange tint is 234, say, half the difference between it and pure red—(255 − 234)/2 = 10.5—could be added on to get 244. (You need whole numbers, so drop the "point 5.") Thus, the two example tints (234,192,111) and (228,186,105) become (244,192,111) and (241,186,105), respectively. This process brightens the craters without making them unnatural, as demonstrated in Figure 11.7(c). The resulting image looks great, and you can attach it to your email to your friends.

Image Processing Summary

Summarizing, we have computed on a digital representation. We have taken a real photograph scanned into the computer and created an artificial image. First, we improved it by removing the smudges. Then, we colorized it by changing white and light gray into orange and corresponding shades of orange-gray. Finally, we boosted the red in the orange-gray tints to make it a little brighter. We discussed these changes as if you were writing a program, which you could do, but image processing software like Photoshop lets you do this through menu choices like Saturation, Brightness, Hue, and so forth. Such software manipulates the pixels with transformations like those described here, as well as in much more sophisticated ways. The result is not the photograph you would have taken had there been color film in the camera, but rather a different image, a synthetic image closer to what you remember or prefer. It is definitely not reality . . . because we could have just as easily made "the man in the moon" smile.

DIGITIZING SOUND

In this section we learn about digitizing, though this time we focus on digitizing sound rather than images because it is slightly easier and equally interesting. The principles are the same when digitizing any "continuous" information.

An object—think of a cymbal—creates sound, as we know, by vibrating in some medium such as air. The vibrations push the air, causing pressure waves to emanate from the object, which in turn vibrate our eardrums. The vibrations are transmitted by three tiny bones to the fine hairs of our cochlea, stimulating nerves that allow us to sense the waves and "hear" them as sound. The force or intensity of the push determines the volume, and the **frequency** (the number of waves per second) of the pushes is the pitch. Figure 11.8 shows a graph of a sound wave, where the horizontal axis shows time and the vertical axis shows the amount of positive or negative sound pressure.

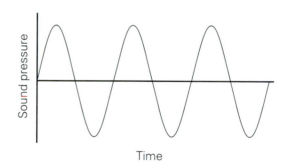

Figure 11.8. Sound wave. The horizontal axis is time; the vertical axis is sound pressure.

From a digitization point of view, the key is that the object vibrates *continuously,* producing a continuously changing wave. That is, as the wave moves past, say, a microphone, the measured pressure changes smoothly. When this pressure variation is recorded directly, as it was originally by Edison with a scratch on a wax cylinder, or with the more recent vinyl records, we have a continuous (**analog**) representation of the wave. In principle, all of the continuous variation of the wave has been recorded. Digital representations work differently.

Analog to Digital

To digitize continuous information, we must convert to bits. For a sound wave, we can record with a binary number the amount by which the wave is above or below the 0 line at a given point. But at what point do we measure? There are infinitely many points along the line, too many to record every position of the wave.

Sampling. So, we **sample**, which means we take measurements at regular intervals. The number of samples in a second is called the **sampling rate**, and the faster the rate, the more accurately the wave is recorded (see Figure 11.9).

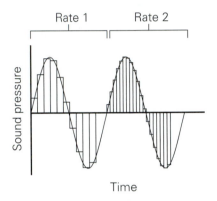

Figure 11.9. *Two sampling rates; the rate on the right is twice as fast as that on the left.*

How Fast a Sampling Rate? To get a good recording of the wave, we need a sampling rate that is related to the wave's frequency. For example, if a sampling were too slow, the sound wave could "fit between" the samples: we'd be missing important segments of the sound.

Fortunately, we have guidelines for the sampling rates. In electrical engineering, the Nyquist Rule says that a sampling rate must be at least twice as fast as the fastest frequency. And what is the fastest frequency we should expect? Because human perception can hear sound up to roughly 20,000 Hz, a 40,000 Hz sampling rate fulfills the Nyquist Rule for digital audio recording. For technical reasons, however, a somewhat faster-than-two-times sampling rate was chosen for digital audio, 44,100 Hz.

ADC, DAC. The digitizing process works as follows: The sound is picked up by a microphone, called a transducer because it converts the sound wave into an electrical wave. This electrical signal is fed into an **analog-to-digital converter** (ADC), which takes the continuous wave and samples it at regular intervals, outputting for each sample binary numbers to be written to memory.

The process is reversed to play the sound: The numbers are read from memory into a **digital-to-analog converter** (DAC), which creates an electrical wave by interpolation between the digital values—that is, filling in or smoothly moving from one value to another. The electrical signal is then input to a speaker, which converts it into a sound wave, as shown in Figure 11.10.

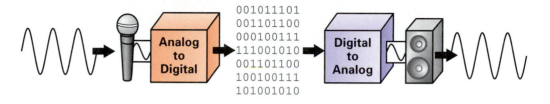

Figure 11.10. *Schematic for analog-to-digital and digital-to-analog conversion.*

How Many Bits per Sample? The problem of digitizing is solved except for describing how accurate the samples must be. To make the samples perfectly accurate, we would need an unlimited number of bits for each sample, which is impossible. But to start, we know that the bits must represent both positive and negative values, because the wave has both positive and negative sound pressure. Second, the more bits there are, the more accurate the measurement will be. For example, with only 3 bits, one of which is used to indicate whether the sign is + or −, we could encode one of four positions in either direction (they align at 0). With so few bits, we can only get an approximate measurement, as shown in Figure 11.11(a). If we used another bit, the sample would be twice as accurate. (In Figure 11.11(b), each interval is half as wide, making the illustrated crossing in the "upper" half of the interval.)

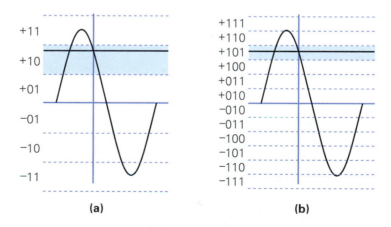

Figure 11.11. *(a) Three-bit precision for samples requires that the indicated reading be approximated as +10. (b) Adding another bit makes the sample twice as accurate.*

Using more bits yields a more accurate digitization. The digital representation of audio CDs uses 16 bits, meaning that $2^{16} = 65,536$ levels are recorded, $2^{15} = 32,768$ for positive values and $32,768$ for negative values.

> **FITBYTE**
>
> **Unforgiving Minute.** How many bits does it take to record a minute of digital audio? There are 60 seconds of 44,100 samples of 16 bits each, times 2 for stereo. That's 84,672,000 bits, or 10,584,000 bytes, more than 10 megabytes! An hour is 635 MB!

Advantages of Digital Sound

A key advantage of digital information (as demonstrated in the last section) is that we can compute on the representation.

MP3 Compression. One computation of value would be to *compress* the digital audio; that is, reduce the number of bits needed to represent the information. For example, an orchestra produces many sounds that the human ear can't hear—some too high and some too low. Our ADC still encodes these frequencies—not to annoy our dog, but simply as part of the encoding process. By computing special functions on the digital audio representation, it is possible to remove these waves without harming the way the audio sounds to us. This is the sort of compression used for MP3. In MP3 we typically get a **compression ratio** of more than 10:1, which means that the number of bits has been reduced to less than one-tenth what it was. So a minute of MP3 music typically takes less than a megabyte to represent. This makes MP3 popular for Internet transmission, because it has lower bandwidth requirements. We discuss bandwidth—the rate at which bits are transmitted—shortly.

We can "fix" a recording in the same way we "fixed" our moon picture. If someone coughs during a quiet moment of Verdi's *Requiem,* we can remove the offending noise from the recording. Performances can be sped up or slowed down without affecting pitch, and so on.

> **FITBYTE**
>
> **MP3.** The "sound track" of a digital video in the MPEG representation is known as MPEG level 3, or MP3.

Reproducing the Sound Recording. Another key advantage of digital representations over analog is that they can be reproduced exactly. We can copy the file of bits that make up an audio performance, without losing a single bit of information. Further, when the original and the copy are played by the same system, they will sound exactly the same. With analog storage, the copy is never as exact as the original, and a second (or third or hundredth) playing of the same version is never as good as the first because of wear. Digital recordings never have these problems as long as the bits remain stable.

DIGITAL IMAGES AND VIDEO

Recall from our discussion of the moon picture that an image is a long sequence of RGB pixels. Of course, the picture is two-dimensional, but we think of the pixels stretched out one row after another in memory, which is one-dimensional. How many pixels are there? For an 8 × 10 image scanned at 300 pixels per inch, there are 80 square inches, each requiring 300 × 300 = 90,000 pixels for a grand total of 7.2 megapixels. At 3 bytes per pixel, it takes 21.6 MB of memory to store one 8 × 10 color image. That's more memory than personal computers came with until recently. Sending such a picture across a standard 56 Kb/s modem—that's kilo*bits* per second—would take at least 21,600,000 × 8 / 56,000 = 3085 seconds, or more than 51 minutes (longer than the average college class). So, how can we see screen-size pictures in seconds when we're surfing the Web?

JPEG Compression

First, a typical computer screen has only about 100 pixels per inch, not 300, which is a factor of 9 savings in memory. But this isn't quite the simplification we need, first because a picture that size still takes more than five and a half minutes to send, and second because once received, we might want to print the picture out, requiring the resolution again. Luckily, electrical engineers invented the **JPEG** compression scheme. *JPEG* stands for "Joint Photographic Experts Group," a nickname for an International Standards Organization (ISO) team that guides the development of digital representation of still photographs.

Compression means to change the representation to use fewer bits to store or transmit information. For example, faxes are usually long sequences of 0's and 1's encoding where the page is white or black. Rather than sending all of the 0's and 1's, we can use run-length encoding to take advantage of the fact that there are long sequences of 0's and 1's. **Run-length encoding** uses binary numbers to specify how long the first sequence (run) of 0's is, then how long the following sequence of 1's is, then how long the following sequence of 0's is, and so on. This works best for long, not short, sequences of 0's and 1's, and most of the time run-length compression is a big win. Run-length encoding is a **lossless compression** scheme, meaning that the original representation of 0's and 1's can be exactly reconstructed. The opposite of lossless compression is **lossy compression**, meaning that the original representation cannot be exactly reconstructed from the compressed form. MP3 is lossy because the high notes cannot be recovered—but it doesn't matter since we can't hear them.

JPEG compression is used for still images. Our eyes are not very sensitive to small changes in hue (chrominance), but we are quite sensitive to small changes in brightness (luminance). This means we can store a less accurate description of the hue of a picture (fewer bits) and, though this compression technique is lossy, our eyes won't notice the difference. With JPEG compression we can get a 20:1 compression ratio or more, compared to an uncompressed still image, without being able to see a difference. For example, if there is a large area of very similar hues (for example, sky), they can all be "lumped together" as the same hue without our noticing. Then, we can apply run-length compression, which wouldn't have worked well with many slight variations in hue, to get further compression. The handy feature of JPEG compression is that we can control the amount of compression: Image compression software will give us a control—a slider or dial, say—so we can choose the amount of compression. Fiddling with the control allows us to determine visually how much more compression can be applied without seriously affecting the look of the image.

MPEG Compression Scheme

MPEG, the compression scheme of the Motion Picture Experts Group of the ISO, is the same idea applied to motion pictures. On the one hand, it seems like an easier task because each image—each frame—will not be seen for very long, so we should be able to get away with even greater levels of single-image compression. On the other hand, the problem seems worse because it takes so many stills to make a movie. In MPEG compression, JPEG-type compression is applied to each frame, but then "interframe coherency" is used. That is, because two consecutive video images will usually be very similar, MPEG compression only has to record and transmit the "differences" between frames. This results in huge amounts of compression, so MPEG only needs moderate amounts of bandwidth.

OPTICAL CHARACTER RECOGNITION

On toll roads now, computers watch cars going by, read their license plates, find accounts for the car in a database, and deduct the toll from the "car's" account. It sure beats stopping every few miles to pay a few more coins! The interesting aspect of this technology is that there is no bar code or electronic transponder; a computer simply recognizes the letters of the license plate. Reading license plates is very easy for humans, but it's a big deal for computers.

Consider some of the difficulties. First, the computer needs an image of the license plate, but the camera is pointed at the highway, getting many images that are not license plates—the scene, parts of cars, trailers, litter, road-kill before it is road-kill, and so on. An electronic device called a **frame grabber** recognizes when to "snap" the image and ship it to the computer for processing. Assuming a frame with a license plate in it has been snapped, the computer must next figure out where in the image it is, because there is no standard location for a license plate on a vehicle, and even if there were, the vehicle could be changing lanes. Looking for letters and numbers doesn't work, because some vehicles display bumper stickers or advertising. Once the license plate is found, recognizing its characters is the most significant challenge, because they're not yet characters, but thousands of pixels.

Happily, license plate colors are chosen to be high contrast, for example, dark letters on a light background. The computer scans groups of pixels looking for edges where the color changes. It forms these into features. A *feature* is a part of a character to be recognized. For example, a *P* might be described by the features of a "vertical stroke" and a "hole" at the top of the stroke, because lines and holes are patterns that could be recognized by noting where color changes. Given the features, a **classifier** matches the features to the alphabet to determine which are close, perhaps finding a strong correlation with *P*, a weaker one with *9*, and a still weaker one with *D*. Finally, after picking the most likely characters, an optical character recognizer usually checks the context, trying to decide if the combination makes sense; for example, has a license been issued with that combination of letters? Finding the number in the database, the computer figures it has read the plate right and debits the account.

FITBYTE

> **Beginning Reader.** In 1954, J. Rainbow demonstrated an optical character reader that could recognize uppercase typewritten characters at the rate of one letter per minute.

OCR Technology

Optical character recognition (*OCR*) is a very sophisticated technology that enables a computer to "read" printed characters. OCR's business applications are sorting mail and banking. The U.S. Postal Service uses a system that locates the address block on an envelope or card, reads it in any of 400 fonts, identifies its ZIP code, generates a nine-digit bar code, sprays the bars on the envelope, sorts it, and, with only a 2 percent error rate, processes up to 45,000 pieces of mail per hour. In banking, where the magnetic numbers at the bottom of the check have been read by computers since the 1950s, OCR is now used to read the *handwritten* digits of the numeric check amount to verify that a data entry person has interpreted the amount correctly.

VIRTUAL REALITY: FOOLING THE SENSES

The ultimate form of digital representation is to create an entire digital world. The idea has become known as virtual reality (VR). So far, VR has less to do with representing the world and more to do with fooling our senses into perceiving something that doesn't exist.

Rapidly displaying still images is a standard way to fool our eyes and brain into seeing motion. Virtual reality applies that idea to our other senses and tries to

Text-to-speech technology >>

Perhaps the most significant application of optical character recognition is Raymond Kurzweil's text-to-speech reading machines developed for the blind and partially sighted. Produced in 1976, the reading machine uses a flatbed scanner—a technology originally developed by Kurzweil—to scan reading material, recognize it as text, and then speak it using a voice synthesizer. Scanning, font-independent optical character recognition, large-vocabulary dictionaries, and speech synthesis are by now standard technologies that Kurzweil had to create for his devices. For the disabled, the reader, and its inverse, the speech-to-text machine, have dramatically improved personal lives and career opportunities. Says the blind musician Stevie Wonder, who credits the reader with changing his life, "It gave blind people the one life goal that everyone treasures, and that is independence."

Raymond Kurzweil received the National Medal of Technology and the Lemelson–MIT Award for Innovation, which is like a Nobel Prize for inventors.

eliminate the cues that keep us grounded in reality. For example, when we see a TV scene of a train coming toward us, we know by various cues, such as peripheral vision, that we're watching a TV; we see the motion but we're not fooled. However, if we're wearing a helmet with a TV in front of each eye that shows the train in a complete scene, gives us three-dimensional vision, and fills in our peripheral vision as well so that when we move our head we can look at other parts of the scene, the cues are reduced or eliminated. Add high-quality audio in each ear and a treadmill so that we seem to be walking or running through the scene, and it's easy to imagine how a computer could effectively fool us into thinking the train is chasing us.

Haptic Devices

Certain deceptions are more useful. **Haptic devices** are input/output technology for interacting with our sense of touch and feel. For example, a haptic glove enables a computer to detect where our fingers are and to apply force against them. When we bring our fingers close enough together, the glove stops their movement, leaving us with the feeling of holding something. With haptic gloves and the VR helmet, a computer can show us Legos in space, which, when we grab them, gives us the sensation of holding them and makes us think we are assembling them. When the glove pulls down on our fingers, we think the Legos are heavy, perhaps made of metal. Though the world is virtual, it is credible to us. Such technology can be used to train surgeons for complex operations, for example.

FITBYTE

Virtual Meaning. The term *virtual* is used often in IT—for example, virtual memory—because the computer produces a believable illusion of something that doesn't exist. *Virtual* means "not actually but just as if."

The Challenge of Latency

The challenge with virtual reality and other sophisticated output devices like video is for the system to operate fast enough and precisely enough to appear natural. We know that when still images are presented in an animation too slowly, the illusion of motion is lost. When that happens in a VR system—when we turn our head but the scene doesn't smoothly change—we can get dizzy, maybe even sick. Our sensation of touch and feel actually operates faster than the 30 Hz standard for visual perception, closer to 1000 Hz. Thus, when we "see" our virtual hand going to pick up a virtual Lego, we must "feel" it before we "see" it if the illusion is to work.

This phenomenon is called **latency**—the time it takes for information to be delivered. We are familiar with long latencies when Web pages are not delivered instantly, but the phenomenon arises wherever information must be transmitted or generated. In most cases, as with Web pages, long latencies just make us wait, but in video, VR, voice communication, and so on, long latency can ruin the medium. Reducing latency is a common engineering goal, but there is an absolute limit to how fast information can be transmitted: the speed of light. Eventually, the virtual world is constrained by the physical world.

The Challenge of Bandwidth

Closely related to latency is **bandwidth**—a measure of how much information can be transmitted per second. Bandwidth is related to latency in that a given amount of information (for example, 100 KB) transmitted with a given bandwidth (for example, 50 KB/s) determines the (best) latency by dividing the amount by the bandwidth; in this case, 100 / 50 = 2, or 2 seconds of latency. Other delays can extend the latency beyond this theoretical best. Higher bandwidth usually means lower latency. (The rule eventually fails for speed-of-light and switching-delay reasons.) So, faster modems mean that Web pages load faster.

VR is a developing technology. It is still challenged by both latency and bandwidth limitations—it takes many, many bytes to represent a synthetic world. Creating them and delivering them to our senses is a difficult technical problem. Nevertheless, it is an exciting future application of IT.

BITS ARE IT

Looking back over this and previous chapters, we have seen that 4 bytes, say, can represent many kinds of information from four ASCII keyboard characters to numbers between zero and about 4 billion. This is not an accident, but rather a fundamental property of information, which we will summarize in this principle:

> **Bias-free Universal Medium Principle:** Bits can represent all discrete information; bits have no inherent meaning.

Bits: The Universal Medium

The first half of the principle—all discrete information can be represented by bits—is the universality aspect. Discrete things—things that can be separated from each other—can be represented by bits. At the very least, we can assign numbers to each one and represent those numbers in binary. But, as we saw with color, it is possible to be far smarter. We assigned the RGB colors so the intensity could be increased or decreased using binary arithmetic. This representation of color is much more organized than simply saying, "Black will be 0, purple will be 1, yellow will be 2, puce will be 3," and so on. As a result of organizing the representation in a sensible way, we can *easily* compute on it, making changes like brightening the image. Of course, if the information is continuous—that is, if it is analog information like sound—it must first be made discrete by an analog-to-digital conversion. But once digitized, this information, too, can be represented by bits.

Bits: Bias-Free

The second half of the principle—bits have no inherent meaning—is the bias-free aspect. Given a bit sequence

0000 0000 1111 0001 0000 1000 0010 0000

there is no way to know what information it represents. The meaning of the bits comes entirely from the *interpretation* placed on them by us or by the computer through our programs. For example, the 4 bytes could be a zero byte followed by the RGB intensities (241,8,32) ■. Or, the 4 bytes could be an instruction to add two binary numbers. As a binary number, the bits work out to 15,796,256.

So, bits are bits. What they mean depends only on how the software interprets them, which means they work for any kind of information. Storage media need only store one pair of patterns: 0 and 1. The principle explains why, for example, a single transmission medium—the TCP/IP packet—is all that's needed to deliver any kind of information across the Internet to your computer: text, photos, MP3 tunes.

Bits Are Not Necessarily Binary Numbers

Since the public first became aware of computers, it's been "common knowledge" that computers represent information as binary *numbers*. Experts reinforce this view, but it's not quite right. Computers represent information as bits. Bits can be *interpreted* as binary numbers, as we've seen, which is why the experts are not wrong. But the bits do not always represent binary numbers. They can be interpreted as ASCII characters, RGB colors, or an unlimited list of other things (see Figure 11.12). Programs often perform arithmetic on the bits, as we saw when we modified the moon image; but often they do not, because it doesn't make sense with the intended interpretation of the information. Computers represent information with bits. They are an amazing medium.

0000 0000 1111 0001 0000 1000 0010 0000 = 15,796,256 interpreted as a binary
number

= interpreted as an RGB(241,8,32)
color (last 3 bytes)

= ADD 1,7,17 interpreted as a MIPS
machine instruction

= ^N_U ^B_S ñ ␢ interpreted as 8-bit ASCII—
null, backspace, n-tilde, blank

= L: +241, R: +280 interpreted as sound
samples

= 0.241.8.32 interpreted as an
IP address

= 00 F1 08 20 interpreted as a
hexadecimal number

Figure 11.12. Illustration of the principle that "bits are bits."
The same 4 bytes shown can be interpreted differently depending on context.

SUMMARY

In this chapter we have considered how different forms of information are represented in the computer. In the case of RGB color, we learned that each intensity is a 1-byte numeric quantity represented as a binary number. Binary representation and binary arithmetic are like decimal but are limited to two digits. We found the decimal equivalent of binary numbers by adding up their powers of 2 corresponding to 1's; and by using a simple algorithm, we did the reverse to find binary from decimal. We used arithmetic on the intensities to "compute on the representation," making gray lighter and colorizing a black-and-white picture of the moon. Much more exotic computations on images are possible in photographic software, but the principles are the same.

Next we considered how to digitize sound as an illustration of all analog-to-digital conversion. Sampling rate and measurement precision determine how accurate the digital form is; uncompressed audio requires more than 80 million bits per minute. We learned how compression makes large files manageable: JPEG for still pictures and MPEG for video. These more compact representations work because they remove information people don't miss. We took a quick look at optical character recognition, and noted that it is a technology that makes the world better. Our discussion of virtual reality illustrated the complexities of conveying information to all of our senses at once. Finally, we emphasized that much of the magic of computers is embodied in the universality of bit representations and the unbiased way they encode, the Bias-free Universal Medium Principle.

EXERCISES

Multiple Choice

1. Each RGB color intensity ranges from:
   A. 0-15
   B. 0-255
   C. 1-16
   D. 1-256

2. The RGB setting for blue is (0 is off, 1 is on):
   A. 0000 0000 0000 0000 0000 0000
   B. 1111 1111 0000 0000 0000 0000
   C. 0000 0000 1111 1111 0000 0000
   D. 0000 0000 0000 0000 1111 1111

3. Analog information is:
   A. discrete
   B. continuous
   C. random
   D. digital

4. According to the Nyquist Rule, the sampling rate of sound is roughly:
   A. half of what humans can hear
   B. the same as what humans can hear
   C. twice what humans can hear
   D. three times what humans can hear

5. The accuracy of a digitized sound is determined by:
   A. the sampling rate
   B. the bit rate
   C. the size of the digitized file
   D. all of the above

6. A digital-to-analog converter:
   A. changes digital information to analog waves
   B. converts continuous sound to digital sound
   C. converts sound to an electrical signal
   D. sets approximated values

7. MP3 is the sound information of
   A. MPEG movies
   B. all digital movies
   C. all computer sound
   D. all digital computer sound

8. Jessica Simpson's "A Little Bit" is 3 minutes 47 seconds long. How many bits is that?
   A. 1,411,200
   B. 40,042,800
   C. 84,672,000
   D. 320,342,400

9. OCR is used in all of the following areas except:
   A. text-to-speech recognition
   B. ZIP code recognition
   C. supermarket checkout
   D. bank account recognition

10. Raymond Kurzweil is known as the inventor of:
    A. OCR
    B. text-to-speech recognition
    C. image compression
    D. virtual reality

Short Answer

1. When all the RGB color settings are set to 0, the color displayed is _____.

2. The first digit of a binary number is always _____.

3. _____ is the term used when digital values are converted to create an analog sound.

4. _____ sound removes the highest and lowest samplings as part of its compression algorithm.

5. A(n) _____ is used to convert analog sound to digital values.

6. _____ is a compression scheme for digital video while _____ is the scheme for digital images.

7. _____ is the group that oversees the development of digital media standards.

8. On the computer, _____ means to store or transmit information with fewer bits.

9. A process that allows the computer to "read" printed characters is called _____.

10. Conversion of the written word to speech is called _____.

11. The creation of a digital representation of the world is called _____.

12. JPEG is to still images what _____ is to motion pictures.

13. _____ are used with computers to control a person's sense of touch.

14. _____ is the time it takes information to be delivered.

15. The _____ states that bits can represent all discrete information even though the bits have no meaning of their own.

Exercises

1. Write the algorithm for converting from decimal to binary.

2. Write the algorithm for converting from binary to decimal.

3. Add 1492 and 1776 in binary and display the answer in binary.

4. In binary, add 1011, 1001, 110, and 1100.

5. Convert RGB 200, 200, 200 to hex C8C8C8 by converting it to binary and then to hex.

6. Add 168 and 123 in binary. How many bytes does it take to represent each number? How many bytes are needed for the answer? What happens if there aren't enough bytes to store the answer?

7. Software is now in use that can let you "try on" a dress virtually. What process would be used to change that bright red, taffeta dress into a soft pink? What would be needed to change it to sea foam (light green)? What would it take to turn it into a color to match your eyes?

8. Explain how a picture at 300 pixels per inch could be converted to a picture with 100 pixels per inch.

9. Most music is now sold on CD-ROM. Explain how a singer's voice in the recording studio goes to the earphones on your computer? Why are both processes needed for this to succeed?

10. Digitally, what would need to be done to raise (or lower) a singer's voice an octave?

11. Why are JPEG, MPEG, and MP3 considered algorithms?

12. To the computer, bits are bits. To a page, letters are letters. Use this to explain the meaning of the Bias-free Universal Medium Principle.

RAY KURZWEIL was the principal developer of the first omni-font optical character recognition, the first print-to-speech reading machine for the blind, the first CCD flat-bed scanner, the first text-to-speech synthesizer, the first music synthesizer capable of recreating the grand piano and other orchestral instruments, and the first commercially marketed large-vocabulary speech recognition. Ray has successfully founded and developed nine businesses in OCR, music synthesis, speech recognition, reading technology, virtual reality, financial investment, medical simulation, and cybernetic art. In addition to scores of other national and international awards, Ray was inducted into the National Inventors Hall of Fame, and received the 1999 National Medal of Technology, the nation's highest honor in technology, from President Clinton. Ray's Web site, KurzweilAI.net, is a leading resource on artificial intelligence.

Do you have a "favorite story" to tell about one of your inventions?

We announced the Kurzweil Reading Machine, which was the first print-to-speech reading machine for the blind, on January 13, 1976. I remember this date because Walter Cronkite, the famous news anchor for CBS News, used it to read his signature sign-off that evening "And that's the way it was, January 13, 1976." It was the first time that he did not read this famous phrase himself.

I was subsequently invited to demonstrate this new reading machine on the *Today Show*. We only had one working model and we were nervous about demonstrating it on live television since there was always the possibility of technical glitches. They responded that it was live or nothing.

We arrived at the Today Show studio very early in the morning and set up the reading machine. Sure enough, it stopped working a couple of hours before show time. We tried various easy fixes which failed to rectify the problem. So our chief engineer frantically took the machine apart. With electrical pieces scattered across the studio floor, Frank Field, who was to interview me, walked by, and asked if there was a problem. We said that we were just making a few last minute adjustments.

Our chief engineer put the machine back together, and it still was not working. Then, in a time honored tradition of repairing delicate technical equipment, he picked up the machine and slammed it into the table. It worked perfectly from that moment on, and the live demonstration and interview went without a hitch.

Stevie Wonder happened to catch me on the broadcast, and called our office wanting to stop by and pick up his own reading machine. Our receptionist did not believe it was really the legendary musical artist, but she put him through anyway. We were just finishing up our first production unit, so we rushed that to completion. Stevie stopped by, stayed several hours to learn how to use it, and went off with his new Kurzweil Reading Machine in a taxi. That was the beginning of a nearly thirty-year friendship which continues to this day. A few years later, Stevie was instrumental in my launching Kurzweil Music Systems, Inc.

Your inventions range from the Kurzweil 250 to a nutritional program that cured you of type II Diabetes. Is there a tie that binds your many inventions?

My original, and still primary, area of technology interest and expertise is a field called "pattern recognition," which is the science and art of teaching computers to recognize patterns. It turns out that the bulk of human intelligence is based on our remarkable ability to recognize patterns such as faces, visual objects, speech and music. Most of my technology projects are related to recognizing patterns, for example character recognition and speech recognition. Even my work in music synthesis was influenced by pattern recognition. We had to answer the question as to what patterns cause humans to recognize sounds as coming from a particular type of instrument, such as a grand piano.

I quickly realized that timing was important for my inventions, and began to develop mathematical models of how technology develops over time. This endeavor took on a life of its own. By using these models, I was able to make predictions about technologies ten to thirty years into the future, and beyond. From these efforts, I realized that the twenty-first century was going to be an extraordinary time in advancing human civilization. This insight has been a major motivation for me to find the means to live long enough, and in good health, to experience this remarkable century.

I also realized that one of the areas of technology that is accelerating is health and medical technology. Therefore the tools we will have to keep ourselves healthy will grow in power and sophistication in the years ahead. It is important, therefore, to keep ourselves healthy using today's knowledge so that we are in good shape to take advantage of the full flowering of the biotechnology revolution, which is now in its early stages.

Many of your past predictions about the future of technology have "come true". How is it that you are able to make such specific and accurate predictions?

Most futurists simply make predictions without a well thought out framework or methodology. I have been studying technology trends for at least a quarter century, and have been developing detailed mathematical models of how technology in different fields evolves. I have a team of people gathering data to measure the key features and capabilities of technologies in a wide array of fields, including computation, communications, biological technologies, and brain reverse engineering. From this work, it has become clear that technologies, particularly those that deal with information, are growing at a double exponential rate (that is the rate of exponential growth is itself growing exponentially). Typically, an information-based technology at least doubles its capability for the same unit cost every year.

The other important issue is that very few people realize that the pace of technical change, what I call the paradigm shift rate, is itself accelerating. We are doubling the pace of technical change every decade. I spoke recently at a conference recently celebrating the fiftieth anniversary of the discovery of the structure of DNA. We were all asked what changes we foresaw for the next fifty years. With very few exceptions, the other speakers used the amount of change in the last fifty years as a guide to the amount of change we will see in the next fifty years. But this is a faulty assumption. Because the rate of change is accelerating, we will see about thirty times as much change in the next fifty years, as we saw in the last half century.

In your book *The Age of Spiritual Machines*, you foresee a future where computers have exceeded human intelligence. How and when do you expect this to come about?

We can separate this question into two questions: when will computers have the computational capacity (the "hardware" capability) of the human brain? Secondly, when will we have the content and methods (the "software") of human intelligence?

In my book, *The Age of Spiritual Machines*, which came out in 1999, I said we would achieve the computational capacity of the human brain for about $1,000 by 2019. I estimate this capacity to be about 100 billion neurons, times about 1,000 interneuronal connections per neuron, times 200 calculations per second per connection, or about 20 million billions calculations per second. This was considered a controversial projection in 1999, but there has been a sea change in perspective on this issue since that time. Today, it is a relatively mainstream expectation that we will have sufficient computational resources by 2019. Computers are at least doubling their speed and memory capacity every year, and even that rate is accelerating.

The more challenging issue is the software of intelligence. A primary source of what I call the "templates" of human intelligence is the human brain itself. We are already well along the path of reverse engineering the brain to understand its principles of operation. Here also we see exponential advance. Brain scanning technologies are doubling their resolution, bandwidth, and price-performance every year.

Knowledge about the human brain, including models of neurons and neural clusters, is doubling every year. We already have detailed mathematical models of several dozen of the several hundred regions that comprise the human brain. I believe it is a conservative projection to say that we will have detailed models of all the regions of the brain by the mid 2020s.

By 2029, we will be able to combine the subtle powers of pattern recognition that the human brain excels in, with several attributes in which machine intelligence already exceeds human capabilities. These include speed, memory capacity, and the ability to instantly share knowledge. Computers circa 2029, possessing human levels of language understanding, will be able to go out on the web and read and absorb all of the available literature and knowledge.

Will these computers of the future have human emotions?

Indeed, they will. Emotional intelligence is not a side issue to human intelligence. It is actually the most complex and subtle thing we do. It is the cutting edge of human intelligence. If a human had no understanding of human emotions, we would not consider that person to be operating at a normal human level. The same will be true for machines. Already, there is significant interest in teaching computers about human emotions: how to detect them in humans, and how to respond to them appropriately. This is important for the next generation of human-machine interfaces. As we reverse engineer the human brain, and understand how the different regions process information, we will gain an understanding of what our emotions mean. A very important benefit of this endeavor will be greater insight into ourselves.

What drawbacks do you foresee for the future you envision?

Technology is inherently a double-edged sword. All of the destruction of the twentieth century (for example, two world wars) was amplified by technology. At the same time, we are immeasurably better off as a result of technology. Human life expectancy was 37 years in 1800 and 50 years in 1900. Human life was filled with poverty, hard labor, and disease up until fairly recently.

We are now in the early stages of the biotechnology revolution. We are learning the information processes underlying life and disease, and are close to developing new treatments that will overcome age-old diseases, such as cancer, heart disease, and Diabetes. This same knowledge, however, can also empower a terrorist to create a bioengineered pathogen. There is no easy way to separate the promise from the peril, as both stem from the same technology. We will see similar dilemmas with nanotechnology (technology in which the key features are less than 100 nanometers) and with artificial intelligence.

The answer, I believe, is to substantially increase our investment in developing specific defensive technologies to protect society from these downsides. We can see a similar battle between promise and peril in the area of software viruses. Although we continue to be concerned about software viruses, the defensive technologies have been largely successful. Hopefully we will be able to do as well with biotechnology and other future technologies.

Could you offer some advice to students with regard to keeping pace with information technology and perhaps with regard to inventing it?

This is a very exciting time to be embarking on a career in science and technology. The pace of change and the expansion of new knowledge is greater than at any time in history, and will continue to accelerate. The impact of science and technology goes substantially beyond these subjects themselves. Ultimately, new technological advances will transform every facet of human life and society.

I would advise students to:

1. Obtain a strong background in math, as this is the language of science and technology. Math also represents a way of thinking that leads to discovery and understanding.

2. Become an ardent student of technology and technology trends. Build your inventions for the world of the future, not the world you see in front of you today.

3. Focus on a particular area of science or technology that particularly fascinates you. The days when one person could master all of science and technology are long gone. However, as you focus, don't put on the blinders to what is going on in fields around you.

4. Follow your passion.

interview
RAY KURZWEIL

HTML REFERENCE

The following brief descriptions form an alphabetical list of the HTML tags used in this book. Check Chapter 4 for further explanation or consult `www.w3.org/hypertext/WWW/MarkUp/MarkUp.html`.

FITCAUTION

Text Only! Remember, HTML source files must contain only standard keyboard text (ASCII). Word processors include fancy formatting that confuses browsers. Use simple text editors only, such as Simple Text, BBtext, or Notepad. Also, the file name extension—the characters after the last dot in the file name—must be html.

HTML Document Structure

Every HTML source file must contain the following tags in the given order:

```
<html>
   <head>
       All header content goes here
   </head>
   <body>
       All body content goes here
   </body>
</html>
```

HTML Tags

Anchor (`<a>` `</a>`): Defines a hyperlink using the `href="`*fn*`"` attribute, where *fn* is a file name. The text between the two tags is known as the link and is highlighted.

```
<a href="nextPage.html">Click here for next page</a>
```

Body (`<body>` `</body>`): Specifies the extent of the body of the HTML document (refer to the preceding section to see the HTML document structure). Useful attributes include

> `background="`*fn*`"` fills the page background with the image (possibly tiled) from the file *fn*

> `bgcolor="`*color*`"` paints the background the specified *color*

> `text="`*color*`"` displays text the specified *color*

> `link="`*color*`"` displays links the specified *color*

Bold (`<b>` `</b>`): Specifies that the style of the enclosed text is to be bold font.

```
<b>This text prints as bold</b>
```

Caption (`<caption>` `</caption>`): Specifies the caption of a table, and must be enclosed by Table tags. See "Table" in this list for an example.

Comment (`<!--`*comment goes here*`-->`): The comment text is enclosed within the angle brackets; avoid using angle brackets in the comments, which can confuse browsers.

```
<!-- This text will not be displayed -->
```

Definitional List (`<dl>` `</dl>`): Defines a definitional list, which is composed of two-part entries, called the definitional-list term (`<dt>` `</dt>`) and the definitional-list definition (`<dd>` `</dd>`). Terms are on separate lines and the definitions are on the line following. A useful attribute is `compact`, which displays terms and definitions on the same line.

```
<dl>
  <dt>First term</dt>
  <dd>First definition goes here</dd>
  <dt>Second term </dt>
  <dd>Second definition goes here</dd>
</dl>
```

Font (`<font>` `</font>`): Defines a range of text in which the style of the font is to be adjusted from the prevailing style. Useful attributes include

> `color="`*color*`"` displays the text the specified *color*

> `face="`*type*`"` displays text the specified *type* face

```
<font face="Helvetica"> This text is san serif </font>
```

Header (`<head>` `</head>`): Defines the extent of the header of the HTML document, which must include a Title. Refer to the first section, "HTML Document Structure," for an example.

Headings (<hi> </hi>): Specifies that the enclosed text is to be one of eight levels of headings. The smaller the number the larger and more prominent the text will be.

```
<h1> Heading level 1 </h1>   Most prominent
<h2> Heading level 2 </h2>
     ...
<h7> Heading level 7 </h7>
<h8> Heading level 8 </h8>   Least prominent
```

Horizontal Rule (<hr>): Defines a line that spans the window, though it can be reduced in size using the `width="p%"` attribute. The attribute `size="n"` specifies the (point) thickness of the line.

```
<hr width="75%">
```

HTML (<html> </html>): Defines the beginning and end of the document. Refer to the first section, "HTML Document Structure," for an example.

Image (<img>): Causes an image—specified by the `src="fn"` attribute—to be placed in the document at the current position. Positioning information uses the `align` attribute to specify the position on the line—`top`, `middle`, `bottom`—and the position in the window—`left`, `center`, `right`. Also, `height` and `width` attributes specify the displayed image's size in pixels.

```
<img src="prettyPic.html" align='left' height='200' width='140'>
```

Italics (<i> </i>): Specifies that the syle of the enclosed text is to be italic.

```
<i>This text is emphasized by italics</i>
```

Line Break (<br>): Ends the current line and continues the text on the next line.

```
This text is on one line.<br> This text is on the next line.
```

List Item (<li> </li>): Specifies an entry in either an ordered or an unordered list. See examples in the "Ordered List" and "Unordered List" definitions.

Ordered List (<ol> </ol>): Specifies the extent of an ordered list, whose entries are list items. The list items are prefixed with a number.

```
<ol>
  <li>First list item</li>
  <li>Second list item</li>
</ol>
```

Paragraph (<p> </p>): Specifies the extent of a paragraph. Paragraphs begin on a new line.

```
<p> This text forms a small paragraph</p>
```

Title (`<title> </title>`): Defines the title for the page, and must be given in the Header section of the HTML source.

```
<title> Titles display at the top of the browser window
</title>
```

Table (`<table> </table>`): Defines a table of Table Rows; the rows contain Table Data. The first row of the definition can optionally be formed of Table Heading tags. A useful attribute is border, giving the table a border.

```
<table border>
  <caption>Description</caption>
  <tr>
     <th>Head Col 1</th>
     <th>Head Col 2</th>
     <th>Head Col 3</th>
  </tr>
  <tr>
     <td>Row 1, Cell 1</td>
     <td>Row 1, Cell 2</td>
     <td>Row 1, Cell 3</td>
  </tr>
  <tr>
     <td>Row 2, Cell 1</td>
     <td>Row 2, Cell 2</td>
     <td>Row 2, Cell 3</td>
  </tr>
  <tr>
     <td>Row 3, Cell 1</td>
     <td>Row 3, Cell 2</td>
     <td>Row 3, Cell 3</td>
  </tr>
</table>
```

Table Data (`<td> </td>`): Specifies a cell in a table, and must be enclosed by Table Row tags. A useful attribute is `bgcolor="`*color*`"`. See "Table" for an example.

Table Heading (`<th> </th>`): Specifies a cell in the heading row of a table, and must be enclosed by Table Row tags. A useful attribute is `bgcolor="`*color*`"`. See "Table" for an example.

Table Row (`<tr> </tr>`): Specifies a row in a table, and must be enclosed by table tags. A useful attribute is `bgcolor="`*color*`"`. See "Table" for an example.

Unordered List (`<ul> </ul>`): Specifies the extent of an unordered list, whose entries are list items. The list items are prefixed with a bullet. A list item can enclose another list.

```
<ol>
  <li>First list item</li>
  <li>Second list item</li>
</ol>
```

RGB Colors

Table A.1 shows the hexadecimal coding for commonly used colors. The numbers, when used in attribute specifications, should have the form "#dddddd".

Table A.1 *Web-Safe Colors for Web Page Design*

990033 153:0:51	FF3366 255:51:102	CC0033 204:0:51	FF0033 255:0:51	FF9999 255:153:153	CC3366 204:51:102	FFCCFF 255:204:255	CC6699 204:51:153
993366 153:51:102	660033 102:0:51	CC3399 204:51:153	FF99CC 255:153:204	FF66CC 255:102:204	FF99FF 255:153:255	FF6699 255:102:153	CC0066 204:0:102
FF0066 255:0:102	FF3399 255:51:153	FF0099 255:0:153	FF33CC 255:51:204	FF00CC 255:0:204	FF66FF 255:102:255	FF33FF 255:51:255	FF00FF 255:0:255
CC0099 204:0:153	990066 153:0:102	CC66CC 204:102:204	CC33CC 204:51:204	CC99FF 204:153:255	CC66FF 204:102:255	CC33FF 204:51:255	993399 153:51:153
CC00CC 204:0:204	CC00FF 204:0:255	9900CC 153:0:204	990099 153:0:153	CC99CC 204:153:204	996699 153:102:153	663366 102:51:102	660099 102:0:153
9933CC 153:51:204	660066 102:0:102	9900FF 153:0:255	9933FF 153:51:255	9966CC 153:102:204	330033 51:0:51	663399 102:51:153	6633CC 102:51:204
6600CC 102:0:204	330066 51:0:102	9966FF 153:102:255	6600FF 102:0:255	6633FF 102:51:255	CCCCFF 204:204:255	9999FF 153:153:255	9999CC 153:153:204
6666CC 102:102:204	6666FF 102:102:255	666699 102:102:153	333366 51:51:102	333399 51:51:153	330099 51:0:153	3300CC 51:0:204	3300FF 51:0:255
3333FF 51:51:255	3333CC 51:51:204	0066FF 0:102:255	0033FF 0:51:255	3366FF 51:102:255	3366CC 51:102:204	000066 0:0:102	000033 0:0:51
0000FF 0:0:255	000099 0:0:153	0033CC 0:51:204	0000CC 0:0:204	336699 51:102:153	0066CC 0:102:204	99CCFF 153:204:255	6699FF 102:153:255
003366 0:51:102	6699CC 102:153:204	006699 0:102:153	3399CC 51:153:204	0099CC 0:153:204	66CCFF 102:204:255	3399FF 51:153:255	003399 0:51:153
0099FF 0:153:255	33CCFF 51:204:255	00CCFF 0:204:255	99FFFF 153:255:255	66FFFF 102:255:255	33FFFF 51:255:255	00FFFF 0:255:255	00CCCC 0:204:204
009999 0:153:153	669999 102:153:153	99CCCC 153:204:204	CCFFFF 204:255:255	33CCCC 51:204:204	66CCCC 102:204:204	339999 51:153:153	336666 51:102:102
006666 0:102:102	003333 0:51:51	00FFCC 0:255:204	33FFCC 51:255:204	33CC99 51:204:153	00CC99 0:204:153	66FFCC 102:255:204	99FFCC 153:255:204
00FF99 0:255:153	339966 51:153:102	006633 0:102:51	669966 102:153:102	66CC66 102:204:102	99FF99 153:255:153	66FF66 102:255:102	99CC99 153:204:153
336633 51:102:51	66FF99 102:255:153	33FF99 51:255:153	33CC66 51:204:102	00CC66 0:204:102	66CC99 102:204:153	009966 0:153:102	339933 51:153:51
009933 0:153:51	33FF66 51:255:102	00FF66 0:255:102	CCFFCC 204:255:204	CCFF99 204:255:153	99FF66 153:255:102	99FF33 153:255:51	00FF33 0:255:51
33FF33 51:255:51	00CC33 0:204:51	33CC33 51:204:51	66FF33 102:255:51	00FF00 0:255:0	66CC33 102:204:51	006600 0:102:0	003300 0:51:0
009900 0:153:0	33FF00 51:255:0	66FF00 102:255:0	99FF00 153:255:0	66CC00 102:204:0	00CC00 0:204:0	33CC00 51:204:0	339900 51:153:0
99CC66 153:204:102	669933 102:153:51	99CC33 153:204:51	336600 51:102:0	669900 102:153:0	99CC00 153:204:0	CCFF66 204:255:102	CCFF33 204:255:51
CCFF00 204:255:0	999900 153:153:0	CCCC00 204:204:0	CCCC33 204:204:51	333300 51:51:0	666600 102:102:0	999933 153:153:51	CCCC66 204:204:102
666633 102:102:51	999966 153:153:102	CCCC99 204:204:153	FFFFCC 255:255:204	FFFF99 255:255:153	FFFF66 255:255:102	FFFF33 255:255:51	FFFF00 255:255:0
FFCC00 255:204:0	FFCC66 255:204:102	FFCC33 255:204:51	CC9933 204:153:51	996600 153:102:0	CC9900 204:153:0	FF9900 255:153:0	CC6600 204:102:0
993300 153:51:0	CC6633 204:102:51	663300 102:51:0	FF9966 255:153:102	FF6633 255:102:51	FF9933 255:153:51	FF6600 255:102:0	CC3300 204:51:0
996633 153:102:51	330000 51:0:0	663333 102:51:51	996666 153:102:102	CC9999 204:153:153	993333 153:51:51	CC6666 204:102:102	FFCCCC 255:204:204
FF3333 255:51:51	CC3333 204:51:51	FF6666 255:102:102	660000 102:0:0	990000 153:0:0	CC0000 204:0:0	FF0000 255:0:0	FF3300 255:51:0
CC9966 204:153:102	FFCC99 255:204:153	CCCCCC 204:204:204	999999 153:153:153	666666 102:102:102	333333 51:51:51	FFFFFF 255:255:255	000000 0:0:0

GLOSSARY

This glossary contains a partial listing of the bold key terms in the book. For a complete list, visit **www.aw.com/snyder**.

Acronyms have their letters spoken, as in H-T-M-L, unless pronunciation is indicated, as in *JAY·peg*.

1-way cipher, see one-way cipher

2-tier, see two-tier

3-tier, see three-tier

A

absolute pathname, navigation information for locating files in HTML using complete URLs

abstract, to remove an idea, concept, or process from a specific situation

administrative authority, see superuser

algorithm, a precise and systematic method for producing a specified result

alphanumeric, describing characters or text as being composed solely of letters, numbers, and possibly a few special characters like spaces and tabs, but not punctuation

ALU, acronym for arithmetic/logic unit

analog signal, a continuously varying representation of a phenomenon, e.g., a sound wave

anchor, the HTML tag that specifies a link, or the text associated with the reference that is highlighted in the document

applet, a small application program, often written in Java, that is executed on a client

argument, a value provided for a parameter in a function call

arithmetic/logic unit (ALU), a subsystem of a computer that performs the operations of an instruction

array, in programming, a variable having multiple elements named by the composition of an identifier and an index

assembly language, a symbolic form of a binary machine language

assignment statement, a programming command expressed with a variable on the left and a variable or expression on the right of an assignment symbol, usually =

asynchronous communication, indicates that the actions of senders and receivers occur at separate times, as in the exchange of email

attribute, in HTML, a parameter used within HTML tags to specify additional information; in databases, a property of an entity; also called a field

B

b, abbreviation for bit, e.g., Kb is kilobits

B, abbreviation for byte, e.g., KB is kilobytes

bandwidth, the bit-transmission capacity of a channel, usually measured in bits per second

binary, having two related components

binary number, a quantity expressed in radix 2 number representation

binary operator, an operator such as addition (+) having two operands

binary representation, any information encoding using symbols formed from two patterns; also called PandA representation in this book

bit, basic unit of information representation having two states, usually denoted 0 and 1

bit-mapped, as in bit-mapped display, indicates that the display's video image is stored pixel-by-pixel in the computer's memory

bookmark, to record a URL locally to simplify referencing it again

Boolean, having the property of being either true or false

boot, to start a computer and load its operating system

broadcast, a type of transmission of information from one sender to all receivers

bug, an error in a computer, program, or process

byte, a sequence of eight bits treated as a unit

C

cable, a bundle of wires carrying power and signals between computer components; also called cord or wires

cancel, a command button that stops a dialog or series of operations without penalty or effect

card, a small printed circuit board usually plugged into a socket on a motherboard to provide additional functionality; also called a daughter board

CGI, acronym for Common Gateway Interface

character, an upper- or lowercase Latin letter, Arabic numeral, or English punctuation; can be used more generally to include the alphabet and punctuation for other natural languages

classifier, a component of an optical character recognition system that ranks characters by the probability that they match a given set of features

cleartext, information before encryption or after decryption

click, to press and release a mouse button

click-with-shift, in selection, to maintain the selected status of all items except the clicked item, which is either selected if it is not selected or vice versa; also called shift-select

client, a computer that receives the services in a client/server structure

client/server structure, a relationship between two computers in which the client computer requests services from the server computer

close, to terminate a GUI window and, if the window is the primary or only window, to terminate the application

collating sequence, an ordering for a set of symbols used to sort them; for example, alphabetical ordering

command button, a synthesized image of a GUI appearing to be a 3D button used to cause some operation to be performed; the HTML button input control

Common Gateway Interface (CGI), an extension to HTML allowing browsers to cause a Web server to run programs on their behalf with specific data

compile, to translate a programming language into a language the computer can interpret (machine language)

compression, encoding information with fewer bits than a given representation by exploiting properties of regularity or unimportance

compression ratio, the factor by which compression reduces an encoding from its uncompressed size

computable, a task that can be performed by computer, algorithmic

computer, a device that deterministically follows instructions to process information

conditional, a programming statement, usually identified by `if`, that optionally executes statements depending on the outcome of a Boolean test

continuation test, a Boolean expression to determine whether an iteration statement will execute its statement sequence again; also called a termination test

control, a subsystem of a computer that is the hardware implementation of the Fetch/Execute Cycle

cookie, information stored on a Web client computer by an http server computer

copyright, the legal protection of many forms of intellectual property

cracker, a person attempting to break a code

crawler, a program that navigates the Internet, cataloging and indexing the Web pages by the words they contain for use by a query processor

CRT, acronym for cathode ray tube, a video display technology

cryptography, the study of encryption and decryption methods

cycle power, to turn a computer off, wait a moment, and then turn it back on

D

daemon, a program that periodically "wakes up" to perform some system management task

data controller, in Fair Information Practices, the person who sets policies, responds to individuals regarding their information, if any, and is accountable for those policies and actions

Data Fetch, third step in the Fetch/Execute Cycle, the action of retrieving the instruction's operands from memory

data type, a set of values for which operations are defined, e.g., number

database scheme or **schema**, the declaration of entities and relationships of a database

debugging, the act of discovering why a system is not working properly

decrypt, to recover the original information from a digitally encrypted representation

definiteness, a property of algorithms that requires a specific sequence of steps be defined

DF, in processor design, an acronym for Data Fetch

digital signal, a discrete or "step levels" representation of a phenomenon, varying "instantaneously"

digitally decrypt, see decrypt

digitally encrypt, see encrypt

digitize, originally to encode with decimal numerals, now to encode in bits

directory, a named collection of files or other directories; also called a folder on Mac and Windows operating systems

discrete, distinct or separable, not able to be changed by continuous variation

display rate, in animation, the frequency with which the images are changed

domain, in networking, a related set of networked computers, e.g., `edu` is the set of education-related computers

Domain Name System (DNS), the collection of Internet-connected computers that translate domain addresses into IP addresses

dual booting, loading two operating systems at once

E

eCommerce, electronic commerce, the use of electronic data communication to conduct business

effectiveness, a property of algorithms requiring that all instructions be performed mechanically within the capabilities of the executing agent

element, an indexed item; also called array element

empty string, a character sequence of zero length

emoticon, a character sequence written to express by its physical form an emotion, common in email; for example, the "smiley face"`:)` to express happiness or humor

encrypt, to transform a digital representation so the information cannot be readily discerned

ER diagram, Entity-Relationship diagram, a visual presentation of some or all of a database schema

escape symbol, a character, often `&` or `\`, prefixing another character or word to enlarge a character encoding, e.g., `&infinity` to encode ∞

EX, in processor design, the abbreviation for Instruction Execution

execute, to perform the instructions of a program, usually by a computer; to run a program

Extensible Markup Language (XML), a W3C standard for structured information encoding

F

factor of improvement, the amount by which a first measurement must be multiplied to be equivalent to the second measurement when computing scale of change

fair use, a concept in copyright law in which copyright limitations are waived for explicitly listed, socially valuable purposes

feature, a component of a character in a optical character recognition system

Fetch/Execute Cycle, the basic instruction execution process of a computer

field inputs, character input such as telephone numbers with a specific structure

finiteness, a property of algorithms requiring that they terminate with the intended result or an indication that no solution is possible

firmware, instructions incorporated into the hardware, usually changeable by external means with difficulty

flame-a-thon, email battle; also called flame war

floppy disk, a storage device providing persistent memory using (removable) diskettes; also called floppy drive

for statement, a common programming structure for iterating a sequence of instruction over a regular range of index values

formal language, synthetic notation designed for expressing algorithms and programs

frame, in animation, one of many images rapidly redrawn to create the illusion of motion

freeware, software available on the Web at no cost

full backup, a complete copy of a body of information usually as of a specific point in time

function, a programming structure with a name, optional parameter list, and a definition that encapsulates an algorithm

function body, the definition of a function's computation

function declaration, the specification of a function, including its name, parameters, and body

G

game tree, a conceptualization of the possible future configurations of a multiperson game

generalize, to formulate an idea, concept, or process so that it abstracts multiple situations

GIF, file extension, e.g., `picture.gif`, specifying a graphic image format, pronounced with either soft or hard *g*

giga-, prefix for billion; pronounced with a hard *g*

global variable, a variable declared outside the scope of a function, usually at the start of the program

graphical user interface (GUI), the synthesized visual medium of interaction between a user and a computer

GUI, acronym for graphic user interface, pronounced *gooey*

H

Halting Problem, the problem of determining if a computation halts for a given input, a problem that cannot be solved by computer

handle, in programming, a binary value returned by a function or server to be used for subsequent references

haptic device, an input/output technology interfacing with the sense of touch

hard disk, a storage device providing persistent memory; also called a disk or hard drive

hardware, the physical implementation of a computer, usually electronic, including the processor, memory, and usually its peripheral devices

heuristic, a guideline to help solve a problem but one that does guarantee a solution; for example, "when looking for a lost article check the last place you used it"

hex digit, one of the sixteen numerals of hexadecimal, 0, 1, 2, 3, 4, 5, 6, 7, 8, 9, A, B, C, D, E, F

hexadecimal, radix 16 number representation

hierarchical index, a structure for organizing information using descriptive terms that partition the information

hierarchy, an organizing structure composed of a sequence of levels that partition all items so that those of one level are partitioned into smaller groups at the next level

hit, for a Web search, a match to a query; for a Web site, a visit

hop, in networking, the transfer of a packet or message to an adjacent router

Hypertext Markup Language (HTML), a common notation for specifying the form of a Web page to a browser

hypertext transfer protocol (HTTP), the rules governing interaction between client and server on the World Wide Web

Hz, abbreviation for Hertz, cycles, or repetitions per second

I

ID, in processor design, an acronym for Instruction Decode

identifier, a legal sequence of letters, numerals, or punctuation marks forming the name of variable, file, directory, etc.

IF, in processor design, an acronym for Instruction Fetch

`if` statement, a programming a structure allowing the conditional execution of statements based on the outcome of a Boolean test

index, in information structures, a organizing mechanism used to find information in a large collection; in programming, the number that together with an identifier forms an array reference

index origin, the number at which indexing begins; the least index

index value, the result of evaluating an index expression; the number of an array element

indexing, in programming, the mechanism of associating a number and an identifier to locate an element

infix operator, a binary operator, e.g., +, whose syntax requires that it be written between its operands, as in 4 + 3

Input Unit, a subsystem of a computer transferring information from the physical world via an input device to the computer's memory

instance, the current values of an entity, table, or database

Instruction Decode, second step in the Fetch/Execute Cycle, the action of determining which operation is to be performed and computing the addresses of the operands

Instruction Execution, the fourth step in the Fetch/Execute Cycle, the action of performing a machine instruction

Instruction Fetch, first step in the Fetch/Execute Cycle, the action of retrieving a machine instruction from the memory address given by the program counter

integer, a whole number; in programming, a data type for a whole number, either positive or negative

integration, in silicon technology, the ability to fabricate both active and connective parts of a circuit using a family of compatible materials in a single complexity-independent process

intellectual property, creations of the human mind that have value to others

Internet, the totality of all wires, fibers, switches, routers, satellite links, and other hardware used to transport information between named computers

Internet Service Provider (ISP), a utility that connects private and business computers to the Internet

interpolation, the smooth movement from one discrete value to another.

intractable, a description for computations solvable by computer in principle, but not in practice

invocation (of a function), to call the function

IP, acronym for Internet Protocol

IP address, the address of an Internet-networked computer composed of four numbers in the range 0–255

IP packet, a fixed quantum of information packaged together with an IP address and other data for sending information over the Internet

ISO, acronym for the International Standards Organization

ISP, acronym for Internet Service Provider

iterate, in programming, to repeatedly execute a sequence of statements

iteration variable, any variable controlling an iteration statement such as a `for` statement

J

JPEG, acronym for the nickname Joint Photographic Experts Group, a committee of the ISO; pronounced *JAY·peg*

JPG, file extension, e.g., `picture.jpg`, for JPEG encoding

K

key, in databases, field(s) that make the rows of an entity (table) unique; in cryptography, selectable code used to encrypt and subsequently decrypt information

kilo-, prefix for thousand; if prefixing a quantity counted in binary, e.g., memory, prefix for 1,024

L

LAN, acronym for local area network, usually pronounced

latency, the time required to deliver or generate information

LCD, acronym for liquid crystal display, a video display technology

length (of an array), the number of elements in an array

lexical structure, a specification of the form of character input; for example, telephone numbers in North America are formed of ten Arabic numerals with a space following the third and a hyphen following the sixth

local area network (LAN), a network connecting computers within a small physical space such as a building

local variable, a variable declared within a function

logical operators, any of the connectives *and*, *or,* or *not*

lossless compression, the process of reducing the number of bits required to represent information in which the original form can be exactly reconstructed

lossy compression, the process of reducing the number of bits required to represent information in which the original cannot be exactly reconstructed

M

machine language, computer instructions expressed in binary, respecting the form required for a specific machine

mask, in fabrication technology, a material similar to a photographic negative containing the pattern to be transferred to the silicon surface in the process of constructing a chip

mega-, prefix for million; if prefixing a quantity counted in binary, e.g., memory, prefix for 1,048,576

memory, device capable of storing information, usually in fixed size, addressable units; a subsystem of a computer used to store programs and their data while they execute

memory address, a whole number designating a specific location in a computer's memory

menu, a list of available operations from which a user can select by clicking on one item

metadata, information describing the properties of other information

microprocessor, see processor

middleware, software intermediating between Web clients and databases or other systems for producing online services

mnemonic, any aid to remembering

moderator, a person responsible for deciding what is to be sent out to a mailing list

monitor, a computer's video output device or display; also called a *screen*

motherboard, a printed circuit board containing the processor chip, memory, and other electronics of a computer

MPEG, acronym for the nickname Motion Picture Experts Group, a committee of the ISO, pronounced *EM·peg*

MPG, file extension, e.g., `flick.mpg`, for MPEG encoding

multicast, a type of transmission of information from one sender to many receivers

N

***n*-tier**, a multilayer system design, usually for providing Web services

name conflict, the attempt to give a different definition, e.g., variable declaration, to an identifier with an existing meaning

navigation, in searching, to follow a series of links to locate specific information often in a hierarchy

nested loop, the condition of a loop (inner loop) appearing in the statement sequence of another loop (outer loop)

netiquette, etiquette on the Internet

NP-complete, a measure of difficulty of problems believed to be intractable for computers

Nyquist Rule, a digitization guideline stating that the sampling frequency should exceed the signal frequency by at least two times

O

OCR, acronym for optical character recognition

one-way cipher, a form of encryption that cannot easily be reversed, i.e., decrypted, often used for passwords

operand, the data used in computer instructions; the value(s) on which operators compute

operating system (OS), software that performs tasks for the computer; it controls input and output, keeps track of files and directories, and controls peripheral devices such as disk drives and printers.

operator overloading, a property of some programming languages in which operators like + have different meanings depending on their operand data types, e.g., + used for both addition or concatenation in JavaScript

optical character recognition (OCR), a computer application in which printed text is converted to the ASCII letters that it represents

Output Unit, a subsystem of a computer that transfers information from the computer's memory to the physical world via an output device

overflow exception, an error condition for operations such as addition in which a result is too large to be represented in the available number of bits

P

PandA, in this book, a mnemonic for "present and absent encoding," the fundamental physical representation of information; also called binary representation

parallel computation, the use of multiple computers to solve a single problem

parameter, an input to a function

partial backup, the new information copied to another medium that has been added to a system since the last full or partial backup

PC, acronym for program counter, for printed circuit (board), and for personal computer

photolithography, a process of transferring a pattern by means of light shown through a mask or negative

photoresist, a material used in a silicon chip fabrication process that is chemically changed by light, allowing it to be patterned by a mask

picture element or **pixel**, the smallest displayable unit of a video monitor

pins, stiff wires in a cable's plug that insert into sockets to make the connection

pixel, contraction for picture element

placeholder technique, a searching algorithm in which strings are temporarily replaced with a special character to protect them from change by other substitution commands

plaintext, synonym for cleartext

point-to-point communication, a type of transmission of information from one sender to one receiver

pop-up menu, a menu that is displayed at the cursor position when the mouse is clicked

precedence, the relationship among operators describing which is to be performed first

prefetching, in online animation the process of loading the images prior to beginning an animation

primary source, a person who provides information based on direct knowledge or experience

privacy, the right of people to choose freely the circumstances under which and the extent to which they will reveal themselves, their attitudes, and their behaviors to others

procedural abstraction, the encapsulation of a sequence of instructions (algorithm) into a function or procedure

processor, the component of a computer that computes, that is, performs the instructions

program, an algorithm encoded for a specific situation

program counter, a register in a computer that stores the address of the next instruction to be executed

public domain, the status of a work in which the copyright owner has explicitly given up the rights

public key, a key published by the receiver and used by the sender to encrypt messages

pull-down menu, a menu positioned at the top of a GUI window, also called a drop-down menu

Q

QBE, acronym for Query by Example

query, database command defining a table expressed using the five database operators

Query by Example, a method for defining queries in a database

query processor, the part of a search engine that uses the crawler's index to report Web pages associated with keywords provided by a user

quotient-remainder form of division, a means of expressing the division of *a/b* as the solution to the equation $a = b \cdot c + d$, where *c* is the quotient and *d* is the remainder

R

radix, the "base" of a numbering system; equivalently, the number of digits in each place

RAM, acronym for random access memory, pronounced

random access, to reference an item directly; contrast with sequential access

random access memory, memory; a subsystem of a computer used for storing programs and data while they execute

reboot, to restart a computer by clearing its memory and reloading its operating system

reckon, archaic term for performing arithmetic calculations

reference, in HTML, the displayed and highlighted portion of an anchor tag

refresh rate, the frequency with which a video display is redisplayed

relational operator, one of six operators ($< \leq = \neq \geq >$) that compare two values; in JavaScript programming, one of the six operators ($<$ $<=$ $==$ $!=$ $>=$ $>$)

relationship, a correspondence between two tables of a database

relative pathname, local navigation information for locating a file in HTML

replacement string, in editing, the letter sequence that substitutes for the search string

Result Return, the fifth and final step of the Fetch/Execute Cycle, the action of storing to memory the value produced by executing a machine instruction

RGB, acronym for red, green, blue, a color encoding method

ROM, acronym for "read only memory," permanently set memory, pronounced

row, a set of values for the fields of a table, also called a *tuple*

RR, in processor design, an acronym for Result Return

RSA, a public key encryption method invented by Rivest, Shamir, and Adelman

run-length encoding, a representation in which numbers are used to give the lengths of consecutive sequences of 0s or 1s.

S

sample, to take measurements at a regular intervals as in sound digitization

sampling rate, the number of samples per second

scope, in programming, the range of statements over which a variable or other defined object is known

screen saver, a changing image or animation that displays on a computer's monitor while the computer is idle

scroll bar, a slider control appearing at the side and/or bottom of a window when the information cannot be fully displayed

SCSI, acronym for "small computer system interface," pronounced *scuzzy*

search engine, a software system composed of a crawler and a query processor that helps users locate specific information on the World Wide Web or specific Web site

search string, the information being sought in a text search

seat, to firmly insert a plug into a socket after an initial alignment

secondary source, a person providing information without direct knowledge or experience of the topic; contrast primary source

self-describing encoding, a representation using meta-data tags that embeds its own structure, as in XML

sequential access, a memory reference pattern in which no item can be referenced without passing (skipping or referencing) the items that precede it; contrast random access

serialized behavior, a property of transactions that execute simultaneously stating that only a single result is produced no matter in what order their constituent operations are performed

server, a computer providing the services in a client/server structure

shareware, software available on the Web, paid for on the honor system

shift-select, a GUI command in which the shift key is pressed while the mouse selects an item, to avoid deselecting the items already selected; also called click-with-shift

slider control, a synthesized slot in which a bar can be moved to select a position in a continuous range

software, a collective term for programs

source, in context of the World Wide Web, the HTML or other text description of how a Web page should be displayed

SQL, acronym for Structured Query Language

string, in searching, a sequence of characters; in programming, a data type for a sequence of characters

Structured Query Language, a standard notation for defining tables from tables in a database

subscript, a synonym for index

substitution, in searching, the result of replacing a substring of a character sequence with another string

superuser authority, the capability to access all functions of a computer or software system, including overriding passwords, also called administrative authority

symbol, an information code formed from a specific sequence of base patterns; for example, 01000001 is the ASCII symbol for *A* formed from patterns 0 and 1

synchronous communication, indicates that the actions of senders and receivers occur at the same time, as in a telephone call

T

table, an organizing mechanism for database entities

tag, a word or abbreviation enclosed in angle brackets, usually paired with a companion starting with a slash, that describes a property of data or expresses a command to be performed; e.g., `<italic>You're It!</italic>`

TCP/IP, acronym for Transmission Control Protocol, Internet Protocol

template, the structural information of a document with placeholders for content that is filled in to produce a complete document

tera-, prefix for trillion; in prefixing, a quantity counted in binary, e.g., memory, prefix for 1,099,511,627,776

termination test, synonym for continuation test

text, a sequence of characters; in searching, the material being searched

text editor, basic software to create and modify text files; contrast with word processor

three-tier, a three-layer system design, often the client/server structure extended with a backend database

toggling, reversing the state of an item, as in to toggle between selected and deselected

token, a symbol sequence treated as a single unit in searching or languages

transducer, device converting waves of one form into waves of another, usually electrical

translate, as an image, to move an image to a new position unchanged; in programming, to convert a program from one formal language to another, usually a simpler one; a synonym for *compile*

triangle pointers, small triangles indicating hidden information; clicking on the triangle pointer displays the information

Trojan horse, a useful and apparently innocuous program containing hidden code that allows the unauthorized collection, exploitation, or destruction of data

tuple, a set of values for the attributes of an entity, also called a *row*

Turing Test, an experimental setting to determine if a computer and a person can be distinguished by their answers to a judge's questions

two-tier, a two-layer system design, usually the client/server structure

U

unary operator, an operator such as negation (-) with a single operand

Universal Resource Locator (URL), a two-part name for a Web page composed of an IP address followed by the filename, which can default to `index.html`

universality, a property of computation that all computers with a minimal set of instructions can compute the same set of computations

V

vacation message, an automated reply to email when there is a planned delay in reading it

variable, a named quantity in a programming language

virtual, a modifier meaning not actually, but as if

virus, a program that "infects" another program by embedding a (possibly evolved) copy of itself

volatile, the property of integrated circuit memory in which the stored information is lost when the power is removed

W

W3C, acronym for World Wide Web Consortium

WAN, acronym for wide area network

Web, short form for World Wide Web

Web browser, a software application that locates and reads HTML pages. Modern browsers can display sound and video, as well as text and graphics (although plug-ins may be required for multimedia).

Web client, a computer requesting services from a Web server; a computer running a Web browser

Web server, a computer providing pages to Web clients; a computer hosting a Web page

wide area network, a network connecting computers over a wider area than a few kilometers

word processor, software to create and modify text files that include formatting tags; contrast text editor

work-proportional-to-*n*, a description of the time required to solve a problem with input of size *n*

World Wide Web (WWW), the collection of all HTML servers connected by the Internet and their information resources

World Wide Web Consortium, a standards body composed mainly of companies that produce Web software

worm, an independent program that replicates itself from machine to machine across network connections

WYSIWYG, acronym for "what you see is what you get," pronounced *WHIZ·ee·wig*

X

XML, acronym for extensible markup language

ANSWERS TO SELECTED QUESTIONS

Chapter One

Multiple Choice

1. A. Monitors use bit-mapped technology generated by the computer whereas TVs use recorded images.
3. C. A laptop has an LCD display and uses RGB color.
5. D. Follow the acronym, PILPOF, plug in last, pull out first.
7. B. A display has over 750,000 pixels that are generated and controlled in memory.
9. D.

Short Answer

1. microprocessor
3. screen saver
5. 786,432 or 1024 × 768
7. tip of the arrow
9. Execute
11. abstraction
13. word processor
15. generalization

Chapter 2

Multiple Choice

1. A. Those with computer skills are sometimes called digerati.
3. D. Both A and B are correct. Ease of use is one of the driving forces behind software development and one of the reasons for the popularity of some software.
5. B. You'll find all except door handles in a typical GUI.
7. B. In Windows, you can close a subwindow, such as a spreadsheet or word processing file, and the application will keep running.
9. A. Open and Print will bring up a dialog box. The Open dialog lets the user select the file to open and the Print dialog lets the user select printing options.

Short Answer

1. digerati
3. analogies
5. Triangle pointers
7. menus

9. Help

11. drop-down menu

13. gray

15. command

Chapter 3

Multiple choice

1. D. The Internet is a great medium for asynchronous communication.

3. B. The ability to create and publish Web pages has made it easier for people to express their opinions and creativity.

5. C. For every n computers attached to the Internet, an additional computer adds n connections.

7. B. The right side shows the domain. That will get the message to the correct location. From there, the mail server will have to get it to the correct address. This is very similar to the postal service.

9. C. The government, educational institutions, and big business put together the first system in the late 1960s.

Short answer

1. electronic commerce

3. multicast

5. peers

7. channel

9. gateways

11. Web servers

13. FTP

15. Hypertext Markup Language

Chapter 4

Multiple choice

1. C. The commands used in HTML are called tags. They are enclosed in `< >`.

3. A. The first one has the tags properly paired.

5. C. These are paragraph tags and put a double space around the text to set it off from the rest of the page.

7. B. As you move left or right in an address across the slash marks, you move up or down a directory.

9. A. `img src = "filename.ext"` will get the image. Then use `align` = and enclose the proper alignment in quotes.

Short answer

1. Web authoring software
3. `<pre>`
5. attributes
7. relative
9. Graphics Interchange Format
11. 000000

Chapter 5

Multiple choice

1. A. Some use the Web for their own gains and slant their content accordingly.
3. C. ERIC has citations covering over 750 professional journals.
5. B. The query processor looks at the search information and performs the search.
7. C. Google was the first search engine to get its keywords from the anchor tags of Web pages to identify content on a page and to find pages to crawl.
9. C. Use the minus sign (–) in front of the word to exclude pages that have that word.

Short answer

1. library
3. Single links
5. Google
7. logical (or Boolean) operators
9. hierarchy
11. hits
13. AND
15. InterNIC

Chapter 6

True/False and Multiple Choice

1. F. A tertiary source is removed from the source by time or space. A tertiary source reports what happened but isn't an eyewitness.
3. D. In addition, mistakes in print tend to stay mistakes.
5. B. An eyewitness and a participant are examples of primary sources.

Short Answer

1. Curiosity-driven research
3. History
5. primary source

Chapter 7

Multiple Choice/Short Answer

1. B. The computer doesn't understand the information it was given. This usually means the user didn't understand what the computer wanted or the user simply entered the wrong information.
3. B. See if the error repeats itself. If it doesn't, then you're in the clear. If it does, then you need to work through the debugging process.
5. A. Look again for the error. See if you can duplicate the problem.

Short Answer

1. Field inputs
3. b
5. bug
7. workaround

Chapter 8

Multiple Choice

1. C. 6 times 6 is 36 and 6 times 6 times 6 is 216.
3. D. The Tab key can work alone. The other keys are used in conjunction with another key.
5. A. A clock with hands is analog. If the clock displays digits, it is digital.
7. D. It's called a syllogism. From the two statements, I can deduce the third statement.
9. A. The coating on floppies and hard disks is an iron compound that can store a magnetic charge.

Short Answer

1. molecules
3. Present and Absent
5. collating sequence
7. escape character
9. Bit
11. Hex
13. ASCII code

Chapter 9

Multiple Choice

1. A. The computer executes its instructions literally. There is no allowance for free will, creativity, or intuition.
3. D. The fastest personal computers can sustain speeds even higher than that, and each generation of computers is faster.
5. A. The ALU gets instructions and .returns their results.

7. B. Branch and jump make the computer switch tasks so it doesn't always grab the next instruction.

9. B. The correct order is thousands, millions, billions, trillions.

Short Answer

1. Computers
3. RAM
5. deterministically
7. information processing
9. keyboard
11. Programming
13. Instruction interpretation
15. gate

Chapter 10

Multiple Choice

1. C. There are five basic requirements: inputs specified, outputs specified, definiteness, effectiveness, and finiteness.
3. A. A natural language lacks the rigorous structure and precise meaning of the others.
5. C. These steps must be repeated in order to put the whole set of CDs in order.
7. A. You took a specific example and generated an idea from it.
9. D. The *Alpha* sweep organizes the first item. The Beta sweep organizes the rest, one at a time.

Short Answer

1. algorithm
3. algorithm, program
5. *Beta* sweep
7. nonredundant
9. loop

Chapter 11

Multiple Choice

1. B. Each intensity has a range from 0–255. That gives you 256 possible settings for each color or 16,777,216 possible colors.
3. B. Analog information is not discrete. It can always be divided into a smaller sampling.
5. B. The larger each sampling is, the closer it can be to the true sound. The size of each sample is the bit rate.
7. A. MP3 is the audio layer of MPEG movies.
9. C. A supermarket uses UPC codes, the little sets of numbers and black and white lines on packages.

Short Answer

1. black
3. Interpolation
5. transducer
7. ISO
9. optical character recognition (OCR)
11. virtual reality
13. Haptic devices
15. Bias-free Universal Medium Principle

INDEX

A

absolute pathnames, 99–100
abstract thinking, 56–57
abstraction, 18–19
   algorithms, 281–284
   Alpha Sweep, 283–284
   Beta Sweep, 281–283
accent marks, 95
access, 15
   Web sites, 140–141
acronyms, 5–6
addresses, 240
   errors, 181–182
   Internet, 68–72
   protocols, 73. *See also* protocols
   Web servers, 84–85
algorithmic thinking, 17
algorithms, 17
   abstraction in, 281–284
   example of, 274–281
   Exchange Sort, 280–281
   overview of, 269–274
aligning
   images, 102–103
   text, 96
Alpha Sweep abstraction, 283–284
Alta Vista, 130. *See also* searching
alternative representations of digits,
   205–206
America Online (AOL), 77
American Standard Code for
      Information Interchange
      (ASCII), 219–222
analog-to-digital converter (ADC), 302
analytical thinking, 21–25
anatomy of computers, 239–244
anchor tags, 97–101
anchor text, 97
applications, 16. *See also* software
   differences between algorithms, 273
   executing, 245–248
arithmetic/logic unit (ALU), 242
ASCI Red, 23
assembly languages, 253
assembly, freedom of, 66
assessing research progress, 158–159
assigning symbols, 219
assumptions, algorithms, 280

asynchronous communication, 66
Atanasoff Berry Computer (ABC), 236
attributes, Hypertext Markup Language
      (HTML), 95–97
audio, digitizing, 301–305
audio clips, Chronfile information,
   160–161
authoring tools (HTML), 115

B

bandwidth, 309
benefits
   of analytical thinking, 24
   of freedom of speech and assembly,
     66
Beta Sweep abstraction, 281–283
binary representations, 293–295
binary systems, 213
bit-mapping, 7
bits
   encoding, 223
   magnetic media, 214
   memory, 215–216
   multimedia, 309–311
   patterns, 216
black and white colors, 293–295
blazing away, 43–44
bold text tags, 91
bookmarking links, 151–152
booting, 18
   operating systems, 253–254
bootstrapping, 18
brackets, Hypertext Markup Language
      (HTML), 95
branch and jump instructions,
   244–245
   executing, 244–245
broadcast communication, 67
browsers, 79–80. *See also* interfaces
   Source View feature, 193, 195
building. *See* design; formatting
buttons
   coordinating with the mouse, 11
   creating, 12
byte-size memory location, 240
bytes, 15
   ASCII, 220

C

cables, 8
   red, green, and blue (RGB), 8
Cancel button, 35
cards, 13
case sensitivity, 48
   errors, 181–182
cathode ray tubes (CRTs), 7
CD Player, executing, 32–33
characters, 47
   digitizing information, 205–206
   optical character recognition (OCR),
     306–307
Chronfile information, research,
   159–162
classification of hierarchies, 123–129
classifiers, 307
clicking, 41–42
   mouse, 11
clocks, 248–250
closing windows, 35
collating sequences, 206
colors
   black and white, 293–295
   computing on representations,
     298–301
   digitizing, 291–298
   Hypertext Markup Language
     (HTML), 104–107
   increasing intensity, 295
   modifying, 295–300
   pixels, 9
   red, green, and blue (RGB), 8, 679
     binary representations, 291–293
   RGB color specification, 104
combining
   bit patterns, 216
commands
   buttons, 33
   Edit menu, 38
   executing, 36
   File menu, 37–38
     New, 39–40
   Find, 47–51
   troubleshooting, 183–184
communication
   types of, 66–68
   understanding IT terminology, 5–6